COLONIAL 'REFORMATION' IN THE HIGHLANDS OF CENTRAL SULAWESI, INDONESIA, 1892–1995

Albert Schrauwers

The To Pamona, the people of the highlands of Central Sulawesi, Indonesia, exhibit the effects of a complicated history of colonial contact. In this anthropological study, Albert Schrauwers examines the profound impact of a Dutch Protestant Mission on the religion and culture of the To Pamona.

Schrauwers reveals how a unique discourse on religion in the Netherlands was exported to its colony, Indonesia. The missionaries fostered a religious nationalism that ultimately transformed the region's cultural and political identity over the course of the subsequent century. The role of the church in Dutch and Indonesian affairs of state is established and the historical roots of this 'pillarization' are unearthed. Central to this phenomenon among the To Pamona, says Schrauwers, was the influence of Dutch missionary Albert C. Kruyt, who used ethnographic methods to impose upon the people a foreign religion and social structure.

Schrauwers has based his study on extensive archival research conducted in the Netherlands, as well as two years of field work in Sulawesi. He presents a dynamic view of the evolution of religious practice among the To Pomona, and brings new material to the scholarship on identity and religion in Indonesia.

(Anthropological Horizons)

ALBERT SCHRAUWERS is a lecturer in the Department of Anthropology, London School of Economics.

ANTHROPOLOGICAL HORIZONS

Editor: Michael Lambek, University of Toronto

This series, begun in 1991, focuses on theoretically informed ethnographic works addressing issues of mind and body, knowledge and power, equality and inequality, the individual and the collective. Interdisciplinary in its perspective, the series makes a unique contribution in several other academic disciplines: women's studies, history, philosophy, psychology, political science, and sociology.

Published to date:

1 **The Varieties of Sensory Experience: A Sourcebook in the Anthropology of the Senses**
  Edited by David Howes
2 **Arctic Homeland: Kinship, Community, and Development in Northwest Greenland**
  Mark Nuttall
3 **Knowledge and Practice in Mayotte: Local Discourses of Islam, Sorcery, and Spirit Possession**
  Michael Lambek
4 **Deathly Waters and Hungry Mountains: Agrarian Ritual and Class Formation in an Andean Town**
  Peter Gose
5 **Paradise: Class, Commuters, and Ethnicity in Rural Ontario**
  Stanley R. Barrett
6 **The Cultural World in *Beowulf***
  John M. Hill
7 **Making It Their Own: Severn Ojibwe Communicative Practices**
  Lisa Philips Valentine
8 **Merchants and Shopkeepers: A Historical Anthropology of an Irish Market Town, 1200–1986**
  Philip Gulliver and Marilyn Silverman
9 **Tournaments of Value: Sociability and Hierarchy in a Yemeni Town**
  Ann Meneley
10 *Mal'uocchiu*: **Ambiguity, Evil Eye, and the Language of Distress**
  Sam Migliore
11 **Between History and Histories: The Making of Silences and Commemorations**
  Edited by Gerald Sider and Gavin Smith
12 *Eh Paesan!* **Being Italian in Toronto**
  Nicholas DeMaria Harney
13 **Theorizing the Americanist Tradition**
  Edited by Lisa Philips Valentine and Regna Darnell
14 **Colonial 'Reformation' of the Highlands of Central Sulawesi, Indonesia, 1892–1995**
  Albert Schrauwers

ALBERT SCHRAUWERS

Colonial 'Reformation' in the Highlands of Central Sulawesi, Indonesia, 1892–1995

UNIVERSITY OF TORONTO PRESS
Toronto Buffalo London

© University of Toronto Press Incorporated 2000
Toronto Buffalo London
Printed in Canada

ISBN 0-8020-4741-6 (cloth)
ISBN 0-8020-8303-X (paper)

Printed on acid-free paper

Canadian Cataloguing in Publication Data

Schrauwers, Albert
   Colonial 'reformation' in the highlands of Central Sulawesi, Indonesia, 1892–1995

   (Anthropological horizons)
   Includes bibliographical references and index.
   ISBN 0-8020-4741-6 (bound)   ISBN 0-8020-8303-X (pbk.)

   1. Reformed Church – Missions – Indonesia – Celebes – History.   2. Missions,
   Dutch – Indonesia – Celebes – History.   3. To Pamona (Indonesia people) –
   Missions – History.   4. Celebes (Indonesia) – Church history.   I. Title.
   II. Series.

   BV3350.S37 1999   266'.425984   C99-931974-4

University of Toronto Press acknowledges the financial assistance to its publishing
program of the Canada Council for the Arts and the Ontario Arts Council.

This book has been published with the help of a grant from the Humanities and
Social Sciences Federation of Canada, using funds provided by the Social Sciences
and Humanities Research Council of Canada.

University of Toronto Press acknowledges the financial support for its publishing
activities of the Government of Canada through the Book Publishing Industry
Development Program (BPIDP).

Canada

Contents

MAPS, FIGURES, AND TABLES   ix

ACKNOWLEDGMENTS   xi

Introduction: On Origin Stories in a Postmodern World   3

Church and State   4
'Returning to the Origin': Colonial Incorporation   8
The Discipline of Anthropology   10
Self-Representation   13
Rationalizing Religion   16
Structure and Agency   20
Elites and Fieldwork   23
The Persistence of Tradition   26

PART ONE: COLONIAL INCORPORATION

Chapter 1: Missions in Colonial Context   31

The Dutch Tribe   33
Verzuiling in the Netherlands   35
Ethical Policy, Missions, and Imperialism in the Outer Islands   40
Imperialism and the Incorporation of Central Sulawesi   45
Dr A.C. Kruyt and Dr N. Adriani, Missionary Ethnographers   51
Animisme and *Spiritisme*   54
Religion in a Colonial Context   58

Chapter 2: The Reformation   60

Peoples without History   64
Dismantling the Village Confederacies   70
Church and State as Village Institutions   77
The Republican Interlude   82
Tentena in the 'New Order' Administrative Context   88
A *Volkskerk* in Transition   90

PART TWO: THE PERSISTENCE OF TRADITION

Chapter 3: The Household, Kinship, and Shared Poverty   97

Shared Poverty and the Moral-Economy Model   100
Sombori and *Santina*   104
The Commodification of Wet-Rice Production in Tentena   110
Kinship and the Household   116
The Household Developmental Cycle   120
Peasantization and 'Discursive Traditionalism'   127

Chapter 4: Marriage, Kinship, and *Posintuwu* Networks   129

The 'Traditional' Marriage Process   133
Posintuwu   145
The Control of Social Reproduction   152
The Women's Christian Organization   157
Class and Marriage   160
The Role of Church and State in Marriage   165

PART THREE: HIGHLAND CHRISTIANITY

Chapter 5: Ritualization   171

Ritual Theory, Ritual Practice   173
The Indigenous Form of Ritualization   179
Inculturation and *Monuntu*   183
Dominance and the Protestant Worship Service   187
Transformations   192

Chapter 6: The Rationalization of Belief   197

Conversion and Shared Belief   198
The Construction of Ritual as Text   206
Rationalization   211
Church Discipline   214
Institutional Rationalization   218

Chapter 7: Rationalizing Religion in Indonesia   225

Colonial Discourses on Religion in Indonesia   230
Post-Colonial Discourses on Religion in Indonesia   237
Culture as Contested Territory   241
What Next?   245

NOTES   247

BIBLIOGRAPHY   253

INDEX   273

Illustrations follow   146

Maps, Figures, and Tables

Maps

Map 1.1 The Kingdom of Poso, Central Sulawesi   49
Map 2.1 Kruyt's Division of the East, West, and South Toraja
      (Village Confederacies in Italics)   66

Figures

Figure 3.1 The Family Compound of Ngkai and Tu'a Bose   108
Figure 3.2 Household Development Cycles in Tentena   121
Figure 3.3 Genealogies of Ngkai and Tu'a Bose   122
Figure 3.4 Street Map Showing Houses 1 and 2 and Their Division   123

Tables

Table 3.1 Household Composition in Study Group   118

Acknowledgments

Preparing the acknowledgments for a book is a humbling and potent reminder of the number of people who freely give the assistance necessary for any research project to come to fruition. In these acknowledgments, I cannot hope to include all those to whom I owe a debt of gratitude. I do hope that anyone I may have omitted by accident will forgive me. *Ne'e ndikitanaka.*

I have benefited from almost a decade of instruction in the Department of Anthropology at the University of Toronto, much of that time under the supervision of Professor Shuichi Nagata. The debt I owe Professor Nagata, who has shepherded this project from inception to completion, is incalculable. Similarly, I thank Professor Peter Carstens, who introduced me to anthropological approaches to religion, and Professor Michael Lambek, the final member of my core committee, for broadening my theoretical perspective beyond my own narrow concerns. Professor Krystyna Sieciechowicz is in many ways the 'godmother' of this book, and to her I extend my continued appreciation. At various times, Jerome Rousseau, Joel Kahn, Glynis George, and Tania Murray Li have provided crucial feedback on various elements of this book.

I owe an equally large debt of gratitude to Professor Timothy Babcock of the now defunct CIDA 'Sulawesi Regional Development Project,' which operated out of the University of Guelph. Professor Babcock, the 'dean' of Sulawesi studies, was unstintingly supportive. Drawing on the breadth of his own long-term and intimate knowledge of the Indonesian situation, he offered invaluable academic insight to my proposed project, as well as a practical support network through the various project offices in both Sulawesi and Ontario. Lastly, his home in Jakarta provided a welcome respite from the rigours of fieldwork. This book would not have been completed without his aid.

The largest debt I owe, and one that is difficult to convey in this form, is to those people of the kecamatan Pamona Utara in Sulawesi Tengah who accepted a stranger with gracious hospitality and thus made this project possible. I have frequently heard of other anthropologists' disagreeable experiences in the field, experiences for which I have no comparison. Rather, my hosts ignored my own clumsy and disagreeable behaviour and responded with Christian compassion, turning the other cheek.

In particular, I wish to thank the Majelis Sinode of the Gereja Kristen Sulawesi Tengah. Although not sponsors of my research, the church was open and supportive of my efforts and provided the fruits of its own research. They provided access to meetings not generally open to the public, as well as introducing me to many individuals central to my project. I hope that the results of my research bear out their faith in me. In particular, I would like to thank Ibu Pdt. A. Lumentut, the chair of the Synod Commission, and Bapak Pdt. H. Ruagadi, Bapak Pdt. Langkamuda, and Bapak Pdt. Hx. Sigilipu, for their moral support and practical assistance. I would also like to thank Bapak P. Posende of the church's Research and Planning Board for sharing his own research and reflections on the church.

At a more personal level, I bear a debt of gratitude to the people of Tentena. The keluarga Tumonggi-Ta'uno accepted me within their household and introduced me to the pace of village life. Almarhum Bapak Ds. Az. Tumonggi provided me the benefit of his considerable knowledge and experience. Ds. Wan Djendjengi was an able translator and research assistant, and a valued friend. His parents, Ngkai and Tu'a A'an, taught me what little I know of farming, and much about its pleasures. Fredrik Ta'uno also proved a valued assistant and friend, and introduced me to a different arena of To Pamona life. Ibu Lurah Parewa-Narendo and her husband, Bapak Pnt. A. Parewa-Narendo (or as I more commonly knew them, Tu'a and Ngkai Eda), were also unqualified in their acceptance and support. Bapak Pdt. R. Mbio-Mowose, his wife, and her father, Ngkai Osi, entertained me for hours as I listened to Ngkai Osi's reflections on a full life. Bapak Tiladuru deserves many thanks for his patient tutoring in Bahasa Pamona. To all, my thanks.

Tentena pai Kanada
Morante ewa kapala
Mau kita mombelawa
Ne'e bali mawo ndaya

I also owe a debt of gratitude to Henk and Marian van der Veld, missionaries for the Overseas Missionary Fellowship; Ted and Joanne Koopmans, of the Mennonite Missionary Fellowship; and Gert Noort, of the Nederlands Hervormde Kerk, for their hospitality and openness in the field.

Fieldwork is only one phase in the production of a book. In the long writing period, I received the support of family and friends. My thanks go especially to my mother, who has always made a home to come back to. I dedicate this work to her in the memory of my father, and to my sister, Diane, the anchors in my life. The thesis on which this book was based could not have been completed without the support of Jane Zavitz-Bond. Wanda Barrett and Leslie Jermyn know my feelings of gratitude, a debt which I lack the ability to convey on paper.

In Indonesia, sponsorship for my research was provided by LIPI (Lembaga Ilmu Pengetahuan Indonesia [The Indonesian Academy of Sciences]), and the Universitas Tadulako, in Palu, Sulawesi Tengah. Funding for my studies was provided by a number of institutions. The Joint Centre for Asia-Pacific Studies at University of Toronto, and the SEASSI program jointly sponsored my Indonesian language training at Cornell University. Funding for the Sulawesi phase of field research was provided by a Social Sciences and Humanities Research Council fellowship. Funding at other stages in my program was provided by Ontario Graduate Scholarships, and University of Toronto Open Scholarships.

COLONIAL 'REFORMATION' IN THE HIGHLANDS
OF CENTRAL SULAWESI, INDONESIA, 1892–1995

Introduction:
On Origin Stories in a Postmodern World

In the beginning God created the heaven and the earth.

Genesis 1: 1

In the beginning was the word, and the Word was with God, and the Word was God.

John 1: 1

Secular humanism so completely dominates the political landscape of our time that a key concept in Christian missiology, 'the Kingdom of God,' is reduced to mere metaphor. The division of church and state is considered essential to the preservation of freedom of religion within a democratic polity. And it is precisely its transgression of this dictum that makes 'fundamentalist Islam' such a potent symbol of arbitrary fanaticism, so easily demonized. Yet, within the history of the Netherlands and its colony Indonesia, these comfortable truisms are turned on their heads. In the nineteenth-century Netherlands, the rise of a constitutional democracy is associated with the intrusion of religion into politics under the banner of forging the Kingdom of God (*Het Koninkrijk God*) here, now. The same icon inspired Dutch missionaries to preach the gospel in the unexplored periphery of the Indonesian archipelago, their 'imperialistic' efforts in the name of God frequently outstripping the expansion of the *Pax Neerlandica* of the more cautious colonial state. This book examines one such model mission on the island of Sulawesi in the context of these broader religious and political transformations, and points to the factors that shaped and moulded its *bête noire*, Darul Islam (the Islamic state), in its own image.

These representations lie at the core of the self-reflexive intent of this study, since anthropology as a discipline is implicated not only in my representations, but in the very self-definition of the people with whom I worked. The religious mission led by Albert C. Kruyt from 1892 in the Poso River depression of Central Sulawesi innovated a 'sociological mission methodology' that drew upon the anthropological methods and theory of the time: this anthropological discourse was intimately tied to the particular form of indirect rule (later 'self-rule') then taking shape in the colony. Kruyt's anthropological representations thus played a key role in defining a legal-administrative unit that was simultaneously a dependent 'kingdom' within the Netherlands East Indies, as well as a *volkskerk*, a people's church (connoting nationhood), a local manifestation of the Kingdom of God. The ideological debates on the boundaries between church and state within the Netherlands were frequently invoked in determining administrative competence in the colony; and anthropological models derived from ethnographic fieldwork were utilized in the metropole as a means of developing a particular definition of religion that suited the religious politics of the era. The To Pamona (people of Pamona) are the product of these diverse discourses, discourses that individuals contextually draw upon to inform their social identities in a complex multi-ethnic population.

Whose image? is thus a key problematic in this book; the concept of 'the' culture and 'tradition' of the group now called the To Pamona needs to be disaggregated, its origins traced, its administrative uses highlighted. By focusing upon how these representations – the word is used both in the sense of 'image of' and as 'speaking for' – have been constituted, I try to underscore the relationship between politics and culture in much of Indonesia. Since 'culture' was key to the working of both indirect rule and the sociological mission method, local, usually elite, voices were quickly implicated in the competing colonial visions. This involvement does not, however, imply the passive reception of colonial categories, and this book is not intended as a Eurocentric recounting of the history of colonial conquests and treaties, or of mission successes. It is less a metahistorical narrative than a contextualization of key areas of cultural debate that emerged over the course of my fieldwork. The very diverse interpretations of key cultural concepts underscores the fact that the To Pamona are not a homogeneous group, and that active resistance through overt and covert means is a crucial aspect of how these concepts can be utilized.

Church and State

These highly visible, continuing conflicts between church and state in the politics of representation are played out in a variety of contexts. Take, for example, the expansion of the annual Independence Day celebrations in the otherwise sleepy church town of Tentena by the government of Indonesia in

1989, just before I arrived in the field. This regional cultural exhibition, the first annual 'Lake Poso Festival,' was a concerted attempt to develop the potential of the nation's '22nd designated tourist destination.' Tentena lies at the head of the Poso River, the heart of Kruyt's mission territory, nestled between mountains and a large lake, and more important, on the Trans-Sulawesi Highway, which links it to Tana Toraja, the second most popular international tourist site in Indonesia, after Bali. The festival grounds were constructed at considerable expense; fifteen exhibition buildings were built for the short, three-week festival, and the telecommunications and transportation infrastructure of the area was upgraded. Like the Independence Day celebrations out of which it grew, the festival was marked by colourful presentations of the *asli* (authentic) arts, songs, and dance of Central Sulawesi. The festival grounds were constructed across the river from two new hotels with Western amenities such as flush toilets and satellite-TV reception. Paddleboat swans rescued from a bankrupt Javanese amusement park, and Christmas lights that blinked *Selamat Datang* (Welcome), provided an odd contrast to the 'traditional' spectacle being mounted across the river.

The festival quickly drew the ire of some in the local church hierarchy who objected to the now Protestant To Pamona, the dominant ethnic group in the area, being characterized by resurrected animist songs and dances associated with headhunting. When I arrived in 1991, the Church Synod, which owned the land upon which the festival grounds were built, had just requested its return and announced its own plans to use the site for religiously oriented events. The following year, a monument to Christian youth was constructed atop a rock outcropping overlooking the festival site. In 1992, the site became the centre of a Dutch-funded centennial celebration of the arrival of Albert Kruyt, the first missionary to the area. Representatives from each of the church's three hundred congregations flooded into the village, dwarfing earlier festival attendance.

In response, the government expropriated the rice fields 200 metres to the west, and began construction of new festival buildings, this time in the shape of the traditional temples of the highlands in the previous century, at a reported cost of 12 billion rupiah (almost $7.5 million Can.). Each of the major ethnic groups of the highlands was represented by their own building, leading one local wag to dub the complex 'Taman Mini Sulawesi Indah' (Beautiful Sulawesi-in-Miniature Gardens) in reference to the popular Jakarta cultural theme park where each of Indonesia's twenty-seven provinces is represented by a pavilion in the shape of its indigenous traditional structures. Shortly thereafter, the church answered with the construction of Banua mPogombo, the Meeting House, an enormous conference centre.

At the root of this impressive construction boom in a backwater of the archipelago (population 8,000) lies a contest of representations; the national motto of Indonesia, 'Various, yet one,' expresses the ethnic, racial, and religious tensions against which the proclaimed unity of the nation must be achieved. With twenty-five distinct languages spoken in the province of Central Sulawesi alone, this is no easy task. This has required the artful manipulation of ethnic identities by the state. The 'Beautiful Sulawesi-in-Miniature Gardens,' like its inspiration in Jakarta, represents a sustained attempt by the New Order government of Suharto to preserve a timeless local tradition within the context of 'Beautiful Indonesia' as a whole – a process Pemberton dubs 'mini-ization' (1994, 12). Using the cultural theme park 'Mini' as a motif, Pemberton underscores the tendency of current state cultural policy to circumscribe ethnic identities as local manifestations of 'shared' pan-Indonesian ideals. 'Mini' is an attempt to recover the 'authentic origins' of the state and re-present them as a timeless legitimization of the current national cultural order. The state's assumption that the local and particular can be translated into core national values defines at once the content of local 'cultures' as well as the role of 'culture' in the production of social order.

These same cultural policies, variously dubbed 'mini-ization' (ibid.), 'discursive traditionalism' (Kahn 1993), 'showcase culture' (Kipp 1993), and 'adat spectacle' (Acciaioli 1985), have been redeployed in the periphery to fix its relationship to the centre; the representations created through cultural centralization in Jakarta have been re-exported to their original sites to redefine not only their content, but also their function. This amounts to a redefinition of ethnicity in Indonesia in terms of 'part-cultures,' as 'folk' traditions that can be understood only in relation to the new 'great' tradition defined by the Indonesian state (cf. Redfield 1960). The original Lake Poso festival grounds were laid out near the legendary village of Pamona, the village of origin of those now called the To Pamona (people of Pamona). The reconstruction of traditional structures and the resuscitation of the animist songs and dances of the To Pamona – now as high art rather than religious ritual – defined a previously diverse group in terms of its now uniform, 'authentic' traditions, as well as its place within a larger Indonesian cultural mosaic composed of similarly shaped and coloured tiles.

The variety of local meanings and intents of these 'tourist productions' merits repeated emphasis; these traditions are not being developed as a convenient cultural pidgin for foreign tourists intent on sampling from a performative smorgasbord. Although foreign tourists are sought as a valued source of foreign exchange, the Indonesian government views domestic tourism as a way of promoting 'national culture' (Adams 1998; Hitchcock 1998). The Five Year Development Plan of 1988 clearly articulated that 'domestic tourism continues to be developed and focused to encourage a sense of love of the country and nation and to build feeling, spirit, and noble national values in order to strengthen a national *persatuan* (unity) and *kesatuan* (togetherness) and to develop the economy. The attempt to nurture and develop domestic tourism has also led to upgrading the quality of the national culture ...' (cited in Hutajulu 1995, 640). The festival is thus clearly a nationalistic project, an attempt to shape and mould a multi-ethnic citizenry into a unified whole. But while there is now a wide-ranging literature on the effects of the New Order's cultural policies, less attention has been paid to the similar role being played by religious organizations with their own 'nationalist' strategies. The Christian Church of Central Sulawesi is equally concerned with its relationship to local culture, as demonstrated by its concerns about the Lake Poso Festival. It is the universal nature of the church's precepts which sets it off from the particular (*adat*, culture) and establishes it as religion (*agama*) as opposed to mere *kepercayaan* (culturally specific 'beliefs'). The state has mandated that each Indonesian citizen have a 'religion,' so defined. Such universalistic religions cut across the commitments of family and ethnicity, and provide for a unified civic consensus for the modern nation-state (Hefner 1989, 2). Ethnic religions (*kepercayaan*) that might prove a resource for alternative forms of 'national' identity face discriminatory penalties. But since the church stands, by definition, outside of culture, it, like the state, must redefine local traditions within its own universal precepts. The To Pamona are overwhelmingly Protestant, a Christian minority in a largely Islamic province and nation. The clash of state and church over how the To Pamona are represented (while simultaneously being reformed) manifests itself through contests like that related to the festival grounds.

The irony of the scale of this contest of representations is the very vagueness of the group to which they are said to apply. The Indonesian government collects no statistics on an ethnic basis, nor is ethnicity listed on an individual's citizenship card (although religion is). The 'To Pamona,' no less than the 'Minahasans' of North Sulawesi, 'consisted of a sizeable group of communities which shared some basic cultural patterns, recognised a common genealogical origin, and expressed their unity in the sphere of ritual and religious belief. The cultural emphasis, however, was upon systematic and complementary differences rather than upon homogeneity and solidarity, and the *ethnie* as a whole had no name' (Henley 1996, 143).

'To Pamona' ethnic consciousness is a relatively new phenomenon, the product of efforts like those of church and state described above. There is some confusion over to whom the designation applies. The state has phrased ethnic identity in terms of disused songs and dances, or as local manifestations of pan-Indonesian values embodied in the state itself. By the same measure, the church has sought to define To Pamona ethnicity in terms of Christianity, a larger category within which the distinctive cultural features of the group recede. These ironies, and the large sums of money involved, lead to several questions: Why does the New Order government persist in constituting To Pamona identity in terms of a *dead* past? And, if it is a dead past, why is the church threatened by it?

These questions can only be answered by looking at the history of how the 'To Pamona' have come to be an object of discourse, both locally and within the anthropological literature, and how this discursive object has been integrated with subjective identities. Both church and state have sought to 'represent,' that is, speak for, a 'community' that they have defined culturally. These representations draw on the political, economic, and cultural discourses through which the people of this area socially reproduce themselves and their communities. 'To Pamona' ethnicity cannot be rooted in 'primordial' (that is, pre-church, pre-state) sentiments and opposed to nationalism. Rather, the divergent ethnic discourses of church and state are themselves part of larger emancipatory nationalist discourses. One nationalist discourse is tied to the theological conceptualization of a *volkskerk* (people's church); the other to the Indonesian nationalist project 'Various, but one.' Both nationalist discourses posit unique and frequently contradictory solutions to the problem of the relationship among 'nation,' church, and state.

'Returning to the Origin': Colonial Incorporation

To understand these variant nationalisms, we must return to their origin, the moment of colonial incorporation. To Pamona ethnicity has its roots in anthropological representations utilized descriptively, and prescriptively, by both the colonial state and the colonial missions. This particular case is of interest because of the role that ethnographic representation played in salvaging distinct cultural forms within the colonial and, later, independent Indonesian state. Anthropological studies were used to reify culture as traditional *adat* (customary) law, itself a means of integrating indigenous peoples within the state. Similarly, mission attempts to 'inculturate' Christianity, to effect conversions while preserving the *adat*, utilized the same anthropological methodologies and genres to the same ends within the church. The To Pamona are the product of these salvage methods, a reinterpretation of an essentialized 'culture' whose content church and state cannot agree on.

Rather than add a new twist to old representations, and thus both solidify conceptions of this discursive object and, perforce, take sides in the contesting visions of who the To Pamona 'really' are, my aim here is to deconstruct the very notion that an authentic To Pamona culture can be uncovered (cf. Kahn 1993, 15–20). That is, I do not deny that there are local contests which seek to shape and mould *local* cultural boundaries and establish authentic local traditions. But, following Scott (1994), I distinguish between local debates that fix boundaries, and the anthropologist's postmodern anti-essentialist agenda. The To Pamona, like any ethnic group, are internally differentiated. They are not homogeneous, but purposely set apart in larger social arenas by contested cultural markers. These ethnic markers, and the internally coherent 'cultures' they are said to represent, are themselves the product of the universalizing discourses of competing authorities.

Given the cultural heterogeneity of the To Pamona, I have shifted the ethnographic focus of this book away from a description of a bounded social entity, a 'culture,' to those groups of individuals who have played key roles in establishing the hegemonic discourses by which the 'To Pamona' have come to be defined. It is for this reason that I discuss at length missionary A.C. Kruyt's now dated theories. Kruyt arrived on the southern shores of the Bay of Tomini in 1892 and began the work of establishing a mission empire that eventually extended across the island to the Bay of Bone. Viewed in its early stages, the mission was a dismal failure; not a single convert was made for fifteen years. But, during these years, Kruyt devoted himself to ethnographic fieldwork and published extensively in the scholarly journals of his day. His crowning achievement was the publication of a three-volume ethnography (with fellow missionary Nicolaüs Adriani) in 1912, for which he was given an honorary doctorate in theology from the University of Utrecht in 1913.

His years of ethnographic study and mission failure had convinced him that the conversion of the heathens (*alfuru*) was less a spiritual than a political matter; it was not until the highlands were severed from the lowland kingdoms that Christianity could make its mark. Kruyt's newly acquired academic credentials and his intimate knowledge of the highlands made him a key player in the colonial incorporation of Central Sulawesi within the Netherlands East Indies after 1905; indeed, much of his ethnographic work was used to legitimate the initial invasion. As a trusted government adviser, he worked in close association with the Binnenlands Bestuur, the Ministry of the Interior, in determining policy and priorities for the newly conquered territory. Beginning in 1908, a series of mass conversions swept the highlands, and the mission rapidly expanded.

The ultimate success of Kruyt's mission made it, and the sociological mission method upon which it was based, a model that was widely emulated throughout the archipelago. His mission was visited by many, from a variety of denominations, who sought to open their own mission fields, and he later taught at the Missionary Training School at Oegstgeest (Horsting n.d.; Randwijck 1981, 392–5). His method called for respect of other cultures, and for alternative cultural interpretations of the scriptures; conversion no longer meant 'becoming Dutch.'

Rather, the scriptures had to be translated into terms adapted to the 'mental' and 'cultural' capabilities of the new converts. And conversion itself was no longer measured according to some abstract theological standard, but according to the sincerity of the convert. He called for the development of 'indigenous' Christianities, that is, for a *volkskerk*, a church that simultaneously manifested the cultural spirit of 'a' people (Kruyt 1936b). An implication of Kruyt's method is that religion became a key factor in the 'imagined community' (the brother-hood [*ja'i*] of Christ) of the heterogeneous groups amalgamated within the Church (cf. Anderson 1983a).

Kruyt's mission methodology was deeply influenced by new currents in colonial policy that solidified the system of indirect rule within the Netherlands East Indies state. The 'Ethical Policy' introduced in the throne speech of 1901 similarly called for respect for indigenous custom, and the repayment of the Dutch 'debt of honour' to its colonies for centuries of exploitation. *Adat* law studies similarly used ethnographic methods, and were conducted to codify the customary practices of the traditional polities within the Netherlands East Indies state through which the Dutch ruled; Kruyt's emphasis on ethnography, respect for tradition, and the development of 'indigenous polities' was thus an adaptation of colonial practice to meet mission ends. The confluence of methods does not, however, imply a confluence of interests; the Dutch, no less than the To Pamona, were riven with political, cultural, and religious divisions. The contesting ethnic 'nationalisms' arising out of the Lake Poso festival grounds have their origins in these divisions.

The Discipline of Anthropology

By self-critically examining the role of anthropology in an active, political process concerned with the definition and preservation of distinctive 'cultures,' I question the assumptions usually held about the relationship between ethnographer and ethnographic subject. Despite theoretical challenges to primordialist or essentialist definitions of ethnic identity (beginning with Barth 1981), most ethnographers continue to define their subjects with a naturalistic verve for classification.[1] By softening the focus on the ethnographic Other, greater attention can be directed at the political and academic dialogues through which the reification of ethnicity in Indonesia takes place. It is then possible to evaluate the motives of the specific actors who have actively supported these competing processes of ethnogenesis. I make no attempt to provide the cultural 'essence' of the To Pamona, or even to catalogue the distinctive elements of 'their' culture. This has already been done at considerable length during the colonial period by the missionaries Albert Kruyt, Nicolaüs Adriani, and Kruyt's son Jan, whose books have become the primary resource for current indigenous scholarship on 'traditional *adat*' (Gintu 1991; Magido 1987; Pangku 1987; Santo et al. 1990; Sigilipu 1993). Rather, this book is concerned with those political, religious, and academic discourses that made such representations possible; hence, its conclusions have implications for discussions of ethnicity, religion, and 'custom' throughout Indonesia. Pemberton refers to this as the 'culture effect,' the production of knowledge called 'culture' which 'is devoted to recovering the horizons of its power by containing that which would appear otherwise' (1994, 9; cf. Asad 1979). The culture effect would erase from memory all that is not contained within its universalizing discourse.

This shift in focus underscores not only the role of literary representation in the formation of colonial subjects, but also its reflexive importance in defining key elements of Western subjectivity. In their study of South African missions, Comaroff and Comaroff note the one-sided nature of anthropological analyses of the encounter between missionaries and indigenous peoples (1991, 54). Europeans are seldom scrutinized in the same way as the ethnographic Other, a methodological legacy of anthropology's birth in the study of 'primitive societies.' If one contextualizes the ethnographic work of Kruyt and Adriani in terms of the dominant intellectual and political currents of the Netherlands at the turn of the century, the ethnographer is revealed as a social actor whose literary efforts made a difference in a number of distinct spheres. Among other things, the ethnographic text, an 'objective' portrait of an Other, was used to legitimate ideological positions in both the colonies and the mother country. Kruyt's and Adriani's work was intended to defend a particular definition of religion; a definition that had a great deal of practical importance for their missionary endeavours, as well as for how religion was conceived at home. This unique Dutch discourse on religion is not simply an outdated scholarly tradition of little practical import, but one that must be situated in the political and class context of both the Netherlands and the Netherlands East Indies at the turn of the century. This scholarly tradition informs not only Dutch colonialism and the trajectory of its reformist efforts, but also the hegemonic discourses that transformed the Netherlands itself. A single framework that encompasses the people of both nations as both historical subjects and objects is required.

Focusing, as this work does, upon colonial religious missions, my concern is to differentiate mission discourses from those of the colonial state. Whereas Pemberton has concentrated upon what he dubs the 'culture' effect, this analysis seeks to recover a parallel 'religious effect.' I ask the question posed by Asad, 'How does power create religion?' (1983, 252). Asad's approach, like Pemberton's, begins with 'authoritative discourse' (1979, 621) rather than with the 'systems of meaning' that are the product of this process. Such a conception of authoritative

discourse allows us to examine the interrelationship between a particular religious discourse – itself the product of a historically produced configuration of
knowledge and power – and the theoretical discourse of anthropologists on
religion. It is this last that is usually passed over in silence; the very practice of
asking the questions we, as anthropologists, do about the discourses and practices of others itself requires the 'context of tradition' – our own anthropological
tradition, a form of 'local knowledge' (Scott 1994, xxii). Anthropology as an
authoritative discourse was utilized in colonial and mission circles as part of a
particular constellation of power and knowledge whose practices can be examined not only in terms of the 'system of meanings' it produced, but also as a
hegemonic discipline that sought to shape and mould – to itself authorize – the
particular religious discourses of the ethnographic Other. It is in this vein that I
approach Kruyt's treatment of 'animistic religion' and his attempts to effect
Christian conversions.

This double-edged approach is required if we are to avoid confusion on the
true subject of this enquiry: this is less an ethnography than an analysis of the
colonial transmission of a particular religious discipline of power/knowledge
(Foucault 1980); this is less a village ethnography than an examination of a
volkskerk, a 'people's church' (which, by definition, encapsulates 'the' people as
well). Totalizing representations of the To Pamona as 'To Pamona' are part of
the authoritative discourses of the state, the church, and Western social sciences.
In contrast, I would emphasize that the 'To Pamona' are not a homogeneous
mass, nor easily characterized by a checklist of cultural features. As I write of the
To Pamona, my intent is to emphasize the contingent nature of the universalizing
discourses encapsulating their individual agency. In this way I hope to situate my
argument within current debates on the role of structure and agency in the
formation of cultural traditions without in any way attempting to 'speak for' or
'represent' them. As the Comaroffs argue,

> improperly contextualized, the stories of ordinary people past stand in danger of
> remaining just that: stories. To become something more, these partial, 'hidden
> histories' have to be situated in the wider worlds of power and meaning that gave
> them life. But those worlds were also home to other dramatis personae, other texts,
> other signifying practices. And here is the second point: there is no basis to assume
> that the histories of the repressed, in themselves, hold a special key to revelation; ...
> the discourses of the dominant also yield vital insights into the contexts and
> processes of which they were part. (1992, 17)

By focusing on State, Church, and academic discourses, rather than on the
'indigenous voices' of those excluded from positions of power, I hope to spare

those who wished to speak but feared being 'involved' (*dilibatkan*) in the, to them, unknown political ramifications of such speech. Given their experience with the Dutch, the Japanese occupation, the subsequent Permesta rebellion, as well as the traumatic period following the 'attempted communist coup' that gave rise to the New Order state, such fears must be respected: 'Otherwise we are pushed back to an anthropology that is little more than a description of the quaint or violent customs of other people, or a social history that calls talking to each other about the vulnerable giving them voice' (Sider and Smith 1997, 14).

Self-Representation

This book is entangled in the same questions about representation as Kruyt's work; who does it seek to describe and for whom does it speak? In answering the first question, I argue that this book is about the conflicting discourses of church and state; it is they who claim to represent their constituencies, not I. I have tried to emphasize that the To Pamona are a disparate group caught within larger encompassing bureaucratic structures. It is these structures, not the *volk*, upon which attention should be focused. I offer no riveting portraits of village life, no complete (and totalizing) discussions of 'the' kinship system, gender, or cosmology. I was constantly reminded of whom I did and did not speak for by one of my primary informants, who interrupted every interview several times with the plea 'Don't write this down yet.' Though proud to be treated as an expert, he had been the victim of successive violent changes in local political circumstances and he feared being 'implicated' in a project whose ultimate purpose he did not understand. His experience had been that those with pencils ultimately wrought the most damage.

This, however, explains only one aspect of my focus upon the conflicting discourses of church and state rather than upon an individualized, exoticized ethnographic Other. Anthropology's current fixation with reflexivity has led me to re-examine what 'social disciplines and social forces ... [make *my*] particular religious discourses, practices and spaces possible.' Just as Kruyt's background and education moulded his approach to religion and ethnography, so, too, has my own. In part, this study of To Pamona religiosity is my attempt to self-reflexively examine and critique my own cultural background. I, no less than my ethnographic 'subjects,' have been 'subject to' these religious discourses and practices. Born and raised within the Christian Reformed Church, a North American incarnation of Dutch Calvinism, I had firsthand experience of many mission practices long before I arrived in Indonesia. Whereas most current ethnography seeks to disrupt Western common-sense cultural presuppositions through a strategy of 'defamiliarization by epistemological critique,' the representation of an exotic cultural reality that implicitly disrupts our own, this work is an example of a less common comparative technique that places as much emphasis on 'us' as 'them'; and which teases out similarities rather than just highlighting differences (Marcus and Fischer 1986, 137–64). Such an approach would seem appropriate in an era of globalization. 'Salvage anthropology' is dead.

In the ensuing chapters I tack between the Netherlands and Indonesia in an effort to clearly delimit the encompassing structures that have shaped both Dutch and To Pamona agency in the Indonesian context. This presentation revolves around the unique role that 'religion' plays within the Dutch, and later Indonesian, state formations. The Netherlands of the period was said to be 'pillarized' (Dutch: *verzuild*) on a religious basis. The metaphor of 'pillarization' is perhaps less well known in North America than that of apartheid, which it resembles in origin, spirit, as well as effects. Pillarization refers to the religious apartheid that characterized Dutch society in the late nineteenth and early twentieth centuries. To refer to a specifically religious apartheid, however, obscures the redefinition of religion involved, and its consequent social divisions. Orthodox Protestant and Catholic social pillars hindered the development of a universal liberal, secular state apparatus, and created a plural non-state administration on a religious basis (Bank 1981; Kruijt and Goddijn 1968; Lijphart 1968; Steininger 1977; Stuurman 1983; Wintle 1987; Zahn 1989). These deep religious cleavages resulted in the development of separate religious school systems, religious political parties, and a host of religiously oriented service agencies such as housing developments, unions, newspapers, radio stations, and hospitals, which elsewhere in the West were sponsored by a secular state. Earlier in this century, typical pillarized Dutch working-class citizens would, for example, rent a house in a Protestant church–sponsored housing development, send their children to a church-sponsored school, read Protestant newspapers, and vote for the Anti-Revolutionary Party (the Orthodox Calvinist party). This social reformation was phrased as an 'emancipatory struggle' similar to the battles of national liberation then sweeping Europe. Placed against this background, the post-independence development of religious pillars (*aliran*) in the Indonesian social formation appears less exotic, and more an effect of colonial intervention (cf. Geertz 1960, 1963b, 1965). While this similarity between the Dutch and Indonesian cases has been noted in the past (largely in the Dutch literature [see Gunawan and Muizenberg 1967; Gunawan 1968, 1971; McVey 1971; Wertheim 1973]), it has been treated descriptively, not analytically (Kahn 1978).

It was personal 'colonization' of this type that led me to question the prevalent view of religious pillarization as a political phenomena. Living in Canada, an unpillarized nation, I was nonetheless a member of a denomination whose extension into civil society matched that of the Dutch and Indonesian churches

(Schryer 1998). The Christian Reformed Church in North America has some 875 congregations and 310,000 members (including baptized children), of whom approximately one-quarter are Canadian. It directly supports its own denominational magazine, as well as radio and television broadcasts (which originate in the United States). The church also directly supports its own missions (both home and foreign), and a third-world development agency. Each congregation has denominationally sponsored social groups for men, women, 'young people,' and youth (including the Calvinist Cadets, a church-centred version of Boy Scouts). In Ontario, it also supports a private system of Christian day schools from kindergarten through high school; the only degree-granting liberal arts college not affiliated to a state-sponsored university; as well as a post-graduate Institute for Christian Studies, which, though bordering on the campus of the University of Toronto, is affiliated with the orthodox Calvinist Free University of Amsterdam. (There are also two denominationally supported colleges and a seminary in the United States.) It also supports a nursing home for the elderly and a counselling centre. The church is affiliated with the Christian Labour Association of Canada, a union predicated upon conciliation rather than labour conflict (and hence not recognized by the Canadian Labour Congress). The church directly supports a political lobby group, the Citizens for Social Justice, and indirectly supports the Christian Heritage Party of Canada, a right-wing federal political party predicated upon Christian principles. It is thus possible for church members to engage in a Christian 'lifestyle' in all aspects of civil society.

By juxtaposing these three examples – Canadian, Dutch, and Indonesian – I aim to de-exoticize the concept of pillarization and draw attention instead to the reasons for the variable success of their common strategies in the political realm (cf. Stuurman 1983). The Christian Heritage Party of Canada has been marginalized as effectively as Parkindo in Indonesia without in any way hindering either group's ability to pillarize Christians; that is, rationalize the disciplinary mechanisms through which they reform their subjects in civil society. Indonesia, in particular, has moved from being politically pillarized by religion during its short-lived democratic period, to a policy of 'floating masses' under the New Order that effectively marginalizes the political power of the religious parties. The 'floating masses' policy argues that an unsophisticated rural population should not be distracted by politics except during short pre-election campaigns, and that no political party should have a grass-roots organization below the regency level. The case of Indonesian Christians thus seems to resemble that of the Netherlands late in the last century, before the extension of the electoral franchise, in that its religiously pillarized citizens have no political voice. Politics are thus played out in the 'cultural' sphere – in schools and in the social organizations through which social reproduction is accomplished. It is in this light that the 'contest of representations' centred around the Lake Poso Festival must be interpreted.

The issues of representation and voice are thus not simply 'political' matters, but invoke complex questions about the very nature of our analytic categories. The roots of pillarization (and hence its cultural politics) lie, rather, in the disciplinary strategies of the church; strategies which, like those of the liberal state, aim to inform their subjects with a distinctive 'nationalist' identity. The similarity between the Dutch word for 'pastor' (*dominee*) and its cognate, 'dominate' (*domineren*), is somewhat ironic. This domination is not achieved through the 'shared beliefs' of the congregation, but through the rationalization of the application of discipline – the voluntary surrender of a voice within a ritual setting that priorizes the interpretation of Truth provided by the minister. The *volkskerk* thus constitutes its subjects as a *volk* and seeks to speak to, and for, them. The Indonesian state directly contests the church's right to do so, and through its political wing, Golkar, similarly attempts to inform local identities and speak for its religious constituents. The state's intrusion in civil society, or, more accurately, the lack of a distinct civil society, thus confounds our preconceptions of 'state,' 'church,' and 'politics.'

Rationalizing Religion

What has excited the political scientists and sociologists who developed the pillarization model is the invasion of the political realm by organized religion, a breach, as it were, in the otherwise solid bastion of secular modernization. Pillarization offers a point of entry for the study of 'religious fundamentalism,' whether Christian or Muslim. Yet, by conceiving religious pillars as a political phenomenon, organized from the top down as a means of mobilizing voters, they have equated a self-defined 'religious' movement, with 'religious' goals, reached by 'religious' means, and a mere disguise for power politics. A single political framework is used, pushing square 'religious' pegs in round 'secular' holes, and so producing contradictory definitions of religious pillars as both 'political parties with ancillary religious organizations' and 'religious groups with political facets.' These two conceptualizations are not mirror images of each other. A consequence of this particular formulation in terms of political parties is the view that religious pillars in Indonesia have disappeared (or that their importance has been marginalized) with the elimination of the Communist party and the restructuring of the Indonesian political system under Suharto's New Order regime. Viewed as 'religious groups with political facets,' such marginalization is not so readily evident.

It is more productive, I would argue, to recast the discussion of religious pillars in terms of an alternative literature, that of the rationalization of religion. Rationalization is a key concept in the sociology of Max Weber, who used the term in multiple senses (Weber 1963). On the one hand, rationalization was used in reference to an intellectual trend towards the 'disenchantment of the world,' the replacement of magical elements of thought with more systematically coherent ideas. Alternatively, rationalization was used in reference to institutional specialization and differentiation, and the development of hierarchical, bureaucratic forms of social organization. The concept was introduced into the Indonesian literature in a now classic paper by Clifford Geertz, '"Internal Conversion" in Contemporary Bali' (1973c [1964]). Geertz described the imminent transformation of Balinese religion from a conceptually disorganized 'animist hodgepodge of feckless ritual' into a coherent, 'rationalized, self-conscious and worldly-wise' belief system that addresses the eternal 'problems of meaning – evil, suffering, frustration, bafflement, etc.' head-on. The main force behind the rationalization of Balinese belief systems was the nobility, who had found their ceremonially based authority challenged by republican ideology. What was once ritual habit unquestioningly supporting noble prerogatives now required its reasons – its doctrines. As Geertz notes, 'to see in all this a mere Machiavellianism however, would be to give the young nobles both too much credit and too little. Not only are they at best partially conscious of what they are doing, but, like my village theologians, they too are at least in part religiously rather than politically motivated' (Geertz 1973c, 186). The rationalization of the belief system was thus accompanied by the reorganization of the Balinese nobility, and the Brahmana caste in particular, within the rational bureaucratic order of the republican state. The rationalization of Balinese Hinduism under the auspices of the 'Balinese Ministry of Religion' has regularized the qualifications of Brahmana priests, classified temples, and established a training school and 'even a small religious political party centred around a ranking noble and dedicated to forwarding these changes' (Geertz 1973c, 189).

Easy parallels can be drawn between the class composition and activities of this religious rationalization of Balinese religion with its attendant creation of a political wing, and the religious revival (*reveil*) that swept the Dutch aristocracy during the 1850s, giving birth to the Orthodox Calvinist Anti-Revolutionary Party. Yet my point is that both cases of religious rationalization have the structural effect of creating religious pillars. Geertz, surprisingly, does not himself draw the parallel between the rationalization of Balinese religion and pillar formation in Java (1963b, 14–16, cf. 21). In focusing upon the emotional and attitudinal changes associated with rationalization as an autonomous cultural process, Geertz ignores one-half of Weber's original formulation, which clearly placed the rationalization of beliefs in the context of the bureaucratization of religious establishments. This Weberian rationalization of Balinese religion, prompted as much by proximate issues of national religious politics and changing patterns of local authority as by the perennial problems of meaning, was as much social-organizational as it was a systemization of doctrine (Atkinson 1983).

The growing literature that has emerged out of Geertz's pioneering work has fastidiously addressed this one-side interpretation of the processes of rationalization. Similar cases of the self-conscious rationalization of 'belief systems' (*kepercayaan*) as worldly-wise religions (*agama*) have been described among numerous groups in the Outer Islands since Geertz's article first appeared in 1964. Religious transformations have been described among the Ngaju Dayaks (Weinstock 1981, 1987; Schiller 1997) and the Meratau (Tsing 1987) of Kalimantan (Borneo); the Tenggar of highland Java (Hefner 1985, 1987); and among the Sa'dan Toraja (Crystal 1974; Volkman 1985; Waterson 1984), Mappurondo (George 1996), and To Wana (Atkinson 1983) of Sulawesi. These examples have all drawn attention to the 'politics of *agama*' (Kipp and Rodgers 1987), and rooted the rationalization of animist traditions in the political demands of the New Order government's civil religion. This literature is, however, a diversion from the parallel I wish to emphasize between rationalization and pillar formation.

While the literature on the 'politics of *agama*' has sought to underscore the social roots of religious rationalization, it implicitly accepts that only 'irrational' animist traditions can be 'rationalized.' The literature thus focuses upon the still animist, isolated groups (*suku terasing*) of the Outer Islands, rather than upon the followers of world religions in the Javanese heartland who are incorporated within religious pillars. While this literature has sought to ground religious rationalization in social and political processes, its static view of the end state towards which their ethnographic subjects are working prevents parallels being drawn with the 'already rational' world religions (for exceptions see Hefner 1987 and Bowen 1993). Even where a world religion is treated within the rationalizing religion framework, it is the act of conversion from animism to Christianity that constitutes the process (Hoskins 1987). The *aliran* of Java are treated as static social structures, not as a dynamic religious process comparable to the transformations undergone by those 'who do not yet have a religion.' This book, in contrast, specifically attempts to examine the historically rooted rationalization of a world religion in the periphery and its attendant establishment of an indigenous 'Kingdom of God.'

The key to this examination are the authoritative discourses I discussed earlier, the specific constellations of power and knowledge that define the boundaries of religiosity. This approach draws on the seminal reworking of the Weberian rationalization thesis by Michel Foucault (1980) and Jürgen Habermas (1984). Both of these approaches extend the Weberian problematic beyond the workings of the bureaucratic 'iron cage' into the operations of society as a whole. What Foucault refers to as the 'capillary action' of modern forms of power/knowledge, and that which Habermas refers to as the 'colonization of the Lifeworld,' is the reorganization of social life through the internalization of 'normalizing' disciplinary practices whose power lies in the ways in which they mask how they work. This was referred to by Pemberton as the 'culture effect,' and by me as a parallel 'religious effect,' the development of a discourse that constantly seeks to authoritatively define itself by pre-empting the space of radically opposed utterances.

It is these disciplinary practices that are rationalized as a means of regularizing and extending their relations of colonizing power. This book seeks to explore how the mission church in Central Sulawesi and the colonial state established a discourse on 'religiosity' that has since infused, reorganized, and rationalized a discursive realm they identified as 'culture' (*adat*). I argue that the architect of this discourse was Kruyt, whose sociological mission methodology applied Dutch conceptualizations to the *alfuru*, the 'not yet Christians, not yet Muslims,' of Central Sulawesi, who lacked a word for religion. The sociological mission method combined the systematic collection of ethnographic knowledge with a retargeting of the subject of conversion from individual to *volk*. Kruyt's progressive model of conversion worked towards the Christianization of indigenous 'culture'; as 'culture' was Christianized, individual members of that 'culture' would be also. 'Culture' was a totalizing concept that encompassed both group (as defined by the mission) and individual (caught within the bureaucratic structures through which 'culture' was abstracted, reified, and legislated).

The rationalization of religion fostered by Kruyt's method was founded on the problematic relationship between a universal 'religion' and a particular 'culture.' This distinction was necessitated by the administrative logic of the secular liberal colonial state. The colonial state governed through indirect rule, through the reification of culture (*adat*) as law. Indigenous political elites were co-opted and incorporated within a bureaucratic colonial state as a means of divide-and-rule, as a means of establishing and maintaining a traditional order that cross-cut and undermined a militant pan-archipelagic Islam. This policy, which emerged out of the lengthy war in Aceh, in Sumatra, at the turn of the century, often created traditional elites where none had previously existed. Such was the case in Central Sulawesi, where the To Pamona were 'feudalized' and given a *raja* (king). Kruyt's attempt to Christianize indigenous 'culture' thus refers to a colonially constituted *adat* discourse and not to a contextless tradition. It is out of these often conflicting, bureaucratically rooted colonial discourses that the current contest of representations of the To Pamona arose. The Hervormde Kerk (Reformed Church) in the Netherlands was by no means a state church; hence the parallel development of religious pillars in Indonesia offered the opportunity for counter-hegemonic movements. The boundary between 'religion' and 'culture' is contested terrain subject to frequent incursions and skirmishes.

The root of the conflict lies in the scope and competence of the bureaucratic orders established by church and state. In the Netherlands, traditional rural elites had rationalized the bureaucratic order of the church as a means of preserving their prerogatives from the rapid expansion of a Napoleonic civil bureaucracy. The pillarization of the Netherlands grew out of the progressive successes of these elites in rationalizing a religious sphere that included large parts of what became the secular state elsewhere in the West. In the Indonesian case, both colonial state and mission church sought to domesticate local elites within their bureaucratic orders, with differential success, drawing upon these Dutch precedents. For those resistant to the heavy hand of the colonial government, the church became the sole political institution that could successfully challenge the state (the incontestable 'loyal opposition' [Haire 1981]). Developing strategies first utilized in the Netherlands, the church has sought to reclaim as much of tradition as possible from a Netherlands East Indies' state that sought to rule through an *adat* discourse.

It should be clear, then, that both church and state must be viewed within a common rationalization framework. The state, no less than the church, rationalized its bureaucratic order to regularize and refine the application of its discipline into all aspects of 'traditional' life. Both church and state have attempted to regularize and centre the realm of To Pamona culture within their hierarchical polities. This commonality of underlying social and cultural processes, however, does not entail a common agenda; although both church and state are rationalizing institutional orders, the rationality that drives them differs. These divergent rationalities must be rooted in the political and class dynamics of those drawing on their particular strategies. This is necessary because, ultimately, what must be accounted for is not just the process of rationalization, common to both church and state, but the relative success of church over state.

Structure and Agency

In discussing the church, state, and their 'rationality,' I hope to underscore that their institutional logic is rooted in the agency of historically constituted subjects, the people I came to know over two years of fieldwork in the subdistrict of Pamona Utara. On the one hand, the To Pamona have been shaped by the demands of these foreign institutions; on the other, their choices have been moulded by class relations which themselves affected how particular individuals were able to situate themselves within these institutional orders and, in so doing, transform and rationalize them. The local elites incorporated within the colonial government's invented kingdom of Poso and the mission's cadres of preacher/teachers were originally selected precisely because of their traditional status; mission and state hoped to co-opt these individuals of influence and use this status to their own ends. Yet, in the process of incorporation, these traditional elites gained resources whose exploitation increasingly involved them in new class relations, in the developing markets in rice, land, and labour; these elites were at the forefront of the commodification of the local economy. It is the relationship among class, tradition, and institutional order, I would argue, that is crucial in accounting for the relative success of the church over the state in the reformation of the highlands.

The local elites of Pamona Utara characterize themselves by their modernity, in large part reflected in a style of consumption made possible by cash incomes. And yet, they ironically continue to present themselves as the experts on Pamonan tradition, a role they have assumed as local patrons, as well as through their role as shapers of State and Church discourses on tradition. In highlighting this divide, they juxtapose the processes of development as represented by them-selves, with the 'perpetuation of tradition' typical of local farmers who are therefore the authors of their own poverty. The divide, however, is never com-plete since the modernity reflected in consumption rarely extends to relations of production; as local patrons, they continue to exploit a transformed tradition that makes their own modernity possible. It is this image of duality that has character-ized the literature on the Indonesian peasantry since the initial implementation of the Ethical Policy, although the location of the dividing line has always been subject to elite definition, as this case suggests. The Dutch colonial economist J.H. Boeke drew this line between highly capitalized Dutch corporations and peasant agriculture (1953). The peasant economy, he argued, was embedded in 'social needs' determined by tradition. This dual-economy approach was given new life by Clifford Geertz (1963a), who saw peasant economy as characterized by 'shared poverty' and the 'involution of tradition.'

Rather than root local poverty in the imperfect penetration of capitalism or the perpetuation of tradition, I argue that peasant agriculture is by no means eco-nomically irrational, or tradition-bound. Detailed discussions with local peasants convinced me that, as a group, they were highly conscious of the costs of tradition, and they pursued such avenues only when they were cost-effective. It is this cost-consciousness and the selective use of non-commodified 'traditional' farm inputs that similarly characterized elite economic strategies and pointed to a crucial ambiguity of capitalism in peasant production; hence, Kahn states, we should not 'rely on characterizing rural relations solely in terms of class (in the classical Marxist sense) or in terms of the survival of pre-capitalist traditions. Instead, rural differentiation ... has to be conceived of as a modern process, in which traditionalization and modernization are inseparably intertwined' (1993, 62).

It is this selective use of 'tradition' and the transformation of this 'tradition' to meet the specific need for uncosted labour in a commodified economy that tie 'modern' elites and 'traditional' peasants together in a common, Janus-faced economic system. Church and state have played different, but important mediating roles in how locals have situated themselves in this economy. Both state and church have been agents of modernity through the introduction of wages and in establishing a standard of consumption to be emulated. The state, however, has been the primary purveyor of development and has been responsible for the enforced cultivation of wet-rice terraces and the introduction of local markets in land, labour, and agricultural goods. The state, through its development policies, has defined a standard of economic modernity against which local 'failings' can be measured as 'the perpetuation of tradition,' that is, poverty for which locals are themselves to blame. The church has been equally involved in the transformation of agriculture in an effort to root out its animist elements, but has had a different attitude towards some economic aspects of tradition. The church has offered an institutional home for an alternative gift economy that stands in ideological opposition to the market and makes the patterns of patronage upon which local leadership is based possible. This opposition of the gift and the market cannot, I argue, be viewed as a natural opposition between 'primitive' and modern economy; rather, the very opposition is the product of the processes of modernization (cf. Parry and Bloch 1989). Both church and state view themselves as modernizing institutions.

This gift economy has in large part become synonymous with kinship and an injunction against the strict accounting of the costs and benefits of kinship relations; it could easily, if erroneously, be treated as a 'traditional' means of 'sharing poverty' (cf. Geertz 1963b). However, this gift economy, *posintuwu* exchange, is a particularly modern innovation, intimately tied to a cycle of feasts incorporated within the institutional boundaries of the church. These feasts occur on a rotating basis among the members of the church's various worship groups, and are the means by which these worship groups define specific individuals as kin, the ideological character of kinship ties, and hierarchical relations within the group. The kinship ties and exchange relations found within these groups also establish the basic forms of patronage upon which leadership in the church is founded. And these same patrons utilize this kinship ideology in their agricultural and business endeavours, thus linking the institutional logic of the church and worship with the 'tradition' by which poor peasants attempt to guarantee the viability of their households.

It is the ideological importance of feasting in the social reproduction of these peasant households that makes it a key area of cultural contestation between the institutional logics of church and state. Like the annual Lake Poso Festival, feasting, and the wedding feast in particular, has become the terrain through which political and economic struggles have been given their cultural cast. The wedding is the largest of the cycle of domestic feasts, and the only feast that involves separate state, church, and 'traditional' ceremonies. Each of these ceremonies attempts to define the newly formed household in a way that reflects distinct institutional priorities; it is precisely because they envision the household as a natural unit of production and consumption, as the natural site of the social reproduction of kin and of gendered identities, that Church and State have sought to 'modernize' the 'traditional family' and its place within their larger institutional orders (Li 1996, Schrauwers 1995). The differing modernities offered by Church and State are thus indicative of a broader, unresolved political conflict being addressed through cultural means, as discussed earlier.

Elites and Fieldwork

The prominence this book gives to the interpretations of local elites reflects, in large part, the circumstances under which my fieldwork was conducted. If, as has frequently been argued (e.g., Moore 1994, 112–16), the travel narrative has been an essential literary tool for establishing the ethnographic authority of anthropologists in their texts, then it is appropriate that my tale recounts the chain of government and church officials along which I was passed on my way both in and out of the field. Whereas the archetypal anthropological travel narrative was an essential means of establishing the cultural difference that separated the West from the rest, my narrative is one about those who control access to even the smallest, most isolated of areas within a well-mapped, and perhaps over-administrated, state. My travel narrative begins almost a year before I arrived in Tentena, as I sought to navigate the Indonesian bureaucracy, rather than the high seas, to obtain a research visa.

These negotiations are handled by the Indonesian Academy of Sciences, who assist in finding the essential local academic sponsor, and also seek the consent of the six independent bureaucracies, including the Department of Immigration and the various security forces whose permission is needed, for a long-stay research visa. The frustrations of the process, involving as it does so many independent agencies, is aptly summarized by John Pemberton's experience, whose research permit appeared 'on February 19, 1982. But the permit also expired on the same date' (1994, 1). My initial experience was by no means as traumatic, and after several months of faxing, phoning, prodding, and waiting, I arrived in Jakarta.

A bureaucratic pilgrimage followed. I was given a series of letters to be delivered to various ministries, where I was registered and processed, and issued with other letters directed at those further along the bureaucratic chain. The days of shuttling between departments, the rendering of letters, and the wait for further permits was then repeated at the provincial level of those bureaucracies, in Palu, Central Sulawesi. And then, at the district level, in Poso. And then at the subdistrict level, in Tentena. There, I registered with the local police, and reported to the subdistrict head (the *camat*), who issued me further letters for the heads of those villages in which I was working. It is important to underscore (given Western attitudes towards bureaucracy) that I recite this bureaucratic litany not as a complaint of unjust treatment, but to emphasize the bureaucratic web within which all Indonesian citizens live. My travel narrative simply recapitulated the governmental links that flow from centre to periphery.

My travel narrative also includes a parallel stream, flowing from the Mission House in Oegstgeest, near Leiden, in the Netherlands, where I had conducted archival research on Albert Kruyt and the Netherlands Missionary Society. There I was given contact information for the chair of the synod of the Christian Church of Central Sulawesi (Gereja Kristen Sulawesi Tengah [GKST]), the Reverend A. Lumentut. I was surprised to learn that Reverend Lumentut was in Jakarta, attending a meeting of the Indonesian Council of Churches (PGI) when I first arrived. We planned to meet, but tight schedules kept me playing catch-up on the trip to Tentena, the site of the GKST's headquarters. I missed our planned meeting at a church in the provincial capital, Palu, and arrived in Tentena several days behind her. The Reverend Lumentut graciously supported my research, and introduced me to Henk and Marian van der Veld, Dutch missionaries from the Overseas Missionary Fellowship, and Ted and Joanne Koopmans, of the Mennonite Central Committee. Ironically, Joanne was the sister-in-law of the minister of the Dutch Calvinist church in my home town. I arrived just in time to attend the biennial Church Synod sessions, at which the issue of the festival grounds was avidly discussed. It was through these ties that I was eventually introduced to Bapak Az. Tumonggi, the son of a minister, an elder in the local church, one-time member of the Church Synod, and then an upper-level bureaucrat in the Ministry of Education, with whom I lived, on and off, for a two-year period.

A simple reading of anthropology's 'participant observation' methodology would have led me to flee farther afield, seeking a more authentic (i.e., exotic) experience in some village where chance meetings with bureaucrats, ministers, and missionaries were less likely. Yet, as I have tried to emphasize here, these now global links are part of everyday life in the highlands of Central Sulawesi. Arriving amid the synod sessions, I was quickly made aware of how politically contentious local 'culture' was, and the importance of elite discourses in negotiating the boundaries of local agency. And given the contentious nature of the debates, each side was more than willing to explain and elaborate on their perspectives. Rather than ignore them, I made them a subject of inquiry.

Overcoming this patron's-eye view remained a priority, but my method of entry to the field sensitized me to my own elite position and the difficulties of establishing rapport. I quickly learned that ignoring ties of patronage and attempting a more direct approach inevitably prompted fears of contradicting the 'experts' and brought such responses to even the simplest of questions as: 'I really wouldn't know. Don't you think you should ask someone like Bapak Tumonggi?' Local opinion had placed me in the generic category of *orang balanda* (Dutchman, a Westerner), and hence most likely a missionary (a positive, valued status in the Christian community). This presumed status had its advantages. As a local curiosity, I was invited to meetings not normally open: as a man, to the meetings of the Women's Commission; though unmarried, to the meetings of the Evangelization Group (for married couples); though a *bapak* (father, but more generally an honorific for those of status), to the meetings of the Youth Group. By attending such meetings widely in the houses of all villagers, I was slowly able to acquire a growing (if incomplete) reputation as someone who 'doesn't choose his people,' which opened further doors down the road for more intimate participation.

Given the wide latitude allowed me, this initial entry into village life meant attending four or five meetings for worship a week (rather than the three meetings attended by the local devout), which further strengthened local assumptions of my 'mission'; unsurprisingly, the worship service became a central focus of my work. What might seem an excessively narrow (and formal) focus rapidly broadened, since meetings for worship are also the opportunity for a series of feasts; the largest of this series of feasts is the wedding, of which I attended about two per month, on average. My voyeuristic role as 'participant observer' was made locally meaningful, especially at these weddings, as I was gradually incorporated as the *seksi dokumentasi* (documentation section) in the village committee structure by which such performances are staged, a role that neatly met both my own and my hosts' needs. As the 'documentation section,' I photographed the bride and groom in the myriad rites and ceremonies by which they were wed. Since the wedding includes separate church, civil, and traditional ceremonies, it proved an important site to examine the cultural struggles of church and state in determining the boundaries of local culture. These events also brought me far afield, as wedding expeditions over the two-year period led me to almost every village within the subdistrict, and many outside of it.

A large part of every wedding was the complicated series of gift exchanges (*posintuwu*) that took place. The ideology of these gift exchanges is a crucial aspect of local definitions of kinship, and of kinship distance. The documentation of exchanges was thus one means of approaching this difficult subject. To Pamona kinship is cognatic; the absence of unilineal kinship groups, combined with a teknonymic naming system whereby an individual changes his or her name with every change in life status, made it extremely difficult to interpret the thousands of dyadic exchanges that take place at each wedding. I might obtain records from a number of sources about what appeared to be three different people, who were in reality one and the same. Few people, however, had knowledge of all the teknonyms since they are age-graded, and it is extremely impolite for a younger person to use an older person's 'real' name. I was lucky, therefore, to have been introduced to Ngkai Osi early in my fieldwork. Ngkai Osi was already six years old when the Dutch first invaded the highlands; despite his advanced years, he was able to link the names I discovered in the church baptismal records with the various teknonyms, and hence provide the key to understanding the pattern of exchanges I saw occurring at weddings, as well as the early history of the village.

It was this emerging pattern that directed my attention towards agriculture; kinship, as I have noted, was solidified by a myriad of dyadic exchanges that established patterns of patronage and dependence. Patrons were able to give more because they had greater resources of land and labour. Yet, as I examined these questions in detail, I discovered that more than *posintuwu* was being exchanged within these kinship groups. Households that I had assumed were rather straightforward units of production and consumption turned out to have 'fuzzy' boundaries, allowing for the transfer of labour and consumables between patrons and their dependants, guaranteeing the viability of them both. The investigation of these patterns quickly acquired a historical dimension, since the landownership that lay at the root of this patronage system had been created within living memory. The surveying of the fields, the investigation into the forms of labour utilization, and the changes in household form over time took me further and further away from the rather static discourses on 'tradition' of church and state, and hence provided me with the resources to challenge their interpretations.

The Persistence of Tradition

The ultimate aim of this book is to challenge the core secularization thesis of

Weberian rationalization. The post-Enlightenment secular social sciences have been eager to trace the path of the 'disenchantment of the world,' the path from religious speculation to secular science, from mythology to theology, from culture to practical reason. These implicitly evolutionist progressions are based on the false assumption that institutional rationalization has necessary cognitive consequences; that, once set in motion, institutional rationalization leads to a particular way of thinking inimical to the flawed reasoning, the irrationality, which lies at the core of religious faith in 'things unseen.' This inherently individualized rationality is linked with capitalist economic individualism, freed from its social shackles by the Enlightenment. It was the specific 'ethic' of Protestantism, its cultural predisposition towards the practices of capitalist accumulation, which enlarged the space of civil society, fostered the growth of the market, and 'disenchanted' the world by removing unruly cultural forces from an increasingly mechanistic model of the way things work.

It is crucial to challenge the linkage between institutional and cognitive rationality because of its implications in development discourse. Despite converting to Protestantism, the To Pamona have apparently not been infused by either the 'spirit of capitalism' or economic individualism. Within the modernization model, their failure to either 'develop' economically or secularize would be treated as evidence of their entrapment in 'irrational' tradition, and outmoded, superstitious modes of thinking. An easy reading of Kruyt's mission methodology could be invoked in explanation; since the sociological mission methodology specifically sought to preserve indigenous 'tradition' within the Christian *adat*, the original cultural impetus of Protestantism was lost. Yet, I would argue that this explanation is fundamentally flawed. We must remember that the *adat* preserved by the state and the church is a 'discursive' traditionalism; it does not describe an implicit cultural logic of practice, but is a textually derived 'tradition' infused with the dominant colonial discourses' assumptions of secularization and modernization. It is this discursive tradition that has been rationalized, systematized, and bureaucratized, and put in its place. As 'tradition,' it stands by definition as a persistence of the past, as an isolated, untouched remnant.

In contrast, I would argue that this discursive traditionalism is not the persistence of the past in the present, the implicit logic of practice of the group defined as the 'To Pamona.' Rather, as a discursive tradition, it is a resource equally available to local manipulations and adaptations, and pressed to other purposes. While the dominant discourses of colonialism were able to establish the basic hierarchical relations between 'modernity' and 'tradition,' and discursively inscribe and describe the 'To Pamona' in 'traditional' terms, their practices, in contrast, frequently bend these 'traditions' in new ways to their suit their needs in a modern, cash economy. No radical divide, no dual economy, can be drawn between the old and the new. Rather, 'tradition,' as a discursive resource, becomes a convenient means for the state of 'blaming the victims' for their own underdevelopment; and 'tradition' becomes a means of survival that provides rational (calculable) benefits for those trapped in the impoverishing development initiatives of the state that are predicated upon capital accumulation for some and progressive poverty for others. This ethnography thus aims to disrupt the development discourses of the state that are used to blame the victims for their poverty by demonstrating how the 'rational' utilization of these discursive traditions exceeds the boundaries of that discourse. In no way can I claim to wholly represent the real or authentic culture of the To Pamona. I can, however, clearly describe the failure of dominant discourses to encapsulate diverse individual reasons and practices without implicating those individuals in political projects not their own.

The progression of this book thus reflects these general concerns. As I have striven to root my analysis of these hegemonic authoritative discourses in the constitution of rural class structure, the progression of chapters moves from an historical analysis of the development policies of the Netherlands East Indies state to the transformations of local 'culture' and 'religion' that resulted. Part One of this book analyses the terms under which Central Sulawesi, and the village of Tentena, in particular, were incorporated within the bureaucratic orders of the state and mission church. Part Two undertakes an analysis of local responses to these encompassing policies. It focuses upon the local creation of a kin-centred moral economy and its relationship to 'traditional leadership' and feasting. The introduction of landed property and the slow commodification of agricultural production have not followed the developmental path laid out by the state. The local elites' dependence upon this kin-centred moral economy constituted through feasting has been incorporated within the church, although not without contradictions. The evolution of the wedding feast is thus examined as an arena within which these conflicting interests are expressed. Part Three examines the rationalization of To Pamona Christianity, rooting this process in the class dynamics of feasting that resulted in an autonomous religious bureaucracy and a 'religious nationalism' with important implications for state formation. The final chapter returns to the general arguments presented in this introduction: that the failure of secularization does not represent a basic irrationality that can be used to blame the victims for their poverty. The historical argument presented in the bulk of this book is supplemented by a comparative analysis with the other religions in Indonesia, including Islam. This contrast is intended to highlight the importance of the historical study of Christianity in the Netherlands to the study of religion in Indonesia.

PART ONE

COLONIAL INCORPORATION

1

Missions in Colonial Context

And he said unto them, Go ye into all the world, and preach the gospel to every creature.

Mark 16: 15

... modern Orientalism, unlike the precolonial awareness of Dante and d'Herbelot, embodies a systematic discipline of accumulation. And far from being exclusively an intellectual or theoretical feature, it made Orientalism fatally tend towards the systematic accumulation of human beings and territories.

Said 1979, 123

In 1886, J.G.F. Riedel, a Dutch colonial official based in Manado, in North Sulawesi, published the first ethnographic sketch of Central Sulawesi. The report, based upon information provided by the rulers of the coastal kingdom of Parigi, is noteworthy less for the accuracy of its literary characterization of the 'Dog Eaters' of the highlands than for the fanciful map that accompanied it. Carefully circumscribed by mountain chains, a circle was drawn around the 'heart of darkness' at the island's centre. This boundary, shored up by an imaginary geography, marked a colonial lacuna filled only by Orientalist 'scholarship.' And as Said has pointed out, such scholarship was driven less by theoretical interests than by imperialist needs to assert claims over human beings and territories. Riedel's map is thus noteworthy in that, for the first time, it spelled out an arena of colonial desire, a bounded territory defined by Dutch interests. The inhabitants of this nebulous region were granted the name 'Toraja.'

Introduced by Riedel, the name was popularized by missionary-ethnographer A.C. Kruyt, who used it to replace the pejorative term *alfuru,* previously used to describe the non-Christian, non-Islamic islanders of the eastern half of the Netherlands East Indies (NEI). This new ethnic category could not long remain defined by an imagined geography; hence, Kruyt predicated his cultural categorization upon 'religion.' An ethnic categorization based upon religion was of practical importance to Kruyt, a missionary charged by the NEI government to create a Christian bastion against the spread of a highly politicized Islam to the highlands. Kruyt identified the religion of the highlanders as animism and produced a number of theoretical works that placed it within a wider evolutionary framework (1906, 1918, 1919, 1920). Identifying a 'religion,' however, is a conceptual exercise; Kruyt differentiated the Islamic coastal peoples from highlanders on the basis of their religion even though they both shared many of the same animistic beliefs. Kruyt's definition of animistic religion necessarily took Christianity and Islam as its starting point, since, as Adriani noted, 'there is no word for religion in the Toraja language. We view their religion as self-evident, hence it is not seen as something separate. Toraja Animism is thus unorganized; it has no tenets, no developed doctrines about gods or man; it doesn't propagate itself, and belongs totally to the social circumstances within which the Toraja people have found themselves for some time' (1919, 60).[1]

Kruyt's definitions and theories were directed towards a specific readership, a colonial audience which shared his assumptions about what constituted a religion, and hence where the boundaries could be drawn around the 'Toraja.' Atkinson notes that the 'invention of religion' in the ethnographic encounter is

> predicated on, and [a] part of, a series of ideologically charged debates involving Western theology, science, morality, and much more. For this reason, the anthropologist's extension of the label to populations that some in Western society view as pagans in need of conversion is hardly a neutral application of value-free terminology. From the 19th-century evolutionist who imagined religion would be superseded eventually by science, to the 20th-century cultural relativist combating Western ethnocentrism, to the politically sensitive researcher of recent years who opposes cultural hegemony – all speak to their own society when they speak about other societies. (1983, 685)

Atkinson argues current anthropological theory is no less bound to the truisms of today. For this reason, rather than attempt to define the 'religion' of Kruyt's 'Bare'e Speaking Toraja' (Downs 1956), a subject of dubious ethnographic utility, I will attempt to analyse how Kruyt's own definitions of religion emerged out of the particular assumptions guiding him in the ethnographic encounter. We begin, in other words, with the question 'How does power create religion?' (Asad 1983, 252). Such an analysis must begin in the Netherlands with the distinctive role religion played in the Dutch state. Once the conditional, socially rooted nature of religion as Kruyt conceived it has been examined, it will then be possible to establish the linkages between the 'inculturated' form of Christianity currently found in Central Sulawesi with the colonial discourses that created it.

The Dutch Tribe

Kruyt was raised and trained during a pivotal historical transformation of the Netherlands that had attendant consequences for religious missions and colonial policy. The development of the modern democratic Dutch state is intimately tied to the process of *verzuiling* (pillarization). *Verzuiling* refers to the complex social process by which religion came to cut across class and status distinctions to create political blocs that divided national social programs on a religious (pillar) basis. This division of Dutch society into pillars was the result of the doctrine of 'sovereignty in one's own sphere' (*soevereiniteit in eigen kring*), by which was meant the division of power between Church and State in a pluralistic society:

> In a Christian (non-religionless) state, the government, as the servant of God, is to glorify God's name by (1) removing all administrative and legislative hindrances to the full expression of the Gospel in national life; (2) refraining from any direct interference with the spiritual development of the nation, for that is beyond government's competence; (3) treating equally all churches, religious organizations, and citizens regardless of their views on eternal matters; and (4) recognizing in the conscience a limit to state power in so far as conscience is presumed to be honorable. (Dutch prime minister A. Kuyper, cited in Langley 1984, 28)

The confessional (religious) political parties who adhered to this standpoint attempted to prevent state interference in the 'religious sphere,' which included education, welfare, health care, and family law. While in power, these parties provided the legislative basis by which denominational organizations could fulfil their religious mission of directing their adherents' spiritual development through denominational schools, unions, newspapers, hospitals, political parties, and a host of other services. The vertical division of Dutch society on a religious basis ministered to the needs of Orthodox Calvinists and Catholics from cradle to grave. Secularism, as an ideology, was marginalized.

The moralizing tone of confessional politics is clearly evident in their introduction of an 'ethical' colonial policy, a variation on the 'white man's burden' (Locher-Scholten 1981). Highly critical of the liberal party's policy of open-door capitalist expansion in the archipelago and the abuses it engendered, the Confessionals (following the socialists) accepted the debt of honour the Netherlands owed the NEI for the millions of guilders extracted from the colonial economy. They did not, however, abdicate the Netherlands' right to rule the archipelago nor the basic form of private capitalist exploitation. The policy was marked, rather, by new concerns for 'native welfare' and 'development,' and the repatriation of some of the funds regularly transferred from the colony. The paternalistic development policies instituted on Java, where most of the abuses had taken place, were accompanied by a new 'ethical imperialism' in the Outer Islands, where the notion of the 'white's man's burden' came to replace the policy of abstention as the Dutch deposed 'despotic' indigenous leaders for the greater good of their subjects. It was under the confessionally conceived Ethical Policy that Central Sulawesi was directly incorporated in the Netherlands East Indies in 1905.

The Ethical Policy also marked a new stage in the relations between the Netherlands East Indies government and the religious missions. The Confessional parties argued that their religious freedoms extended to the archipelago, and that the state should remove 'all administrative and legislative hindrances to the full expression of the Gospel ...' This move was opposed by the civil service of the Netherlands East Indies government, who were fully cognizant of the political repercussions of Christian missions in Islamic areas (Randwijk 1981, 215–33). The newly acquired non-Islamic areas, however, were generally opened to the missions without hindrance. These new missions fully accepted the doctrine of the debt of honour. In response, they reworked their 'Ethical Theology' to emphasize respect for indigenous cultures (Randwijk 1981, 146–8). Earlier missions had often treated religious conversion as the first step in the social conversion of the 'native' (*alfuru*) into a Dutch citizen. This meant the use of non-native languages (Bahasa Malayu [Indonesian] or Dutch) in church services, the strict adherence to Dutch liturgies, and attempts to culturally tranform the new converts. The Ethical theologians argued that such converts simply acquired a Christian 'lacquer'; there was no real transformation of the essential being of the new converts, the end result being a syncretic and impure Christianity. The advocates of Ethical theology thus called for missions in the vernacular and a respect for indigenous *adat* (culture). This necessitated new mission methodologies. A.C. Kruyt stood at the forefront of such developments, his sociological mission method becoming a standard in Dutch missions during the early twentieth century (Randwijck 1981, 392–4).

The process of *verzuiling* in the Netherlands thus had a dual effect upon Kruyt, his theories, and his missions. First, pillarization opened up large areas of the Indonesian archipelago to Christian missions but did so under the terms of the Ethical Policy. This new respect for indigenous cultures created new problems as missionaries were faced with understanding radically different societies and deciding what was, and wasn't, compatible with the 'essential' Christian message. It is in this problematic area that pillarization's impact was felt yet again. The practical decisions of missionaries in the encounter with an alien culture were guided by the ideologically charged theological, political, moral, and scientific debates of the Netherlands. The missionaries' practical decisions reflected Dutch concerns, giving the new culture-specific Christianities a pillarized form.

Verzuiling in the Netherlands

To understand Kruyt's mission and its social and cultural effects, it is necessary to understand the relationship between church and state in the Netherlands. The development of the modern Dutch state, and *verzuiling*, are two sides of a single process wherein the existing social, economic, and political structures of the Netherlands were transformed by the reconstructive forces of industrial capitalism. *Verzuiling* was the unintended product of a number of political and social strategies adopted by Dutch elites to combat the attendant woes of capitalist development such as secularization, urbanization, class strife, feminism, and divorce. None of these religious strategies was unique to the Netherlands, although their success was. This success can be related only to the peculiarities of the Dutch social formation, not to the strategies themselves (Stuurman 1983, 324–6). An oligarchic political system, relatively late industrial capitalism without a strong pre-existing landed nobility, the slow growth of urban centres, a decentralized form of industrial growth in the late nineteenth century – all worked to pillarize Dutch society.

Verzuiling, a concept rooted in political science, was first used to describe the particular form of confessional politics in the Netherlands during the 1950s. These studies emphasized the political side of *verzuiling*, rooting its attendant social phenomena (the religiously based social-service organizations) in the political culture of Dutch elites. They then applied this explanation retrogressively to the emergence of the system in the late nineteenth and early twentieth centuries (Lijphart 1968; Kruijt and Goddijn 1968). Such explanations are less than satisfactory, however, since the pillarization of Dutch society occurred at a time when only 10 per cent of the adult male population of the Netherlands had the vote, and hence preceded the widespread extension of the electoral franchise through which the confessional parties gained parliamentary control (Stuurman 1983, 67–9). Political pillarization is only one aspect of the wider process of social pillarization. *Verzuiling* can be rooted in certain elite strategies designed to combat specific social problems, but this does not imply that *verzuiling* is the product of an elite conspiracy or that elite strategies were not contradictory. In fact, the Dutch elite was internally divided and frequently worked at cross purposes. *Verzuiling* was the *unintended* product of specific strategies utilized in specific social conflicts (Stuurman 1983, 47–50). While functional explanations can be provided for these strategies in those conflicts, doing so does not imply that these strategies were intended to pillarize Dutch society. Historical arguments that root *verzuiling* in the Catholic and Orthodox Calvinist pillar's struggle for 'emancipation' read *verzuiling* backwards in time, assuming that the religious pillars (as opposed to the religious denominations) existed before the struggle and aimed to assume a role in government through that struggle.

An examination of these elite strategies must attend to the class interests that they served to protect, keeping in mind that neither the nineteenth-century political elite nor the strategies they adopted were homogeneous. The Confessional movement was composed of an alliance of aristocrats and the disenfranchised petty bourgeoisie (*kleine luyden*), and thus assumed the same structural position as the Conservatives in Britain. However, it is precisely because the franchise was so limited that we must attend to the non-political, voluntary organizations and societies by which the disenfranchised were either incorporated in these elite strategies or made the *subject* of these strategies. Such voluntary societies were created in great numbers throughout the nineteenth century to address the attendant ills of 'modernism,' represented by, for the Confessionals, 'Liberalism' and 'Socialism.' New social movements, such as Home Missions and Confessional labour unions, were religiously based attempts to address the problem of the new working class.

There is now an extensive literature on the development of similar Continental movements. Foucault's analysis (1979, 1980; Martin et al. 1988) of the development of 'disciplinary technologies' in the evolution of the modern state clearly links capitalism and the 'enlightenment sciences' to a new micropolitics of power that sought to create a docile subject/worker. Prison, poorhouse, and hospital reforms; the professionalization of medicine; the emergence of the social sciences – these are all elements of an extension of the civil hegemony of the state through a refinement of the techniques of governance (Burchell, Gordon, and Miller 1991). Foucault's analysis, however, pays scant attention to the role of religion in the development of these technologies of power. Foucault makes clear that these technologies of power differ from earlier political ideologies precisely in that they are treated as practical 'techniques,' and hence are an administrative, not a political, revolution (Dreyfus and Rabinow 1983, 136). Religious organizations, including those explicitly opposed to the 'secular humanism' of the Enlightenment, could and did utilize these new administrative techniques. Although the Dutch Reformed Church was highly decentralized in the eighteenth century, vesting real power in the congregation, and in particular the *collators* (the nobility with the right to select the minister), Napoleonic reforms established a centralized ministry of religion that usurped many of these rights and introduced a modernist movement within the church. The modernists instituted liturgical, theological, and organizational changes that paralleled reforms in other departments of the state.

Foucault's reticence about the disciplinary aspects of religious organizations is generally reflected in anthropological theory. Anthropological theory has tended to treat the practical activities of religious rituals as 'systems of meaning' that require 'interpreters' to 'translate' the exotic ritual idiom into terms we can understand (cf. Leach 1964, 12; Asad 1988, 87; Bell 1992, 30–1). What is translated, however, is not one symbol system into another, but *practice* into text. The reduction of religious practice to such an interpretation ignores exactly those disciplinary techniques that Foucault saw as crucial to the Enlightenment transformation of the state. Just as the social sciences had generally failed to analyse the new disciplinary techniques, they have similarly failed to analyse the specific role of religion in that transformation. To examine the disciplinary power of ritual is to examine the means by which it creates the mental and moral dispositions appropriate to a Christian: to see religion as a 'technology of the self' (Martin et al. 1988). Interpretations are multiple and easily changed; 'disciplinary practices, on the other hand, cannot be varied quite so easily, because learning to develop moral capabilities is not the same thing as learning to invent representations' (Asad 1988, 87).

The new disciplinary technologies introduced by the Enlightenment sciences fundamentally transformed the state, and so, too, state churches. Because these techniques were seemingly 'ideologically neutral,' they were as equally accessible to the religious conservatives as to the Liberals who first initiated them. In the Netherlands we see a pattern of Liberal transformation of the state apparatus (which *included* the state church), followed by a confessional reaction that utilizes the very same techniques. Thus, *verzuiling* is not a radical departure from the Liberal democratic state, but the particular form that it took in the Netherlands. The only thing that remains to be explained is the *success* of the religious parties in applying these techniques, and the weakness of the Liberals who first introduced them. The strength of the confessional parties can be explained only through the peculiarities of the Dutch social formation.

Like most other northern European nations, the Netherlands was transformed from an 'undeveloped' nation into a capitalist liberal-democracy during the nineteenth century. The scope of the changes involved ranged from the creation of a unified, rational legal system (which meant, among other things, the universal adoption of family names); the introduction of a land registry that literally mapped the Netherlands for the first time; and the establishment of a transportation network of roads, canals, and railways (Woud 1987). The pace of these changes was, however, noticeably slower in the Netherlands than elsewhere. As natural resources and cheap labour were lacking, the pace of industrialization was slow; the Dutch economy remained dominated by agriculture well into the late nineteenth century. Urbanization was correspondingly slow, and industrialization, when it finally occurred, tended to be more evenly spread over the countryside, forestalling the development of worker enclaves and the development of widespread class conflict (Stuurman 1983, 189).

The profoundly rural nature of the Netherlands and the slow pace of changes ensured that central reforms were tested and contested by the local oligarchies that had held sway during the eighteenth century. Only in so far as these oligarchies were incorporated in the evolving state were reforms enacted. However, not all of these local oligarchies were dominated by landed aristocracy; much of the Netherlands had never been under feudal tenure. These non-feudal areas tended to be dominated by the *nouveau riche*, merchant capitalists elevated to the nobility. They retained the same rights as the landed aristocracy although their class interests differed. The pattern of incorporation thus reflects class interests; the bourgeoisie, dependent upon the development of the state, were at the forefront of the 'enlightenment,' whereas the landed aristocracy resisted those changes that infringed on their local prerogatives. Many of these prerogatives, such as their control over poor relief and education, were exercised through the 'state' church. Centralized 'rational' reforms in the church considerably weakened their authority and, in their eyes, the very social fabric of rural society (Stuurman 1983, 326–9).

Conservative resistance to modernist reforms was expressed through a religious revival between 1845 and 1854 in the cities of Den Haag (the capital) and Amsterdam by those wedded to the royalist notion of the 'Great Protestant Nation' (*Groot Protestantse Natie*) (Rasker 1974, 75; Wintle 1987, 22). This revival was limited to aristocratic circles, and can be characterized as a romantic rejection of sterile, modern intellectualist theology for a pietistic emphasis on the individual's personal, emotive relationship with God. Although theologically Orthodox in inclination, the revivalists were not interested in doctrine or dogma, but the moral reformation of post-revolutionary Dutch society. Although originally an aristocratic movement, the revival had broader social impact through aristocratic control of the pulpits of the nation, as well as through their 'Christian Philanthropy' (Wintle 1987, 23). Two figures, Otto G. Heldring and Guillaume Groen van Prinsterer, played leading roles in defining the thrust of this conservative 'reformation.'

Otto Heldring was a leading figure in the Home and Foreign Missions movement, which grew out of the revival (Reenders 1991). Home Missions were a religiously oriented attempt to apply the new administrative techniques of the modern state. Heldring helped organize the revivalists into groups of 'Christian Friends' who undertook specific philanthropic projects to address the problems of the new working class. He thus encouraged the establishment of Christian schools to combat illiteracy, rationalized diaconal poor relief through the formation of poorhouses, established an asylum for women and children as part of a broader campaign against prostitution, and resettled the unemployed on newly reclaimed agricultural land. This emphasis on the practical application of Christian principles gave rise to an 'Ethical Theology' that later had enormous implications for colonial policy and colonial missions.

Groen van Prinsterer attempted to politically organize the revival through the Anti-Revolutionary Party (Rasker 1974, 94). The Anti-Revolutionaries were formed in 1850 as a response to the 1848 Liberal constitution, which introduced universal suffrage – on a limited basis – to extend the franchise to some Catholics, ended the relationship between the Protestant church and state, and allowed the re-establishment of the Roman Catholic hierarchy. Prinsterer, like most of his aristocratic backers, was wedded to the eighteenth-century political vision of the Netherlands as a 'Great Protestant Nation' and opposed to the liberal reforms ushered in by the French Revolution – hence, the name of the party. The explicit religious cast of the political party is explained by the traditional source of authority of the Dutch aristocracy, the Protestant Church. The revivalists proved the obvious clientele. Home Missions extended traditional aristocratic prerogatives, education and poor relief, in the changed circumstances of the nineteenth century. The Anti-Revolutionary Party created the political framework within which these efforts at aristocratic renewal could take place.

The first real test between the Liberals and the Anti-Revolutionaries was on the issue of public education. Liberal visions of a unified state included mandatory, secular public education with a rationalized curriculum. The system in practice then was an amalgam of locally run church and public schools that offered a religious (Protestant) education. Liberal success in Parliament, however, was dependent upon Catholic support. When the newly restored Catholic hierarchy resisted the introduction of secular education and backed away from their alliance with the Liberals, educational reform was not shelved but enacted by the religious conservatives. The conservative fraction of the Dutch elite rationalized the educational system by creating not one secular national school system, but a number of religiously based national systems (Stuurman 1983, 105–39).

The natural extension of the struggle for a religious educational system was the creation of the Free University, an orthodox Calvinist university created specifically to train conservative ministers untainted with theological modernism. When the state church (controlled by the modernists) refused to acknowledge the credentials of the Free University's graduates, a large number of orthodox congregations seceded from the church, creating the second bulwark of the new orthodox Calvinist social pillar. Unlike the debate on the reformation of the public school system, the schism was not a 'political' struggle, and hence is not usually considered in discussions of *verzuiling*. An unintended result, however, was the increasing institutional cleavage of Dutch society and the social pillarization of the Protestants. Similar struggles were also being fought on other non-political, 'non-religious' fronts, such as the trade union movement (Stuurman 1983, 148–91). In this case, the development of socialist trade unions was followed and opposed by denominational trade unions based on an ideology of conciliation, which admitted both workers and owners. About half of all unionized labourers were incorporated in confessional labour unions.

The religious and social cleavages that divided the Netherlands into pillars were less important politically than the divide between the two major religious pillars and the Liberals (the so-called *antithese*). These pillars were politically mobilized by the conservatives to gain a parliamentary majority. Rather than engaging in traditional mutual hostilities, orthodox Protestants and Catholics were politically (if not socially) united in seeking guarantees of religious freedom, which limited central state control. Religious freedom ensured a continuation of the particularist power base of the conservative elite, a coalition of landed aristocracy and petty bourgeoisie who had the vote. Having successfully organized the conservative elite along Confessional lines, the Confessional parties sought to extend the franchise to those who had been socially 'pillarized' through the efforts of Home Missions and religious schools. The development of mass democracy in the Netherlands is thus the product of the specific social forces that led to pillarization, not the other way around.

Ethical Policy, Missions, and Imperialism in the Outer Islands

The transformation of the state in the Netherlands in the late nineteenth century was matched by similar changes in the colonial bureaucracy. Just as *verzuiling* was the particular form that Liberal democracy took in the Netherlands, so too, it was under the Ethical Policy that the liberal reforms of the NEI government took shape in the twentieth century. Although the Indies had seen more than three hundred years of Dutch colonialism, Dutch rule had been a sporadic affair. Until the English interregnum, Dutch rule was extended through the Vereenigde Oostindische Compagnie (VOC [United East Indies Company]) and colonial policy was synonymous with trade policy. From 1816 until 1864, colonial policy was an entirely royal prerogative, and designed to provide an independent source of state revenue for the House of Orange. Under the Culture System, exactions in kind were obtained through indirect rule, and state mechanisms were particularist, not universal. The opening of the colonies to capitalist enterprises under parliamentary Liberal guidance necessitated the creation of a rationalized legal-bureaucratic system to ease the operations of highly capitalized Dutch corporations. Since the Dutch lacked manpower and were bogged down in an expensive war in Aceh, Sumatra, this legal-bureaucratic state apparatus was simply superimposed on earlier patterns of indirect rule, giving rise to the so-called dual economy. The rationalization of the NEI state was thus predicated upon rationalizing the system of indirect rule, *not* the imposition of a unitary legal-bureaucratic state. The Netherlands East Indies was as pluralist as the Netherlands itself. Under the Ethical Policy, this pluralist approach was further developed through *adat* law studies, ethnographic studies that defined 'tradition,' and hence the structure of indirect rule. The 'Ethical Theology' of the missions paralleled this process in many ways. It was under these policies that the Outer Islands, and Central Sulawesi in particular, were incorporated in the Netherlands East Indies state in the early twentieth century.

The introduction of the Ethical Policy in 1901 surprisingly met with widespread approval from all parliamentary factions, primarily because of the vagueness of the term and the scope of interpretation it allowed. It is thus important to differentiate the specific policy objectives of the Confessional parties who implemented it from those of the Liberal (later Socialist) who had coined the term (Locher-Scholten 1981, 209). The Anti-Revolutionary Party had recognized the debt of honour of the Netherlands to the East Indies in its 1878 party program (Verkuyl 1990, 35). The terms of this recognition, however, were paternalistic and served to limit the rights of subject peoples as Dutch citizens. Abraham Kuyper, then leader of the Anti-Revolutionaries and the prime minister under whom the Ethical Policy was introduced, emphasized that the Netherlands East Indies were not an integral part of the Kingdom of the Netherlands. They were, rather, an obligation inherited from the bankrupt United East Indies Company. Subject peoples in the Netherlands East Indies were *not* Dutch citizens, and had no rights under the Dutch constitution. The Dutch did, however, inherit a responsibility for the archipelago, an ethical call to protect and shepherd the colony until it could take its place among the nations. The ethical responsibility of the Dutch was explicitly formulated in terms of *state formation*. State formation was, however, to be a Dutch prerogative.

State formation in the Netherlands East Indies, thus equated with ethical responsibility, meant the introduction of modern liberal administrative techniques of the sort applied to the Dutch state itself, as described earlier. Indirect rule was to be rationalized along the lines of Western statecraft, not along indigenous lines as in the past. Much of this transformation was under the hand of A.W.F. Idenburg, who served as both Minister of Colonies (1902–5, 1908–9, 1918–19) and Governor General (1909–16) (Kuitenbrouwer 1991). It was under Idenburg that direct Dutch rule was extended over the entire archipelago for the first time, establishing the *Pax Neerlandica*. This entrenched the first requirement of administrative efficiency in the eyes of the Ethical Policy advocates: tranquillity and order (*rust en orde*). This spatial extension of the state was accompanied by the expansion in the number of governmental departments and their programs: 'Education, religion, irrigation, agricultural improvements, hygiene, mineral exploitation, political surveillance – all increasingly became the business of a rapidly expanding officialdom, which unfolded more according to its inner impulses than in response to any organized extra-state demands' (Anderson 1983b, 479). The rapid expansion of the state apparatus raised its own problems. Lacking manpower, the NEI government was increasingly forced to turn to the religious missions for implementing specific programs, especially in education and health. When coupled with the Confessional parties' insistence that the doctrine of 'sovereignty in one's own sphere' extended to the archipelago, it could be argued that the Netherlands East Indies state was also being pillarized. Such an easy parallel, however, is confused by specifically East Indies issues, in particular a militant Islam. Indigenous opposition to Dutch rule in the archipelago was increasingly phrased in terms of a call for observance of *shari'ah* (Islamic) law. Dutch indirect rule through indigenous elites and the codification of *adat* law was, in fact, aimed at curtailing Islam's unifying power (Lev 1985, 66). By strengthening traditional non-religious elites and inventing them where none existed, the process of divide-and-rule continued in new guise. The rigour with which the Dutch sought to preserve 'tradition' within a colonial state legitimated by its obligation to 'develop' its subject peoples is a clear indication that it was the practical, administrative logic of state formation that determined the content of the Ethical Policy, not vice versa.

There is an added tension between *adat* and religion that did not exist in the Netherlands and that further complicated the definition of the proper sphere of 'religion' in the colony. The missions pressed for the same religious rights they enjoyed in the Netherlands. However, as in the case of Kruyt's Toraja, the separation of 'religion' from indigenous government was unclear. By strengthening the position of *adat law* for the non-Islamic peoples among whom the missions had been granted permission to work, the government worked against mission efforts at *religious* conversion, since these peoples made no distinction between the two. This left the missions with two options: the first, to oppose the policy of indirect rule through indigenous *adat*, would have meant an untenable alliance with Islam. The second option was to embrace *adat* studies as a means of defining 'religion' in the East Indies social formation. This second option was adopted by the Ethical Theologians who utilized secular liberal social sciences in the service of missions. Their ethnographic work took place within the common framework established by *adat* law studies.

These *adat* law studies provided the particularist information that the colonial administration required to function efficiently. It defined the distinctive 'ensemble of a population' to which various state administrative and disciplinary could be applied, and the range of variation of practices which could be safely tolerated (cf. Gordon 1991, 220). The Netherlands East Indies state was predicated upon a basic legal distinction between Dutch citizens subject to Dutch law, and indigenous peoples subject to *adat* law (de Kat Angelino 1931, 3: 102–35). The administration of *adat* law was left to the Ministry of the Interior (Binnenlands Bestuur), which established the bureaucratic mechanisms for indirect rule. Although the substantive law applied in each *adat* law area (*adatrechtkring*) differed, the bureaucratic mechanisms by which it was administered were rationalized along Western lines. Indirect rule required the codification of 'tradition' in such a form that it could be administered as law; since the law was being defined substantively, the abstraction of 'law' from 'religion' became problematic, and it was this administrative problem that gave rise to the theoretical debate about the universal features of 'religion.' This ideologically charged debate was influenced not only by the prevailing political debate in the Netherlands, but also by the administrative logic of the colony. Since 'religion' and 'law' were administered by two different departments of the NEI government, the ultimate resolution of the theoretical debate in turn determined departmental competence. More important, it also set legal restrictions on the actions of missionaries.

Mission response to these restrictions was shaped by the administrative logic of the colony, as well as the distinctive politico-theological ideology dominant among the Confessional parties, and led to the missions' adoption of 'neutral' administrative procedures to mission ends. As noted above, mission ethnography was the product of Ethical Theology, which had its roots in the Dutch revival of the nineteenth century. The revivalists placed greater emphasis on the reformation of the self than on denominational organization. They emphasized the ethical nature of truth, which therefore required not only understanding (correct belief), but that the entire personality be reformed on biblical principles so that one was visibly centred on the word of God. This emphasis on the individual was no cult of individualism; its ethical emphasis was predicated upon the subsuming of the individual within a spiritual community. The Ethical Theologians conceptualized the role of the church specifically in terms of that spiritual community, as a *volkskerk* ('people's' church, in a sense, defining nationhood); they, too, were concerned to define an 'ensemble of a population,' although on a religious basis. This conceptualization of the church thus involved a relativization of the church's tenets, a recognition that cultural norms should not be confused with biblical principles; different peoples could have different cultures and different churches, but still dwell in God's truth as long as those traditions were evaluated from a biblical perspective (Randwijck 1981, 146–9, 447–9).

There are three implications of Ethical Theology pertinent to the colonial setting. First, their conceptualization of the church as *volskerk* implies a 'people.' The word *volk*, like 'nation,' was based upon cultural or racial criteria and hence stood in opposition to 'the state.' In the colonial setting, a 'people' could be defined on the basis of 'objective' cultural characteristics even where no indigenous sense of ethnic identity existed and indigenous political divisions could be ignored; such was the case with the Toraja. Such cultural categorization worked hand in hand with *adat* studies in that a 'people' were said to share an *adat*, and hence became an administrative unit in the colonial bureaucracy. The second implication of Ethical Theology was its paternalism. The emphasis on individual reformation and the disregard for denominational organization ensured that the *volkskerk* so defined remained under mission control. This paternalism was masked by mission relativism; they insisted that the transformation of the *adat* under Christian principles had to emerge through self-examination and self-reformation and would lead to a distinctive form of indigenous Christianity. This ignored, of course, Dutch control of church administration, and mission efforts to document the Christian *adat* within the larger legal-administrative system of the colonial service. The third implication of Ethical Theology, its cultural relativity, gave rise to a widespread attempt to understand other cultures in their own terms. Missionaries were thus an integral part of the development of Dutch anthropology in its pre-professional phase.

Mission ethnographies, as empirical studies, explicitly sought to situate their ethnographic subjects in universalist (usually evolutionist) terms, and thus bear no outward sign of these ideologically charged colonial debates; the uses of ethnography were separated from the *act* of ethnography, hence validating their objectivity and universal conclusions. We have seen, however, that such abstract theoretical considerations had practical implications in the division of administrative competence within the bureaucracy, as well as defining the rights of missions vis-à-vis that bureaucracy within the larger state formation. In particular, the definition of religion and the establishment of ethnic boundaries (*adatrechtkring*) were not simply abstract theoretical issues, but an exercise of power by which subject 'peoples' (as collections of individuals, yet as a *volk*) were co-opted and integrated within the emerging Netherlands East Indies state.

Imperialism and the Incorporation of Central Sulawesi

Central Sulawesi, like most of the Outer Islands, had been of peripheral interest to the Netherlands East Indies government. The Confessional parties who implemented the Ethical Policy had consistently defended the prior policy of abstention (or non-interference) in the Outer Islands, fearing that an expansion of Dutch rule would further involve the Dutch in costly wars like that in Aceh, Sumatra. The imperialist expansion into the Outer Islands is a turnabout that again indicates that the logic of East Indies state formation determined the content of the Ethical Policy, and not vice versa (Fasseur 1979, 184–5; Goor 1986, 12–17). Ethical imperialism was not necessitated by any change in the circumstances in the Outer Islands, which had been profitably exploited under the policy of abstention. What changed were the forms of exploitation. The needs of merchant capitalism were adequately met by the policy of abstention that guaranteed a Dutch trade monopoly, if nothing else. Capitalist investment in the form of mines and plantations, however, required a state infrastructure that could guarantee the factors of production. This is not to imply that ethical imperialism was directly driven by investment. Rather, it was fear of the loss of potentially exploitable territories to other imperialist powers that led the NEI government to establish a legal-bureaucratic state recognized by those powers in the Outer Islands. The incorporation of Central Sulawesi follows this pattern in its broad outlines (Locher-Scholten 1991). The specifically 'ethical' cast of Dutch imperialist expansion ensured that development, religion, and *adat* played a prominent role in the new state formation.

By the late nineteenth century, treaties had been signed with indigenous polities throughout Sulawesi, establishing three basic types of rule: first, the 'government lands' such as Makassar, which were directly ruled; second, the allied states such as Bone, which had signed the Treaty of Bungaya and helped the Dutch conquer Makassar, which were ruled indirectly; and, lastly, the 'feudal lands' with whom individual contracts or treaties were signed (Blink 1905–7, 2: 441). Most of the Bay of Tomini (and hence Central Sulawesi) fell within this last category. Contracts were signed with the indigenous polities of the bay with the dual intention of establishing Dutch suzerainty and regulating trade without involving the Dutch in direct rule. The establishment of suzerainty through treaties was a cost-effective though weak means of forestalling the imperialist claims of other colonial powers (primarily Britain and Australia). Although exploratory trips to Lake Poso had been undertaken by Dutch civil servants (*controleurs*) – J.C.W.D. A van der Wijck, in 1865, and W.J.M. Michielsen, in 1869 – there was no permanent post in the southern half of the Bay of Tomini (Adriani 1932, 1: 371–406).

Private corporations first gained the right to obtain mining concessions in the islands during the liberal period, after 1870. However, G.W.W.C. Baron van Hoëvell, the Assistant Resident of North Sulawesi, had concluded that, 'as long as the political circumstances in the various kingdoms of the Bay of Tomini are not notably improved, and order and tranquillity established in place of plundering, murder and arbitrariness, the time has not yet come to open these regions to European capital and industry ... the choice for the Bay of Tomini must be: no permission for private industry whenever there is no opportunity to establish a governing civil servant at the same time' (quoted in Arts 1985, 87). Between 1890 and 1910, Northern Sulawesi underwent a gold rush that sparked widespread prospecting throughout the Bay area, including those areas where the Dutch had not yet established direct rule (Beurden 1985). In 1890, Australian prospectors explored the southern end of the Bay without Dutch permission, raising the spectre of other colonial claims on the area. The Sarasins, Swiss zoologists, made an extensive exploratory journey through the highlands between 1893–6 and 1902–3 (Sarasin and Sarasin 1905). Gold increased the value of the area to both the Dutch and other colonial powers, necessitating a new relationship between the indigenous states and the Netherlands East Indies government. Although no mines were ever established in the southern end of the Bay, gold fever and foreign interlopers provided sufficient incentive to expand Dutch rule in the area.

Actual expansion into the area, however, was stymied by the expense, a shortage of manpower, and the policy of abstention (Arts 1985, 101). A temporary solution was found in the Netherlands Missionary Society (Nederlandsch Zendeling Genootschap [NZG]). The setting up of a mission post served a dual function; first, it established actual Dutch occupation of the territory, and hence a Dutch eye for interlopers. Second, the mission would actively work to stem the growing influence of Islam and the indigenous states in the highlands. Van Hoëvell thus recommended the area as a mission field to the NZG in 1889, and Albert C. Kruyt established a post at Poso in 1892 (Randwijck 1981, 658). A *controleur* was placed at Poso in 1894, but it was not until 1895 that a ten-man garrison was established. Despite the additional manpower, the *controleur* remained a powerless figurehead, his hands tied by the policy of abstention, and by ignorance of the language and culture of the area.

This situation changed after the Dutch invasion in 1905. Seeking funds to pay for the new state apparatus, the Dutch sought to impose a universal import/export tax system on all ports in the archipelago. Similar taxes had been the primary source of state revenue for most of the kingdoms of South Sulawesi; hence, it is not surprising that the kingdoms of Luwu and Bone resisted and refused to sign new contracts. It was this act of 'rebellion' that led to the Dutch military expeditions of 1905, and the incorporation of the entire island of Sulawesi within the Netherlands East Indies state (Locher-Scholten 1991, 161).

Although the imperialist expansion into the highlands was for economic (gold mining) and political reasons (establishing the tax system, pre-empting other colonial claims), the expeditions were justified in terms of 'ethical' responsibility. Kruyt and the missions served their part in the legitimation of the invasion. Whereas, in 1898, Kruyt felt the conversion of the Toraja 'awaited the Holy Ghost,' a few years later he viewed it as 'less a spiritual than a political process' (Arts 1985, 111). W.G. Engelenberg, the Assistant Resident of Central Sulawesi, justified the expansion against 'ethical' critiques and in so doing helped redefine the very meaning of 'ethical' in the colonial context.

> I have the opportunity to point out a danger to those who engage in ethical politics. Mr. Abendanon on returning to the motherland, points to the labour of peace and of love of a Kruyt, of an Adriani, praising them and disapproving of our violence in so many areas of the outer possessions. These friends of peace well know that a Kruyt, an Adriani, have pointed out in their public writings the duty of the Government to forcefully seize Luwu. The rottenness of the political circumstances makes their work unfruitful. And the rottenness could only be cut away by the violence of a Government. Violence is in itself neither good nor bad. Everything depends upon the motives for our deeds. The greater or lesser morality does not depend upon the deed, but on the inner grounds that drive us. If our motives are good, moral, then the fruits of these motives, i.e. our deeds, are good. We are confronted with abuses which can only be eliminated with a rough hand and we need to clean it up because the interests of this people themselves bid us. (Engelenberg MVO 1906, 14)

The Netherlands East Indies government had not expected armed resistance from the 'Toraja' once the ruler of Luwu, their nominal sovereign, had been subjugated. Thirteen ships, being 3,000 men, invaded Bone and Luwu in the summer of 1905 (Arts 1985, 102), establishing Dutch control by September. However, in the ensuing months numerous military expeditions were required in the highlands calling forth images of a 'new Aceh.' In September 1905, Engelenberg held a meeting of village chiefs from Napu and Pebato to explain the new regime. A military force had to be sent out, however, after two chiefs refused to attend; sixty To Napu died in the resultant battle. The Resident of Manado organized a two-pronged attack on the highlands, from Poso in the north and Wotu in the south, meeting at Lake Poso. This expedition reached the lake on 29 October. On 11 November, the indigenous leaders from around the lake were called to a meeting to hear the reading of a letter from the ruler of Luwu renouncing all title to the highlands. However, when a promised visit by the crown prince of Luwu was late to materialize, a fortification was constructed at the village of Tamungkudena at the head of the lake (near Tentena). After a short battle, the village fell. Only sporadic resistance followed. By January 1906, 'tranquillity and order' had been established in the highlands, with total casualties among the highlanders in the hundreds.

Following the pacification of the highlands, indirect rule was established in the flowing phrases of the Ethical Policy. Education, economic development, responsible and rational government, and ultimate independence were the 'good' motives which justified the military action.

> What is the future of these lands? Our interference in the lives of these people can only be defended if our intention is to educate them for independence. If our motives are selfish, then we are being imperialistic; if we exploit this land and people for our own benefit, our ambitions here are to be disapproved. I foresee our task as that of educators. I seek to bring here the power for self-determination ... What is self-government? Does it not imply the competence to foresee the needs of the people? This self-government must learn to understand what a territory, a people need to develop, to extend their own power, to exploit their own capital. It must learn to find the means to develop. Income must be found and the regulation of their finances must be set up such that a broad economic development therefore results. How do I guarantee this future? I propose to form a federation of self-governors in this division, which will have a single common exchequer. Should this federation be recognized by the Government as a corporate body then it will have the competence to handle matters of law. (Engelenberg MVO 1906, 27–8)

The colonial reformation of the highlands belied 'indirect rule.' Engelenberg's optimistic proposal of a federation of 'self-governors' was based on limited knowledge of the number of autonomous groups in the highlands. Engelenberg was thus forced to amalgamate a number of groups to create a viable bureaucratic unit, the district (map 1.1). Bureaucratic amalgamation entailed actual resettlement. Between 1906 and 1908, the small scattered villages located on mountain ridges in the interior were forced to relocate to larger, oftentimes mixed villages located along a planned road in the river valleys. Raiding and secondary burials were banned, eliminating the core ritual by which indigenous leaders had solidified their kin following. These leaders now became colonial appointees, deriving their power and authority from the new system of 'self-rule.' Village headmen (no women were appointed) were subordinated to a district chief, who, in turn, was ultimately subordinated to a *raja*, or king, appointed by the Dutch in 1917

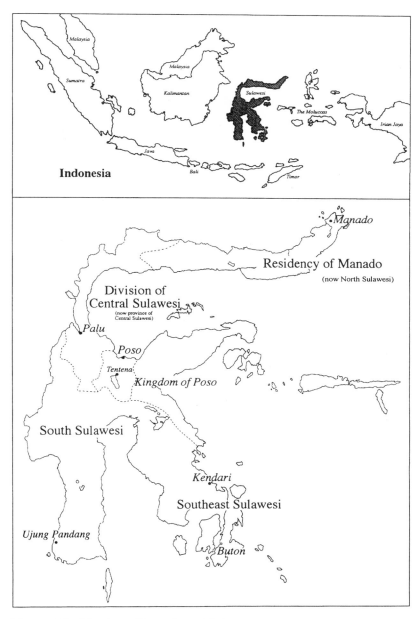

Map 1.1 The Kingdom of Poso, Central Sulawesi

(*Regeerings-Almanak* 1918). The replacement of the proposed 'Poso Federation' with the creation of a non-existent feudal tradition simply highlights the authoritarian and paternalistic vision of the Ethical Policy. 'Self-governance,' 'development,' and 'tutelage' did not imply 'self-determination.'

This colonial bureaucracy was charged with the administration of *adat* law. The definition of *adat* law was complicated by the first conversions to Christianity in the highlands after 1909. *Adat* law studies presumed a cultural homogeneity, which the conversions challenged. Had conversion to Christianity implied the adoption of Dutch culture as in the past, the problem would not have existed, since the 'Dutch *adat*' would apply to converts. However, the missions, working within an Ethical framework, specifically sought to divorce religion from culture; the *adat* was to be preserved, such that an indigenous Christianity took shape, distinctively 'Toraja' but subject to universal biblical precepts (see Adriani 1932, 1: 359–70). The abstraction of 'religion' from *adat* was required so that *adat* law would be applied in 'civil' matters only (cf. Steedly 1993, 70). Religious freedom was to be guaranteed, and converts spared from persecution under *adat* law by non-Christian headmen, district chiefs, and the *raja*. As already noted, the appropriate division of civil and religious spheres was a contentious issue within Dutch society itself and not one easily resolved when applied in the colonial context. The paternalistic bias of both NEI government and the missions ensured that the definitions of *adat* law and religion would lie in Dutch hands:

> To mix in the affairs of a people a fixed program is required wherein the one thing is allowed, the other not, which is primarily a political matter and thus not something offered with free choice. Only knowledge of a people, and love for a people give insight in that which we may interfere in ... We cannot know beforehand what a people really needs, but we can discover it. This applies to both civil servants as well as missionaries, and the best service they can offer each other is to stand by each other in the search for that which they still need to become good leaders of the people who are entrusted in their care. (Adriani 1932, 2: 183)

The contentious issue of where to draw the boundary between church and state highlights the differing interests of the missions and the colonial civil service. Both, however, regarded it a political matter to be settled by the Dutch alone. This settlement was to be based upon knowledge of subject peoples, making ethnography a key component of indirect rule. Ethnography thus linked Ethical Theology to the missionaries, and *adat* law studies to civil servants, and oriented both their efforts towards the new ethnic group, the 'Toraja,' forming under their prescriptive tutelage.

Dr A.C. Kruyt and Dr N. Adriani, Missionary Ethnographers

Almost twenty years after Riedel had defined the 'heart of darkness' in the centre of Sulawesi, the territory was incorporated in the Netherlands East Indies state. The gold rush, the desire for Christian converts, the need to establish administrative control over a potentially profitable territory – all hastened the slow pace of Dutch intrusions in the area. I have argued, however, that the administrative methods adopted to incorporate this territory were not uniform in their effect; missions were not the simple 'handmaiden of colonialism.' The adoption of *adat* law studies by the missions was one means by which they could foster their own interests over that of the state. This use of ethnography by the mission was a radical innovation adopted through the efforts of three pivotal men: Professor P.D. Chantepie de la Saussaye, Albert C. Kruyt, and Nicolaüs Adriani. These three scholars established a discourse on 'tradition' in Central Sulawesi that was to have great impact on the development of To Pamona ethnicity, and on the specific means by which this 'traditional people' were to be incorporated into the modern NEI state.

The Netherlands Missionary Society and the Netherlands Bible Society had first settled upon Central Sulawesi as a new mission field in 1890, in consultation with G.W.W.C. Baron van Hoëvell, Assistant Resident of the Residency of Manado (Arts 1985, 86; Kruyt 1970, 56). Two missionaries, then in training, were designated for the field: Albert Christiaan Kruyt (1869–1949), the son of a Netherlands Missionary Society missionary in Java (Brouwer 1951, 11–16), and Nicolaüs Adriani (1865–1926), son of the director of the Utrecht Missionary Association and a nephew of the director of the Netherlands Missionary Society (Kraemer 1935, 12). These two men, each from a strong mission background, embodied the new currents affecting missions in the Netherlands East Indies. Ethical Theology and Ethical Policy were combined in these men to produce a new mission methodology, the 'sociological method,' in which ethnography played a key role. Between them, Kruyt and Adriani produced no fewer than four lengthy ethnographies of the 'East (or Bare'e-speaking) Toraja' (Kruyt 1895–7; Adriani and Kruyt 1912–14; Adriani 1919; Kruyt 1950 [1912]), theoretical studies on 'animism' (Kruyt 1906; Adriani 1932, 2 [1919], 283–353), two dictionaries (Kruyt 1894; Adriani 1928), an extensive grammar (Adriani 1931), as well as articles too numerous to mention (see the bibliographies in Brouwer 1951 and Adriani 1932). This flood of information about the previously unknown 'Toraja' provided a showcase for the new missiological method that became a standard for the next generation of missionaries.

Albert C. Kruyt was the youngest son of Johannes Kruyt and Dorothea van der Linden, Netherlands Missionary Society (NZG) missionaries at Mojo-Warno in

Java. The family played a prominent part in the small world of Dutch colonial missions; Kruyt's uncle and aunt on his mother's side were also missionaries in Java, and five of his six sisters and brothers became missionaries as well (Brouwer 1951, 14–15; Kipp 1990, 49–96). Although born on Java, Kruyt was repatriated to the Netherlands at age eight and educated in the Mission School in Rotterdam. In 1884 he entered the missionary training program, graduating, aged twenty, in 1889. The first few years of this program merely completed the students' secondary education, whereas in the last five years the students were taught theology, mission history, missiology, Indonesian languages, anthropology, and comparative religion (Brouwer 1951, 23). Kruyt had no university education, nor was he a minister; the NZG was a private corporation, not a church, and therefore could not ordain ministers. However, Kruyt did have to pass the examinations set by the Haagse Commissie, which admitted assistant ministers for the state church, the Protestant Church of the Netherlands East Indies (the Indische Kerk). Kruyt's doctorate in theology was honorary, presented in 1913 by the University of Utrecht in recognition of his ethnography 'De Bare'e Sprekende Toradja's van Midden-Celebes.'

Nicolaüs Adriani came from a very different social circle. Adriani's father, Ds. M.A. Adriani, was a minister, and director of the Utrecht Mission Association. His mother came from the Gunning family; his uncle J.H. Gunning, with whom he lived as a high-school student, was an influential theology professor who laid the groundwork for 'Ethical Theology' (Rasker 1974, 139–52; Kraemer 1935, 12–13). His aunt was the sister of Professor N.G. Pierson, at one time president of the Netherlands State Bank, the minister of finance, and the minister-president (Randwijk 1981, 47). Another uncle, J.W. Gunning, became director of the NZG and its Mission School in 1897. Indeed, few of Adriani's family did not hold academic or pastoral positions; therefore, it should be no surprise that Adriani became a theology student at the University of Utrecht in 1886. Adriani's theological studies were interrupted in 1887, when he joined the Netherlands Bible Society, a mission that sent trained linguists to the Netherlands East Indies to study Indonesian languages and translate the Bible (Kraemer 1935, 16). Adriani entered the University of Leiden in 1887, graduating with a doctorate in East Indian Languages and Literature in 1893 (Kraemer 1935, 19).

The figure linking the key players and organizations that led to Kruyt and Adriani's placement in Central Sulawesi was Professor P.D. Chantepie de la Saussaye. De Saussaye was Professor J.H. Gunning's successor, a prominent Ethical Theologian who was the chairman of the board of both the NZG and the Netherlands Bible Society. He was an ardent opponent of the Enlightenment and liberalism. His doctoral thesis was entitled 'Methodological Contributions to the Study of the Origins of Religion' (1871), one of the first comparative studies of religion in the Netherlands; it made heavy use of ethnographic studies (Rasker 1974, 235). He was named to the chair in comparative religion at the University of Amsterdam in 1878. It was his knowledge of comparative religion that led to his involvement in mission organizations, and his academic position that guaranteed his influence in the continuing debate on the nature and boundaries of 'religion' in the Netherlands East Indies. De Saussaye thus gave the missions of the NZG and the Netherlands Bible Society their ethical imperative, as well as directing their ethnological studies. It was he, in consultation with Assistant Resident G.W.W.C. Baron van Hoëvell, who decided to open the mission field in Central Sulawesi, and, as chairman of both NZG and Netherlands Bible Society, ensured the close cooperation between the two missions.

Kruyt's sociological method was a practical application of Ethical Theology as embodied by de Saussaye. Ethical Theology conceptualized the role of the church in terms of a spiritual community, the *volkskerk*, a concept that grew out of the distinction between Christianity and culture, Christianity being universal, and culture, specific. The sociological method was thus a means of 'inculturating' Christianity within a non-Christian people in such a way that their culture was Christianized without necessarily losing its distinctive ethos. This concern to inculturate Christianity sprang from the revivalist emphasis on the emotional bond between the believer and God; personal piety could emerge only where Christianity was not perceived as an alien imposition.

> How must we approach the *adat*? When we truly recognize the *adat* as the form wherein the Indonesian shows his inner being, when we view the *adat* as the result of a perhaps age old history and development, if we know that the *adat* is the formulation of the most appropriate rules of living for the people, then we stand with respect towards the *adat*, even if it does differ from our opinions. Then we will study it to understand how it works, and that which people cannot retain as Christians we do not cut off in rough fashion, but rework the thoughts and feelings of the native Christian through preaching the Gospel, through Christian education, so that whenever their circumstances have changed, become Christian, they themselves will alter their *adat*, so that they, in their Christian state, become an expression of what lives within them. Only then will the double-sidedness of their being, of which I spoke, be left behind. (Kruyt 1937, 48)

The sociological method involved a process of ethnographic study followed by the selective utilization and reworking of indigenous rituals within the framework established by the mission. Study of the *adat* was considered essential to understanding the religious feelings and thoughts of Indonesians, since these emotions and symbol systems were rooted in 'pre-logical' thought (see, for example, Kruyt 1937b, 22–39; Kruyt 1925, 182). Kruyt recognized that the message of the gospel was not self-evident and that Indonesian converts often interpreted his message in their own cultural terms. Kruyt saw such attempts as encouraging, as a sign that converts were seeking to find the relevance of the gospels within their cultures. He did not view conversion as an all-or-none, individual phenomenon, but as a developmental process in which a culture was Christianized, thus providing a supportive social context. This process was characterized by preaching the gospel, its reception, and the evocation of questions about its application in their lives followed by the selective reworking of the *adat* by the Indonesians themselves. Kruyt refused to issue a set of rules; he insisted on the reformation of the old *adat* through a dialogue with the mission (Kruyt 1925, 134–57). The actual form this 'Christian *adat*' took is discussed in greater detail in subsequent chapters.

The definition of religion in the Indonesian context thus emerged out of a three-party dialogue. The first party consisted of the Indonesians, whom the mission claimed were the ultimate arbiters of what parts of their *adat* were compatible with Christianity. The missionaries, in turn, defined Christianity for the Indonesians. This Christianity presumed a separation of church and state, although neither of these parties agreed on the boundary. As already noted, the NEI government contested mission claims on a number of counts. Adriani argued that setting this boundary was a political matter, and a political matter that was to be settled by the Dutch alone. This abstract debate had practical implications which ensured that mission and government interests did not coincide. The production of ethnographic knowledge as part of the sociological method was one of the practical means by which the debate was settled. By documenting the traditional 'religion' of the Toraja, the missions could redefine the debate about the boundary between church and state in terms of 'animism' and *adat*. By establishing the boundaries of a pre-existing religious tradition within the *adat*, they established their own sphere of competence.

Animisme and *Spiritisme*

Kruyt's major concern was thus to define the 'religion' of the 'Bare'e speaking Toraja' (later known as the To Pamona), and so place them within the larger evolutionary framework that structured *adat* law studies as an academic discourse. The mission's use of ethnography was situated within a growing international debate on the nature of 'primitive society' by lawyers, theologians, and philologists. The fruition of this debate defined the field of research of a new science, anthropology. Although few anthropologists would now accept their definition of 'primitive society,' by the end of the nineteenth century an 'orthodoxy' had emerged; 'primitive society' (an evolutionary category) was ordered on a kinship basis and was divided into exogamous descent groups related by a series of marriage exchanges. Their religion was 'animism,' the belief that natural species and objects had souls. These basic institutions preserved 'cultural survivals' like fossils of long-dead practices. With the development of private property, descent groups were displaced by the emergence of the territorial state (Kuper 1988, 6–7). Kruyt's ethnographic work was firmly fixed in this tradition; it clearly ordered the strategic questions facing the mission, 'the origin of the family, the state and religion' (ibid., 9). Further, its conclusions offered him the rhetorical means he needed to justify the role of the mission in the newly acquired territory of Central Sulawesi.

Kruyt's education at the Missionary Training School had included lessons in the new science. J.W. Roskes, the school's director, was the brother-in-law of G.A. Wilken, who in 1894 became the first Professor of Geography and Anthropology of the Netherlands Indies at the nearby University of Leiden. Wilken was the son of a North Sulawesi NZG missionary and had served for several years in the Indies civil service before he was repatriated in 1881 to continue his education. Roskes taught the new missionaries his brother-in-law's theories, which disseminated the growing international orthodoxy on 'primitive society' within the Netherlands (Brouwer 1951, 24). Wilken's work was heavily influenced by the then current theories of unilinear evolution, especially those of J.J. Bachofen. Wilken postulated four evolutionary stages of human history: the first, a stage of communal promiscuity, was followed by the development of matriarchy, as a woman and her children formed the first exogamously marrying social groups. Matriarchy developed as a result of the first incest prohibition, that between siblings. Matriarchy in turn gave way to patriarchy, as men sought to strengthen their ties with their outmarrying children (sons). As the importance of communal ownership diminished, the patrilineage lost its importance, giving way to the highest evolutionary stage, the nuclear family (Koentjaraningrat 1975, 29–30).

Wilken's work on animism closely followed that of E.B. Tylor, who claimed that it was the philosophic basis of primitive religion. Animism consisted of two unformulated propositions: all parts of nature had a soul, and these souls are capable of moving without requiring a physical form. The first proposition, that all natural objects have a soul, gives rise to fetishism, the worship of visible objects as powerful, spiritual beings. The second proposition, that souls are independent of their physical forms, gives rise to spiritism, the worship of the souls of the dead and the unseen spirits of the heavens (Wilken 1912a, 3: 3–5).

Kruyt's original contribution to the debate was made in a lengthy comparative study, *Animisme in den Indischen Archipel* (1906), published just after the military incorporation of Central Sulawesi in the Netherlands East Indies state.

Kruyt combined Wilken's two paradigms, linking the four stages of social evolution to a parallel religious evolution from pre-animism to animism to spiritism to Christianity. Kruyt argued that most discussions of animism failed to distinguish between animism proper, characterized by a belief in 'soul substance,' and spiritism, the belief in and worship of an enduring soul. Kruyt noted that the To Pamona had two concepts that could be translated as soul; the first, *tanoana*, was impersonal, a life force that filled all nature (cf. Ind. *semangat*). As it is only loosely tied to objects, an individual's store of it could be increased or decreased through ritual action. The amount of *tanoana* possessed by an individual relates directly to that person's degree of consciousness; the more conscious the individual, the more forceful he or she is, the more *tanoana* he or she possesses. The complete absence of *tanoana* leads to death. This impersonal notion of 'soul substance,' he noted, was typical of 'natural man' still living in tribal communalism – hence, without a strong conception of individuality, individual responsibility, or a personal afterlife.

The belief in 'soul substance' differed from a belief in *angga*, the souls of the dead. These souls retain their individuality after the person died. This degree of individuality differentiates the *angga* from *tanoana*, an impersonal force. Spiritism, the worship of the souls of the dead and other spirits, can thus be distinguished from animism proper. This notion of an enduring soul develops in proportion to the individual's self-consciousness; hence, only the souls of the most individualistic, the chiefs, were worshipped as *anitu* (ancestral guardian spirits).

Kruyt proposed four types of religion – pre-animism, animism, spiritism, and Christianity – which fit Wilken's four evolutionary stages of social development. This religious and social evolution can be presented through a set of opposing pairs: communalism versus individualism, kinship versus the state, matriarchy versus patriarchy, immorality (e.g., promiscuity) versus morality (e.g., monogamy). Kruyt qualified the bold assertion of evolutionary sequence, however, by noting that *all* of the earlier types of religions co-existed simultaneously within Toraja society as 'cultural survivals.' He argued that elements of animism and spiritism had similarly survived within Roman Catholicism until purged by the Reformation. The evolutionary sequence provides the criteria for evaluating the elements of every complex society; Protestantism, the superior religion, represents individualism, patriarchy, and morality, whereas all that Protestants should find reprehensible is a cultural survival which must be cleansed, as during the Reformation, by adherence to biblical principles alone.

Conversion to Christianity was thus not a mere change in religion, but an implicit evolutionary advancement. The Toraja were ripe for this transition, their religion being a combination of animism and spiritism. Christianity would originally be interpreted through the thought patterns associated with spiritism (i.e., 'dynamism'), and only slowly would the remnants of the older form disappear. Conversion to Christianity was not a simple all-or-none individual event, since these thought patterns were rooted in culture. It was only as Toraja culture as a whole was Christianized that it would provide the supportive atmosphere needed for the advancement of individual rationality. Until that time, rational Dutch missionaries would be needed to provide guidance and ensure that the purity of Protestantism was protected.

Kruyt's unique formulation of this evolutionary sequence had enormous practical implications for the mission, especially in its relationship with the women of the highlands. According to Kruyt, both animism and spiritism simultaneously existed in Pamonan society, as women's and men's 'religions,' respectively. Women were the priestesses of the cult of *tanoana*, reciting litanies that brought them to the heavens, where they sought the lost *tanoana* of the sick (Kruyt 1906, 446). Men, on the other hand, stood at the centre of the ancestor cult, hunting the heads necessary for the secondary funeral needed to transform an *angga* into an *anitu* (an honoured ancestor). Christianity was capable of making inroads in the ancestor cult since the pre-existing notion of spirits and gods were easily incorporated. On the other hand, animistic beliefs, women's religion, in this case, had no place in Christianity and were thus to be driven into the background, where they continued in truncated form as 'superstition.' The incorporation of highland religion within Christianity through the sociological method thus selectively excluded women from positions of authority.

Second, Kruyt acknowledged that pre-animism, animism, and spiritism were Western abstractions that highlanders did not distinguish as separable systems of thought, primarily because their thinking was 'pre-logical.' The abstraction of animism as a specifically 'religious' form separable from *adat* law thus awaited the 'development' of their logical capabilities through religious education. At the turn of the century, no word existed for 'religion' or 'animism' in Pamonan, until the missions introduced the words *agama* (from Bahasa Malayu, religion) and *molamoa* (to worship the spirits, gods). By implication, the highlanders did not distinguish between religion and *adat*. To them the *adat* was simultaneously the religious and civil code established and enforced by the ancestors of a group. They were thus unable to distinguish the roles of mission and colonial service. Kruyt argued that, when the highlanders converted to Christianity, they did not automatically gain the 'sophistication' to make this distinction. To their minds, was not the colonial service Christian too? Governmental subordination to the word of God was thus not a concept the mission had to teach, but a shared assumption of the highlanders and missionaries contested by (some) of the civil service: 'By Christian *adat* we mean both the civil as well as the religious *adat*. We don't pull the civil *adat* within the sphere of religion, but leave it as large a terrain as possible. Both are to be viewed as the Christian *adat*. Out of this observation it follows that the civil and religious *adat* cannot conflict with each other. The one must be called Christian as much as the other' (Adriani 1932, 1: 369). A Christian *adat* was a legal fiction in the same way as *adat* law. It was cast as somehow 'traditional,' a preservation of that which uniquely defined a *volk*, yet somehow amenable to reform. The new and derivative Christian *adat* was to be based upon the old, shorn of all 'heathen, unjust or unchristian elements' (Adriani 1932, 1: 370). The largest part of this truncated *adat* was to be left in the civil sphere where it could be adapted as needed to suit new economic circumstances. That part of the *adat* that touched on specifically religious matters was separate from civil law, and to be regulated by the church. Kruyt gave the marriage *adat* as one pertinent example (1937b, 46–7). Unjust practices were first eliminated: the death penalty for marriage between a slave and a free woman was commuted to banishment. The exchange of bridewealth traditionally marked the conclusion of a marriage, but was not specifically Christian and thus was left in the civil sphere. The marriage was not to be recognized, however, unless it was sanctified in the church, 'before God.'

Religion in a Colonial Context

Comaroff and Comaroff have elegantly summarized the one-sided nature of anthropological analyses of the encounter between missionaries and indigenous peoples. Europeans, they note, are seldom scrutinized in the same way as the social and cultural orders of the ethnographic Other, a methodological legacy of anthropology's roots in the study of 'primitive society.' 'As a result, we persist in treating the evangelists not as individuals possessed of socially conditioned biographies that make a difference but as a taken-for-granted, faceless presence on the colonial stage' (1991, 54). They note two methodological implications. First, this encounter must be regarded as a two-sided historical process in which missionaries, no less than indigenous peoples, are affected by the terms under which they met. Second, that a comprehensive study of the missionary encounter ought to begin in Europe.

In this chapter I have tried to demonstrate that this encounter was fraught with complexity, and that anthropology itself served to mediate among ethnographic subject, colonial government, and missions. Rather than engage in conventional ethnographic analysis (which lends itself to the same process), I have sought to examine the 'historical conditions (movements, classes, institutions, ideologies) necessary for the existence of particular religious practices and discourses' (Asad 1983, 252). 'Religion' in the Netherlands was a problematic issue in the history of this mission. The very lack of Dutch consensus on what constituted a religion and where the proper bounds between church and state lay combats any simple presuppositions about the relationship between missions and colonial rule. The process of *verzuiling* in the Netherlands had multiple sensitive effects on how religious missions were to be conducted. The mission developed its own forms of religious colonialism distinct from, and often in conflict with, the Netherlands East Indies state.

A key element of my argument is that, by adopting the *adat* law discourses of the colonial Ethical Policy, the missions embarked on a project of 'nation building' (emancipation), of which they were not always conscious. Kruyt's academic studies of the 'Bare'e-speaking Toraja' were not simply descriptive, but also prescriptive, since they became the basis for the *adat* polity established by the Netherlands East Indies state. His ethnography was situated within an evolutionary framework that not only analytically determined where they were on this scale, but also predicted what they were to become. The current conflict between Church and State on what constitutes an authentic To Pamona 'culture' thus has its roots in this ethnographic discourse.

Once the role of anthropology is introduced into this process, the epistemological status of anthropological knowledge becomes problematical. In this chapter, I have side-stepped the issue by treating ethnology as but one of the 'historical conditions' necessary for the emergence of a 'religious' sphere in Toraja 'culture.' The focus of analysis has been placed on the *uses* of ethnographic knowledge. Traditional culture no longer exists and is not recoverable, having been reduced to 'just' text, tainted by colonial expediencies. Unlike the broader subject of 'culture,' Kruyt's programmatic assertions, his theories, his ethnographies, have not been reduced to text, but are text. Kruyt, as missionary, explicitly stated his intended *use* for the ethnographic knowledge he was collecting, and this chapter has contextualized his interests in terms of the 'movements, classes, institutions, ideologies' of the Netherlands East Indies. In the next chapter, the application of these discourses over the last eighty years is examined, as the various contests between church and state were resolved, contested, and fought over again.

2

The Reformation

Verily I say unto you, Except ye be converted, and become as little children, ye shall not enter into the kingdom of heaven.

Matthew 18: 3

When capitalism expands and penetrates rural areas, the dominant classes will attempt to establish the political, legal and ideological forms necessary for its functioning and stability. In this process they will encounter ideological practices which originated in social relations now subordinate to capitalism. To explain this situation it is useful to introduce the concept of 'ideological articulation' in order to avoid static ones such as 'survivals' and 'persistence of tradition.' 'Ideological articulation' allows for a dynamic and historical analysis because it does not assume – as classical modernisation theory did – that the disappearance of non-capitalist ideological practices is a precondition for modernisation, nor does it adhere to Marx's over-enthusiastic view in the Communist Manifesto that 'the bourgeoisie, whenever it has got the upper hand, has put an end to all feudal, patriarchal, idyllic relations.'

Muratorio 1980, 40

Fabian argues that space was the fundamental notion underlying colonial linguistic and cultural projects: languages, and hence 'peoples,' were treated as 'strange regions to be explored, as bounded systems to be monographically described, as the possessions of territorially defined groups (so that linguistic, ethnic and geographical labels could become interchangeable)' (1986, 79). This geographic containment of distinctive differences was easily mapped in time, as the distance from 'civilizing centres' was translated into an earlier stage in the master evolutionary schema legitimizing imperialist expansion (Kearney 1996, 29). Whereas Riedel was able to define his unknown ethnographic subjects with a simple circle of mountains drawn on a map, Kruyt and Adriani began their massive three-volume ethnography of the 'Bare'e-speaking Toraja' (1912–4) with four lengthy chapters describing the various groups they sought to capture with the designation. Such was the detail of their accounts that they could not agree on where to draw the boundaries of their imagined community (Pakan 1986). Kruyt outlined a threefold division of East (or Bare'e-Speaking), West, and South (Sa'dan) Toraja, based upon a combination of factors such as language and the presence or absence of arbitrarily selected cultural traits such as the mutilation of teeth, house type, and slavery. Adriani based his threefold division upon a more refined linguistic analysis (Adriani and Kruyt 1912–14, vol. 3). Walter Kaudern, a Swedish anthropologist, divided the area into four, rather than three, subgroups (1925a).

Their inability to agree was rooted in their need for larger units of cultural homogeneity and solidarity in an area where the inhabitants systematically stressed complementary differences. Kruyt's initial adoption of the name 'Bare'e-speaking Toraja' (later known as the To Pamona) was meant to emphasize the ties between the various, still pagan highland groups, and so rationalize a single Toraja *volkskerk* to a colonial audience (End 1992, 18–20). His arbitrary application of the name 'Toraja' resulted from the absence of any pre-existing sense of shared ethnicity among those so designated. 'Bare'e speakers' in fact identified themselves as speakers of Are'e, Ae'e, Iba, and Aunde'e, where differences of dialect signified group boundaries; each of these groups was said to have a distinct *adat*. Although many (but not all) of those designated 'Bare'e-speaking Toraja' shared a common myth of origin in the kingdom of Pamona, the myth stressed their common subjection to the kingdom of Luwu, a symbol that simultaneously emphasized their diaspora, their diversity rather than their ethnic unity (Kruyt 1950, 16). The kingdom of Pamona consisted of a single large legendary village located across the river from Tentena, whose ruler was ultimately conquered by the kingdom of Luwu to the south, and led off in servitude (Sigilipu 1993, 2). Since they no longer had a leader, the people of the kingdom dispersed, each group leaving behind a stone (*Watu mPoga'a*) as a remembrance of their origin there. The division of this original unity served to legitimate frequent intergroup warfare under the impetus of the coastal kingdoms.

In the post-colonial era, the myth of Pamona has been reinterpreted as an ethnic charter for Kruyt's Bare'e speakers. The cultural construction of this particular identity was in large part constrained by the anthropological discourses of Church and State (cf. Steedly 1996; Henley 1996). A 'collective subject' was called into being through the 'discursive traditionalism' of the colonial state's system of *adat* law, in combination with the mission's attempts to 'inculturate' Christianity within this discursive tradition. Theirs was not the descriptive project that they claimed; through the selective designation, demarcation, and delineation of cultural and linguistic practices, they established new boundaries, as real yet as imaginary, as the chain of mountains used by Riedel to encircle his unknown 'Toraja.' This new ethnic identity, as 'To Pamona' (people of Pamona), grew less from the myth of their common origins than out of a legal fiction, the *resurrected* colonial kingdom of Poso/Pamona,[1] which had been utilized by the Dutch as a means of indirect rule through *adat* law among the various highland groups.

When I arrived in Tentena in November 1991 it was with the intention of researching the incorporation of indigenous political structures of this 'people without history' (Wolf 1982) within the church and state. I quickly found that Wolf's epithet for those excluded from the grand developmental histories of the west was oddly true of the To Pamona; not only was their voice missing in the historical literature of the region, but they had little knowledge or concern for the kinds of 'events' that provide the grist of Western historical discourse (cf. Parmentier 1987, 5). Instead, they ground their history, that is, their social charter of who they were and where they came from, in the maintenance of old hamlet boundaries within the administrative village. These historical hamlets, rooted in common kinship, were relevant as signs of current divisions and unions and a template for their re-creation. In other words, these signs were living history, a specifically ethnic idiom or 'local knowledge' for 'imagining the real' (Geertz 1983, 184). My own interests in institutional history and the process of incorporation thus contrasted with their notion of history as *adat*, 'the way of the ancestors,' a timeless set of the correct relationships that should exist between people.

In government eyes the timelessness of *adat* as a 'historyless history' made it an ideal expression of ethnic identity because it simultaneously defined a group for whom *adat law* is applicable. These two images of the *adat*, as moral knowledge and as law, parallel the contrast between nation and state, *volk* and government. As specifically moral knowledge it is rooted in everyday relationships and derives its strength from a set of non-state sanctions. To participants, *adat* law, as the legal codification and rationalization of 'the way of the ancestors,' partakes of the timeless quality of the moral knowledge they daily enact without serious questioning. *Adat* law is a relatively successful assertion of the state's hegemony in so far as *adat* law has come to be accepted as an appropriate ideological expression of villager's common-sense moral ethos (Geertz 1973a, 126–7). Nonetheless, the ideology of *adat* law differs from that ethos in that it simultaneously expresses political facts and the distribution of power (cf. Williams 1976, 145). *Adat* law delineates who constitutes an expert and who may appropriately adjudicate *adat* disputes. The timeless ethos is thus translated into a body of legal knowledge husbanded by the village *dewan adat* (adat council) and periodically subjected to debate, refinement and reformation by the state (see, for example, Santo et al. 1990).

It is this process of refinement and reformation of the *adat* that I would like to address in this chapter. That is, at this point I am concerned to document the transformations in official '*adat* discourses,' not the moral knowledge or practices of villagers. The state and church have played key roles in the emergence of ethnic identity among the To Pamona. Kruyt's sociological mission method, discussed in the previous chapter, is one means by which they did so. His work has been supplemented by that of a number of local ministers who have written their graduating thesis on the relationship between culture and Christianity (for example, Gintu 1991; Pangku 1987; Tanggerahi 1983). Similarly, the government's Department of Education and Culture has produced a number of ethnographic publications on various aspects of 'To Pamona' *adat* (1977/8, 1983, 1983/4, 1984, 1985, 1986) under its 'Inventory and Documentation of Regional Culture Project.' Since the *adat* has always been characterized as 'unwritten' or 'uncodified' law, the diligence with which both church and state have documented valid expressions of To Pamona culture reflects their own concerns to form a seamless identity bridging all aspects of civil society. To paraphrase Adriani, these are the concerns of government, not of the governed; of those 'good leaders of the people who are entrusted in their care' (1932, 2: 183).

My analysis of To Pamona ethnicity is intended to problematize this 'seamless identity.' Unlike Kruyt and Adriani and the NEI state, I do not treat the To Pamona as a natural category, and hence focus on the role of ethnography in creating and managing ethnicity. Key to the analysis of Pamonan ethnicity is the concept 'ideological articulation,' by which the ironic 'preservation of tradition' by the forces of modernization is accomplished. My aim is not to uncover the 'real' *adat*, that is, some idealized 'culture' untainted by colonial expediencies; rather, my goal is to underscore the diversity of those captured within the administrative strictures of *adat* law and to dwell on the colonial expediencies themselves. This is not an ethnography of a distinct culture, but a history of an ethnographic tradition and its administrative uses by church and state in an area being incorporated within the wider capitalist economy of the Dutch East Indies. As such, it is largely a history of a single village, Tentena, on the shores of Lake Poso, and hence at the centre of Riedel's 'imagined community' of 'Toraja.'

Tentena is by no means representative of the wider community of To Pamona; it is, however, an exemplary centre. It is a locus of ethnic identity since it incorporates the ancient village of Pamona, the *puse lemba*, the 'navel' of the region. It is also the headquarters of the independent Christian Church of Central

Sulawesi (Gereja Kristen Sulawesi Tengah [GKST]) which grew out of Kruyt's mission. And lastly, as the capital of the administrative district of Pamona Utara, it is the governmental centre through which national policy decisions are funnelled. It is here that we can see the long-term implications of colonial strategies that ultimately created a 'pillarized' Christian society not unlike the 'Great Protestant Nation' then forming in the Netherlands.

An examination of religious pillarization in the New Order period requires a change in focus from the explicitly political actions of religious parties to the rationalization of 'culture' by the politico-bureaucratic regimes of specific religious organizations. It is this task that is pursued throughout the remainder of this book. The New Order's cultural policies specifically aim to depoliticize both ethnic and religious identities. But if one redefines the self-image of the To Pamona in terms of 'animist' songs and dances, their Christian identity is challenged. The New Order's definition of *adat* in terms of pre-Christian traditions and the Church's own definition of a Christian *adat* are inherently contradictory. Government policy is thought to encourage communalism within the church, threatening Christian unity and abetting the creation of ethnic churches. The church has already undergone a number of these painful ethnic secessions. Driven by its own imagined community, the 'Brotherhood of Christ,' the church has shored up its identity by directly contesting the state's representations. These contests only confirm the state's fears of religion as a destablizing force and strengthen its resolve to root ethnicity in an alternate depoliticized 'cultural' arena.

Peoples without History

Kruyt, Adriani, and Kaudern's inability to arrive at a common classification of the peoples of Central Sulawesi is not surprising. The province's scant population was divided among no fewer than five language groups and twenty-five languages (Noorduyn 1991). It is a sparsely populated mountainous region with few alluvial plains. Rivers formed the major means of communication, and oriented the highlanders towards coastal kingdoms such as Luwu, Parigi, and Tojo, which dominated the interior through their control over the interisland trade in forest products. These political and trade ties varied from simple *masintuwu*, friendship, to *mepue*, to recognize as Lord (Tideman MVO 1926, 40–1). Political systems among the highland groups themselves varied from relatively egalitarian polities to highly stratified chiefdoms. Various cultural traits, whether of house type or the presence of institutionalized slavery, were widely if unevenly diffused throughout the region. Although the highlanders were exceptionally diverse, both the mission and the colonial government chose to highlight specific common cultural and political elements in the process of incorporation while systematically eliminating many of the differences. As an ethnography of that incorporation, this brief description of the diversity of the pre-colonial period ironically focuses upon these cultural similarities of colonial concern, while ignoring the more exotic, now banned practices such as headhunting, which were of such importance for the Dutch in emphasizing their moral superiority, and hence right to rule.

The core settlement areas of the To Pamona identified by Kruyt lie in three major river basins: the Poso, which empties into the Bay of Tomini to the north; the Laa, which empties into the Gulf of Mori to the east; and the Kalaena, which empties into the Gulf of Bone to the south. The Poso and Laa river valleys are separated by the Pompangeo mountains. The Poso and Laa river valleys are separated from the Kalaena river valley by the Takolekaju mountains which run from the southeast (where it forms the southern barrier of the Laa basin) in a northeasterly direction (ultimately forming the western barrier of the Poso basin). Nestled between these mountain barriers is Lake Poso, the second-largest lake in Sulawesi, which drains into the Poso River; it is 34 kilometres in length and 12 kilometres at its widest. The major axis of To Pamona settlements was north/south, stretching from the Bay of Tomini to the Gulf of Bone. The lower reaches of the Laa river basin were settled by the To Mori.

The small, hilltop hamlets found throughout these three river basins formed larger named political confederations, which varied in their degree of stratification (map 2.1). These groups were generally limited to the valley of one of the feeders of the major rivers; they derived their names from their village of origin, settled by refugees from Pamona. Examples of these groups include the To Lage, who settled in the upper Tomasa river valley; the To Pebato, in the Puna river valley; and the To Wingke mPoso, on the upper reaches of the Poso River. These groups of settlements were said to share a common set of ancestors, and hence a common *adat*. In reality, they were internally as diverse as the To Pamona as a whole. For example, the hamlet of Wawo Ndoda, which was eventually incorporated in the village of Tentena, was a part of the centralized chiefdom of the To Onda'e in the Laa river valley. Wawo Ndoda was known, however, for not having any slaves, and for having a woman as its leader. As a result, these collections of hamlets should not be treated as units of cultural consistency, as groups that shared customs (*adat*), but as nascent political confederations that emphasized their unity through shared descent.

Adriani clearly stated that it was shared descent which made both group unity and leadership possible: 'It is not actually the chief that brings about this unity between the otherwise loosely bound and neighbouring, independent villages. If the closer family ties served to strengthen traffic between the villages, then the

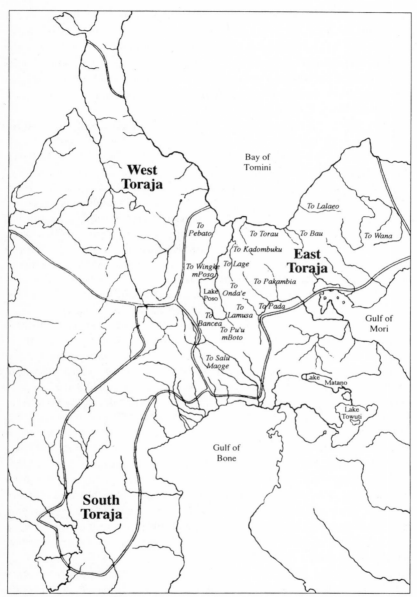

Map 2.1 Kruyt's Division of the East, West, and South Toraja (Village Confederacies in italics)

chiefs of these villages will also have more to do with each other. They will involuntarily organize themselves, and one will become first amongst them' (1932, 2: 92). The general process of decision making reflects the lack of centralized power. Decisions on matters of village-wide significance were made by consensus in open meetings. Any adult could attend and participate, but women usually sat behind their husbands, and younger men usually remained silent. Their seating arrangement, in nested concentric circles, emphasized the importance of those sitting in the inner circle, who did most of the talking. Kruyt asserted that such consensus-seeking resulted from a general fear by all, including the village leadership, of taking individual responsibility for a decision (1950, 114). The leader (kabosenya, literally, 'big one') of a village was that person who would pronounce the decision consensually arrived at. However, anyone could bypass this forum if he or she was willing to accept sole responsibility for the outcome, as in the settlement of a dispute. In the more hierarchical village confederacies, individual kabosenya were more willing to assume this burden.

The internal harmony (mosintuwu) of these confederations of hamlets was less dependent upon their degree of political hierarchy than upon alliances between their constituent kinship groups. Each hamlet was composed of from two to ten banua, longhouses,[2] occupied by two to six matrilineally related households. Each household farmed its own swiddens (slash-and-burn fields left to lie fallow every few years), and had its own hearth. Land was freely available, even to slaves. The longhouse served as the matrilineal core of a corporate group that collectively inherited and owned specific kinds of elite goods such as cloth, water buffalo, and copper plates. Ties between longhouses were maintained through ritual exchanges (posintuwu) of these elite goods between kin during wedding and funeral feasts. These ties were extensive (counting siblings to the third degree) and cognatically calculated. Internal harmony (mosintuwu) within confederations was thus maintained through overlapping membership in these corporate groups and the posintuwu exchanges among them (Schrauwers 1997).

Political leadership and social stratification both emerged out of these exchanges of elite goods. A kabosenya acquired this role by being the genealogical senior of a corporate group, and therefore the one who managed its collective property. The term thus distinguishes the rank of seniors from juniors within their own kin groups. Second, in an extension of this usage among the slaveholding village confederacies, it refers to the rank of free-born, distinguishing them from slaves or permanent juniors. Slaves (watua), like genealogical juniors, were subordinated through the kabosenya's control of the elite goods necessary for bridewealth. Slaves were those without siblings, either because they were cut off for incurring recurrent debts, or because they were war captives. Lacking a family of their own, their (reduced) bridewealth had to be paid by their 'owners' – a corporate group, not an individual. Slaves and their children remained the genealogical juniors of this corporate group in perpetuity. Lastly, the term is an indication of status, referring to that one *kabosenya* from among the many in the village (the *wa' a ngkabosenya* [council of elders]) to whom most of the villagers turned for assistance. Those with little politically significant standing, in contrast, were called 'chief of their own house' (Kruyt 1950, 114). Politically significant status accrued to those of the rank of *kabosenya* only.

Kabosenya acquired status through feasting, the arena within which 'power' was husbanded and translated into leadership. Like the Javanese notion, the To Pamona concept of power (*tanoana*) is of that creative energy which suffuses the 'entire cosmos,' including both 'organic and inorganic matter' (Anderson 1972, 7). *Tanoana* is 'that which animates'; hence, its absence results in illness and death. The primary means of acquiring and maintaining one's stock of *tanoana* was simultaneously a ritual and a political act (cf. Atkinson 1989). Ritual action was addressed to husbanding power, either through initiations (*mampapotanoana, momparilangka*), marriage (*morongo*), thanksgiving (*padungku*), or secondary funerals (*mompemate, motengke*). The liturgy of these rituals differs, but the staging, staffing, and supplying of the events remained the same: a feasting complex. Feasts utilized a standard ritual repertoire, merely increasing in size as the ritual beneficiaries moved through life. The largest feast was thus the secondary funeral by which a deceased *kabosenya* was transformed into an honoured ancestor (*anitu*). This series of feasts reproduced the animistic 'power' that signified life in ever larger units: longhouse, village, cognatic kinship group, and village confederacy. Politically, this graded set of feasts served to reproduce the exchange networks of people with whom the members of a longhouse lived in harmony while it simultaneously established a status hierarchy among the kin group's leading *kabosenya*.

The means by which the exchange of elite goods established this status hierarchy among the *kabosenya* can best be illustrated through the largest of the feasts, the secondary funeral (*mompemate, motengke*). The secondary funeral was performed to end mourning and could occur several years after the death, once the flesh of the deceased had rotted from the bones. The ritual was performed for all the dead within a village and was the means by which their souls were led from the underground realm of the dead to their ultimate resting place (*Wawo maborosi*, the many mountains). The souls of the recent dead were considered of great danger to the living until the secondary funeral has been performed for them. They frequently stole the *tanoana* of the unharvested rice, or of their relatives, causing illness and death. The staging of the secondary funeral was of considerable difficulty and required the scalp (also called the *tanoana*) of an enemy, the contribution of numerous gifts of *posintuwu* from related groups of sibling sets, as well as the building of temporary shelters for the hundreds of guests. It was for this reason that the ceremony was frequently postponed until such a feast was required to aid a deceased *kabosenya* join the ranks of the founding ancestors of the village (*anitu*).

Each feast had a host, usually the longhouse of the deceased, whose *kabosenya* organized the building of the feast huts for the guests, the slaughtering and cooking, and performed the ritual. The *kabosenya* (male or female) performing the ritual assumed the *posintuwu* obligations of the deceased as well as those incurred through the ceremony itself. Their repayment of these *posintuwu* debts was cardinal to the survival of the 'occasional kin group,' the alliance of longhouses. These ties were forgotten by those of descending generations if their *kabosenya* did not maintain exchange relations with more distant relatives; a stingy *kabosenya* found his family shrank over time. If, however, the *kabosenya* maintained relations with a broad network of relatives throughout his lifetime, and continued to exchange with second, third, and fourth cousins, these latter attended this *kabosenya*'s secondary funeral, and recognized their common kinship ties. That funeral, however, would be organized by one of the *kabosenya*'s children, who must demonstrate the abilities by which their parent became prominent: organizational ability and generosity.

The political system of the highlands was thus predicated upon the mainte-nance of exchange relations among various longhouses. Leadership emerged in the niches of the exchange system. A *kabosenya* could attain prominence through the size and extent of his gifts of *posintuwu* to the feasts of those with whom he was related. Renown for generosity was a cardinal feature of a true *kabosenya*, whose house ladder should be well worn by the feet of supplicants. Yet a truly outstanding leader, as Adriani wrote, could emerge only where closer family ties 'strengthened traffic between villages' (1932, 2: 92). A prominent *kabosenya* would follow a strategy of arranging 'centripetal marriage alliances' (cf. Errington 1989, 258–62) between members of his kin to reinforce the network of familial ties upon which his political influence depended. These overlapping marriage alliances also marked the boundaries of the village confederacy, which was ideally endogamous.

While this feasting complex was evident in all of the village confederacies which Kruyt identified as 'Bare'e-speaking Toraja,' the degree of political stratification varied immensely. Some, such as the To Onda'e, had a hereditary slave class and an institutionalized village-confederacy leadership role. Others, such as the To Wingke mPoso, lacked a slave class, village-confederacy leader, or firm boundaries. In this discussion, I have also failed to address relations between the highlands and the coastal kingdoms from whom they acquired the elite goods necessary for *posintuwu* exchanges; or the relations between the various village confederacies, characterized by ceaseless headhunting raids (see Schrauwers 1997). Rather than being an attempt to homogenize the diversity of the highlands, this brief discussion has tried to outline a particular set of practices that were to become of central importance in the colonial period. In particular, it has sought to underscore the relationship among the feasting complex, *posintuwu* exchange, and the basis of leadership. Both church and state sought to incorporate the *kabosenya* within their new bureaucratic orders. They differed, however, in their understanding of the nature of 'traditional' leadership, and hence in their success.

Dismantling the Village Confederacies

The district officer charged with incorporating the highlands of Central Sulawesi within the Netherlands East Indies saw himself as an 'educator' who ironically sought to 'bring the power for self-determination' (Engelenberg MVO 1906, 27). Such self-determination was not individualistic, but nationalistic in intent, and implied the existence of a *volk* that would ultimately come to political maturity under the tutelage of the Dutch. As I have pointed out, no such *volk* existed. Thus, to reach that end, he had to implement a host of policies that served to permanently inscribe boundaries around the 'collective subject' defined by Kruyt and Adriani as the 'Bare'e-speaking Toraja.' The kingdom of Poso established the administrative framework within which the linguistic, ethnic, and geographical labels applied by the Dutch could become interchangeable. It was the mission, however, that ultimately assumed the paternalistic role of educator; they served as cultural brokers explaining puzzling state directives, established schools, and proclaimed the message of Christ from their pulpits. Here I emphasize that the terms and conditions by which these political subjects were granted rights within the larger bureaucratic structures of the Netherlands East Indies state were based upon their collective membership in the ethnie defined for them by the Dutch, a *volk* (cf. Steedly 1996, 451). That is, the concern expressed here is less with self-identity than with the means by which local power relations were bureaucratically incorporated and 'governmentalized ... elaborated, rationalized, and centralized in the form of, or under the auspices of, state institutions' (Foucault 1991, 103).

In the introduction, I pointed out that my aim was to document how the practices of the people so incorporated exceed the limits of the 'culture effect' that 'is devoted to recovering the horizons of its power by containing that which would appear otherwise' (Pemberton 1994, 9). In this section I begin to address exactly how the 'culture effect' worked through the creation of an *adat* discourse that ignored the administrative practices within which it was embedded. The codification of a discursive traditionalism, *adat* law, which delineated the substantive differences separating this *volk* from others within the Netherlands East Indies, can be contrasted with homogenizing socio-economic and political transformations introduced under the Ethical Policy with the aim of shepherding these new colonial charges along a unilinear path to 'modernity' and 'self-determination.'

Engelenberg, the colonial official charged with pacifying the highlands, had originally planned to rule indirectly through a league of village confederacies. His plan was stymied by the colonial government's need for a clear chain of command. Since most village confederacies (with the exception of the To Onda'e) had no recognized head and were small kinship-bounded polities, the Dutch ultimately abandoned the plan for a federation of indigenous leaders and imposed a 'kingdom' like that of neighbouring Mori and Tojo on the regency. The various village confederacies were amalgamated in five large districts, each governed by a district headman (*mokole*) subordinated to the newly appointed king (see map 1.2). Tentena became the seat of a similarly named district which incorporated members of the To Wingke mPoso, To Onda'e, To Tino'e, and To Lage. Since the kingdom was ruled according to *adat* law, yet each district was an amalgam of several village confederacies, each with its own *adat*, a process of government rationalization of *adat* law began almost immediately and has continued until today. The *adat* of each village confederacy has increasingly been subordinated to a new legal entity, the *ada mPamona*, the Pamonan *adat*.

The homogenization of *adat* law within the kingdom complemented agricultural development policies, which had the advantageous effect of increasing the governability of their subjects. The Dutch considered swidden agriculture as practised in the highlands to be ecologically destructive; their agricultural development projects and settlement policies were directed towards the creation of a uniform peasantry of wet rice or *sawah* cultivators tied to their land and their villages. Following the consolidation of their control of the highlands between 1906 and 1908, the Dutch began a massive resettlement plan, forcing all the highlanders to abandon their hilltop hamlets and construct larger villages in the few alluvial plains suitable for wet-rice agriculture (Kruyt 1970, 91–105, 144–55). All of these villages were to be situated along a single road stretching from the coastal town of Poso to Tentena, through the Laa river valley, to the southern end of Lake Poso. Given the hilly topography of the area, sites suitable for *sawah* cultivation were few; swidden agriculture is actually better adapted to local conditions. The government's policy had its greatest success along the coast, in the alluvial plains at the north and south ends of Lake Poso, and in the Laa river basin, where the bulk of the population is now concentrated; whole territories in the interior were depopulated. The implementation of the policy has thus resulted in the consolidation of a number of different village confederacies in the same or neighbouring villages, often at· a great distance from their traditional lands. Those village confederacies forced to abandon their hilltop hamlets have found that they have no secure legal tenure to their traditional lands, further decreasing the saliency of village confederacy membership.

The legitimacy of Dutch political control in these new villages was in large part dependent upon incorporating traditional forms of political leadership. However, the hierarchical polity envisioned by colonial officials involved a central misunderstanding of the role of the *kabosenya* as well as the importance of the consensual village council. Unsurprisingly, the newly appointed village headmen proved a general failure. Kruyt described how *kabosenya*, when appointed as village headmen, inevitably disappointed Dutch officials through their inability to command. The crucible of contention was inevitably the newly imposed corvée labour demands, the four days a month of roadwork expected of every adult male (Adriani and Kruyt 1912, 1: 151). The failures of these village headmen were interpreted as the recalcitrant refusal to obey, and they were summarily replaced; their substitute was usually a village leader of even less influence, leading to the regular rotation of increasingly ineffective functionaries (Kruyt 1924c, 1924e, 32). It was in this context that many unconverted highland villages, including Tentena, asked for a mission school. The mission-appointed Manadonese teachers played a prominent role as cultural brokers between villagers and the colonial bureaucracy. Although phrased in terms of 'cooperation' with the state, this role as cultural broker gave the mission a great deal of leverage in how it interpreted state policy (Arts 1985; Coté 1996).

Tentena, for example, was formed about 1907–8 on the alluvial plain on the east bank of the Poso River, about 2 kilometres downstream from Lake Poso. It was an amalgamation of approximately six villages, comprising about two hundred households stretched along a single road parallel to the river. The village proved too large for a single *kabosenya* to control and was soon divided into two administrative villages, Tentena and Sangele, each with about one hundred households. Even though the two villages shared a single church, members sat on opposite sides. They shared few kinship ties, and their residents rarely mixed. The village of Tentena, composed of the hamlets Wawo Lembo, Dulungi, and Mogumpo (the last two from the west side of the river), was later expanded with the addition of a number of households from the Onda'e village of Wawo Ndoda. Wawo Lembo was the numerically largest hamlet, and the village headman was generally chosen from its *kabosenya*.

The mission, striving to acquire voluntary 'converts,' was forced to work within the limits of traditional forms of social organization. Although the Dutch had amalgamated numerous hilltop hamlets to form larger directly administered villages, there were no recognized indigenous political leaders at that level; rather, each hamlet retained distinct boundaries within the village, and hamlet affairs remained the concern of its unrecognized consultative hamlet council. Kruyt had noted as early as 1912 that the *kabosenya* needed to be incorporated within the church, since they were already taking charge of the organization of most church festivities (Kruyt 1970, 312). He recommended that these leaders be officially recognized as church elders, although their duties were to differ somewhat from the Dutch model. Within the presbyterial system of the Dutch Reformed Church, the Council of Elders, or consistory, is the decision-making body of the congregation. Kruyt argued that, in the case of the To Pamona, the village council (*wa' a ngkabosenya*) functioned as the decision-making body, and he hoped that a specifically To Pamona type of consistory could eventually be formed from it. However, at that time not all members of the village council were Christian, hence its members could not automatically assume the status of church elders, even if, as was the case, they were arranging Christian events in an effort to *mosintuwu* with their Christian neighbours. As a result, Kruyt institutionalized the role of elder without institutionalizing a decision-making consistory (which informally remained the unrecognized consultative hamlet council). The elder, like the *kabosenya* of old, was consensually selected by the villagers (both Christians and non-Christians).

These elders were considered church headmen, a role paralleling that of the village headman appointed by the colonial government (Kruyt 1970, 313). An early Pamonan teacher in Tentena, L. Molindo, stated that this proved a consistent problem for villagers in distinguishing the sphere of competence of church from that of state. The missions emphasized that the role of elder was more like that of the traditional, non-coercive *kabosenya*, rather than the village headman. Although a church leader and organizer, the elder was not a decision maker as decision making was still the function of the village council, the as-yet-unformed consistory advised by the teacher. As more adults converted to Christianity, the number of elders was increased. In Tentena, an elder was selected for each of the original three hilltop hamlets. Each of these elders preached weekly to the members of their hamlet, now officially designated an 'Evangelization Group" by the mission. The Evangelization Groups thus served to perpetuate the boundaries between these groups within the village of Tentena as a whole.

The old hamlets had been defined as '*adat* communities,' which meant they shared common ancestors who were worshipped in the hamlet temple. This shared descent had practical implications in *posintuwu* exchanges and in the formation of agricultural work groups. Within the new heterogeneous Christian villages, the ritual expression of kinship through the worship of the ancestors was increasingly untenable after the banning of headhunting and secondary funerals by the colonial government. Since the basis for the authority of the *kabosenya* largely rested on kinship ties, the Evangelization Groups became an alternative ritual vehicle within which these ties could be perpetuated. The mission's intent to evangelize through these groups can be contrasted with the manner in which they were implemented so that they were consonant with the different ends of pre-existing social groups and forms of leadership.

The Evangelization Group was thus influenced by the dynamics of exchange between kin articulated through ritual feasts, which embodied relations of authority and dependence. It demonstrates, in other words, a historical continuity with the feasting complex marked by *posintuwu* exchanges described earlier in this chapter, although these feasts were given a Christian context. Such linkages between a 'universal' religion and a local feasting tradition can also be seen in the *slametan*, which plays a similar role among the Muslim Javanese (Keeler 1987, 142–57). The Javanese comparison is intended to underscore the point that such 'borrowings' are not indicative of 'incomplete conversion' or syncretism. Woodward argues that 'it is impossible to evaluate the "Muslimness" or "Hinduness" or "Christianness" of a local tradition unless the analysis of local custom and ritual is informed by knowledge of the textual tradition in question' (Woodward 1989, 52). He ably demonstrates how the Javanese *slametan* is rooted in local interpretations of Sufi (rather than modernist) doctrine. Similarly, in chapters 5 and 6, I deal more explicitly with the Christianization of To Pamona rituals.

The Evangelization Group service, at its most basic, is a formal occasion hosted by households on a rotating basis, after which coffee and cakes are served. This, in itself, is a major burden and great pride is taken in one's hospitality, in providing a number of different types of cakes, such that the attenders feel honoured by the effort taken on their behalf. The commensal eating of even the most basic of foods designates the participants as living in harmony (*mosintuwu*). The larger the feast, the greater the fellowship. Many families take advantage of their turn to host the group as an opportunity for a thanksgiving service. The thanksgiving service may be held for many reasons: for example, a birthday, the completion of a house, a successful harvest, graduation, the cure of an illness. The thanksgiving service is also an expression of a household's ability to feast, of its prosperity. The form of the thanksgiving service is similar to that of a regular religious service, except that a minister (instead of elder) will usually be asked to preach, and the food offered is correspondingly luxurious; a chicken or pig may be slaughtered, supplemented by fish and eel. Indeed, meat is rarely eaten except at such events. The expense of even the smallest thanksgiving service is often out of bounds for the poorest families, but social pressure is so intense that everyone will attempt to host at least one. Even households that do not normally attend the Evangelization Group will take their turn to host it.

The performance of these feasts is phrased in the language of *posintuwu* (cf. Ind. *gotong royong* [mutual assistance], esp. in regards the Javanese *slametan* [Keeler 1987, 143]). The *posintuwu* may consist of simple attendance, a contribution in kind (esp. of rice) or of labour. *Posintuwu* in kind is always considered as a gift to the holder of the feast and is intended to defray the costs involved. Exact reciprocity is not expected, but the relationship must be maintained by a return gift. Even attendance is appreciated as such. The closer the family, the greater its contribution. Contributing labour is usually restricted to the closest of the host's family (*to saana*), supplemented by those well known for their generosity, who tend to play supervisory roles. The larger the thanksgiving service, the more labour is required since people are needed to slaughter the pig, build the temporary shelter for the guests, cook, serve food, and clean up afterwards. Thus, although all present at the feast are *mosintuwu* (have provided *posintuwu*, and are eating together), the performance of the feast simultaneously serves to differentiate the group that hosts the meal from the more extensive kin-group members (*santina*) who attend as guests.

That the performance of a feast clearly establishes lines of authority and dependence within the wider kin group can be seen in the case of two newly married brothers, Tukaka and Tua'i, each of whom wished to celebrate his child's first birthday with a thanksgiving service, which I attended. Tukaka, the older brother, began planning the feast shortly after the birth of his child, purchasing a piglet that he raised specifically for the event, held in conjunction with an Evangelization Group service. In contrast, Tua'i approached his family a week before the birthday and stated he wanted to hold a feast but couldn't afford it. The family responded to his plight with sufficient *posintuwu* to celebrate a small feast for the immediate family. During the latter feast, the father of the brothers gave a short speech emphasizing the event as a small sign of prosperity and independence. He stated that Tua'i, who already had two children, could at last hold a feast of his own, even though humble in its offerings. The speech clearly underlined the significance of feast-giving as an assertion of independence and ability even if circumstances undermined the substance of the message. Tukaka, on the other hand, planned his feast in such a way as to lessen his dependence on his family and so demonstrate his abilities and prosperity to them. He thus became someone whom Tua'i could approach for assistance. By holding a feast, Tua'i was asserting his household's status as a *posintuwu* exchange partner, although one in a dependent position. Their father's contestable assertion of Tua'i's independence had to be stated since his dependence in performing the feast was obvious to all attending.

Feast-giving, kin ties, *posintuwu*, authority, and dependence are thus interwoven in Evangelization Group structure. The group is linked by ties of kinship and *posintuwu* exchange, which are simultaneously ties of prestige and dependence. This system is dynamic, emerging out of the weekly series of feasts, whether a simple family service with coffee and cookies, a thanksgiving service of simple or grand proportions, or the largest of feasts, the funeral or wedding. In all cases the feast is carried out under the tutelage of the church, which transforms the brute expression of the economic ability to host a large number of people to a sumptuous meal into praise for the blessings of God. Similarly, feasting transforms generosity within a kin group into church-sanctioned leadership roles. Through their display of piety in feasting and their generosity in *posintuwu*, these individuals emerge as candidates for elder, the leader of the Evangelization Group.

The end effect of colonial intervention in the highlands was to ameliorate the social, political, and cultural differences among the various village confederacies and so marginalize their importance. These peoples were administratively reordered within new modernizing bureaucratic polities, the mission church, and the kingdom of Poso, ironically ruled by 'traditional' law (the *ada mPamona*). By eliminating or modifying the ancestor cult and shifting the emphasis of the *adat* away from shared descent to customary law, village confederacies lost their identity as bounded kinship units. In contrast, the weakening of differences, the elimination of warfare, and the introduction of a uniform *adat* have all served to foster a larger regional identity. The kingdom of Poso, composed of districts and administrative villages, increasingly came to replace the hamlet and the village confederacy as the primary forum for indigenous kinship-based politics.

I will argue that it is these new political forums which gave birth to the religious and ethnic nationalism of the To Pamona. The model for the To Pamona was Minahasa in Northern Sulawesi, where similar policies had been followed in the previous century, resulting in a similar polyglot 'nationalism' among the diverse linguistic groups of the interior highlands around Menado (Henley 1996, 42). The content of this polyglot To Pamona regional identity, specifically defined in terms of 'tradition,' was negotiated by the *kabosenya*, who were directly incorporated in mission and state bureaucracies. These *kabosenya* bent these bureaucracies to meet their own needs and preserve their own status, as described in the case of the Evangelization Group. Importantly, the terms under which the colonial state and missions incorporated the *kabosenya* differed; it was the mission that successfully incorporated feasting and kinship within its boundaries. The irony of this Dutch administrative and social revolution utilizing 'traditional' leaders ruling by 'traditional' law requires repeated emphasis. The irony can be tied to the central contradiction of the Ethical Policy, which mandated that the colonial state at once respect 'tradition' yet shepherd its wards towards a mythical end-state of modernity.

Church and State as Village Institutions

The bureaucratic orders of both mission and state were predicated upon nationalist projects in which a *volk*, the 'Bare'e-speaking Toraja,' were 'educated' to the point of 'self-determination.' Here we turn, then, from an encapsulated 'tradition' to a new type of political figure whose authority lay in educational qualifications created and moulded within Dutch institutions. Although the Dutch appointed a *kabosenya*, Papa Besi, as village headman of Tentena in 1908, the settlement was under the direction of a Manadonese civil servant, Be'a Nayoan. Both the colonial administration and the missions initially used acculturated Protestant Manadonese from North Sulawesi in these roles. As soon as the To Pamona acquired basic educational qualifications, they quickly replaced the Manadonese, the first step in their 'national self-determination.' The test case for this method of rapid replacement with only minimal acculturation was Kruyt's adopted son Pancali Sigilipu, who became the schoolteacher in Tentena in 1910. However, the ideological divisions of the Netherlands, in particular the contested boundary between church and state, created similar confusion in the new institutions taking shape in Tentena. Since the mission controlled the educational system (as it did in the Netherlands), the church became the entry point for the larger political system established by the colonial government. It was the church's Christian national ideology of a *volkskerk*, rather than an attenuated *adat*, which was to dominate the self-identity of this bureaucratic elite.

Unlike in the coastal areas, where schools had been established a decade before the extension of Dutch rule and villages converted *en masse* to Christianity, the conversion process in Tentena was individualized, and focused upon issues of faith. There was a significant animist segment of the population until the Second World War. The first converts were two schoolgirls who were baptized in 1910. Although the number of Christians grew marginally to about twenty by 1915, most converts were of similar junior status, recent graduates of the new school. It was only because of mission toleration of the *adat*, the hallmark of Kruyt's methodology, that these new Christians could practise their faith. Low-status converts whose families remained largely animist were expected to take part in the ritual expression of kinship and labour-exchange relationships. It was difficult for converts to farm their fields as Christians; their elders made no distinction between 'agricultural technique' and 'animist religion,' since animist rituals stereotyped established practice in a point-for-point manner without there being a clear differentiation between secular practice and religious principle.

The process of conversion thus involved learning a new category of experience, 'religion.' Whereas both Adriani and Kruyt note that the To Pamona originally had no word for religion, by the 1920s, the word *molamoa* (to worship the spirits) came into use as indigenous debates emerged about what practices Christians could and could not engage in. The word is indicative of the rationalization of a traditional religion, its transformation from 'fussy ritual acts' into an abstract, more logically coherent set of beliefs (cf. Geertz 1973c; Hoskins 1987; Atkinson 1983). The rationalization of traditional religion into a distinct form of religion (*agama,* from Malay) thus allowed both low-status converts and high-status animists to engage in a common secular *adat* (defined as simple technical action) without either transgressing their 'beliefs' (cf. Steedly 1993, 70).

Although the first converts faced numerous difficulties stemming from their inability to participate in animist rituals, the tide soon turned, as the number of converts blossomed; this tended to cloud a second distinction, that between religion and the state. This distinction was contested in the Netherlands; whereas the minority liberals sought to create a secular state, the dominant religious parties insisted that religion constituted a uniform set of moral principles that were applicable to all spheres of activity which it was the duty of the state to enforce. Applied to the colonial context, Adriani argued, the mission should circumscribe a small part of the *adat* as 'religion,' but the whole should be considered a 'Christian *adat*' since that which lies outside the delimited sphere of religion was nonetheless subject to its moral principles (1932, 1: 359–70). The mission consistently adhered to this position, whereas the civil service varied its policies, depending upon the views of the continually changing *controleurs.* Engelenberg worked closely with the missions, and thus the initial terms under which the To Pamona were incorporated tended to work in the missions' favour and institutionalize their definition of religion (Arts 1985, 115).

From the To Pamona point of view, the ideological distinction that underlies the administrative separation of church and state was blurred; the To Pamona had no experience with the concept of 'secular state' nor of 'religion.' They had considered the mission and its schools 'the tame cow' being used by the colonial state to bait them, the 'wild buffaloes' (Adriani 1919, 178). Kruyt's son (1970, 111) ironically blamed the colonial government for reinforcing the To Pamona 'tradition' of 'the unity of church and state,' fostering confusion. He cited the example of an elderly Christian relieved of his civil corvée labour duties because of age who subsequently stopped coming to church because he had been 'set free.' This man perceived the attendance of church services to be a part of state corvée labour demands. It was the colonial government, not the mission, which had banned reburial of the dead, headhunting, and the execution of changelings (*tau mepongko*), yet these actions clearly worked to benefit the mission by making the practice of traditional religion increasingly impossible. The To Pamona thus correctly perceived that the NEI state wanted them to become Christians (Kruyt 1970, 110–11). It was only with time that the villagers internalized the distinction between the religious and the secular, but, in so doing, they simultaneously learned Adriani's dictum that the secular *adat* was subordinate to religious principles. This was less a 'confusion' than the ideological groundwork of the distinctive form of 'pillarized' Dutch Protestantism described in the previous chapter. This is most clearly seen through mission educational policy and its effects on the staffing of the indigenous civil service. The case of Pancali Sigilipu is instructive in the way that religious education became the gateway to the colonial bureaucracy and local authority.

Sigilipu was born in 1888 in Wawo Ndoda, a To Onda'e village, but shortly thereafter his parents moved to the To Wingke mPoso village of Petirolemba (also known as Sigilipu, which he later used as a last name). About 1894, Sigilipu's parents were killed in a To Onda'e raid on the village, and he alone was taken prisoner 'because he did not cry' and hence knew no fear (Kruyt 1970, 64). He was made a slave, but his new owner, in need of money, offered the boy to Kruyt for *f* 125. Kruyt agreed to buy Sigilipu only if it was possible to restore his *kabosenya* status. The young boy was initially educated in the mission school at Kasiguncu on the coast, but Kruyt later sent him to his brother in Java, where better schools were available.[3] Sigilipu was baptized there in 1905. He was then sent to the Teacher Training College at Tomohon, in North Sulawesi, and graduated in 1909. He was immediately taken into mission employ and became the first schoolteacher minister (*guru injil*) in Tentena in 1910. It was probably his influence that brought other villagers from Wawo Ndoda, relative latecomers, to Tentena. The following year he married Naka Soa'e, the daughter of the first mission convert, Papa i Wunte, the former *kabosenya* of Kasiguncu and new headman (*mokole*) of the Pebato District.

Pancali Sigilipu served as the schoolteacher and preacher in Tentena until 1925 and thus oversaw the initial missionization of the village. Schools had always been one of the mission's primary methods of evangelization, although most teachers were paid by the state not the mission (Arts 1985, 114–15; Kruyt 1923a; Meulin 1923a, 1923b). The education they provided was specifically religious, and the Manadonese schoolteachers also served as preachers on Sunday. Kruyt had a great deal of difficulty in establishing schools in the precolonial period since his Dutch-derived educational model served no function in To Pamona society. *Kabosenya* argued there was no point to learning how to read, and the school would simply undermine the *adat* (Kruyt 1970, 71). After the establishment of colonial rule, many villages such as Tentena asked for a schoolteacher, even though they were as yet unmissionized. They saw the schoolteachers as culture brokers who could explain the new demands being made upon them by the Dutch. As it became clear that the Manadonese teachers, were to be replaced with To Pamona teachers the schools finally acquired a function as a point of entry in the bureaucracies established by the Dutch. Pancali Sigilipu was the trailblazer in this respect. The role of schoolteacher offered young men privileged positions of power as intermediaries with the Dutch, positions of power denied them in the indigenous political system.

The career path of Pancali Sigilipu is illustrative of the options which religious education opened. Sigilipu married the high-status daughter of Papa i Wunte, the district head of the Pebato region. Since post-marital residence was matrilocal, Sigilipu should have moved to his father-in-law's house, where he would have been subject to a host of avoidance behaviours on the part of his wife's kin, thus ensuring his subordination. However, the mission demanded that it have the freedom to place their all male teaching staff where they were needed. To Pamona teachers subject to bride service paid a fine instead. They were thus able to make strategic marital alliances without being subject to daily regulation by their parents-in-law. Sigilipu, for example, gained access to the extensive kinship network of Papa i Wunte while being freed of the greater than ordinary authority of his father-in-law, who lived in a different district.

As noted above, the teachers served as culture brokers whose power derived from their influence within the mission and the mission's influence on the colonial government. This initially set the teachers outside the political arenas in which traditional leadership held sway. However, as more and more villagers became Christian, and as those traditional political arenas were incorporated within the church, the teacher acquired wider authority. L. Molindo, Pancali Sigilipu's replacement, related how he not only served as teacher and preacher, but was called upon to settle disputes and arbitrate on matters of the new 'Christian *adat*.' Molindo, for example, had been instrumental in having the fine for not living matrilocally paid by teachers to their in-laws eliminated.

Lastly, education provided a clear path to power in the civil service established by the Dutch. Previously, the nature of the *kabosenya*'s limited power was described; they were unable to command villagers to follow the innovations ordered by the Dutch. It is for this reason that the teachers assumed prominence in explaining Dutch policy to the villagers and, through the mission, ameliorating the difficulties of chiefs unable to comply with Dutch orders. Even though the colonial government eventually softened in their expectations of village head-men, they did not alter their policy of ruling through 'traditional' leaders. The entire system of *adat* law was predicated upon maintaining the semblance of respect for indigenous political organization. A rational bureaucracy thus had to be established around these headmen and their limited authority. Each headman had an educated (hence usually Christian) subordinate, the *juru tulis* (secretary), who kept the village tax records. The headmen, over time, were themselves subordinated to district heads selected for their educational qualifications. The traditional *kabosenya* had no career path other than as village leader or church elder. The emerging literate Christian elite had numerous options within both mission and state, first as 'culture brokers,' and later as civil servants. Pancali Sigilipu was thus selected as the District Head of the District of Tentena (now Pamona Utara) in 1925 specifically because he was the most educated To Pamona. Sigilipu's replacement as preacher/teacher in Tentena, L. Molindo, was similarly selected as District Head after Sigilipu's internment during the Second World War.

It was among this group of well-educated mission and government workers, not the 'traditional' *kabosenya*, that the church's nationalist discourse, its conception of a *volk* and of a *volkskerk*, took root. Competing with the better-educated Manadonese teachers who preceded them, they could justify their preferential access to mission and government jobs only in terms of an indigenous discourse; 'their' language and 'their' *adat* were the fundament of Dutch rule in Poso (cf. Steedly 1996). Freed of *adat* strictures such as matrilocal marriage, these men were regularly moved throughout the district, and thus derived their authority from their bureaucratic roles, not their kinship ties. By rooting their authority in Dutch institutions predicated upon territorially bounded 'imagined communities' which were said to share a language and culture, they became the first to recognize the 'reality' of Dutch ethnic prescriptions (Anderson 1983a). That is, with their own authority rooted in Dutch-sponsored 'nationalist' projects, mission and government workers actively supported and helped form the ethnic object which only the Dutch had been able to perceive before. As evangelists, they sought to create the 'brotherhood (*ja'i*) of Christ' in the highlands. As civil servants (they were paid by the state), they ruled according to the *adat* prescriptions of Dutch mission and government.

In relating the details of Pancali Sigilipu's career, I have tried to emphasize that a clear separation of church and state did not follow from the creation of a 'religious sphere' in To Pamona society. The abstraction of religion (*agama*) from *adat* was a slow process marked by the ideological subordination of *adat* practices to 'rational moral principles.' The abstraction of a religious sphere did not mean the radical separation of religious and secular spheres, each regulated by distinct institutions. Rather, the mission's definition of religion specifically subordinated both spheres to their set of moral tenets and authority. This definition of religion was contested, of course, by the colonial government, which ambivalently sought to create a distinct secular sphere by, for example, forbidding church elders to serve as village headman in 1919. However, the colonial government's own policies worked against them by favouring Christianity, by leaving education in mission hands, and by the villagers' own unfamiliarity with 'secular' power. The resulting blurring of the boundary between mission and state was thus similar in form to the emancipatory nationalist project, the 'great Protestant nation,' which developed in the Netherlands during the same period.

The Republican Interlude

The echo of Sukarno's unilateral declaration of independence of the Republic of Indonesia from Dutch rule on 17 August 1945 was not easily heard on Sulawesi. Large parts of the island emerged from the Japanese occupation exhausted and were forced to accept the more limited independence being offered by the returning Dutch. By December 1946, Sulawesi had been integrated into the state of East Indonesia. East Indonesia was the first of a number of regional member states of a planned federal United States of Indonesia which the Dutch expected to control from the centre (Steinberg 1987, 421). Although the Dutch regained military control over much of the archipelago thereafter, international political pressure forced them to abandon their claims in late 1949. The newly triumphant republic, which gained Sulawesi as a result of political rather than military conquest, had only a tenuous hold over much of the island. The 1950s were thus characterized by a weak state, numerous regional rebellions, and the creation of religious pillars (*aliran*) within the electoral framework of the new republic.

The relative weakness of the new Indonesian state in Sulawesi was made evident by two rebellions. In the Buginese areas of Southern Sulawesi, the Darul Islam (Islamic state movement)[4] led by Kahar Muzakkar, a low-ranking aristocrat from Luwu, controlled all but the large cities by 1956 (Robinson 1986, 84–93). Muzakkar was a prominent leader of the republican South Sulawesi militia units which had opposed the resumption of Dutch rule. When he was denied a command in the Republican army in 1950, he returned to the jungle and began a successful guerrilla war. By 1953 his group had joined the Darul Islam rebels of West Java in demanding the establishment of an Islamic state (Harvey 1977, 28–33). Darul Islam swept through the Christian areas of Wotu and Malili in South Sulawesi, forcing conversions to Islam and widespread migration of refugees. During this period (1956–63) large numbers of southern Christians moved north to the Lake Poso region. The lowlands of the Kalaena river valley have thus become almost uniformly Muslim. The migration, like the forced resettlement of villages by the Dutch, further mixed the various village confederacies in polyglot Christian communities.

Simultaneously, Tentena was invaded by Protestant Manadonese from North Sulawesi during the Permesta rebellion of 1958–61 (Harvey 1977). Permesta was an army-backed revolt seeking greater regional autonomy and a change in national economic policy which discriminated against the Outer Islands. In 1957 the leaders of Permesta had supported the unilateral declaration of the province of North Sulawesi (until then incorporated in the unitary province of Sulawesi, with its capital at Ujung Pandang in the south) and established a provisional government in 1958. At that time they invaded the Regency of Poso and established command posts in Poso and Tentena. The Christian Manadonese were initially welcomed; their goal of greater regional autonomy found wide-spread support in the highlands, which were still feeling the effects of the Darul Islam rebellion to the south. This support rapidly faded however, after several atrocities were committed by Permesta troops.

In the absence of the national government, a largely To Pamona militia, the Youth Movement of Central Sulawesi (Gerakan Pemuda Sulawesi Tengah [GPST]) was raised in the highlands to combat the invasion. The GPST success-fully expelled the Permesta unit from Tentena after mortar shelling levelled several houses in the village. The formation of the GPST was motivated less by support for the national government than by the same motives of regional autonomy which drove Permesta itself, as its subsequent history shows. The GPST is just one manifestation of the regional nationalisms fostered by colonial state and mission bureaucracies. The GPST assumed local-government functions for several years. Its leader, Asa Bungkundapu, sought to protect local interests in the face of continuing incursions from the north, south, and, finally, the central government. A prominent concern was the loss of land rights. The GPST issued an order to split Tentena and establish a new village, Petirodongi, on the west side of the river in order to pre-empt the national transmigration program that had designated the area a settlement site for landless Javanese peasants. This was the first example of what has become a widespread pattern of internal colonization, although with only equivocal results. Even in those areas where To Pamona have pre-emptively settled, their lands have been expropriated at a later time for transmigration projects (as at Pancasila) on the grounds that the province is sparsely populated and land rich.

After ties were re-established with the central government, the GPST refused to disband unless its members were incorporated as a unit in the National Army. The army refused and sent a Javanese unit of the Brawijaya (an army battalion) to Tentena to forestall further regional unrest. Although central control was eventu-ally re-established, a misunderstanding with the GPST resulted in the accidental shooting of several soldiers stationed in Tentena. In retaliation, the Brawijaya secretly executed eleven leaders of the GPST as they withdrew from the region. The GPST's quest for regional autonomy from North Sulawesi was finally achieved in 1964, when Central Sulawesi was recognized as a separate province by the republic (Department of Education and Culture 1979, 191–2).

The constant civil turmoil that marked this period, as first the Dutch, then the Republic, Permesta, and the GPST struggled for control over the civil apparatus of the state, can be contrasted with the rapid growth and consolidation of the newly independent mission church (Kruyt 1970, 359–72). The Christian Church of Central Sulawesi (Gereja Kristen Sulawesi Tengah) was instituted on 18 October 1947, when the mission transferred its bureaucracy to an indigenous synod. The synod, centred in Tentena, was rigorously democratic and thus constituted a viable political organization that, in the turmoil of the 1950s, provided for the stable administration of To Pamona villages. This synod assumed control over the mission's schools, hospital, churches, and personnel. Also incorporated within the new church were the *kabosenya* who served as elders, and who utilized their authority to settle disputes at the village level. This stable administrative base served the church well as it sought to protect its interests through a political wing, Parkindo (Partai Kristen Indonesia, the Indonesian Protestant Party), which successfully campaigned in the elections of 1955. The To Pamona thus appeared thoroughly pillarized on a religious basis during the republican period. The Christian Church of Central Sulawesi now serves some 328 congregations in two provinces, and has approximately 150,000 members. It is organized on the presbyterial system, a political system that opens the church hierarchy to lay leadership, although always under the tutelage of ministers.

Individual congregations have a limited amount of independence to meet local needs. Elders are nominated by their Evangelization Groups and freely elected by secret ballot from among all the professing members of a congregation. Such elections are of great local interest since these elders serve as the primary link between individual members and the broader church. The consistory is led by the minister as chair, and it is he or she who assigns the elected elders to their various positions. The minister, however, has only a single vote in council decisions, the same as any elder. The consistory's decisions are dominated by the elders, although limited by the policies set by higher bodies such as the classis and synod, where ministers increasingly predominate. Elders also receive direction through an annual congregational meeting in which the elected representatives of each Evangelization Group meet to set congregational priorities. The individual congregation is thus exceedingly responsive to policy suggestions from below.

Each congregation is a part of a larger territorial unit, the classis, composed of about thirty churches. Each consistory will appoint two elders and their minister to attend the classis meetings, usually held twice a year. The classis is led by the classis minister, who supervises the individual ministers of congregations. The classis in turn elects two of its members who, with the classis minister, will attend the biennial synod sessions. The synod is the superior deliberative body of the denomination attended by representatives from all classis meetings. At a minimum, a third of its members are ministers (i.e., the classis ministers), but in practice more than a half of the body may be ministers since many classis meetings will elect a minister as one of their two representatives. The synod decides on general policy and elects the standing Synod Commission. The chair, vice-chair, and secretary of the synod must be ministers but all other positions are open to lay members. Like the classis and synod bodies, hypothetically a third of the Synod Commission are ministers, although the average is more than half. It should thus be evident that the increasingly restricted number of elders taking part in classis and synod meetings leads to the domination of the higher levels of the church hierarchy by ministers such that the proportion of ministers to lay members in the Synod Commission is the inverse of the proportion for the consistory.

The Synod Commission is responsible for the day-to-day operations of the denomination. This includes the appointment of classis ministers and congregational ministers to their posts. The Synod Commission thus has a great deal of power to appoint those who will in the long run elect the Synod Commission. The danger of nepotism is prevented by a strong lay presence at all levels of the hierarchy, and the democratic rigour of the election process. Although ministers are always placed in supervisory roles in consistory, classis, and synod, their election is dependent upon the two thirds of the synod meetings who are not directly dependent upon the patronage of the Synod Commission. The resulting political formation is thus democratic while remaining under the firm tutelage of a strong ministerial presence.

The Synod Commission directly supervises a number of departments charged with evangelizing specific constituencies within the church, such as women, men, and youth; with evangelizing among non-Christians/non-Muslims (*pekabaran injil*); with research and planning; with internal institutional development; and with running a book store. These departments are intimately tied to the congregational structure of the church. The women's, men's, and youth's groups are, for example, organized on a congregational basis. Evangelization is intended to establish new congregations. Research and Planning and Internal Institutional Development (*pembinaan*) are aimed at developing and evaluating church programs at the congregational level. The social-science focus of the Research and Planning Department contrasts with the theological orientation of the Department of Internal Institutional Development.

The congregational hierarchy is but one aspect of the wider institutional make-up of the church, which includes a number of non-governmental organizations (*yayasan*) that run schools, and health and development agencies. These *yayasan* implement the social programs of the church. These incorporated bodies are directly responsible to the Synod Commission, whose members are frequently appointed as the heads of these organizations. The Christian Education and Teaching Foundation (Yayasan Pendidikan dan Perguruan Kristen) operates 68 kindergartens, 35 primary schools, 10 junior high schools, 4 high schools, and an agricultural junior high school serving almost 13,000 students (Inta 1992, 141). The theological college (Sekolah Tinggi Theologia), located in Tentena, is a degree-granting body educating ministers as well as religious teachers for both state and church schools (Papasi 1992). The Social Health Services Foundation (Yayasan Pelayanan Kesehatan Masyarakat) operates a hospital in Tentena and several health-related programs in isolated areas (Tobondo 1992). The Social Development Foundation (Yayasan Pembangunan Masyarakat) is the church's development organization that works in conjunction with a number of international NGOs such as World Vision, the Mennonite Central Committee, the German NGO Brot fuer die Welt, and the Nederlands Hervormde Kerk on a diverse range of projects, most with an economic focus (Langkamuda 1992). They operate a number of occupational schools, teaching carpentry, auto mechanics, and 'life skills' for people from isolated areas (*suku terasing*). They have also engaged in numerous agricultural development projects intended to increase production in both rice and tree crop production throughout the province.

From an organizational perspective, the GKST can thus be divided into a congregational wing 'inculturated' in a local feasting tradition, and a 'modernist' wing implementing educational, economic, and health projects. Both wings articulate at the synod level, in a modern, rationalizing bureaucracy whose interests overlap with the state's. The church's health and growth are, ironically, dependent upon its preservation of tradition within a modernizing project, a *volkskerk*. The thoroughly democratic election of synod members does not imply that the synod is representative of the larger society of which it is a part. There is a substantial difference between the conditions of an elder's initial election to the consistory and his or her later rise through the church hierarchy. Although each elder must demonstrate traditional leadership qualities to be elected by the laity, his or her subsequent rise through the church hierarchy is judged on other criteria, which include both educational qualifications and government connections. Senior civil servants, lawyers, and teachers are most frequently selected to attend classis and synod sessions. A similar set of criteria are applied to ministers and their promotion to classis minister and election to the Synod Commission. The greater one's education, the higher one rises. Given the costs of higher education, the class composition of the upper levels of the church hierarchy is thus uniform and at odds with the wider membership of the church.

In conversation, Synod Commission members cast this opposition in terms of their 'modernity' (associated with their education) versus the 'traditionalism' of the laity, not class. The church was cast in reformist terms, as a meritocracy taking full part in national and political cultures. The church elections, like the national elections, were signs of development and progress, and contrasted with the 'feudalism' of *adat* systems. The class interests of the state and synod overlap, leading to a shared ideology based on keywords like 'modernity,' 'take-off,' and 'development.' For example, the 1990 synod session theme 'The Holy Spirit Grants Strength to Witness' was officially interpreted to mean 'With words and deeds, the members of the Christian Church of Central Sulawesi give shape to the call to raise the standard of living and the struggle for autonomy to bring about (economic) "take-off."' This emphasis on modernity serves to set the church and state elites off from the wider society, and hence legitimate their rule without in any way jeopardizing the institutional continuity of a 'tradition' firmly entrenched in the everyday acts of piety of villagers. The well-educated elder or minister who adheres to the norms of traditional leadership serves as a link between the modern bureaucracy of the synod and the kin-based political units of the congregation. It is the irony of 'modernity' being utilized to perpetuate 'tradition' that Muratorio attempted to capture with the phrase 'ideological articulation' and that is discussed more fully in the following chapters.

This pillarization of the To Pamona demonstrates how successfully the church had come to 'represent' its constituency. As a *volkskerk* it provided a capable political vehicle and administrative means for achieving social goals. Kruyt's sociological mission methodology had emphasized the incorporation of *adat* institutions within the church; this method is now complemented by a new mission method, the 'comprehensive approach,' which emphasized the social tasks of the church. The Reverend Visser, a Dutch missionary in Tentena in the 1970s, argued: 'We get nothing from religion if the people are unhealthy and we get nothing from healthy people if they don't know how to earn money; and you get nothing from people who only know how to earn money, but have a rotten mentality' (Berge and Segers n.d., 1). The church's role thus extended into each of these areas: health, economy, and spiritual development. The church's political efforts were simply an extension of these social concerns, which were conceived as religious, not political issues.

As the Darul Islam rebellion in South Sulawesi makes clear, it was not only the Christians of Sulawesi whose political priorities were dictated by their religious affiliations (Harvey 1977, 27). During the 1955 elections in the Regency of Poso, 61 per cent of the ballots were cast for Islamic parties (with Masyumi receiving the lion's share, 42.49 per cent). The Christian parties (Protestant and Catholic) received 27 per cent of the votes (with Protestants receiving 26 per cent). Secular parties such as the Nationalist (PNI), Socialist (PSI), and Communist (PKI) parties received a combined total of only 10 per cent of the ballots. In the province of North Sulawesi as a whole (which at that point included Central Sulawesi), Islamic parties received 51 per cent of the vote, Christian parties 21 per cent. In South Sulawesi, the figures paint a similar picture: Islamic parties received 64.5 per cent of the ballots, and Christian parties 11.5 per cent. The brand of secular nationalism upon which Sukarno had based the republic received little support in Sulawesi. *Aliran* or religious pillars appear even more pronounced in Sulawesi than in Java, where the term originated.

Tentena in the 'New Order' Administrative Context

It should be clear that, at the birth of the New Order state in 1965, the civil administration of the state in Central Sulawesi lay in tatters and the church had assumed many governmental functions; Sulawesi appears to have been thoroughly pillarized, and organized religious bodies remained the largest threat to the re-establishment of a civil state. The New Order represents a clear break with earlier Dutch policies of ethnic and religious management. The generals of the New Order earned their rank in putting down the Darul Islam (Islamic state) rebellions of Sumatra, Java, and Sulawesi. Themselves committed to a secular, pluralistic society, they have consistently sought to de-politicize religious identities. A uniform policy has been hindered, however, by a contradictory fear of regional, ethnic separatism as manifested, for example, in the Permesta rebellion of North and Central Sulawesi. The colonial policy of utilizing local *adat* to weaken the political power of Islam has thus been made untenable; the Dutch had simply fostered the growth of numerous regional 'nationalisms' as manifested in the Central Sulawesi Youth Movement. The New Order has responded by, on the one hand, subordinating the political aspirations of religious groups to the state ideology, the Pancasila. On the other hand, it has further marginalized the importance of *adat* law, thought to foster ethnic separatism, through the creation of a uniform civil bureaucracy predicated upon national law. *Adat* has been redefined as *kebudayaan* (culture, arts) rather than law.

The isolation imposed on the highlands of Central Sulawesi by regional revolt in the 1950s and 1960s and the destruction of the major means of transport and communication has slowly been eroded by five Five-Year Development Plans (REPLITA). The New Order has strengthened its control over the regions through the expansion, institutional differentiation, and professionalization of the civil service at the expense of the older system of indirect rule through *adat* law. Most government departments now have offices at the regency or district level, and many of these have displaced *adat* processes. This is particularly true of the Ministry of Justice, which has established civil courts. This restructuring of village administration is the product of the 1979 Village Government Law (Undang-undang No. 5 Tahun 1979 tentang Pemerintahan Desa), which established a uniform local administration throughout Indonesia. The goal of the legislation was to increase the effectiveness of village administration and public participation in development policy (Warren 1986, 221; Kato 1989, 92), although the implementation of the law has tended to prioritize an effective and centralized administration over public consultation. The legislation imposed Javanese models of village organization on the diverse *adat* communities of the Outer Islands (Kato 1989, 94). Every village (administratively defined) would have an executive (the *kepala desa* or *lurah*), a Village Deliberation Council (Lembaga Musyawarah Desa [LMD]) as its consultative body (which generally remains unimplemented), and a Village Society Resilience Council (Lembaga Ketahanan Masyarakat Desa [LKMD]), which serves as a village cabinet whose main function is to assist the village head with development planning and projects.

This radical restructuring of village administration has effectively marginalized the older colonial administrative system rooted in *adat* law. The Council of Elders has been displaced by a village *adat* council (*dewan adat*), which functions as a 'poor man's court' rather than as the civil service. Its decisions may be contested in civil court or overturned by the civil bureaucracy. The council is directly subordinated to the village mayor, who is its chair and who is responsible for the conduct of all *adat* ceremonies. Whereas this mayor was once a *kabosenya* from the village, the six villages at the head of Lake Poso have been amalgamated into the 'city' of Tentena, and their mayors replaced with appointed civil servants (*lurah*); this makes the primary *adat* functionary a village 'outsider,' a civil servant who serves on a regular rota basis and whose rulings are increasingly moulded by state policy. Cases that cannot be resolved by the *adat* councils are brought to the subdistrict head (*camat*), a civil servant and superior of the mayors.

The marginalization of *adat* law and the development of a professional civil service has been matched by increased government tutelage of *adat* as 'Culture' (*kebudayaan*) by the LKMD, which sponsors regional competitions of traditional songs and dances. These regional arts competitions are themselves situated within larger national programs broadcast through the state television network, TVRI. *Adat* is being redefined, from law to 'traditional Culture' – and, in particular, an outdated tradition having little day-to-day saliency. The founding of the Lake Poso Festival and the massive construction boom of traditional temples at the festival grounds must thus be examined from this perspective – as part of a policy to marginalize the political saliency of religious and ethnic identities except in so far as they are subordinated to the state. Alternative expressions of ethnicity that might prove a source of social conflict, such as religion or 'race' (or more accurately, Chinese and Papuan ethnicity), have no place in these fora. Hence it is the dead 'animist' tradition, the authentic (*asli*) 'origins' of the To Pamona, which is incorporated within the state's ethnic arts discourse and not the more vibrant, but politically salient, Christian arts tradition.

This is a new strategy of ethnic management that emphasizes 'ethnic blindness and showcase cultures' (Kipp 1993, 108). It specifically defines each ethnic group as a part of the cultural mosaic of a state which is officially 'Various, But One.' Mandatory government identity cards list religion but not ethnicity, and no statistics are collected on an ethnic basis. Ethnic languages are not repressed, but the utilization of Bahasa Indonesia increasingly marginalizes those languages in public life. 'Schools and government are ethnically blind, at least in principle' (ibid., 109). This refusal to delimit ethnic *groups* contrasts with the government's active promotion of 'showcase cultures' or '*adat* spectacles' (cf. Acciaioli 1985). In encouraging the mounting of such spectacles, traditional leadership and *adat* discourse are locked into 'traditional concerns' and made irrelevant to the normal operations of the state. The emphasis on *adat* as culture marginalizes ethnic politics while simultaneously granting ethnic identity a high profile in a limited sphere that emphasizes its relational aspects. This is the crux of the process that Pemberton (1994) describes as 'mini-ization,' in which the 'authentic' origins of each ethnic group are captured in timeless fashion within the overarching unity of 'Beautiful Indonesia' as a whole.

A *Volkskerk* in Transition

I began this chapter by questioning the essentialist roots of expressions of To Pamona ethnicity which claim to represent the group's authentic 'origins.' By focusing upon how these 'representations,' in both the sense of 'image of' and as 'speaking for,' have been constituted, I have tried to underscore the political, economic, and cultural discourses that made the ethnic category 'To Pamona' salient. To Pamona ethnicity cannot be rooted in some 'primordial sentiment' and opposed to nationalism. Rather, the two divergent ethnic discourses I have related here are themselves part of 'emancipatory' nationalist discourses. The one nationalist discourse is tied to the theological conceptualization of a *volkskerk*; the other, to the Indonesian nationalist project 'Various But One.' Both discourses can be traced back to their colonial roots: Ethical Theology and the Ethical Policy. Both projects posit unique and sometimes contradictory solutions to the problem of the relationship among nation, church, and state.

These discourses are key features in the 'ideological articulation' of the capitalist transformation of the highlands and its now subordinate 'traditional' social relations. This 'perpetuation of tradition' is no static 'survival' but a reworking of the feasting complex and *posintuwu* exchange within the confines of a 'modern' bureaucracy. I have argued that this rationalization of tradition within the church has given rise to a social formation characterized as *aliran* in Java and as *verzuiling* in the Netherlands. The health and growth of the church ironically depends upon its preservation of local traditions within its modernizing project. A similar ironic dynamic developed within the colonial state's preservation of *adat* law. The truce between these somewhat complementary colonial projects was disrupted by national independence and its subsequent regional rebellions. New Order strategies pose a more fundamental challenge to the 'traditionalist' roots of the church's modernist national project.

The scope of this challenge was made quite clear on a sunny morning, 10 January 1997, when two turboprop helicopters bearing the Minister of Interior Affairs and the Minister of Defence landed on the grass runway of the Missionary Aviation Fellowship airstrip, which lies precisely between the old festival grounds, now controlled by the church, and the new festival site. They were greeted by Surjadi, the government-sponsored head of the Partai Demokrasi Indonesia, the Indonesian Democratic Party, the state-engineered amalgam of the Nationalist Party and Parkindo, the Indonesian Protestant Party, who had arrived the day before. Come to celebrate the twenty-fourth anniversary of the founding of the party, this convoy of dignitaries proceeded to temporary open-air shelters erected at the new festival grounds – and not to Banua mPogombo, the church's large, modern conference centre a short distance away. After their short speeches, the ministers promptly returned to Jakarta. Short soundbites of their speeches (but not Surjadi's) were duly reported that evening on the national news. These events are typical of state policies intended to disentangle religion from politics, to dismantle the old *aliran* of the republican period.

In broad strokes, the state has endeavoured to sever the link between the religious parties and their religious constituents. The numerous religious parties, both Muslim and Christian, have been amalgamated into two polyglot organizations fraught with internal tensions and disputes. These parties have been shorn of their religious symbols and names. As political parties, they have been banned from maintaining any grass-roots organizations and their leadership is subject to government review. The Indonesian Democratic Party, for example, is approaching the current elections handicapped by an internal leadership struggle between Surjadi, the state-sponsored candidate, and Megawati Sukarnoputri, the popular daughter of past-president Sukarno and an advocate of democratic reform. This internecine struggle erupted in widespread riots in Jakarta, and at the previous party convention in Sumatra.[5] Indeed, it was the fear of further riots that had pushed Surjadi to search for a safe haven for this party convention, the isolated village of Tentena in the highlands of Central Sulawesi. Amidst ministers of state and numerous squads of well-armed soldiers, an affable Surjadi calmly electioneered.

The severed ties between the Indonesian Democratic Party and its associated religious bodies as evidenced here by Surjadi's selection of the open-air festival grounds over the church's conference centre is but one side of state policies intended to depoliticize religious identities. This domestication of religious politics has not meant a rejection of a state role in the religious life of the nation. The first principle of the Pancasila, the five political principles on which the Indonesian state is based, is the belief in 'one God' (*Tuhan*).[6] The New Order state has firmly rejected the politically unpopular defence of secularism; it demands that every citizen have an official religion, and its Department of Religion actively supports the building of churches and mosques. For example, the largest church in Tentena, Gereja Moria, was built with extensive government support. Religion classes are a requirement in all state schools, including university. State support for religion has, however, been on its own terms. Only Islam, Protestantism, Catholicism, and monotheistic variants of Buddhism and Hinduism are recognized as 'official religions' (*agama*) receiving government support. Other 'belief systems' (*kepercayaan*) face discriminatory penalties since they are associated with locally bounded ethnic groups and thought to foster ethnic secessions. And since 1984, all organizations, including religiously oriented ones, were forced to acknowledge the Pancasila, the ideological basis of New Order rule, as their *asas tunggal*, the sole basis of their ideology. This subsumption of the Quran, the word of God, to the word of man evoked widespread but ineffective resistance from many Muslim organizations (Ramage 1995, 35–9). The Muslim political party, the United Development Party (Partai Persatuan Pembangunan), was thus forced to abandon Islam as its 'philosophical' basis and acknowledge the Pancasila as its 'sole foundation.'

The success of the state in ideologically encapsulating religion within its political and administrative order has apparently decimated the religiously based political pillars described earlier in this chapter. Yet, these strategies of containment have had contradictory effects, especially if we view *aliran* as rationalizing religions rather than strictly political phenomena. The New Order state's policies are reminiscent of those pursued by the Ethical Politicians of the Netherlands East Indies under the urgings of prominent Orientalist Snouck Hurgronje. Hurgronje recommended the colonial state actively support Islam as a spiritual and cultural force while strictly prohibiting Islam as a political force (Ramage 1995, 192). I underline this similarity because it was these same 'culturalist' policies that spurred the rationalization of Indonesian Islam through such Islamic organizations as Sarekat Islam, Nahdatul Ulama, and Muhammadiyah. It is thus arguable whether religion can be depoliticized in this manner. Religious pillarization did not emerge out of political action in the 1950s; rather, political action emerged out of a rationalized religious bureaucracy created, like the state, through Dutch colonialism. The authoritarian muting of political debate in Indonesia has by no means decimated the religious pillars; indeed, in some ways they have been strengthened through the active financial support of the New Order (Hefner 1989). Politics in such a repressive atmosphere has simply been displaced into new arenas, such as 'culture,' as my discussion of the Lake Poso Festival indicated.

PART TWO

THE PERSISTENCE OF TRADITION

3

The Household, Kinship, and Shared Poverty

Charity never faileth: but whether there be prophecies, they shall fail; whether there be tongues, they shall cease; whether there be knowledge, it shall vanish away. For we know in part, and we prophesy in part. But when that which is perfect is come, then that which is in part shall be done away. When I was a child, I spake as a child, I understood as a child, I thought as a child: but when I became a man, I put away childish things. For now we see through a glass, darkly; but then face to face: now I know in part; but then shall I know even as also I am known. And now abideth faith, hope, charity, these three; but the greatest of these is charity.

I Corinthians 13: 8–13

Economic progress was impossible. Every family in the community had its property, but the other members made claims upon it in case of a crisis in the community or a clan feast. Then the families who had had the most success with their cattle, had to supply the most animals. If a member of the community was in debt, the richest members were first requested to help him out of the clutches of his creditors. If large quantities of a certain article were stored, for instance salt, so many came and asked for it that the supply was soon exhausted. If a person had acquired a special article or implement, this was borrowed so often that he had very little opportunity to use it himself. Refusals were few and far between owing to the fear of being isolated and also out of vanity, as they liked to hear their praises sung.

Kruyt 1929, 2

This chapter addresses the apparently incongruous processes of economic development and the preservation of tradition, as outlined in the previous chapters. This central contradiction of the Ethical Policy was the conflicting needs of the Netherlands East Indies (NEI) state to shepherd its wards along the clear, unilinear path to 'development' sketched out by early anthropologists such as Wilken and Kruyt, without fostering a pan-archipelagic opposition that might challenge Dutch rule. State policy was thus aimed at fostering the 'development' of the various *volk* of the NEI within the confines of traditional *adats*. It should come as no surprise, then, that the uses of 'tradition' in such changed circumstances should reflect the capitalist transformation of the highlands rather than being a simple perpetuation of the past in the present. I specifically argue against those dual-economy models of peasant economics which hold that an untouched peasant 'moral economy' characterized by 'shared poverty' has remained culturally isolated from the capital–intensive plantation agriculture of Dutch business concerns (Geertz 1963a; Scott 1976). In the crudest form of these models, peasants are thought to be trapped in their subsistence routines, culturally incapable of taking advantage of capitalist markets in land, labour, or products.

Such an argument is by no means limited to the Indonesian case. The moral-economy model and the related concept of the persistence of tradition are often used to characterize relations of production in 'traditional' peasant communities undergoing change. A moral economy is assumed to be a natural, universal characteristic of the peasantry which existed prior to the introduction of capitalist relations. It is characterized by subsistence production and the provisioning of subsistence insurance, and is driven by a risk-averse non-market rationality. It is argued here, however, that this model of peasant economies ignores the historical specificity of agrarian transformations of groups such as the To Pamona. Ahistorical analysis that relies on such models obscures or ignores the mutualistic links between moral and market economies and their co-emergence under colonial tutelage. Too often characterized as a persistence of tradition, the moral-economy model implies historical continuity, yet is usually explained in abstract terms not unlike those models of *Homo Oeconomicus* against which it argues (Peletz 1983, 732). Although the To Pamona appear to be perpetuating a 'moral economy' as an obstacle against capitalist development or as protection from market forces, closer scrutiny indicates that these forms arose in the context of capitalist transformation, class differentiation, and historical attempts to create an economically rational peasantry.

After the villagers of Tentena were resettled from their nearby hilltop hamlets in 1908, they were forced to take up wet-rice, or *sawah*, agriculture on the valley floor, on the shores of Lake Poso. This change in productive technologies was part of a broader program of development that included their political and religious incorporation within the structures of Dutch colonialism. Wet-rice cultivation was but one of the policies intended to create a nuclear-family household peasant economy, a more 'advanced' position along the unilinear path to development proposed by early anthropological models. Multiple-household longhouses (*banua*) were to be broken up into their constituent units, and each of these units was to own and individually work their own property. In this way, 'native communalism' was to be discouraged and an ethic of individual initiative and self-interest introduced, a policy which Dutch liberals considered the only means of bettering native welfare (de Kat Angelino 1931, 2: 517–30; Kahn 1993, 75–81; Kruyt 1924b, 50).

The state appears to have been unsuccessful in its attempts to create either simple family households or an economically rational peasantry among the To Pamona, despite decades of official government policy and pressure. The area is characterized by vague household boundaries, a feasting economy supported by a gift-exchange network, forms of non-waged labour exchange, and patterns of petty merchandising, all of which underscore an apparent economic 'irrationality.' However, this apparent 'irrationality' in the local market economy cannot be explained as the persistence of tradition nor merely as strategies of some pre-existing moral economy. Each of these strategies was adopted through rational economic calculation and uses commodity forms linked to the market. As I noted in the introduction, these economically irrational 'traditions' are a discursive resource which locals, trapped in the impoverishing development initiatives of the state, can bend to their own uses. Relations of production and social repro-duction have shifted in the context of increasing commodification to create a double-faced economic strategy simultaneously dependent upon market and non-market mechanisms.

This is not a simple chicken-and-egg question. Rather, the question of the historical precedence of moral economies has important implications in the discussion of class formation and class conflict. Classical models of the differen-tiation of the peasantry emphasize, first, the household as a unit of production and consumption, and, second, that it is households which are divided into haves and have-nots. They emphasize that class tensions develop between households based on their differential access to resources. However, the To Pamona case shows how this tension was defused through the adoption of 'moral economy' type strategies. These peasants show differentiation without class formation because they have been able to diffuse class antagonisms by blurring household boundaries. These strategies translate potential class antagonisms into hierarchi-cal, kin-based, patron–client relations that preserve the authority of the *kabosenya* while providing a new class basis for their leadership. The success of the church, in turn, was dependent upon the success of these *kabosenya*.

The historicity of this moral economy will thus be inverted by demonstrating how it emerges out of capitalist changes in relations of production and differen-tiation in landholdings. That is, it will be argued that the moral economy is not a survival of some natural economy but a 'discursive traditionalism' that develops in the process of what Kahn calls 'peasantization.' Peasantization is a process whereby farmers seek to 'ensure or even extend the exploitation of the "free" productive inputs available to them' (Kahn 1993, 65). He describes a continuum of divergent peasant economic behaviours spanning the 'traditional' peasant whose activities are made possible only through commoditized inputs, to the 'capitalist' peasant whose success is owed to maximizing the exploitation of 'traditional' uncosted resources such as family land and labour. In each case both commoditized and uncosted 'traditional' inputs are necessary for the reproduction of household production. Yet these peasant forms of production, as distinct from capitalist forms, depend upon the maximization of these 'traditional' uncosted inputs (cf. Friedmann 1980; Smith 1985). Although enveloped in a discursive traditionalism, such inputs are by no means simple perpetuations of pre-capitalist relations (cf. Roseberry 1989, 217–23). These new 'traditions' cannot exist other than in a commoditized economy upon which they depend.

Shared Poverty and the Moral-Economy Model

During the last eighty-five years, economic development around Lake Poso has been accompanied by the fragmentation of landholdings and the commodification of the means and relations of production. The differentiation of the peasantry has, however, been uneven, blunted by 'shared poverty' among kin, to use Geertz's (1963a) phrase for the 'moral economy' model. Geertz used the term to refer to a pattern in which agricultural output was evenly divided among village households through the elaboration and expansion of traditional systems of labour relations, especially sharecropping, rather than through changes in the proprietary control of land (1963a, 98). This ethic of 'shared poverty' limited the differentiation of the peasantry in Java to 'just-enoughs' and 'not-quite-enoughs.'

Geertz's analysis of shared poverty was based upon the 'dual economy' framework of Dutch economist J.H. Boeke (1953). Although Geertz's argument deals with Java, his theoretical formulation has provided impetus for the analysis of the role of culture in the modernization of all Indonesia. Geertz argues that Indonesia had two economies: one, a modern plantation sector; the other, a subsistence-oriented, indigenous sector. These two sectors were distinct, but interrelated because of the unique characteristics of *sawah* fields that allowed for seemingly infinite degrees of intensification of production. Plantation sugar and subsistence rice crops could be cultivated on the same land without decreases in rice yields because of a process he calls 'involution' (i.e., traditionalism). Involution refers to the intensification of prior social patterns of production and a refinement of old agricultural techniques untouched by the highly capitalized Dutch corporate economy. Since traditional production techniques are intensified rather than altered, involution should be contrasted with evolution (the emergence of new forms), and revolution (an abrupt radical change) (White 1983, 20). The involution of the peasant economy was the product of an ethic of 'shared poverty' that sought to divide a reduced economic pie into ever more minute shares, 'if not altogether evenly, at least relatively so' (Geertz 1963a, 97). This egalitarianism manifests itself in the relatively equal distribution of the use of fields (if not ownership), work-sharing, and income-redistributing institutions. Traditionalism, in other words, was associated with a non-market economic rationality rooted in subsistence production.

Even this brief outline of the involution thesis makes clear that Geertz holds a Chayanovian model of the peasantry (Kahn 1993, 90); that is, he asserts that land is in flexible supply to all households, that their production is geared to securing a socially determined minimum income, and that any income beyond this minimum has diminishing marginal utility (Hunt 1979, 248). As the ratio of workers to consumers within a household rises, the amount of labour required from each worker to meet that socially determined minimum income will *decrease*, leaving workers 'spare time' that could be utilized on the plantations. A 'dual economy' with distinct capitalist and subsistence sectors is thus conceptually created. Capitalist agriculture in the plantation sector fails to impinge on the cultural norms and relations of production of the peasant sector, despite its appropriating much of the village rice lands for sugar production. The economic logic of the Javanese peasant remains insulated, entrapped in an involuted subsistence ethic that precludes any radical differentiation of the peasantry and hence an indigenous capitalist revolution.

The situation I found in Central Sulawesi seemed broadly similar, and initially led me to interpret my data as yet another example of shared poverty. In an analysis of sixty-eight related households in four highland villages in Central Sulawesi,[1] differentiation in landownership seemed clear: landholdings varied from those with no *sawah*, to those with up to 6 hectares. There were clear differences in lifestyle between the well-to-do (19 households), middle peasants (19 households), and the poor (30 households).[2] However, like Geertz in Java, I found that differentiation in ownership of land was only an 'indifferent guide to the social pattern of agricultural exploitation' (1963a, 99) and necessitated a careful examination of how agricultural production was distributed. Much of the difference in wealth between households derived from civil-service jobs or pensions. Wealth and landownership seemed to have little to do with relations of production. Members from all three groups took part in 'traditional' labour exchanges, *pesale*, and a significant proportion of all three groups depended on hired agricultural labour to work their holdings. The persistence of 'traditional' labour exchanges and their attendant metamorphosis into new forms among all three groups, the development of sharecropping, and the existence of an ethic of sharing among kin all led me to wonder if shared poverty was typical of the local peasant economy despite the absence of a significant plantation sector, which Geertz thought central to its development in Java.

In transposing Geertz's argument on 'shared poverty' to the highlands of Central Sulawesi, I will argue that Geertz's critics to date have not gone far enough (Alexander and Alexander 1978, 1982; Breman 1982; Collier 1981; Gordon 1992; Knight 1982; White 1983). This transposition allows us to examine the theoretical underpinnings of Geertz's argument and those of his critics, apart from the particular historical example he chose to demonstrate them. These critiques have emphasized the theoretical shortcomings of the 'dual economy' model and rightly questioned the mutualism of sugar and rice cultivation. They have not demonstrated, however, that the differentiation of the peasantry has been a salient feature of the Javanese social landscape or that 'shared poverty' has failed to blunt class polarization. Rather, these critiques have

> appeared in reverse chronological order, pushing the temporal boundaries of the 'traditional' economy further and further back in history. Indeed, the break with Geertz is less radical than his critics would have us believe, since almost all those attempting to demonstrate the demise of involution appear to posit an historical period in which Geertz's model, or something quite close to it, is said to be pertinent. But positing a 'traditional' economy and contrasting it with the 'fact' of commoditisation, inequalities in land distribution and the like is not the same as demonstrating a secular trend towards increased class differentiation. (Kahn 1985, 78)

In contrast, I would argue that shared poverty is not a feature of some earlier 'traditional' period but is itself the product of the processes of differentiation and commodification. That is, shared poverty is the unintended result of liberal policies aimed at creating a class of simple commodity producers integrated in commodity and labour markets. Geertz observes that Javanese peasants had one foot in the plantation economy and the other in a subsistence-oriented peasant sector (1963a, 90ff.). The peasant's ability to obtain a minimum income from subsistence farming reduced the amount of wages that needed to be paid in the plantation sector. Similarly, in Sulawesi, the continued need to engage in subsistence agriculture with only minimal capital inputs and an overabundance of labour led to the reconstitution of To Pamona kinship and the household such that they were excluded from the commodified production process (cf. Smith 1989, 163–6). Shared poverty emerges with the need to maintain a kin-based, subsistence agricultural sphere in an otherwise commodified economy.

Like the other critics of Geertz noted above, my analysis of the commodification of production, consumption, and social reproduction within and between households begins with a repudiation of the dual-economy model underlying Geertz's involution thesis, while accepting his culturalist position that 'tradition' has served to blunt class polarization. By rejecting the dual-economy approach, I reject Geertz's treatment of capitalism as a monolith restricted to the modern sector of the economy; rather, capitalism is treated as a multivariant process in which the commodification of product, land, and labour must be separately accounted for (Kahn 1985, 82). Focusing on the uneven commodification of specific processes should make it apparent why some relationships are subjected to maximizing calculation while others seem to be excluded (Smith 1989, 163–6). I refer to this as the reconstitution of kinship within the constraints of differentiation.

This analysis of kinship begins by questioning the analytic usefulness the concept 'household.' Much of the literature on differentiation assumes that the simple family peasant household is a self-contained unit of production and consumption and that the differentiation referred to is a differentiation of peasant households (Wong 1987, 21). A growing literature has increasingly challenged a number of cardinal presuppositions behind the conception of the household as a bounded and independent unit (Wong 1987, 1991; Yanagisako 1979; Sanjek 1982). It has become increasingly apparent that, like the monolith 'capitalism,' the various facets of the household need to be distinguished. Co-residence, kinship, production, consumption, and social reproduction are all factors that occur within households without being its defining features. The moral valuation of domestic relations similarly fails to delimit household boundaries; supposedly 'domestic' values such as sharing and lack of calculation may bridge households, while the co-resident group itself may be characterized by relations of hierarchy, servitude, or dependency (Harris 1982, 150; Hart 1992).

It is only through attention to the dynamic interplay of these features within the arena of the household that we can escape the constrictions of an ideal type analysis that masks the unevenness of the capitalist reformation of the To Pamona peasantry. By examining patterns of production, consumption, and social reproduction, and their place in the To Pamona 'tradition' of shared poverty, I hope to show how commodification has reshaped the household. I found that *the unequal distribution of land was essential to the creation of viable peasant enterprises, and as a result, that 'kin,' not land, were redistributed.* That is, I invert Geertz's Chayanovian assumptions of stable households and the redistribution of resources. In the remainder of this chapter, I attempt to demonstrate the implications of this statement in terms of shared poverty and interhousehold relations. I hope to show that the To Pamona household cannot be defined in terms of its domestic functions; it is, rather, an amorphous arena whose membership is determined by the synergistic logic of capitalized production and the 'axiom of amity' of kinship (Fortes 1969, 235–7).

Sombori and *Santina*

The household (*sombori*), as it was historically constituted, can be understood only in relation to the *santina*, a cognatic kinship group which extends to include third cousins, and the *posintuwu* networks that tied it together. *Sombori* is a term derived from longhouse life and literally means 'those who live on one side of a hearth' (Adriani 1928, 759). A longhouse would contain four to six separate *sombori*. The *sombori* was created through marriage, and refers primarily to the husband–wife pair. The *sombori* was thus defined in terms of a conjugal relationship rather than as a unit performing necessary domestic functions. This couple would sleep together. The wife would cook for the two of them, and they would eat together but not alone, since they ate and shared their cooked food with others in the longhouse. Unmarried boys and girls slept in communal chambers. Kinship, co-residence, and consumption were intertwined, although the *sombori* was not the clearly delimited unit within which they took place (cf. Sanjek 1982, 98). Related *sombori* within a longhouse performed many of the domestic functions normally attributed to the household. This fits well with To Pamona developmental conceptions of the *sombori*, a unit they see as growing increasingly independent through time as its members gain required skills and resources, but cushioned within a larger kin network which assumes those domestic duties it is unable to accomplish alone.

The word *posintuwu* or one of its cognates provides the ideological underpinning of all interhousehold relations. It is a cultural keyword inextricably bound up with the problems of kinship, production, reproduction, and feasting it is used to discuss. The root of the word is the verb *tuwu* (living). *Katuwu* means life, rank; hence, *sintuwu* means 'of the same rank,' living a similar life. *Mosintuwu*, means to live in friendship, to mutually engage in activities with the implication of a return (favour, gift, labour). The noun form is *posintuwu*, friendship, and its objective manifestations, the gift and mutual assistance. In translating *mosintuwu* I have, in part, followed Adriani (1928). Adriani's selection of the word 'friendship' correctly captures one aspect of the word, the feeling of amity, but ignores both the kinship aspect and its material manifestations. The official motto of the district is *Sintuwu maroso, tuwu siwagi, tuwu malinuwu. Sintuwu maroso* denotes a strong sense of living together, of being together, of doing together. *Tuwu siwagi* denotes a lifestyle of supporting or aiding others. *Tuwu malinuwu* denotes an unending life, one continuously renewed, like a clump of bamboo; though one bamboo plant might die, its roots constantly give off new shoots, giving the clump the appearance of living forever. The motto thus roots life itself in an ideal of communal activity, mutual aid, and relatedness in a common origin. It is this relatedness which provides the rationale for common action and mutual support among *sombori*.

The relatively undifferentiated picture of a 'communal' society presented by Kruyt hides a far more complex social reality. The *sombori* was a potential production unit; that is, a unit that farmed its own fields and engaged in labour exchanges with other *sombori*. A gendered division of labour made husband and wife the *minimal* unit of production, not the *necessary* unit of production. Unmarried individuals were unable to cultivate their own fields since they could not participate in the exchanges of opposite-sex labour required for certain tasks such as cutting the forest by men and planting by women. A newly married couple might continue to farm together with the wife's parents if the bride was too young and inexperienced to assume all domestic responsibilities. Such a multiple-family household was said to be *sanco-ncombori* (from the same root as *sombori*). This relationship would continue as long as required as the couple first cooked separately, then later established its own fields. This household form might also result when parents became elderly. Such a relationship need not imply co-residence, and the couple might continue to cook separately as well.

The responsibility for raising children and the intergenerational transfer of productive resources was assumed by the wider kin group. That is, the *sombori* has been defined in terms of a *relationship*, that of a conjugal partner, rather than in terms of a domestic function, child rearing. This 'domestic' function is a *kin*, not a household, responsibility. This is now most clearly seen through high rates of fosterage within the *santina* (cf. Goody 1971). A three-village survey of more than 500 households found that between 8 and 15 per cent of the households of each village were fostering children. The role of kin in social reproduction was also seen during the creation of new *sombori*, a process which involved the *santina*'s approval of the match, their collection of the bridewealth through gifts of *posintuwu*, and the exchange of bridewealth. Marriage was made possible through a series of bridewealth prestations (*oli mporongo*) which legitimated the groom's *santina*'s rights in the children of the union. The woman's *santina*'s rights followed automatically from birth and required no payments. In the case of both marriage and child rearing, larger kin groups controlled the constitution of the household and its membership.

Production, consumption, and social reproduction are treated separately here because they implied different moral imperatives within and between households. My first criticism of 'shared poverty' is that it assumes a universal moral ethic shorn from the constituent social relations within which it is enacted; it is inherently teleological (Alexander and Alexander 1982, 599). In contrast, my research revealed a more complex moral universe. For example, production was characterized by work exchanges (*pesale*) marked by exact reciprocity between production units within the same agricultural season. Although the harvest from one's fields was dependent upon the labour of others, this exact exchange of labour precluded any later claims being made upon it. One's harvest was one's own, and taking any part of another's harvest was theft (*salaa mpale*). On the other hand, consumption was marked by generalized reciprocity across household boundaries. Although individual *sombori* cooked their own meals, all the *sombori* within a longhouse ate together and shared their food, but not from a common pot; those who had fish or other delicacies would divide these among those present. To be present while someone eats is to be obligated to join them; to leave without eating is an invitation for divine retribution (*kasalora*). Eating together is a symbol of kinship and amity. Such generalized exchange was not limited to cooked foods eaten in the presence of others. Any surplus foodstuff was distributed, with no calculation of an exact return. Such sharing was explicitly phrased in kin terms and should not be interpreted as a universal ethic; as Wong notes, 'in many Southeast Asian societies the cognatic character of the kinship system has accentuated the perception of inter-village relations as being based on sharing, if only because within a few generations the rapid spread of bilateral links tends to extend the kinship ideology of help without calculation to most if not all residents' (1991, 194). My landlord played host to an extensive kin network, but made the following point: 'You have to be sure that all who cross the threshold claiming to be family, really are.'

I would like carefully to distinguish the sharing that occurs in the everyday sphere of consumption from the long-term processes of social reproduction. Social reproduction is also characterized by sharing; but, in this case, it is specific elite goods needed for the creation of new households that are shared. The *santina* provides the means to marriage, a bridewealth consisting primarily of cloth, a water buffalo (or its cash equivalent), and a brass tray, but does not directly provide the means of production that the new household requires for its subsistence. In swidden cultivation, access to marriage determined access to labour. This was tantamount to providing the productive resources the new household required since land was freely available. Importantly, the giving of bridewealth also legitimated the kin groups' rights in relation to the children of the union. With the introduction of wet-rice fields, or *sawah*, these two aspects of social reproduction have been disassociated. While bridewealth continues to legitimate the kin groups' rights in relation to children (and their labour), it no longer guarantees the new household's access to land. One must be generous in providing bridewealth for kin, but such generosity need not extend to providing land. The moral ethic governing *posintuwu* exchange is regulated by the 'axiom of amity' and 'shared poverty'; the moral ethic governing inherited land transfers, though similarly phrased in the language of the 'axiom of amity,' has led to the differentiation of holding size and the emergence of class divisions.

This differential is, however, blunted by the permeability of household boundaries; that is, by the transfer of consumables, kin, and their labour, which Geertz called 'shared poverty.' Wealthier households appear to be generously aiding their poorer kin by providing food and residence for their children. The inequalities created through the processes of social reproduction were mitigated by providing aid. It is important, however, to underscore the difference between the redistribution of productive labour and the redistribution of productive resources, although both had been linked historically through the giving of bridewealth. In aiding members of their *santina*, large landowners gained unpaid 'kin' labour that could be utilized in agricultural production to reduce capital costs and ensure the continued viability of their enterprises. They exploited these 'free' labour inputs to reduce the costs of production. I will argue that these interhousehold kin ties are kept non-commodified through the utilization of 'discursive traditions'; hence, a non-capitalist logic *appears* to be at work, even though production itself is fully commodified. This form of shared poverty is the product of the differentiation of ownership of productive resources.

The following illustrative example is typical of seven groups of sibling sets (*to saana*) I worked with in Tentena. Figure 3.1 gives details of some of the residents of the housing complex on a quiet back street in which I resided. The extended family of Ngkai and Tu'a Bose have complied with government policy by building three separate houses approximately 2 to 3 metres apart in a fenced compound. Although I have limited this description to these three houses for simplicity's sake, this compound is linked to a second compound built on family land on the far side of the village, where several other siblings reside. The relationships between these two compounds are similar to relations within the compound.

Within the first set of houses, the physical buildings only roughly approximated household boundaries, which were purposively left vague. At one level, there were three households resident in the three houses: Household A, living in House 1; Household B, living in House 2; and Household C, living in House 3. Membership in these three households varies, however, depending upon our criteria for defining the household.

In terms of co-residence and the accomplishment of household chores, each physical house comprised a single unit dedicated to the upkeep of that house. Note, however, that in no case is the membership of the house that of a nuclear family. In the case of House 1, for example, a nephew is co-resident, while one of

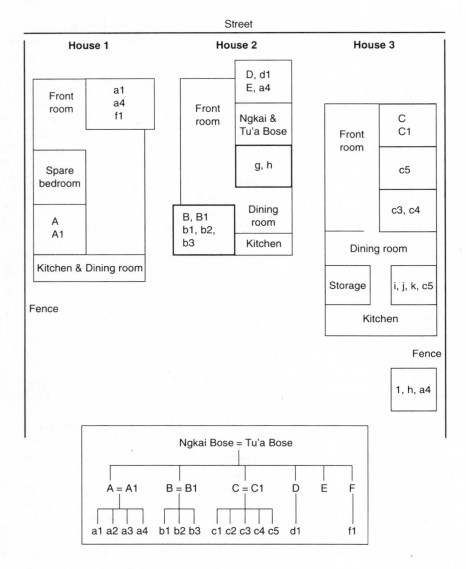

Figure 3.1 The Family Compound of Ngkai and Tu'a Bose

their own sons and two of their daughters are not. House 2 contains a multiple family household: Ngkai and Tu'a Bose, the parents of the sibling set which lived in these two compounds, and two of their married children and their children. House 3, like House 2, contains a number of more distant relatives (signified in the figure by lower-case letters), who aided them in their multiple enterprises.

If we define the household as a unit of consumption, these household boundaries shift. There are still only three households, but House 2 is split (as indicated spatially on the figure by the bold line). A married son and his three children occupied one part of the house, and maintained a separate hearth. But Ngkai and Tu'a Bose and a divorced son (D) eat their meals in House 3, which provided for all their needs. A unmarried son (E) was a dependent of House 1. At a later point in my fieldwork, the divorced son (D) moved out of House 2 and established residence in his own small store. House 3 nevertheless continued to send him regular meals.

House 1 contains one extended household, two children being fostered out and fostering f1, as well as feeding brother E, who sleeps with D in House 1; a4 will frequently sleep with D and E or with l.

House 2 contains one household, that of son B, who are also fostering B1's nephew; h is a member of House 2(i) (see figure 3.4), who sleeps with either g or l. B, D, and another sibling are now the owners of what remains of Ngkai Bose's *sawah*. The resulting plots are too small to be farmed individually; hence, the three brothers take turns farming it.

House 3 is a complex household composed of Ngkai and Tu'a Bose, their divorced son D and his daughter, married daughter C and her family, three 'nieces,' i, j, and k, and C1's nephew, 1.

Inter-household boundaries are purposefully kept vague because of a married couple's explicitly stated responsibility to ensure the social reproduction of their larger kin group, the *santina*. It is this responsibility to their *santina* which accounts for the large number of distant kin living in all three houses. Frequent gifts of cooked food between hearths is rationalized in the same terms. The very vagueness of household boundaries is one strategy used to provide 'subsistence insurance' for the extended kin group; hence, this 'persistence of tradition' could be taken as evidence of a moral economy. Yet, this transfer of kin must be more carefully examined in terms of its uses as a 'free input' in the various productive enterprises of these households - a task that will be undertaken in the next section of this chapter.

We must be careful not to dismiss prematurely this 'moral economy' as fully subsumed to capitalist relations of production. It is, rather, a case of 'ideological articulation' whereby a dominant class has created the social and ideological resources necessary for the functioning of capitalist agriculture in a land- and capital-poor area (Muratorio 1980, 40) As noted, the spread of capitalism has been an uneven process, and the commodification of product, land, and labour must be separately accounted for. A careful analysis of the shift from swidden to *sawah* production is required to determine to what degree agriculture has been subsumed by capitalism. This historical treatment will be limited to Tentena, the village I know best.[3]

The Commodification of Wet-Rice Production in Tentena

Sawah was introduced in Tentena about 1908 by the Dutch (Hengel MVO 1910, 25). Each household was required to cultivate 0.02 hectare of *sawah*, a larger burden than might appear, as neither hoes nor ploughs were available; the ground was worked by driving cattle through the mud. Of little productive value, these plots were viewed as another form of government corvée. Since the work had little productive importance, adults left *sawah* cultivation to their children, who were receiving additional instruction in specially laid school *sawah* (Kruyt 1924b, 44). Tentena's *sawah* has been used to teach other villages the basic techniques involved; hence, Tentena has consistently benefited first from the introduction of new technologies. Ploughs, for example, were introduced in Tentena as early as 1925, but by 1935 had not been adopted elsewhere (Winkelman MVO 1935, 4).

Rice grown on *sawah* was said to be less appetizing; therefore, the small amounts grown were sold to raise the money needed for the new head tax (Kruyt 1924b, 52). Wet-field rice was the first commodity; to this day, dry-field rice is not marketed, despite an acute local demand; my landlady refused to 'waste' a gift I had received of such rice on my dinner, and insisted on saving it for a feast. The government also attempted to commodify the land itself. *Sawah*, unlike the dry fields, was not abandoned and thus remained the property of those who opened it. Villagers, contrary to government desires, continued to treat land like other forms of property such as cattle, which could be owned either by individuals or by several related households (usually sibling sets, *saana*) who worked it together (*ndapojuyu*). The land market remains restricted, and most *sawah* is acquired through inheritance.

The introduction of the plough around 1925 altered the balance between dry- and wet-rice cultivation. Both methods require labour during the brief rainy season. When *sawah* fields were small and left to the care of children, dry-rice cultivation proceeded unhindered. As the *sawah* expanded in size in accordance with government dictates (the original minimum of 0.02 hectare was increased to 0.1 hectare), the labour demands of *sawah* began to impede dry field cultivation. The introduction of the plough increased the amount of *sawah* that could be easily cultivated and gave rise to a land rush, as *sawah* fields were expanded to a maximum of 2 hectares in Tentena, and 12 hectares elsewhere, depending upon population densities and the amount of suitable land. Since the plough couldn't be used on hilly dry fields, those fields were eventually abandoned. Neighbouring villages resort to dry field cultivation only when their *sawah* are insufficient in size to meet both cash and subsistence needs, although this pattern disappeared in Tentena just before the Second World War. Abandoning swidden cultivation did not, however, imply a complete shift to wet-rice production for sale. The *sawah* fields were now producing for both subsistence and sale. As population increased, saleable surpluses grew smaller, and *sawah* was reserved for subsistence production. Thus the switch in farming technologies did not immediately lead to the commodification of relations of production.

Sawah fields were not as responsive to population pressure as swidden production. The limited amount of irrigable land meant a limit of approximately 110 hectares of *sawah* for Tentena (or approximately 0.41 hectare per family these days). Since land could be obtained only through inheritance, *sawah* holdings tended to be fractionalized, as parents divided their *sawah* among maturing children. Parents then cultivated dry fields, or lived in multiple-family households with one of their children. This fragmentation of holdings was combated in a number of ways including the unequal distribution of *sawah*.[4] Some relief was also obtained in the late 1950s, when half the village moved to found the new village of Petirodongi, and during the early 1970s, when the green revolution doubled productive capacity through the introduction of high-yield varieties of rice. By 1991, *sawah* holdings in Tentena varied in size between 0.09 and 2.0 hectares, the result of varying fertility rates between families, inheritance strategies, and resettlement. The relatively small size of landholdings has prevented the emergence of a class of estate-holding *kulak* landowners; as Geertz noted of Java, 'farmers of a dimension and disposition sufficient to qualify as proper *kulaks*, to the degree they appear at all, seem but bubbles in the stream, local, fragile and evanescent, soon engulfed by the central current' (1984, 519).

The initial means by which *sawah* was introduced in Tentena precluded the commodification of the relations of production, while also limiting the impact of the commodification of its fruits. Rather, the impetus for the commodification of all factors of production came from Chinese merchants who settled in Tentena during the 1930s. As holdings were fractionalized, some farmers were forced to engage in wage labour or to sell or rent their holdings. The absolute need for cash to pay taxes, school fees, and bridewealth in an otherwise non-commodified economy created debts that could be met only on these Chinese merchants' terms. By the 1950s, the Chinese had acquired intermediate sized holdings and rented more land, which they cultivated as 'typical' capitalist enterprises. Similarly, the terms under which the peasant sector worked were being increasingly, if unevenly, commodified as a result of peasant debt. The ability to resolve debt with surplus production marks the difference between viable and non-viable enterprises. Those with non-viable holdings (currently below 0.25–0.3 hectares) became increasingly dependent upon wage labour for the primary reproduction of their households. The commodification of labour and land thus began among those with non-viable enterprises, and only peripherally affected those with viable holdings who remained entrenched in a 'subsistence economy.'

The existence of non-viable holdings and the emergence of wage labouring clearly indicate that 'shared poverty' does not operate at the level of land redistribution. Access to 'surplus' *sawah* for the landless has been partially but not completely commodified. Few farmers could afford to purchase land if their own small holdings were the result of fragmentation. The purchase of land may thus be undertaken by a group of siblings who own and work it in common. The terms under which this and other types of 'communal land' are worked vary immensely. In some cases, not all of the siblings reside in the village; hence, the non-residents may receive only a small part of the harvest. This amount may be specifically set (a form of sharecropping) or left to the goodwill of the cultivating relative. An example of how the means by which land was acquired affects the terms of sharecropping relationships was provided by one widow and her sons who cultivated two plots belonging to her non-resident sister. The first plot was her sister's share of their father's inheritance, and the sister had purchased the second. No rent was paid on the first plot, although each year the widow would 'remember' (*ndaendoka*) her sister with a part of the harvest, commensurate with her own circumstances. For the second, purchased plot, she paid a fixed rent of 100 kilograms of rice (close to the market rate).

Few kin demand a rent from siblings or from first or second cousins for the use of inherited land, although they will invariably be 'remembered' in kind after the harvest. If they are forgotten too often, however, or if they are in need of the income, the owners may rent the land out to a non-relative (frequently a Chinese businessman) at market rates. Those with salaried jobs frequently allowed a sibling to work their share of *sawah* and took a plot for a house and yard in the village as their share of the inheritance. If no land of this sort is available, the landless may turn to other villagers with surplus land. They may work the land in common, the harvest being divided on a ratio of 7 to 3 to the benefit of the landowner; or, the land may be granted in exchange for work elsewhere. The land might also be sharecropped, with payment of a cash rent or a third of the harvest. These patterns demonstrate that the landless can obtain access to land on flexible terms, although only in few cases is this access to land granted without a return in kind, labour, or cash. As a result, there is clearly a *net* transfer of wealth from the poorer to the richer households. Significantly, this transfer of wealth can be expressed either in market terms, with fixed rents, or in the language of kinship, with poorer families 'remembering' their benefactors with whatever surplus they can spare.

The commodification of agricultural labour, like land, has occurred as holdings became insufficient for subsistence. Agricultural labour was exchanged through *pesale*, a pattern of labour exchange adapted from shifting cultivation. It is marked by the exact exchange of a day's labour for a day's labour during the agricultural season. The workers bring their own cooked rice, but the host provides fish and coffee for all, creating a festive atmosphere. Many farmers emphasized that they hold a labour exchange to liven up the drudgery of working the fields. The Chinese merchants refused to engage in these work exchanges and offered a wage for the day's work. Indigenous civil servants such as Ngkai Bose were the first to attempt to follow their example; they could afford to hire labour and, because they worked in offices, could not exchange labour. However, since they were caught in a network of kin relationships, it was difficult for these civil servants to hire wage labour from their fellow villagers. Rather, they were forced to hold a labour exchange and offer a cash replacement for the day's labour they were unable to return. They could only issue a general call for labour and wait to see who showed up; the hiring was out of their hands. All who came had to be paid, even if their numbers exceeded that required for the task itself. This added immeasurably to the festive atmosphere of the labour exchange but precluded the widespread hiring of wage labour. Any attempt to limit the number of workers resulted in strained social relations and accusations of stinginess from those increasingly dependent on wages.

Since the larger landholders were unable to reciprocate all the labour required to work their land, they were forced to either rent out part of their holdings (creating the relatively even distribution of field cultivation per household remarked on by Geertz as typical of shared poverty) or expand their households so as to increase the amount of labour available to them. Large landholders such as Ngkai Bose would frequently foster their poorer relatives' children, transferring 'kin' labour from those without resources to those with labour needs. This is the opposite of the Chayanovian expectation that land be redistributed in a 'communal' economy of simple family households, a point to which I will return. Those landholders with viable subsistence farms were not at the forefront of the commodification of labour (i.e., as employers) since their enterprises increasingly drew on domestic labour supplemented by fostered children. Rather, the commodification of labour arose among those with an absolute need for cash who lacked other resources with which to obtain it (a relatively dispossessed proletariat). A pool of daily-wage labourers with insufficient landholdings for subsistence emerged during the late 1950s. Since they did not require labour exchanges to work their own minuscule plots, they began to demand a cash substitute, like that they received from the Chinese merchants whenever they joined in a labour exchange. At about the same time, farmers also began demanding a wage substitute from those who did not return their labour-exchange obligations by the end of the agricultural season. In this way, wage labouring emerged separately from the holding of labour exchanges.

Ploughing has now been completely commodified, but other tasks such as planting, weeding, and harvesting demonstrate a more complex pattern subject to rigorous calculation of the costs and benefits. Labour exchanges continues to occur for planting and weeding, due to its low cash costs. Those with no regular cash income may resort to labour exchanges because they cannot afford to pay for labour, even though, in their own words, 'labour exchanges are not economical' (*tidak ekonomis*). All the farmers I spoke with were quick to commodify the costs involved in a *pesale*: they must provide food for the workers and then must replace each worker day with a day's labour of their own, at a *potential* loss of Rp. 3.500 a day (the daily wage rate of a labourer in 1993). According to these farmers, hiring workers appears more 'economical' (since they do not have to pay for the worker's food), but it requires a greater *up-front* cash outlay – almost three times as much. They are too close to the margins to be able to afford these up-front costs, even if, as they indicated they knew, it was more economical in the long run. Hiring workers is thus adopted only if they have a shortage of household labour to exchange. The opportunity cost of labour exchanges are further reduced since certain kinds of 'kin' labour do not have to be exactly reciprocated. In one case, for example, two cousins with no land joined a third cousin's labour exchange. Since the two had no land of their own, they had no use for the landowner's labour. However, the landowner 'remembered' their unasked-for aid and called on them for help with harvesting, for which they were paid with a share of the harvest. The landowner's plot was barely sufficient for his own subsistence, but his own poverty prevented him from adopting the most 'economic' strategy; as a result, his poverty was 'shared' and his minuscule production divided. As Geertz noted, these are less 'haves' and 'have-nots' than 'just-enoughs' and 'not-quite-enoughs' (1963a, 97).

Those with an outside source of income who could afford to pay wages but who also have surplus household labour demonstrate another strategy for the adoption of labour exchanges. Like the others, they opt for labour exchange because of its lower cash costs. This group tended to have the largest landholdings and hence required the greatest amount of capital for hiring labour. But, because of their larger holdings, they also had difficulty in returning all the labour they required through *pesale*. They thus worked only a portion of their land with labour exchanges and rented the rest out; only if their outside incomes were large enough did they utilize wage labour to farm it all. The largest landowner in Tentena is a teacher in a state school. He could easily recruit labour from among his students, and the labour was returned by a combination of members of his own household and other 'kin' labour that need not be reciprocated.

The commodification of labour has resulted in the emergence of alternative forms of work exchange. *Mombesale* (from the same root as *pesale* but with the prefix *mombe-*, mutually) is labour-oriented, where *pesale* is task-oriented. It developed as the wage-labouring workforce in Tentena grew larger. Five or six labourers form a group, working in turn for each member. Members of this group might include both landless labourers and those with mid-sized holdings. The group's labour is used for the benefit of each member in rotation, who may either use their labour in his or her own fields or *sell* it to the highest bidder. Thus, group members work continuously, but their costs are minimized since each worker provides his or her own food. The system meets the needs of those requiring labour as well as those requiring cash. Similar to *mombesale* is the *partai* (Indonesian 'party'), or *regu* (Pamona 'to play'), which operates on the same principles but with a larger group, of up to thirty workers.[5]

The differentiation of landholdings is thus historically linked to the commodification of production. There are many non-viable holdings insufficient to meet both subsistence and commodified needs, necessitating wage labour outside the household unit of production. The differentiation of holdings has been accentuated by other costs of farming such as the purchase of fertilizer. These costs are often sufficient to prevent smaller landholders from cultivating their land. The need for an outside income for even 'subsistence' production has meant that all households now engage in wage labour to some degree. This includes agricultural wage labour, the collection of forest products on commission, and sending older children to work in distant cities or plantations and depending on their remittances. Multi-occupational households have become the norm.

Given the commodification of labour and the need for cash for even subsistence production, the continued use of 'kin' labour by wealthier farmers is analytically problematic. This problem is usually resolved with reference to 'shared poverty' or 'moral economy' arguments. I similarly attempted to understand the use of kin labour with reference to a non-commodified subsistence ethic but found my informants' 'subsistence-oriented strategy' was based upon rational calculation of the factors of production. In all cases, farmers sought to reduce the costs of production as much as possible so as to minimize their subsistence costs and maximize their cash income from their surplus. However, since incomes are low even among those with larger landholdings, kin ties are mobilized in a variety of ways to reduce these costs. Although the villagers emphasized that the calculation of costs and benefits between kin is improper – *be maya mombereke* (should not be mutually counted) – the decision to utilize kin labour was itself subject to calculation. Villagers refused to commodify specific kinds of 'kin' labour but did calculate the costs and benefits of utilizing those forms of labour. Kin labour could include both household labour and that of other households, given the fuzzy household boundaries. Hence, the teacher mentioned above would reciprocate labour with that of his non-resident father-in-law's temporary ward. The utilization of kin labour is often physically eased by the transfer of kin between households, which is phrased in terms of aiding poorer relatives, of 'sharing poverty' (*tuwu siwagi*). The relationship among kinship, kin labour, and household enterprises thus requires a more detailed examination.

Kinship and the Household

The porousness of household boundaries in Tentena is aptly demonstrated by the use of extra-household kin labour in household-based production; it counters the image of the peasant household as a discrete production–consumption unit. Villagers view the *sombori* in developmental terms, as an increasingly independent unit of production that must be cushioned within a larger kin network that assumes those domestic duties the household is unable to accomplish alone. The fuzzy household boundaries that result from the sharing of domestic functions among kin precludes any analysis of household consumption and social reproduction except in relation to the wider network of households of which it is a part, that is, the *santina* (cf. Sanjek 1982, 98). Yet, given the clear economic pressures, and the readiness to calculate the costs and benefits of various kinds of access to labour and resources, we must be careful to note which features of the social structure 'lead individuals to provide work for other households at the expense of their own' (Alexander and Alexander 1982, 599). While an ideology of shared poverty characterizes Tentena, this egalitarian *ideology* stands at odds with the differentiation of the peasantry and a hierarchical social structure. As Kahn notes, ideologies 'should be objects *of* analysis rather than tools *for* analysis' (1978, 130; emphasis in original). The place of 'kinship' in levelling differences in wealth between households must thus be treated as problematic, rather than explanatory.

We must be careful not to separate morality from the relationships within which it is embedded. Sharing, the redistribution of consumables, must be distinguished from shared poverty, defined in terms of social reproduction. The ideology of sharing in Tentena emphasizes only the obligation to divide a surplus with little emphasis on the needs of the receiver. Independence is highly prized – hence, the gift should not connote 'charity'; one must share equally among all present. Sharing requires no immediate return, but givers will eventually stop sharing if they are not 'remembered' (*ndaendoka*). The return prestation need not be of equal value. Even if the amount shared is small, its value is not decreased since even in a time of scarcity the receiver has been remembered.

Non-market exchanges dominated the local economy until the 1970s. Few goods had a commodity value; hence, their availability was dependent upon personalized ties of sharing. This is no longer the case. 'Sharing' has been replaced with taking goods on credit. Although most goods now have a commodity value, generalized exchange still continues on a more limited scale, especially of items such as home-grown vegetables, and cigarettes. In the newly commodified economy, these persisting exchanges have acquired new emotive importance, emphasizing solidarity.

The generalized reciprocity of consumables can be contrasted with un-balanced reciprocity typical of shared poverty in social reproduction. This distinction is of importance because an individual or household surrenders its independence through its inability to reciprocate. These relationships are marked by a clear hierarchy of dominance and subordination. Harris reminds us that, while the 'language of kinship is concerned with generosity and sharing ... this is only one side of the story ... relations of extreme authority and dependence may be expressed in kin terms. In some cases it has been argued that kin terms and kin relations effectively disguise class differences' (1982, 150). Unbalanced reciprocity may take the form of fulfilling certain kinds of domestic functions, such as the provisioning of a home, clothing, food, or education for another family or their children, as we saw in the family compound of Ngkai and Tu'a Bose.

The redistribution of kin, not land, through widespread fosterage is one important means by which this sharing of poverty is effected. Analysis of the household composition of a group of sixty-eight households in the *santina* of my landlord in four widespread villages showed 44 per cent were nuclear family households, 49 per cent were extended-family households fostering children (or other kin), and a further 6 per cent were multiple-family households living in multiple-family households (table 3.1). These figures show the failure of the liberal development policies intent on creating a peasantry composed of simple family households, each an independent unit of production and consumption, despite its success in eliminating the longhouse.[6] These household forms are not stages in a single-household development cycle but are, rather, the product of a common kinship logic.

Shared poverty follows from specific obligations to aid in the social reproduction of kin. By 'social reproduction,' I intend, on the one hand, the means by

TABLE 3.1
Household Composition in Study Group

Type	Number	Per cent
No family	1	1.5
Simple family household	30	44.0
(denuded)[7]	(10)	(15.0)
Extended-family households	33	49.0
(denuded)	(8)	(12.0)
Multiple-family household (*sanco-ncombori*)	4	6.0

which households are created, and, on the other, the means by which the ties within and between households which I have referred to as 'kinship' are simultaneously created and perpetuated. These processes are cemented by the exchange of bridewealth. That which Geertz characterizes as shared poverty, I see as the specific relationship between kinship (the *santina*) and the household.

The creation of a new household and the acquisition of land were historically accomplished through marriage. The switch from swidden to *sawah* cultivation altered this system, shifting the process of land provisioning from marriage to inheritance, although the inheritance is often distributed shortly after the marriage. The resulting differentiation in landholdings is ameliorated by the transfer of responsibility for the social reproduction of kin to other households. Since this responsibility transcends household boundaries, it is exceedingly difficult to categorize household forms based simply on who is living *within* a *sombori*. The various of household forms encountered in the sample, whether nuclear family, stem family, or lateral or downward extended household, are not the product of a uniform developmental cycle, but the product of this complex reallocation of kinship responsibility in relation to the specific demographic circumstances of the wider kin group and the availability of resources. The household can be defined only in terms of roles, not its domestic functions, since such domestic functions are often assumed by other households in the kin group. The household is not a necessary unit of production, consumption, or social reproduction. The household is, rather, a flexible structure within which the members of a *santina* achieve these ends.

A married couple assume responsibility for the social reproduction of the members of the kin group that paid their bridewealth. They may thus assume the burden of raising the children of others, often as distant as third cousins. Such appeals for help are frequently based upon the prior residence of the householder or their parent in the household of the ward or their parent or grandparent. A significant proportion of the children from extended-family households (net importers of kin) were themselves fostered out. It is important to emphasize that fostering is not the simple transfer of children from poor to rich households (cf. Wong 1991, 201). Fosterage is a means by which the *santina* helps its kin fulfil the domestic functions that some households are unable to provide themselves. For example, a couple may foster a poorer relative's child, providing food and shelter, but require assistance themselves in acquiring higher education for one of their own children.

Fosterage is a relatively new phenomenon among the To Pamona,[8] and must be clearly differentiated from adoption. Goody differentiates fosterage from other forms of pro-parenthood by emphasizing that the nurturing, educational, and sponsoring roles of parenthood are assumed without 'effect[ing] the status identity of the child, nor the jural rights and obligations this entails' (1971, 336). Foster parents nurture children without the jural obligation of sharing an inheritance with them. Their parental role and authority are unchallenged, but the jural status of the ward *may* lead to a clear domestic distinction being made between own and foster children. A young woman, a cousin, living in my landlord's household, for example, assumed a servant role. She was asked to live with the family to prevent her making what they considered an undesirable marriage. She was given a small allowance for doing the housecleaning, but the reason for her stay was always expressed in terms of their parental role in arranging her marriage, and obtaining a job for her. I noted one day that she never rested, that she was always cooking or cleaning; hence, I likened her role to Cinderella's,[9] a reference that she surprisingly understood, having seen the Disney movie. She was horrified at the suggestion and begged that I never repeat it. She insisted that she worked only because she felt she should fulfil her responsibilities as a family member, not because she was forced to do so. My landlord and landlady had assumed a parental role, were attempting to find her a job, and were assuming responsibility for her marriage. By working hard, she showed the depth of her appreciation, as she would to her own parents. Such relationships are cast in kinship terms, and thus invoke patterns of authority as well as amity. Given these patterns of authority, we must be careful in asserting that the transfer of dependents is a 'levelling mechanism.'

The terms under which wards are accepted vary greatly. In the majority of cases, the ward was accepted because he or she was attending a local school. However, that reason often hid more complex situations; in one case, for example, two sisters living in two different towns exchanged their similarly aged children so they could attend the high school in the other town. The exchange of these children hid other motives, such as a discipline problem and the desire to strengthen an emotional bond between the sisters through an exchange of their children. While fosterage may be a means by which resources are redistributed within a kin group, levelling differences in wealth, that is not necessarily its only intent.

One effect of the sharing of domestic functions within a *santina* is that it simultaneously provides 'kin' labour for those with greater resources. While the intent of fosterage may not be to gain such labour, once acquired the labour is utilized in familial enterprises and heightens differences in production and wealth. I have emphasized the ambiguity of fosterage as both leveller and accentuater of differences in wealth because it remains a kinship phenomenon and is therefore regulated by the 'axiom of amity' outside of the cost–benefit analysis now common in many aspects of production. Although several wealthier families have actively sought 'kin' labour for their household enterprises, they have also been asked to aid distant family, to foster a child whose productive labour is inconsequential. A strict calculation of costs and benefits is explicitly ruled out, yet allows those with resources to utilize the domestic labour they acquire to ensure the viability of their peasant enterprises. 'The poor "lose" their children and thus their ability to increase resources, whereas the wealthy can profitably "bind" them by means of their resources in property' (Wong 1991, 201).

The Household Developmental Cycle

Landownership, generally excluded from the redistributive systems of 'shared poverty,' serves to create a permanent economic, and hence political, centre for the extended kin group. Differential access to property simultaneously defines the centre of the kin group and its periphery. Those who possess viable peasant enterprises as a result of their larger holdings serve as the centre of their wider *santina* by guaranteeing the social reproduction of its members. The transfer of kin towards the centre (through fosterage) preserves the viability of the centre while increasing the differential between it and its economically unviable periphery. As a result, the household developmental cycle found among the To Pamona is not unilinear, but follows two major paths, depending upon the viability of the peasant enterprise. In the first case, poorer families dependent upon the market for the social reproduction of their enterprises are more likely to live in denuded simple family households, or *sanco-ncombori*. In contrast, wealthier families with viable landholdings are more likely to live in extended-family households, supplemented with their poorer relatives in characteristically 'peasant-like' enterprises (see figure 3.2).

The case study that follows provides a concrete example of the dual processes described above. In tracing this history, the implications of differential access to

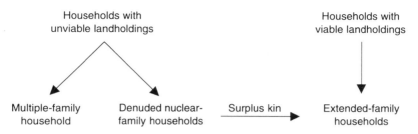

Figure 3.2 Household Development Cycles in Tentena

land on these two household development cycles are emphasized. The point of the analysis, however, is to underscore the political implications of this dual development cycle. As noted in the previous section, fosterage serves a political function as familial patrons assume parental roles for members of their wider kin group. As 'parents' they control access to marriage as well as the household membership of the clients within their *santina*. The political implications of this are discussed more fully in the next chapter.

The history of Ngkai and Tu'a Bose's *santina* can be traced from the initial settlement of Tentena, and lies within memory of its oldest members, including Tu'a Bose's mother. By 1920, some members of this *santina* had been forced by the Dutch to move from the distant Onda'e village of Wawo Ndoda,[10] first to neighbouring Sawidago, then to Tentena; they appeared to have been related to Pancali Sigilipu, the first minister in Tentena, a kinship tie that later led to further intermarriage. Ngkai Bose's grandparents, and Tu'a Bose's grandparents (see figure 3.3), each built a house on one of the many side roads in the village. Ngkai Bose's paternal grandparents, Kaya and Janji, built the first house (House 1); he was born there in 1925. The house on the opposite side of the road (House 2) was occupied by Ngkai Bose's grandmother's brother (Gore), which he shared with his wife's brother (Kina) and family. Ngkai Bose knew them all as 'grandparents,' since no distinction in terms of reference is made between members of a sibling group.

The second couple in House 2 (Kina and Abi) were the maternal grandparents of Tu'a Bose. The marriage of Ngkai and Tu'a Bose thus represents a particularly valued form of marital alliance, the renewal of a tie between two longhouses within the *santina*. The overlapping kinship ties have made Ngkai and Tu'a Bose a focal point for the *santina*, and hence prominent political figures in the village. In the discussion that follows, I note only the semi-permanent occupants of each of these two houses; other *sombori* that lived there for short periods and tempo-

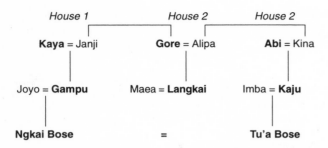

Figure 3.3 Genealogies of Ngkai and Tu'a Bose (Men in bold)

rary residents have been left out to simplify the narrative outline, even though, in practical terms, they served as the social glue of the *santina*. (The domestic migrations of the residents of these houses are shown in figure 3.4.)

By the 1930s, Ngkai Bose's grandparents had died and the house was occupied by his parents and two of his parents' married nieces. The *sawah* opened by the now deceased grandparents was owned in common (*ndapojuyu*) by the three couples, but by that time each *sombori* independently farmed a section and cooked for themselves. Each family lived in their own room, although, as in the longhouse, the unmarried boys (including Ngkai Bose) slept together in the open greeting room of the house. One of the nieces moved to the town of Poso for a short period to open a coconut plantation, but returned to Tentena in the late 1930s when those efforts failed, owing to a drop in copra prices during the depression. By that point the house was crowded with children, so the niece moved to another relative's house nearby. They asked for, and received, a large section (about 80 *are*, 0.8 hectare) of the *sawah* held in common until then, which was officially divided in a family gathering. Ngkai Bose's parents and the other married niece accepted much smaller sections (about 60 *are* in total), because they still farmed dry fields.

By 1924, one set of Tu'a Bose's 'grandparents' (Gore and Alipa) in House 2 were deceased, and their son Langkai had married and was living with his uncle and Tu'a Bose's grandparents (Abi and Kina); both *sombori* established their own independent hearth (*rapu*). None of the *sombori* in the house possessed *sawah*; they were latecomers, and the parents too ill for the strenuous task of opening wet fields. Tu'a Bose's parents married in 1927 and opened their own *sawah* on the far side of the river. Since Abi and Kina were ill and unable to fend for themselves, Tu'a Bose's parents continued to live together with them in a multiple-family household (*sanco-ncombori*). By 1934, with a total of five children (including Tu'a Bose) having been added to the two households, the

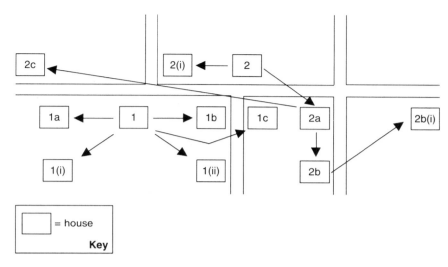

Figure 3.4 Street Map Showing Houses 1 and 2 and Their Division

house was getting small; her parents thus built a new larger house down the road (House 2a) with her father's brother Tolo. Her co-resident uncle, Langkai, retained the old house because 'he had nothing else.' Tu'a Bose's parents and grandparents continued to live in a multiple-family household in the new house (2a), but Tolo maintained his own hearth. Tolo had no *sawah* of his own.

Meanwhile, Ngkai Bose's parents remained in House 1 with their niece and her family. They had four sons, the youngest of which was Ngkai Bose. As each son married, he received a small section of the remaining sawah (about 0.15 hectare apiece) and moved to the homes of his wife's parents. Ngkai Bose, the youngest son, married Tu'a Bose in 1947 and moved to house 2a, where he eventually lived in a multiple-family household (*sanco-ncombori*) with four other *sombori*, including his wife's parents, his wife's childless aunt and uncle, and his wife's married siblings. At the time Ngkai and Tu'a Bose married, Tolo built another house in the backyard (House 2b). Tolo lived in a multiple-family household with his two married daughters, and they together farmed a 0.5-hectare field inherited by one of their foster children, an orphan. The childless aunt and uncle of Tu'a Bose built House 2c at about the same time, and later adopted one of Tua Bose's sister's children.

The tendency for households originating in House 2 to live in multiple-family households can be contrasted with the separate hearths maintained in House 1. The difference appears to be related to the lack of resources, in particular *sawah*, in House 2. Newly created *sombori* were unable to establish their independence because, by this time, swidden agriculture had been abandoned and *sawah* holdings already fractionalized. House 2 had never had a large amount of *sawah*.

Ngkai Bose, however, had an outside income, having become the district secretary shortly before his marriage. With the money he earned, he set about improving his extended household's fortunes. He paid for land suitable for *sawah* on the far side of the river and purchased the material needed to construct a larger house for his burgeoning family. As the husband of the eldest daughter, he assumed a leading role in the management of the household. This, however, brought him into conflict with his wife's eldest brother. This brother ideally should have moved to his wife's family's house; however, as this wife was also from a large, poor family, they were forced to remain in House 2a. This elder brother resented the role assumed by Ngkai Bose, and frequent arguments resulted. After one blow-up, Tu'a Bose's parents advised Ngkai and Tu'a Bose it might be better if they established their own household, as they had the means. They divided the small amount of property they had among all their eight children, giving Tu'a Bose some sago and coconut trees as her share. The elder brother, enraged by the division of the property previously owned in common (*ndaposintuwui*) without his concurrence, sold Tu'a Bose's share behind their backs.

Ngkai Bose thus took the material he had assembled and built a larger house on the site of House 1, where he, his family, his parents, his married cousin (who had always lived with his parents), and their children resided. He retained, as well, the small amount of *sawah* given by his parents; he later purchased additional *sawah* from a Manadonese farmer.

Over the next several years, Ngkai Bose's brothers each built their own home on the lot (houses 1a, 1b, 1c). This sudden house-building spurt was due in part to government policy to reduce the number of *sombori* in each house to a maximum of two. It is normally daughters who build their homes on the parental lot, but since Ngkai Bose's parents only had sons, the land was otherwise unoccupied. This same house-building spurt led one of Tolo's married daughters (House 2b) to build her own home (2b[i]). It should be emphasized that the impetus for this house-building was not a sudden rise in prosperity; indeed, this was recalled as a time of great want, with harvests insufficient for even subsistence. The houses were built at the instigation of the government; it is important to note that both new houses (1 and 2b[i]) were built by civil servants with an outside income.

Shortly thereafter, during the Permesta rebellion, the village of Petirodongi was founded on the far side of the river, and two of Ngkai Bose's brothers and his cousin moved, selling or giving their share of the family *sawah* to him, leaving him with his father's *sawah* intact (0.6 hectare). The other remaining brother (1c) eventually moved to the provincial capital, leaving Ngkai Bose as the sole possessor of the site of the current compound (see figure 3.1). He remained in Tentena because of his job in the civil service.

The childless couple (2c) who had adopted one of Tu'a Bose's sisters later also adopted one of Tu'a Bose's daughters and moved across the river to the new village of Pamona. Tu'a Bose's sister, once married, moved back into House 2a with her parents; her brothers and sisters moved across the river to Pamona, where they farmed the land they had opened with Ngkai Bose's financial help. They divided up the small amount of *sawah* they had, as well as the *sawah* paid for by Ngkai Bose when he was a member of their household, among themselves; Ngkai Bose abandoned all claim to the land. Indeed, this land was still insufficient for the large family; hence, they frequently turned to him for further aid, either in providing cattle or in fostering their children. Ngkai Bose's brother (1c) died quite young, and Ngkai Bose also assumed a parental role towards his children, taking responsibility for their marriages.

This complex case study provides examples illustrating the general conclusions I reached in the analysis of the histories of seven *santina*, compared with the more detailed contemporary economic data I collected on sixty-eight related households. The development cycle of Ngkai and Tu'a Bose's household varies greatly from that of those households at the periphery of his *santina*, such as Langkai (House 2). These two development cycles of what I have glossed as viable and unviable households can be contrasted in terms of the logic that links them. The dual development cycles emerge because of differential access to land within a kin group. Parental property is usually divided as their children marry, enabling each of them to establish an independent simple family household. Problems emerge only if the parental landholding is insufficient to support the families of all the married children. According to inheritance law (*ada mpopanta*), land should be divided equally among siblings, but in practice, since property is divided as children marry, unequal division may be utilized to ensure the viability of the new *sombori*.[11] Younger children are usually given higher education as compensation for their lost share.

Sufficient resources to form an independent household are increasingly in short supply as parental holdings are fragmented. The resources sufficient to support husband and wife may be insufficient when children are added (House 2a), or alternatively, labour may be in short supply if the *sombori* is childless (House 2c). Or, having obtained land, the household may be unable to afford the cash inputs needed for production. In any case, children may be fostered, resulting in a denuded simple family household. In the poorest of families, family lands will not be divided and families will live in a multiple-family household until further resources are found (Houses 2, 2a, 2b, 2b[i]). Every group living in a multiple-family household with whom I spoke emphasized that their ideal was to live in their own house as a sign of their independence. In situations such as this, some families may be forced to foster out some of their children even before they establish an independent household.

Ngkai and Tu'a Bose's household is typical of the second development cycle, that of extended-family households with numerous foster children. This is not easily decipherable from the case study. The characteristics of this cycle emerge more clearly from a survey conducted among sixty-eight related households from a single *santina*. The extended family households, such as that of Ngkai and Tu'a Bose, are a subset of the wealthier simple family households and therefore not a product of the lack of resources that force poor families to live in complex households (*sanco-ncombori*). I found that 63 per cent of the wealthy families in my sample formed extended-family households, whereas only 21 per cent lived in simple family households. Many of the wealthy currently living in these simple family households had fostered children in the past. In contrast, among the poor households, 63 per cent were living in simple family households, while only 37 per cent were living in extended-family households. As noted in the previous section, the more resources a household has at its command, the greater its labour requirements, and hence its willingness to accept foster children.

Ngkai Bose, for example, had one hectare of *sawah* by about 1960. Since he had a civil-service job, he was unable to work his fields himself. It was inordinately expensive for him to hire labour under the guise of labour exchange. However, over a period of twenty-five years, he fostered more than thirty-six children, many to adulthood. These children worked his *sawah* as well as helping him open a clove-tree plantation during the 1970s. In another case, a teacher acquired three foster children almost as old as himself within a year of his marriage. He utilized their labour to grow peanuts, which he sold in a small store he opened and staffed in part with his 'children.'

Although there is no common development cycle, I would like to emphasize that both paths follow a shared logic of social reproduction, since the extended family households could not exist except for the net transfer of children from denuded simple family households. All of the household types noted take shape because of a shared ideology that emphasizes kin responsibility for the social reproduction of the *santina* through the transfer of people. Although there is some sharing of resources among kin, it appears that people are far more mobile than land. Households 2, 2a, 2b, and 2b(i) are all characterized by a lack of resources, a tendency to live in a multiple-family household, and the transfer of kin towards the centre, defined by Ngkai and Tu'a Bose.[12] 'Cinderella,' for example, was the child of one of Tu'a Bose's brothers living in House 2a and originally lived with Ngkai and Tu'a Bose before moving in with my landlord.

The co-residence of often distant kin brings them emotionally closer, and this in turn strengthens the solidarity of the kin group. Children from a number of branches of the group will meet within one household and learn of the wider kinship ties binding them, as well as of the practical limits of 'kinship.' The emotional ties created must, in turn, be contrasted with the hierarchical relations simultaneously established. In raising these children, foster parents may assume parental responsibilities, including control of subsequent marriages. Their advice is frequently sought and their organization of marriage preparations is often essential. The ties that link households of whatever type are thus conceived of in kin terms, with attendant responsibilities, rights, and duties.

Lastly, it is important to note the changes brought about by development, by the commodification of labour, and by the sharpened differentiation of landholdings. The government-imposed shift from swidden to *sawah* cultivation and the resultant fragmentation of landholdings has deprived a number of *sombori* of the resources they need to establish an independent household, a rare phenomenon under swidden cultivation. Living in multiple-family households, which at one time was a means to support elderly parents unable to farm for themselves, has become a parental support of married children unable to establish themselves independently. Similarly, poorer simple family households are denuded of children, and wealthier households expanded. Paradoxically, government policies aimed at creating simple family peasant households have had the effect of increasing the tendency to live in multiple-family households, and of strengthening the wider kinship system that it sought to destroy by eliminating longhouses.

Peasantization and 'Discursive Traditionalism'

That the differentiation of the peasantry should be accompanied by the reassertion of the pertinence of kinship in a commodified economy brings me back to the point with which I began. I noted that 'the persistence of tradition' did not imply a static perpetuation of an earlier mode of production. The penetration of capitalism has been uneven, leaving relations of social reproduction of the ties between households as a domain outside the arena of commodity production. Within the new social formation, kin labour substitutes for wage labour where capital is scarce. The fact that wealthier households have utilized kin labour rather than wage labour makes it apparent that the continuing injunction against strict accounting of costs and benefits of kin relationships works both ways. On the one hand, it gives the ideology of kinship in Tentena the appearance of 'shared poverty,' of a redistribution of wealth. On the other hand, differences in wealth are evident and, if one does not calculate the value of the net transfer of labour to wealthier households, poorer households are deprived of that labour for use in their own enterprises.

One important aspect of shared poverty, as I have developed the concept, is that the redistribution or 'levelling' of wealth simultaneously gives rise to hierarchical kinship relationships. Although class divisions are blunted, and an ideology of economic and political egalitarianism asserted, kin relations translate actual economic inequalities into genealogical seniority. Familial patrons assume parental roles for their extended kin group, and in so doing control the constitution, membership, and access to the means of production of newly formed households within that wider group. Familial clients with non-viable peasant enterprises and few wage opportunities become dependent upon this wider kin network for their own social reproduction. In transferring the responsibility for the social reproduction of their households to their kin group, they acknowledge this dependence in kinship rather than economic terms. That is, they are not employees, but children.

Shared poverty in the Geertzian sense thus requires qualification as a theoretical model, specifically with regard to the failure to define the kinship-bounded groups within which it operates, as well as its treatment of impinging capitalist relations. Although I have inverted Geertz's Chayanovian assumptions, I agree that the differentiation of the peasantry and the resulting reconstitution of kinship and the household is not the result of capitalist 'maximizing individualists.' *Contra* Geertz, I argue that the mechanisms of shared poverty are not 'traditional' but emerge as a response to differentiation and the introduction of capitalist relations of production. This is seen clearly among the To Pamona, who have only recently been reconstituted as a peasantry. I have attempted to show that viable peasant enterprises (Geertz's 'just-enoughs') have maintained their viability by preserving specific types of kinship labour in non-commodified form. A maximal economic surplus is not reinvested in production, but subsidizes a more extensive kin network that serves as a political unit, an issue that is discussed in chapter 4.

4

Marriage, Kinship, and *Posintuwu* Networks

Then said he also to him that bade him, When thou makest a dinner or a supper, call not thy friends, nor thy brethren, neither thy kinsmen, nor thy rich neighbours; lest they also bid thee again, and a recompence be made thee. But when thou makest a feast, call the poor, the maimed, the lame, the blind: And thou shalt be blessed; for they cannot recompense thee: for thou shalt be recompensed at the resurrection of the just.

Luke 14: 12–14

The commodification of agriculture has clearly made household production and reproduction dependent upon extra-household kinship ties that provided 'subsistence insurance' for the wider kin group; this 'subsistence insurance,' viewed as 'non-calculative' compassionate sharing, turns out to have specific economically rational (calculable) benefits that lie outside the narrowly defined kinship 'tradition' codified in Kruyt's ethnographies as 'communalism.' The provisioning of this not necessarily altruistic subsistence insurance is linked to the establishment of hierarchical patron–client relationships within the extended kin group (*santina*).

In this chapter, the manner in which these hierarchical kinship ties are ideologically constituted through feasting and *posintuwu* exchange networks is examined. Feasting is the arena within which kinship, religion, and politics have been articulated. The exchange of *posintuwu* for the larger feasts establishes a gift economy that simultaneously defines the recognized limits of the kin group as well as establishing the special 'altruistic' character of kin relationships. *Posintuwu* exchanges have gained new ideological importance; as free gifts, they serve to contrast the kinship relations maintained through *posintuwu* exchange with the impersonal market exchanges that have come to dominate production. This symbolic contrast is of relatively recent origin. One searches in vain for mention of *posintuwu* in Kruyt's ethnographies, yet, by the time of my fieldwork, *posintuwu* was a constant source of debate in household, church, and government.[1] This debate has emerged as feasting and kinship have been encapsulated within the broader, bureaucratically driven concerns of church and state. *Posintuwu* exchange is one of the *adat* discourses through which these institutions have sought to mould To Pamona identities. However, as noted in chapter 3, this key element of social reproduction has alternative uses for most participants; these uses inflect the expressions of 'kinship' that church and state have reified in *adat* liturgies. The largest of these feasts, the wedding, is thus an ideal site in which to examine the conflicting strategies of the various participants.

In the pre-colonial era, *posintuwu* was given only at secondary funerals (*posintuwu tau mate*) and at weddings (*posintuwu tau tuwu*). It served a dual function; as a material contribution, it made the feast itself possible. The gift, however, also signified that the gift giver and receiver were in *mosintuwu*, living in peace and friendship. The material considerations ensured that these ties were not entered into indiscriminately. The occasions on which such gifts were given ensured that the recipients of such gifts were limited to one's extended kin group. Both of these gift-giving occasions were utilized by *kabosenya* (leaders) to consolidate their extended kin group, albeit in differing ways. In the case of the secondary funeral, *posintuwu* signified a continuing tie between two kinship groups (*to saana*) whose common inheritance had been expended through feasting in the past. *Posintuwu* given at marriage served a different function, since it was used for bridewealth, not just the feast; indeed, the marriage feast was typically small. Marriage served to renew ties within an extended kin group, and the exchange of bridewealth legitimated the groom's family's rights in the children of the union.

Conversion to Christianity, the switch from swidden to *sawah* cultivation, and the resultant changes in kinship and household forms have all served to alter the meaning of *posintuwu* exchanges. The elimination of the secondary funeral had the greatest impact. The missions opposed the *motengke* and *mompemate* funerals because of their associations with ancestor worship, and the colonial government banned the core ritual of the funeral, the cleaning of decayed flesh from the bones, because it was unhygienic. Although *posintuwu* exchanges remain an important part of Christian funerals to this day, the speed with which the body must be buried (usually within twenty-four hours) precludes the organization of a major feast. Marriage, in contrast, has come to assume a greater role in the feasting complex. What had once been a minor feast of interest only to the immediate families of the bride and groom has become a major 'ritual of social location' (cf. Millar 1989); that is, a ritual that serves to fix the relative status of the two families within a larger social universe. The To Pamona have, in fact, adopted many of the Bugis practices described by Millar in their weddings; a continuing highland–lowland dynamic that points to the importance of wider regional and national cultural policies.

Weddings have also become the ideological focus of attempts to maintain kinship as a non-commodified realm. *Posintuwu* collected from the groom's kin is used to pay the *oli mporongo* (price of the wedding, bridewealth [Adriani 1928, 516]). The exchange of bridewealth is thus inherently contrastive, distinguishing *posintuwu* (a voluntary gift) from *oli* (the demanded price), kin from non-kin.[2] This contrast has only slowly developed, as the meaning of the word *oli* has itself been transformed. In the pre-colonial period, a *maoli* exchange (an exchange of goods for a 'price') transferred use rights in an object, not ownership, and thus was the means by which the groom's family acquired rights in his children, or a farmer 'bought' a field in the forest from its spirit possessor. The *maoli* exchange was characterized by direct reciprocity, the trade of spiritually powerful goods for other equally powerful goods. This direct exchange was necessary to protect the 'seller' from the loss of *tanoana,* which could result in illness. The missionaries actively sought to purge these 'animistic' aspects of the term, and its current meaning is 'to buy.' The *oli mporongo* has thus increasingly come to signify the 'price' of the wedding. And as the commodity value of the bridewealth required by the *adat* has consistently dropped in relation to the costs of the accompanying feast, the bulk of current bridewealth payments consists of money to defray these costs (*bila-bila*).

Changes in the form of the wedding feast will thus be examined as an indication of how kinship has been reconstituted in opposition to the commodification of the economy. As the greatest of the feasts, the wedding makes large demands on the resources of the participants; both families must turn to their wider kin groups for *posintuwu*, the money, rice, cattle, and purchased cloth needed to perform the required ceremonies and rituals. *Posintuwu* exchange is a transactional sphere that serves to de-commodify these objects, withdrawing them from their regular circulation in the market (Appadurai 1986; cf. Ferguson 1994, 135–66). *Posintuwu* contrasts with market exchange in that status accrues to those who give the largest gifts. The larger landholders are able to give larger gifts and hence acquire greater status within their kin groups. Such large gifts allow even the poorest member of the kin group to maintain the group's status through an appropriately grandiose feast. Large gifts are, however, a grave burden for the poor since a failure to return an equal amount of *posintuwu* means a loss of status relative to their benefactors; every wedding is composed of a multitude of binary-status competitions between the hosts and the individual members of their kin groups as each attempts to at least equal the other's past contribution. In so far as the poor are able to equal their patrons, they contribute larger amounts than they would to others, thus allowing these patrons to give correspondingly larger wedding feasts that validate their greater wealth and status both within and outside the kin group. Feasting, no less than 'shared poverty,' emphasizes generosity and the sharing of wealth yet simultaneously creates hierarchy within a group bounded by kinship ties.

The increasing importance of *posintuwu* exchange is itself problematic (to both analysts and participants), and linked to the changing political and economic roles of kinship. While *posintuwu* exchanges have become increasingly more important, the extended kin group has ceased to serve as the political framework for village organization, having been supplanted by state and church bureaucracies. If *posintuwu* exchanges have ceased to solidify the extended kin group, what function do they now serve? I would argue that the change in meaning of *posintuwu* exchanges can be related to the extended kin group's continued economic role in providing 'subsistence insurance' through 'shared poverty.' This economic function is not predicated upon endogamy within the extended kin group although endogamy continues to serve as a valued cultural norm. While the quasi-corporate group, the sibling set, has retained its central social importance, the extended kin group is becoming increasingly marginal in determining the alliances between these sibling sets. In arranging and approving marriages, endogamy within the extended kin group is now of secondary importance to other class-related factors. *Kabosenya* are no longer concerned to solidify their extended kin group through arranged endogamous marriages, although arranged marriages remain important in maintaining class ties with other *kabosenya*. That is, *kabosenya* desire their children to 'marry well,' appropriate to their status, so that they can provide their parents with a comfortable life in their old age. What had once been a means of establishing political alliances between leaders in a classless society has been translated into the means by which a landholding class consolidated itself.

The wedding feast and its attendant *posintuwu* exchanges thus play a central role in the constitution of these new class groups. This process, however, has been allowed to develop only within the constraints set by government and mission. The feast is thus an ideal arena within which to examine the articulation of these various interests. The wedding feast is the only instance of a ceremony that is an amalgam of the civil, *adat*, and religious; all other feasts are explicitly religious affairs (*kebaktian*). This is an indication of how successful the church has been in 'inculturating' itself and creating a 'Christian *adat*.' This transformation of the *adat* has had equal effect on the remnants, such as the wedding, purposefully left outside the religious sphere. Although the government and missionaries approached *adat* from two angles, both approaches have tended to emphasize structure over practice in their definitions; that is, to emphasize rules and liturgies over political process and practice. As the church has successfully incorporated feasting, the *adat* has increasingly come to be defined in terms of a set of formal actions stripped of their larger cosmological significance (cf. Steedly 1993, 70). *Adat* manuals (Magido 1987; Santo et al. 1990; Sigilipu 1993), following the mission lead, have defined *adat* in terms of 'liturgies.' There are no explanations of feast organization or of *posintuwu*, and that which is described above as a political process has been specifically excluded. The cosmological significance of feasting is noted only in the numerous theological theses written by ministers-in-training that draw out biblical parallels for current feasting practice (for example, see Gintu 1991 and Tanggerahi 1983). The liturgical encapsulation of feasting is discussed more fully in the next chapter.

The remainder of this chapter elaborates on these basic distinctions and how they have developed. The first section provides a brief synopsis of the 'liturgy' of the wedding feast and how it developed and has changed over the last eighty-five years (cf. Pemberton 1994, 197–235). The remainder of the chapter examines those aspects of the wedding feast that are specifically excluded from this 'liturgy.' The *posintuwu* exchange system is presented in the second section, followed by a discussion of the other means by which patrons exert their control over the social reproduction of their kin groups, and the changes that have resulted from new class dynamics and household forms. The final section describes the strategies utilized by the government, church, and To Pamona to control the kinship and class networks created through the wedding feast.

The 'Traditional' Marriage Process

The marriage process is composed of a number of high-status ceremonies. None of these ceremonies is obligatory, save the civil registration of the marriage with the local *camat* (subdistrict head), which is sanctioned by law. The costs of these ceremonies is such that the successful completion of the whole series forms a test of the financial strength of both families. The inability to complete even one of these ceremonies may have grave implications for the match; at worst, the wedding itself may be cancelled. It is important to emphasize, however, that the size of any of these ceremonies is relative, dependent upon the demands of the bride's parents and in keeping with their abilities and status.

The process is put in motion when the potential groom's parents agree to send a formal marriage proposal (*meoa*) to the parents of the prospective bride. They will organize the first of the numerous deliberative meetings (*gombo*) that mark this cycle of ceremonies. This meeting is intended to obtain the approval of their extended kin group for the proposed match. The parents play only a small public role within these deliberations, which are left to the kin group's *kabosenya* (although few would choose to use that term today). The extended kin group of both parents will be invited, representing four kin groups (i.e., the surviving extended kin groups of the four grandparents of the groom). Members of the *adat* council (*dewan adat*), a group of elected community members knowledgeable in *adat* ceremonies, must also be present. A high-status family member (not the parents) will lead the deliberations. The groom is usually in the kitchen, in the back of the house, and is not normally included in the discussion. This practice made any individual the worst source of information about the organizational details of his or her own wedding. Such matters were the concern of those who were already married, and hence recognized social actors.

The initial point of concern is whether the proposed marriage is permissible. The ideal partner should be *popotu* (a relative of the same generation). Marrying a second cousin is permissible with payment of a fine, although a third cousin is preferred. Marriage between generations is generally discouraged and some types of match are forbidden: a man may not marry a classificatory aunt (although a woman may marry a classificatory uncle) or someone of the grandparental generation. The deliberations are complicated, however, by the cognatic nature of To Pamona kinship and the resultant multiplicity of possible kinship relationships between the potential bride and groom. These rules are applied against the four doors/sides (*aopo nculapa*). That is, a relationship is sought between each of the candidates' parents: groom's father to bride's father, groom's mother to bride's mother, groom's father to bride's mother, groom's mother to bride's father. Should a undesirable degree of relationship be found in any one of these 'sides' (*sanculapa*), the marriage is still permissible with payment of a fine of one piece of cloth. This fine is raised if undesirable degrees of relationship are found on more than one side: two pieces of cloth if two of the sides are related, a pig if three, and a water buffalo if four. Some formerly forbidden marriages (as with a classificatory grandparent) are now allowed with a fine of a water buffalo. It is important to emphasize that none of these prohibitions is legally binding, and payment of the fines is voluntary. Failure to pay the fine simply precludes an *adat* wedding. Civil and religious ceremonies may be performed, as they follow different rules.

The degree of relationship and the desirability of the match ascertained, other factors now come into play. The potential groom is summoned from his hiding place and questioned about his relationships with the potential bride and other women with whom he was known to mix (*momungge*, 'woo'). The express purpose of the questioning is to establish if either the potential bride or another woman is pregnant. If the potential bride is pregnant, the formal proposal process cannot be followed and the two must be summarily married as soon as possible. Should it become apparent that another woman is pregnant by the potential groom after the formal proposal has been sent, the groom's kin will be fined and the marriage may be cancelled.

If the deliberations favour the match, the formal proposal package will then be prepared by one of the members of the *adat* council. This package (*peoa*) contains all the ingredients for chewing sirih, a traditional offering made to guests: seven areca nuts, seven sirih pods or leaves, lime, tobacco and gambier are placed inside a metal container (*salapa*). It is also increasingly common for the proposal package to contain a gold necklace or ring for the potential bride, to signify that she is now 'tied' by the proposal. All of these objects are carefully wrapped within a *koli mbua*, the dried, paper-like base of an areca-palm frond. The bundle must be tied together with a strand of rattan wrapped fourteen times, and knotted seven times, around the package. The proposal must be carefully packaged and its contents unblemished, since any deviation from the prescribed norm is just cause for refusing the proposal. The aesthetics of a proposal package are of considerable interest to the potential bride's kin; a carefully prepared and wrapped package is an indication of the respect of the groom's kin.

The meeting concludes with the selection of the seven individuals who will deliver the formal proposal. The group is led by at least one member of the *adat* council accompanied by other prominent family members. The group cannot include the potential groom or his parents. They will set the date for delivering the proposal and the length of time allowed before an answer is expected. Acceptance of the proposal is signified by opening the package, and this must be done before the contents have rotted. The potential bride's family thus have a maximum of a month to either accept or return the proposal package or face a fine of a water buffalo. This may be the last meeting of the groom's family until the day preceding the wedding.

The seven individuals selected to deliver the proposal will collect at the potential groom's parents' house early in the morning on the appointed day. The recipient of the proposal (not the bride's parents) has by this time been informed that a proposal will be delivered. Delivering the proposal is potentially the most expensive element of the proposal process since the groom's family is hoping to make as good an impression as possible. Since this will be the first formal meeting between the two families, the group should be dressed in expensive *adat* costume; at the very least, the leader, and the young girl who actually bears the proposal package in a sarong on her back, must be in costume. This girl's parents and siblings must all be living, a symbol of the groom's family's hopes for prosperity for the new couple. After breakfast, the group will be brought by taxi to the home of the potential bride's representative. The taxi fare for the group to even nearby (60 kilometres away) villages can equal some families' monthly income. The bride's representative is usually the village mayor or one of the *adat* council, who will be joined by a member of the bride's kin group (but not by her or her parents). They are the ones who will actually deliver the proposal package to the bride's parents.

Although the purpose of the meeting had been established beforehand, the subject of the proposal should ideally be approached through inference and metaphor. The guests will be offered sirih (which few chew any longer) and tobacco in an exaggerated show of hospitality by the potential bride's representative. Traditionally, the potential groom's representative would broach the subject of the proposal with *kayori* (verse), asking if there was still forest land that could be cleared for a new garden. The verbal skills of the messenger, like the *adat* costume, bespeak the groom's family's seriousness and desire to honour the bride's family. The proposal package will be produced from within the sarong, and its recipient named. The reception of the proposal is always non-committal, although respect is shown the bearers by placing the package in a covered woven basket. The meeting is then over. If the group has come any distance at all, the bride's kin group (but not the parents) will then provide lunch and the group will return home.

If the bride's parents are at all serious about accepting the proposal, they will arrange an 'opening' ceremony (*mabulere peoa*) within the allotted time. The opening ceremony mirrors the groom's proposal ceremony. The representatives of the bride's extended kin group are summoned, and their approval for the match sought. Like the groom's family, they will explore the 'four sides' for undesirable degrees of relationship between the two candidates. Other factors may also enter into the discussion of whether to open the proposal package. For example, an outstanding argument between any of the bride and groom's kin members may be enough to prevent the proposal being made (by the groom's kin), or accepted (by the bride's kin). Although the parents of the candidates may subvert this opposition by subsequently arranging another *gombo*, to which they purposefully do not invite the objecting kinsman, such tactics carry heavy costs. First, the permanent enmity of the kinsman may be incurred since their exclusion from the ceremony is a denial of the kinship relationship and its obligations. Second, such tactics often necessitate moving the wedding feast to another location, where the objecting kinsman will not immediately learn of it. This may lead to the humiliation of the groom's kin having to host a wedding feast at which they should be guests.

Should no objections to the match be found, the bride will be summoned and asked if she finds the proposal acceptable. This is an innovation. Kruyt records that traditional marriage negotiations often occurred without the knowledge of the bride (Adriani and Kruyt 1912–14, 2: 26–7). However, both church and civil marriage ceremonies are predicated upon marriage being a voluntary contract of the couple. Seeking the potential bride's sentiments regarding the proposal is a token acknowledgment of this situation. When she is asked, the bride's coy answer should be 'as my parents wish.' Parents and kin thus have the potential to exert tremendous control over marriage, either by refusing to open a proposal package from an unacceptable candidate, or by restricting the child's selection of a spouse to one from a number of parentally approved candidates. Regardless of some parents' stated openness to whomever their child selected, all emphasized that the child's desires were easily thwarted. It is, they argued, disappointment with the *adat* process that leads many young people to get pregnant on purpose, thus forcing their parents' approval of the marriage even if at the cost of embarrassing them, and the village, to whom *adat* fines must then be paid.

After all sides have expressed their approval, an older member of the family will be invited to unwrap the proposal package. The tying technique and contents of the package are carefully examined and are of considerable interest to those attending. A respected woman close to the bride will then take the necklace or ring from the package and place it on the bride. A member of the *adat* council will address the bride, admonishing her to avoid contact with any men, including the groom. The intent of the admonitions and restrictions on her behaviour are to forestal pregnancy, which would result in a fine from the groom's family. The meeting ends with the selection of a number of representatives who will bear the news to the groom's parents. They will also bear the list of the bride's family's bridewealth demands (*bila-bila*).

In the pre-colonial period no such list was necessary, and the bridewealth was indicated by specifying its 'basis' (*pu'u oli*). The bridewealth consists of the *sampapitu* (the 'seven'), and the *wawo oli* (that above the price). The *sampapitu* was the 'magical' part of the bridewealth. Although the items composing the 'seven' varied throughout the highlands, it usually consisted of a copper plate and spiritually powerful cloth (*kolokompa*). The *wawo oli* also varied, depending on the rank of the bride's mother; but, in the Tentena area, it was specified by its basis (*pu'u*), a pig or a water buffalo. This animal formed the first *wia* (counter) of the *wawo oli*. If the basis is a pig, then the *wawo oli* consists of thirty *wia*; if a water buffalo, seventy *wia*. The *wia* have no fixed equivalents but are usually pieces of cloth or other trade goods (*ayapa*). The larger the bridewealth, the greater the status of the bride. Since the exact nature of the *wia* is not specified, even the value of a small bridewealth can be increased with expensive items, to make up for the smaller number of *wia*. Bridewealth inflation is common and it has become increasingly rare to see a pig offered as the basis since the *adat* council determined that a money equivalent could be offered in place of the real thing. This arbitrary sum has not kept up with inflation or the actual cost of either a water buffalo or a pig. As the actual cost of a pig has approached the *adat* valuation of a water buffalo, more and more grooms request permission to change the basis of the bridewealth they pay and so claim a water buffalo for the price of a pig.

The bridewealth specified by the *adat* is forming an increasingly smaller part of the demands of the bride's family. The list of their demands also specifies the financial aid they expect for the wedding. This consists of contributions of money, rice, and meat animals for the feast as well as the 'household basics' for the new couple. The conception of 'household basic' has changed from a machete and clump of sago palm trees, to include a bed, sheets, cupboard, wash stand, and mosquito netting. The total costs born by the groom for a moderately sized wedding may easily reach Rp. 1,000,000 ($666 Can. in 1990) in an area where a very good wage would be $116 (Can.) per month.

By the time of the wedding day, both the bride's and the groom's families will have built temporary extensions to their houses to shelter the expected guests (i.e., the *To Popawawa*, or groom's family). The bride's extended family act as hosts and are referred to as the 'waiters' (*To Peta'a*). The dual meaning of the term in English aptly sums up their role: they 'wait for' the groom's coming, and 'wait on' his procession (although the term has only the first meaning). Most of the *To Peta'a* will have work assignments, although the higher the status of the individual the more likely they are to play a supervisory role.

The groom and his procession are referred to as the *To Popawawa* (the bringers). Perhaps the most important change in the wedding feast is the number of *To Popawawa*. Traditionally, there were two kinds of wedding ceremonies, and only the second was marked by a large feast. The first type of wedding, *mopawawa* (to bring), was a low-key affair in which a low-status groom and the *sampapitu* were brought to the bride's house with only the simplest of ceremonies. The minimum number of *To Popawawa* was seven, and hence the attendant feast small. The payment of the *wawo oli* was deferred to a later date, usually the birth of the first child. The second type of wedding, *mebolai* (to approach the bride's house) was similar in form, but marked by greater ostentation. The term specifically refers to the fact that all of the bridewealth is paid at the time of the wedding. This type of wedding was adopted by wealthier, higher-status families and marked by conspicuous consumption. The demands of the bride's family were greater and designed to test (and publicly demonstrate) the ability of the groom's kin group to pay. The groom's cortège would be stopped along the way (*mobolombongi*) and allowed to pass only on payment of a piece of cotton cloth to a representative of the bride's family. This ritual is performed a predetermined number of times before the cortège reaches the bride's family. The groom's cortège was also numerically larger, demonstrating the size of his kin group. All weddings now follow this second pattern to a greater or lesser degree, which is an indication of the general devaluation of bridewealth. Although technically *mebolai*, they are universally referred to as *mopawawa*. Most kin groups can now afford to pay all of the bridewealth at the time of the wedding, and their cortèges include from 100 to 1,500 people each.

The groom's *santina* will collect at his parents' house, where they will be fed before the trip. If the wedding is in another village, the groom's kin will be brought either to a nearby kinsman's house, where another temporary shelter has been prepared, or to the village *baruga* (town meeting hall). There, the *To Peta'a* will serve the guests refreshments. Women in *adat* costume will first serve the prominent leaders of the groom's kin group with sirih (and sometimes tobacco) from small baskets. The servers must be compensated with some small token, usually money. This 'traditional' welcome (*mepamongoka*) and sign of hospitality is followed by a score of young people in their Sunday best performing the more mundane task of providing the rest of the guests with coffee and cookies. This pattern – of *adat* ceremony for high-status guests followed by the modern functional equivalent for the rest of the guests – continues throughout the wedding.

The official welcome over, the groom and his kin form a procession to the bride's house. The official procession consists of the groom and seven people, all of whom must be dressed in *adat* costume. This procession consists of a leader (*tadulako*) who precedes the group and serves as its intermediary with the bride's family, an umbrella bearer to shade the groom, his parents, and the bearers of the *sampapitu*, his sword (or machete), and his bag. This procession is also accompanied by a number of young men continuously playing gongs and, further behind, the rest of the groom's kin group. Those who are not part of the 'seven' wear their best Sunday clothes. The groom and his *tadulako* will be greeted by the *tadulako* of the bride's family and brought inside the house to the bridal chamber. The bride is locked inside this room with a number of attendants, who have decked her out in the finest *adat* costume. The groom must knock on the door three times, demanding entry. This is refused until the *tadulako* throws a piece of cloth (sometimes money) over the door as compensation to the bride's attendants (*mobolombongi*). This is a tense moment; if the attendants are not pleased with the gift (usually when too small a sum of money has been substituted for the piece of cloth), they may refuse to open the door. When finally granted access, the groom enters the room and claims his bride. Not touching, and suitably subdued, they are escorted to the *baruga*, where the bridewealth will be paid. This is another innovation, in that traditionally the exchange of the bridewealth did not require their presence, and preceded the groom claiming his bride. This alteration was made to accommodate the requirements of the civil registration of the marriage, usually performed at the same time as the exchange of the bridewealth; the civil registration, unlike the surrender of bridewealth, requires the couple's presence.

On reaching the *baruga*, the bride and groom will first be seated in chairs, facing the *camat* (subdistrict head). The civil registration of the marriage requires that the *camat* read the text of the 1975 regulations for the performance of the 1974 marriage law (Peraturan Pemerintah Republik Indonesia No. 9 Tahun 1975 tentang Pelaksanaan Undang-Undang No. 1 Tahun 1974 tentang Perkawinan; see Bakry 1978) and ask if the marriage is freely entered into. The simple ceremony concludes with the signing of the marriage certificate. If the couple live close to the district capital, the civil registration of the marriage may be completed several days before.

The civil ceremony over, the chairs will be cleared away, and the bride's and groom's parents and their representatives will assume positions on mats on the floor, facing one another. They are separated by the bride and groom on one side, and the village mayor (as chairman of the *adat* council) and another member of the *adat* council facing them. The village mayor, dressed in his civil-service uniform, stands out in these transactions marked by colourful *adat* costume. Only the *sampapitu* will be given at this point; this is to spare the feelings of those being married at the same time whose *wawo oli* may be considerably less. The transfer of the *wawo oli* forms the centrepiece of the *resepsi* (reception) that is to follow. There, the generosity of the groom's kin can be displayed to its intended audience, the bride's kin.

The transfer of the bridewealth (*mojiji oli*), like that of the proposal, is carried out through intermediaries, the *tadulako* who led the marriage procession. These *tadulako* should be 'well versed in,' that is, competent in, the *kayori* (verse) that accompany the surrender of the bridewealth. The groom's side will spread out two woven mats between themselves and the bride's side and count out 'the seven.' Until recently, each of the seven items had to be counted using its *adat* name. These names varied between village confederations. An Indonesian government–sponsored *adat* council decreed that, in the name of unifying the *adat* of the area, these names could no longer be used. 'The seven' would simply be counted. This has elicited widespread resentment, and some areas refuse to follow government dictate. All fines incurred by the couple must also be paid at this point. The *sampapitu* will then be wrapped in the uppermost mat by the bride's *tadulako*, while the groom's *tadulako* will retrieve the bottom mat. The ceremony completed, the village mayor and the member of the *adat* council will prepare the *adat* marriage certificate. This document mirrors both civil and religious marriage certificates and is also a recent innovation.

The bride and groom, still looking subdued, will now return to their respective houses and prepare for the church wedding. The church wedding contrasts sharply with the *adat* ceremonies that preceded it and would not look out of place in the Netherlands. The bride and groom change from *adat* costume into suit and resplendent white bridal gown for a wedding ceremony, whose liturgy follows that of the Dutch Reformed Church. The church ceremony is not widely attended since a number of couples are married together and their combined wedding parties could easily overflow the church. The scheduling of the day's activities usually fixes the church wedding for mid-afternoon, the hottest point of the day and the general rest period. The bride's family, burdened with the logistics of preparing the feast, will take advantage of the rest period, since the reception may go on into the small hours of the night. As a result, only the immediate families of the bride and groom who have no feast-related duties will attend.

Following the completion of the wedding, the bride and groom will return to the bride's house for the reception (*resepsi*). As the name indicates, the reception is a modern (*maju*) innovation, a reworking of two older ceremonies. The first of these ceremonies was the *polimbu,* a general term for all communal meals. The rice for such meals may be cooked by individual households, but the meat is cooked communally, and this is what sets the meal off as a feast. Pigs and water buffaloes were slaughtered only on these occasions, and the meat used to prepare a special feast food, *beko,* a stew containing boiled meat and finely chopped up banana tree. It is considered the pinnacle of To Pamona cuisine. During the *polimbu,* the *tadulako* of the groom's kin would offer the new couple advice on the proper behaviour of a spouse (*mepatuju*).

At the turn of the century, a number of couples normally wed on the same day and held a *polimbu* in common. The missionaries originally held these *polimbu* in the church itself, the church thus becoming a functional replacement for the traditional site of the *polimbu* – the *lobo*, or village temple. By the 1930s, the feasts were moved off premises, to the new village meeting halls (*baruga*) out of 'respect' for the church building. By the 1950s, as more and more grooms followed the *mebolai* marriage pattern, with a larger number of guests, higher-status individuals would choose to marry on their own. As the only couple being married that day, they had no competition for guests or labour, and could hold as large a feast as their circumstances allowed. Alternatively, combining weddings on a single day became a conscious strategy for limiting the expense of a wedding, since the cost of the slaughtered animals would be borne by a number of families. Yet, as even poorer families found they could afford to *mebolai*, they began to hold separate *polimbu.* A number of weddings might still be held on the same day to limit the number of guests (and attendant costs), but each would have its *polimbu* at the bride's house. It was at this point that the *resepsi* was introduced, during the early 1970s.

The *resepsi* is a combination of the *polimbu* and another ceremony, the *mompaore* (to bring up), in which the bride and groom climbed up (in the old stilt houses) to the bridal chamber, where they received special instruction. During the *mompaore*, the couple would again be publicly regaled with advice (*mepatuju*), this time by the bride's *tadulako*. The couple would then be shown the bridal chamber (*mantuju paturua*). Two or three elders would bring the couple into the bedroom and explain the proper basis of a marriage. The *paturua* (bridal chamber), they would be told, was the basis of the *sombori*. No one else was allowed within that chamber, including their parents, without their permission. They were never to publicly argue, but to first discuss all their plans together in the bedroom. They were to impartially treat their in-laws as their own parents; if the couple argued, the groom should turn to his in-laws for help, and the bride to hers. After this advice was given, the couple would resume their seats with the other guests, although they switched positions, now sitting with their respective in-laws to indicate their incorporation in their spouse's kin group. The bride's family would close the ceremony with a public apology for any shortcoming in their hospitality. After nightfall, a ring dance (*dero*) would take place. The groom would usually participate, although the bride would not.

Since the early 1970s, the *polimbu* and the *mompaore* have been combined in the *resepsi*. As the word indicates, the reception, like the church wedding, attempts to emulate *maju* (modern) Western norms. This set of practices was first adopted by urban Christians, particularly those from Minahasa in North Sulawesi, and has slowly made inroads in the rural areas. The changes introduced were implemented at the time of the New Order government's first large-scale national development plans. The emphasis on modernization extended beyond agricultural development projects and included *kebudayaan* (culture). The *polimbu*, in which guests ate with their fingers from leaf plates, was thus transformed into a buffet with plates, cutlery, and printed invitations. A similar attempt was made to modernize *adat* costume. What had once simply been clothing was transformed into 'high culture' as Western dress became the norm. This *adat* costume was similarly subject to the new modernizing aesthetic sensibilities. Thus, the short pants of old, now associated with primary-school uniforms, were replaced with trousers. More colourful and plush materials were used, and designs created using sequins instead of paint.

The *resepsi* further differs from the old-style *polimbu* in that it focuses upon the bridal couple. As more and more families followed the high-status *mebolai* marriage form, they held their own *polimbu* at the bride's house rather than communally at the *baruga*. The bride and groom and their parents were now set off from their guests by their colourful *adat* costume and by an increasingly ornate podium in front of their guests. This raised podium and the *adat* costumes are indicative of a change from 'practice to spectacle.' That is, the modernizing aesthetic that now infuses *adat* practice has transformed the value of 'tradition' from 'a matter of practice ... [to] become a matter of consciously adhering to prescribed ceremonial, of performing ritual and acting in accord with an etiquette deemed valuable though not exclusive in its claims to adherence' (Acciaioli 1985, 152; cf. Pemberton 1994, 234–5). Young people seeking to marry a parentally proscribed candidate are quick to point out that the *adat* wedding is only a *pro forma* requirement that can be completed at a later date, while a civil ceremony is all that is legally required. By modernizing the *adat*, specific elements (e.g., *adat* costume, the transfer of bridewealth) have been selected as representative of 'tradition' and placed on display, transformed into spectacle. The assembled guests themselves engage in new social and cultural forms, and watch (rather than participate in) the traditional ceremonies performed before them. Their own appreciation of the spectacle is moulded by its adherence to the 'liturgy' defined by *adat* manuals. This liturgy is increasingly focused on the actions of the bridal couple, their parents, and the *adat* council, leaving their audience free to engage in other activities.

The reception incorporates not only the *polimbu*, but also the transfer of the bridewealth and the giving of advice in the bridal chamber. Since almost all families now follow the *mebolai* marriage pattern, the transfer of bridewealth is performed at the time of the wedding, usually during the reception. The spectacle of the groom's payment of the bridewealth is played out on the 'stage' created by the bride's family; that is, the amount of bridewealth is evaluated by the audience against the number of guests hosted by the bride's family. The mechanics of the transfer of the bridewealth is similar to the earlier transfer of the *sampapitu*. However, more effort is put into the payment of the bridewealth, especially if it is large. *Kayori* will be recited, and speakers evaluated for their cleverness in both delivering and receiving the bridewealth. The emphasis, however, is not on upstaging but on equalling the bridal spectacle. I have seen a well-versed *tadulako* deliver his bridewealth in plain prose rather than embarrass the unprepared representative of the bride. On the other hand, if the amount of bridewealth is large and the guests numerous, the shortcomings of the speakers will reflect badly on the very spectacle they have attempted to create. After the bridewealth has been paid, the bride's kin makes a big show of transferring the bolts of cloth hand over hand into the house. This cloth will later be distributed among the bride's *santina* and those who helped with the wedding.

The reception is also increasingly being used as an opportunity to perform another *adat* marriage requirement, the *motela'a* (first visit of the bride). This ceremony, in which the bride enters the house of her in-laws for the first time, traditionally occurred a few weeks after the wedding. Its incorporation in the reception is an attempt to limit the costs of bringing together and feeding large numbers of guests so soon after the major expense of the wedding. The purpose of the ceremony is to complete the 'exchange of parents' (*motolo ine, motolo papa*) called for in the bridal chamber. During this ceremony, the mother of the groom gives a piece of cloth (the *papepone*, invitation to come up) to the bride to signify she accepts her daughter-in-law as one of her own children. This is followed by the gift of a basket containing a knife and a pinang nut (used in chewing sirih) as her invitation to sit within the house. Having received these gifts, the bride is to consider her mother-in-law's hearth as her own and to assist her there as one of her own daughters. These gifts may now be given during the reception, or, as in the past, held on a separate occasion with the attendance of as large a group of the couple's kin as they can afford.

In this overview of the *adat* marriage process, I have emphasized changes that have occurred over the last ninety years. These changes can be summarized in terms of three general processes. The first process, 'bridewealth inflation,' refers to the increasing value of the bridewealth itself, the universal adoption of the *mebolai* marriage form, and the increasing size of the marriage feast. Marriage ceremonies have evolved from relatively minor feasts into major 'rituals of social location' that draw on symbols and practices whose relevance lies less in tradition than in larger national cultural policies (Millar 1989; cf. Pemberton 1994, 235). Bridewealth inflation is thus bracketed within yet another process, that of the reification of *adat* and the creation of spectacle. *Adat* has been transformed from *the* way of getting married, into an optional set of rule-bound ceremonies that can be performed for a host of other reasons, such as garnering status; it is now only *one* of many ways of getting married. The *adat* wedding plays off of both church and civil weddings, imitating their forms by defining official liturgies and issuing marriage certificates, and yet, is consciously utilized to express particularly local concerns in opposition to the universalizing forms of church and state. Lastly, in so far as the *adat* wedding has been reduced to a liturgical performance, its *audience* has been freed from the *adat* restrictions by which they judge the spectacle; the actions of the majority of guests occur outside the narrow *adat* rules that prescribe the behaviours of the bride, groom, their parents and *tadulakos*. The performance of the *adat* liturgy has become the occasion for a feast but does not dictate the form of the feast itself, with its committees, *posintuwu* exchanges, buffets, and bands. The feast goes on as a sideshow, as it were, enacted by the audience before the gaze of the *adat* ceremony participants. These last two processes, the creation of *adat* spectacle and the modernization of feasting as distinct from this *adat* spectacle, are significant in that they parallel a similar bifurcation of ritual practice within the church. The church liturgy is similarly performed within the context of feasting, yet carefully distinguished from it. In the rest of this chapter and the next, I discuss further how feasting has come to be linked with specific forms of liturgical performance (whether *adat* or religious liturgies), and hence the major means by which the church has inculturated itself.

Posintuwu

Posintuwu exchanges are an aspect of feasting that lie outside the officially sanctioned *adat* wedding liturgy. There is little or no mention of *posintuwu* exchanges in either mission or *adat* manuals, and government publications generally subsume it under the national rubric *gotong royong* (mutual assistance). The exchange of *posintuwu* is thus particularly open to the expression of local concerns outside the explicit framework of *adat* law or the church. In earlier chapters, the role of *posintuwu* exchanges in constituting kinship ties was noted. The emergence of 'kin labour' in opposition to the commodification of the agricultural economy was also described. In this section, these two aspects of kinship are linked as they appear in feasting, showing how *posintuwu* networks simultaneously establish kinship as a distinct ideological sphere in which economic calculation should not enter, as well as establishing relations of hierarchy and subordination between particular individuals (cf. Ferguson 1994, 135–66).

In the previous chapter I discussed how 'shared poverty' in the highlands is expressed in the idiom of *posintuwu*. Given the inclusive nature of the metaphors through which kinship is expressed, it is important to delineate the range of meanings of *posintuwu* and the groups of people to whom they apply. In emphasizing the inclusive nature of kinship (by which it shades into other terms such as friendship), the communal aspect of engaging in these practices (*mosintuwu*) is highlighted. The manner of one's participation is, however, determined by one's relationship to the host. A distant relative may *mosintuwu* through attendance at a feast. Closer family (*santina*) may materially contribute to the feast with rice or meat animals. Lastly, one's near kin (in a geographic, emotive, or genealogical sense) will contribute labour as well. The degree of one's contribution is thus indicative of both inclusion and kinship distance.

The exchange of material contributions is of particular importance since the amount of these contributions determines the size of the feast, and hence the status of the host. Every feast carries the inherent risk that the preparations will be inadequate for the number of people who attend. This disaster implies stinginess and a past failure to *mosintuwu*. The ideal is to apologize for the meagerness of one's offerings but have enough food to send home with as many people as possible. Each host must thus carefully judge how extensive an exchange network he or she will maintain. Their own material circumstances place a limit on the number of their own contributions, and hence on the number of people from whom they can expect a return contribution. Their own material circumstances determine the breadth of those they consider close kin. Wealthier households usually boast more extensive exchange networks and count more people as close relatives. The wealthy are also more likely to sponsor the weddings of relatives other than their own children.

There is an inherent tension in *posintuwu* exchange between its generalized and balanced elements. Theorists of exchange have increasingly argued that the model of 'economic man' that underlies the notion of 'balanced exchange' assumes that return gifts are made to pay off initial gifts and that such an evaluation can be made only once the exchange relationship has been ended. Following Mauss (1970 [1925]), they have come to emphasize that such reciprocal gift exchange is not based upon balance of value (which implies closure) so much as upon the reproduction of social relations through things exchanged (Weiner 1980). A *posintuwu* exchange is not balanced in the sense that a gift given must be reciprocated in equal measure, but in that a failure to reciprocate implies an end of the relationship. My informants emphasized that *posintuwu* was ideally a free gift. Giving such a gift was a risk and one could not demand a return *payment*, or even expect a gift of equal value. They emphasized that such calculation was unbecoming among kin. Such ideological expressions of motivations must, however, be examined as part of a longer exchange history. Individually, each gift is made in generalized terms, freely and without calculation of return. Yet, the person who receives such a gift will remember and feel an obligation to reciprocate *only* if he or she wishes to maintain a relationship with that *posintuwu* partner. Hence, one man explained that he denied his relationship with one set of relatives by refusing to send *posintuwu*. Another neighbour noted that, over the years, he had given five bolts of cloth for the bridewealth of others, and that his aims had been magnanimous; yet when his own son married, 'All five bolts came home! Not one was lost!'

However, models of exchange based upon the 'rational' decision-making calculus of 'economic man' have had increased salience as the local economy has been commodified. Villagers themselves feel this tension between the balanced and the generalized aspects of *posintuwu* exchange, which they say reflects the different motives of the participants. It was common for elders to decry current practice with reference to the *buku posintuwu*, the notebook in which the hosts of wedding or funeral feasts transcribe the names of donors and the amount of their gifts. These elders claim that in the old days one gave what one had without calculation. The offer was made in a public meeting before one's kin group, where one's generosity could be seen. Now, they claim, *posintuwu* (consisting of money) is slipped into envelopes and written in books so that the host will know exactly how much he or she must match in return. According to

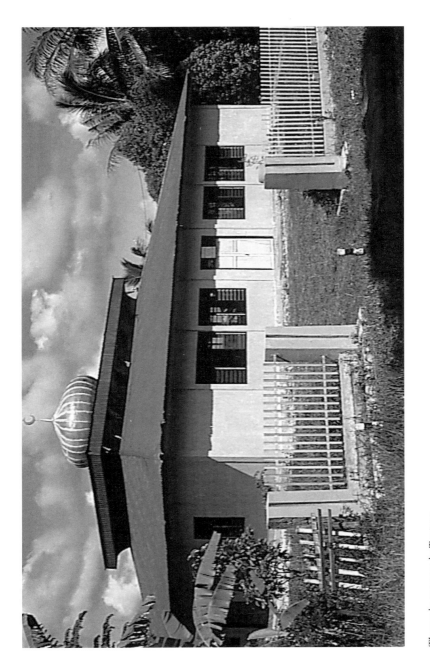

The main mosque in Tentena.

Gereja Moria (the main church in Tentena).

Preparing a wedding proposal.

Throwing cloth over the door to gain admission to the bride.

Paying the brideprice (*pu'u oli*).

The church wedding.

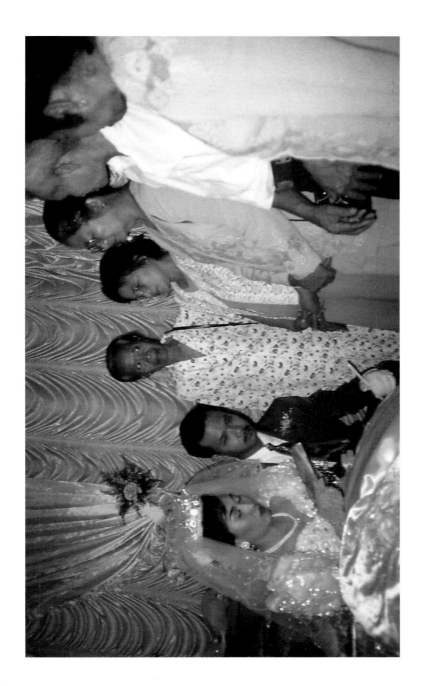

Bride and groom receiving advice in the *paturua*.

Butchering a pig for the feast.

these elders, there has been a noticeable shift from generalized to balanced reciprocity, as evidenced by the gift books.

My younger informants denied this shift in attitude, explaining that the account books were an innovation tailored to a type of *posintuwu* that is itself an innovation. Only *posintuwu umum* (general gifts) are recorded in the gift books. *Posintuwu umum* refers to the numerous small (but hardly negligible) gifts made by more distant family and neighbours. These gift amount to the daily wage for an agricultural worker (i.e., Rp. 3,500 or less, or its equivalent in rice). Poorer families, I noted, gave little *posintuwu umum* outside of their small circle of neighbours. According to my informants, the paradox of *posintuwu umum* is that it is these smaller gifts which are recorded; one farmer bitterly pointed out that it was obvious people didn't check their gift books when making their gifts since he had given a neighbour a sizable gift and had received only *posintuwu umum* in return. Others pointed out that, because the amounts were fairly standard, they gave all that they had on hand, and even borrowed if they had nothing. They referred to their books only when making a return gift to someone who was 'a lazy gift giver.' Such individuals are known to be stingy, not just with their gifts, but also with their participation. Poverty was taken into account as an obviating factor, and those who had little to give often donated inordinate amounts of labour instead.

The emergence of *posintuwu umum* is closely tied to the colonial government's incursions in the marriage process. The colonial government made the village mayor responsible for the delivery of all marriage proposals and for the arrangements for the subsequent mass weddings. In the pre-colonial era, *posintuwu* was collected only by the groom's family for the purpose of bridewealth (*mogulele*). In the colonial period it became the mayor's responsibility to canvas the villagers (including non-kin) for contributions on behalf of the groom. These village-wide contributions formed the basis for *posintuwu umum*. These efforts were clearly supplementary to those of the groom's family itself, who continued to collect bridewealth among their extended kin group for the bulk of the bridewealth. Under Indonesian rule, these colonial incursions into wedding planning have been extended by subsuming *posintuwu umum* under the national rubric *gotong royong* (mutual aid). Bowen has documented how the political construction of this national universal category 'has become a key element in the Indonesian system of political and cultural power through three continuing processes: (1) the motivated misrecognition of local cultural realities; (2) the construction of a national tradition on the basis of those misrecognitions; and (3) the inclusion of state cultural representations as part of a strategy of intervention in the rural sector and the mobilization of rural labor' (1986, 545). The political implications of the subsumption of *posintuwu* exchange to this national category are discussed in the final section; here I continue to focus on the indigenous appropriation of the new 'tradition.'

Posintuwu umum has become of importance only as more and more individuals followed the *mebolai* marriage pattern. *Posintuwu* has been transformed from a means to collect bridewealth *by the groom's family*, to a means of holding the feast *by the bride's family*. The key to the transformation was the 'motivated misrecognition' of feasting and its relationship to *posintuwu* exchange.

The responsibilities of the bride's family for the marriage feast had traditionally been small, and differed from others in that it was the only feast at which the guests did not bring at least a portion of their own food. When a feast such as a funeral, thanksgiving (*padungku*), or *mesale* (labour exchange) took place, the host provided only the meat, each guest bringing his or her own cooked rice. Because the wedding feast was so small, the bride's family had little trouble providing all the food, including the cooked rice. However, as weddings got larger, the bride's family's resources were taxed beyond their limits. It was at this point that supplementary gifts of rice were sought by the village government to lessen the family's burden under the banner of *gotong royong/ posintuwu*. These small gifts of rice (2–3 kilos) involved the subtle misrecognition of bringing one's own cooked rice for one's own consumption rather than bringing a gift of uncooked rice to be followed by a meal. Although *posintuwu umum* is generally given at weddings at which one is a guest, one's gift of rice is not utilized directly to feed the guests. Rather, these gifts are collected and sold, the money being used to defray the costs of rented dishes, roofing, chairs, and so on.

The image of *posintuwu umum* thus conforms with traditional feasting, although, like the *adat* ceremony itself, the practice has been transformed in the process of modernization. Like the modernization of the wedding ceremony and the creation of an '*adat* spectacle' that allows for such innovations as buffet meals and the use of cutlery, *posintuwu umum* utilizes the idiom of 'tradition' while freeing participants from *adat* restrictions fixed in unchanging 'liturgies.' The traditional markers of feasting, the self-provisioning of rice, the *beko* (a meat dish), and eating together are all preserved in modern form, supplemented by chairs, cutlery, and new types of food. This new type of feasting has become the dominant form, not only in weddings, but also funerals and thanksgiving services.

Of central importance to the creation of this new 'tradition' in the shadow of the liturgies of the *adat* spectacle is its dependence upon the commodity form of the gift; that is, the misrecognition of cooked rice to be eaten for uncooked rice to be sold. Indeed, those who no longer farm frequently give cash instead of rice. One would expect that, in such circumstances, the complaints of the elder generation would be borne out with the calculation of 'balances due' at the completion of every feast. Such attitudes do exist, particularly of those branded lazy gift givers. The *posintuwu* exchange network would then more closely resemble an *arisan* (savings club). *Arisans* are held in conjunction with a number of groups that meet periodically on a rotating basis in the homes of their members, such as the evangelization groups. In an *arisan*, every member makes a contribution to the host. This continues every time the group meets, each host receiving the sum collected on that occasion. When one finally serves as host, the exact sum one gave to the prior hosts is received back from each. A treasurer keeps track of the contributions to ensure balanced reciprocity is maintained.

Despite the invented nature of the tradition, *posintuwu umum* is judged by the criteria of *posintuwu* rather than that of the *arisan*. That is, almost every informant emphasized that the ideal remained that of an unencumbered gift (either in material or in labour) in which the emphasis was placed on the generosity of the giver rather than the obligation to return. Such generous individuals were taken to be natural leaders, the people to whom you could turn for help in other circumstances. Those with large *posintuwu* networks thus tended to be elected to the *adat* or church council, despite deficiencies in their oratory or knowledge of *adat*. In giving their own gifts, my informants all noted they gave more to such individuals. Those who give more thus receive more, although such a 'balanced' result originates in 'generalized' motives.

The application of *posintuwu* ideals to *posintuwu umum* has considerably extended the feasting economy while situating it in opposition to market exchanges. As has already been noted, *posintuwu* was given only at secondary funerals and at weddings. *Posintuwu umum*, however, is given on any feasting occasion to which one is invited and is no longer collected by the village mayor. The pattern of feasting established at weddings has thus been extended to all the larger feasts and led to a general elaboration of the size and types. Feasts are now held as general church-sanctioned thanksgiving services for birthdays, graduations, the construction of a new house, recovery from an illness, and similar situations. Most of my informants felt obligated to bring *posintuwu* whenever they were invited on such occasions. They also felt obligated to hold feasts on similar occasions to maintain a similar level of hospitality, leading to the rapid adoption of feasting innovations.

The creation and extension of *posintuwu umum* according to the ideals of *posintuwu* has implications for the older form, now referred to as *posintuwu keluarga dekat* (*posintuwu* from close family). *Posintuwu* was traditionally given by close family, and gifts from this category of individuals continue to be larger. It is these individuals who are intimately connected with the actual planning of a wedding, with collecting the bridewealth or holding the feast. While *posintuwu umum* is now collected on the day of the feast itself, *posintuwu keluarga dekat* is usually pledged in advance at one of the family's planning meetings (*gombo*). Although the giving of *posintuwu keluarga dekat* has become the defining feature of 'close family,' these boundaries are open to negotiation as more distant ties may be emphasized or denied, or fictive ties created. For example, in one upwardly mobile household where both husband and wife were orphans with small kin groups, new 'family' was discovered in a distant village. No tie was known (or possible),[3] but they shared the same last name. The man made a visit to the eldest member of that family, seeking information about a possible blood tie. When he found her and explained his quest, she cried for several hours before revealing that the previous night she had dreamed she would be visited by lost family. Since that time the two families have exchanged *posintuwu keluarga dekat*. Others with similarly small kin groups have changed their last names to emphasize a tie with a larger distant family – for example, using their great-grandfather's rather than their grandfather's name as their patronym; this extends their 'close' family out another degree.

The more people the hosts can include as close family, the larger the feast they can hold; yet such a strategy carries its own risks. Although a larger feast can be given, it is at the cost of having to make a return gift at a later date to maintain the relationship. Further, indiscriminate invitations provide grist for the gossip mill and are portrayed as grasping. The preparation of invitation lists is of great importance to maintaining one's reputation. Despite these risks, an increasing number of hosts have sought to broaden their network of 'close family' in this manner immediately before a feast in the face of escalating wedding costs. One man specifically attributed the problem to the generally low value of *posintuwu umum*, which was not keeping pace with inflation and reflects a general decline in the standard of living over the past decade.

Posintuwu keluarga dekat is usually pledged at a planning meeting for the wedding. It is the conduct of this meeting that has provided the ideological model for *posintuwu umum*. This meeting is supposed to be characterized by spontaneous displays of generosity. Everyone who attends has come with the specific purpose of pledging a gift. Over the past decade, as more hosts have substantially enlarged their 'close family,' they have also taken to specifying a floor amount for this gift. The high-status host who introduced this practice, well known as a generous gift-giver and community leader, stated that he did so in an attempt to modernize the accounting practices of the wedding. To ensure that the wedding remained within budget, it was essential to have an accurate knowledge of one's resources. The application of accounting principles has, however, led to spirited public debate about the very nature of gift-giving as others have utilized the innovation in a calculated manner to increase contributions to their feasts.

The benefits of specifying a floor value for *posintuwu keluarga dekat* are now often hotly contested. As noted, specifying this value is closely related to extending the boundaries of one's 'close family' as well as the low value of *posintuwu umum*. Many thus view this innovation as an attempt to raise the standard of *posintuwu umum*. Yet those who have adopted the innovation have found that calculation begets calculation, not generosity. Thus, by including more people in their family meeting, the hosts feel obligated to provide hospitality to demonstrate their own generosity in the face of public criticism. The family meeting often turns into a feast itself. After the costs of the meeting are deducted, the increase in *posintuwu* pledged seldom nets more than *posintuwu umum*, while obligating the host to give more to all those he has invited as 'close family.' Attempts to gain status by holding a large feast through the calculated manipulation of invitation lists and *posintuwu* networks inevitably backfired as gossip deflated the host's reputation, and hence the size of future gifts.

The introduction of the floor value for *posintuwu keluarga dekat* has added a degree of calculation to the planning of every wedding feast, even if the host does not set a floor value. Each feast-giver is faced with escalating costs resulting from feasting inflation. Like the community leader noted above, wedding hosts find that the ideal of generosity is 'uneconomic,' that they cannot budget appropriately unless they set a *posintuwu* floor value. They also know that the opportunity cost of setting a floor value may outweigh its benefits. The availability of a choice of gift-giving strategies has thus served to highlight the opposition between generosity and balanced reciprocity, kin and non-kin, *posintuwu* and *maoli* exchanges. It is careful calculation that now leads to the adoption of one strategy over the other, including the decision to be 'generous.' In both cases, however, gift-givers find it to their advantage to emphasize the *posintuwu* ideal of the 'free gift.' To the generous gift-givers eager to maintain their reputation, the ideal of the free gift underscores their magnanimity. To the calculating feast-giver attempting to benefit from the generosity of others, the ideal of the free gift limits the obligation to repay an equal amount.

The tension between the generalized and balanced elements of a single exchange system arises from an ideal of generosity that purposefully ignores the reciprocal aspect of gift giving. Although the gift-giver chooses to emphasize that no return gift is expected, the failure to reciprocate effectively ends the *mosintuwu* relationship. The relationship must be constantly renewed with further gifts. Thus, the tension between balanced and generalized reciprocity derives less from the generosity in having given a single gift than from the amount of that gift examined against the history of the exchange relationship. Generosity cannot be demonstrated by giving a gift, but only by giving more than one receives. Generous gift-givers thus strive to return more than they receive; the calculating feast-giver an equal amount or less. Since generosity is a prized cultural ideal, the generous gift-giver gains in reputation, and hence tends to receive larger gifts in return. The economic tension described thus overlays a status competition between the host and the gift-giver. The generous gift-giver wins status because of the size of his gifts, but is almost guaranteed a return gift of equal amount. These larger gifts allow generous gift-givers to hold larger feasts, which further validate their greater wealth, status, and reputation for hospitality. The calculating feast-giver attempts to hold a similarly sized feast, and does so by manipulating the exchange network to his or her own advantage. Their feasts are similar attempts to validate their status, although their reputations suffer in the process. *Posintuwu* networks and their related feasts thus bear a striking resemblance to the *potlatch* of the North-West Coast Indians (Mauss 1970[1925], 31–7).

By emphasizing that these two strategies both depend upon the amounts given, I hope to underline the similarities between the *posintuwu* system and 'shared poverty,' as described in the previous chapter. There I discussed how indigenous conceptions of shared poverty appeared to benefit poorer kin without altering the general process of the differentiation of the peasantry. The appearance of generosity by wealthy kin was balanced by the transfer of 'kin' labour to their households. So, too, in *posintuwu* exchanges, wealthy kin appear to aid their poorer kin by more generous gifts. Yet the size of the gift is misleading, since a return prestation of equal amount is almost guaranteed. The failure to match the value of the original gift carries with it a loss of status and a recognition of dependency, much like the transfer of kin to wealthy households. Poorer families that attempt to utilize the generosity of others' *posintuwu* to hold larger feasts to validate their own status relative to other feast-givers find their reputations tarnished and all future gifts strictly balanced.

The Control of Social Reproduction

Both the strategies of 'shared poverty' and *posintuwu* exchange make specific linkages between kinship and an ethic of generosity that simultaneously establishes relations of hierarchy within a *santina*. Wealthy households, enlarged with fostered children, serve as centres, where a number of branches of families will meet and learn of the wider kinship ties binding them. The co-residence of often distant kin brings them emotionally closer, or *mosintuwu*. These networks are reflected in *posintuwu* exchanges between the constituent households of the extended kin group. These wealthy households have the ability to exchange gifts of greater value. Their gifts thus allow their poorer kin to hold larger feasts than would otherwise be possible, and so maintain the status of the kin group as a whole. Their wealth also enables them to recognize and participate in more weddings as 'close kin.' This generosity may extend to sponsoring the weddings of their poorer kin, especially of children they have fostered. Yet, their generosity is not quite the free gift they claim it to be, since they will receive a substantial amount of it in recompense in a return gift, thus allowing them to hold larger feasts that validate their generosity to a larger audience through an '*adat* spectacle.' Hence, whether an equal amount of *posintuwu* is returned or not, a difference in status is created that reflects differences in wealth.

Feasting and *posintuwu* exchanges thus continue to serve many of the same functions as in the pre-colonial period. At that time, exchanges performed at a feast articulated patterns of authority and dependence. The exchanges occurred between groups of people who had shared a common inheritance that had been dispersed through feasting. The exchanges perpetuated existing social ties and ensured continuing harmony among these groups. The feast itself served to embody the social relationships created through the exchanges, to make manifest genealogical ties within a framework that simultaneously defined political relations. By performing a secondary funeral rite, a *kabosenya* proved able to shoulder the *posintuwu* network of the deceased ancestor; the ancestor served as the genealogical centre of the extended kin group, whereas the *kabosenya* hosting the ritual proved capable of being its political centre. However, this centre required constant renewal through continuing *posintuwu* exchanges because the common inheritance of the kin group was dispersed in the feast itself (Schrauwers 1997). Although the primary occasion for feasting has changed to the wedding ceremony, the relationships embodied through exchange continue unabridged. Through their sponsorship of the marriages of distant kin, the wealthy maintain an extensive kinship-oriented patronage network. The introduction of *sawah* and commodity exchange has not radically altered the system. *Posintuwu* exchange and shared poverty in the ideologically insulated 'kinship' sphere continue to be used to control of the entire process of social reproduction, including access to marriage itself. Control of social reproduction by seniors thus refers to a complex of kin-related economic, political, and ideological mechanisms.

A closer examination of the *adat* wedding process described earlier demonstrates the principles by which genealogical seniors were able to assert their control over social reproduction through their control of the resources required to host a wedding. Within the proposal process, the candidate and his parents cannot present arguments in favour of the proposed match. They must depend on an influential family member who possesses the genealogical knowledge to defend their interests. Genealogical knowledge is itself symbolic capital. The teknonymic naming system fosters genealogical amnesia among the young; they are generally incapable of specifying exact relations within their extended kin group. Knowledgeable elders are the sole repository of this knowledge, and it is they who evaluate whether the 'four doors' are open. Since any two individuals can be related in a number of ways, the emphasis these elders place upon particular ties reflects their more general evaluation of the suitability of the match. Those opposed to a match need only place emphasis on a proscribed relationship, such as a marriage between a man and his classificatory aunt or grandmother. The candidate's representative must thus command enough authority to sway the rest of the kin group. This authority is predicated upon their reputation for generosity, their *posintuwu* networks, and hence their ability to sponsor the wedding feast. A prominent kinsman is able to translate their *posintuwu* network into a work crew and to provide the material resources needed to stage the feast. The staging of the feast in turn validates their generosity and authority, providing a visible demonstration of their control of the *adat* liturgies by which the wider audience will judge the spectacle, as well as the solidarity of the kin group of which they are the centre.

The organization of a wedding feast thus mirrors the same patterns of authority and dependence found in household organization and *posintuwu* exchanges. Many of the wealthier householders boast of the number of kinsmen they have raised to marriage, noting that they, not the parents, sponsored the wedding feast. These familial patrons' opinions carry inordinate weight in the constitution of new households, but also, through continuing aid and *posintuwu*, on the continuing viability of that household. The following two examples relate the diverse experiences of two young women cared for by my landlord, Papa Ian, and demonstrate his power over their social reproduction. The first woman contested this patron's control over her marriage and paid the price. The second woman, in contrast, benefited fully from her patron's largess.

The first woman, whom I dubbed 'Cinderella' in the previous chapter, had been a member of the households of either Papa Ian or Ngkai Bose for most of her life. She had most recently entered Papa Ian's household at his invitation to discourage her from making what he considered a bad marriage. Her suitor proved quite persistent and was able to sway the girl's father (but not Papa Ian) to approve of the match. A proposal was thus sent, but Papa Ian was specifically excluded from the opening ceremony (although Mama Ian was allowed to take the car, implying his tacit knowledge). Shortly after the proposal was opened, news arrived that the young man had impregnated a second woman and that this woman's family was insisting on marriage. Cinderella soon after moved from the house, knowing that Papa Ian was now intransigently against the union. The young man paid an *adat* fine instead, and he and Cinderella proceeded with their wedding. Although Cinderella's family should have hosted the wedding, these revelations made it impossible to conduct the marriage in the village, where the family breach might have resulted in public disagreement. Cinderella and a very small number of supportive kin thus travelled in secret to the young man's village, where one of his kinsmen acted as the host of the bride's party. The humiliation of hosts acting as guests allowed the wedding to proceed, although it signified a serious breach between the young woman and her kin.

In the second case, Ana, another long-standing member of the household, received a marriage proposal from a man in her natal village. She sought and received the blessing of Papa Ian, who then sponsored her wedding feast. Although formally deferring to Ana's parents, he stated that she had been a member of his household so long that he considered her as one of his own children; he would marry her off. It was he who called and led the meeting of close family to arrange the wedding, he who provided the single largest contribution, he who collected *posintuwu* from his far larger *posintuwu* network to help fund the feast, and he who brought a considerable number of workers to ensure the feast went off without a hitch. The resulting feast was far larger than the bride's parents could have afforded otherwise, and served to maintain the status of the wider kin group as well as of its sponsor.

Control over the social reproduction of the wider kin group is thus dependent upon two factors: the traditional *adat* process for determining the acceptability of a match, and having both the financial and social resources to sponsor the expensive *adat* feast. The first factor was paramount in the traditional system and served as the means by which *kabosenya* arranged marriages to suit their own ends. Arranged marriages are now illegal, and the *adat* wedding has been transformed into an *optional* spectacle. It is increasingly common for young women to purposefully subvert the *adat* process by simply getting pregnant. Although carrying a heavy social stigma, it is now so common that one *adat* council president estimated only 30 per cent of all proposals followed the *adat* procedure. Control over social reproduction is now more dependent upon having the financial and social resources to sponsor the wedding feast *and* to provide continuing support to a new family with few economic resources. Control of social reproduction is thus less dependent upon the *adat* processes in which it was traditionally vested (especially the exchange of bridewealth) and increasingly vested in the processes of shared poverty and *posintuwu* exchange.

This increasing marginalization of *adat* processes has ironically been linked with their transformation into an '*adat* spectacle.' Since the state now rules through the civil service, it had to carefully distinguish the roles of the village mayor as civil servant, subject to national *law* through which the state ruled, and the mayor as *adat* functionary responsible for the performance of adat *ceremony*. The 1975 marriage law established a civil wedding registry and ceremony separate from church and *adat* weddings, making the latter optional. To further formalize the separation of powers, the government also established the village *adat* council (*dewan adat*), a body led by the mayor but separate from the civil service (Wignjodipoero 1983, 34–9). This seven-member council has been vested with powers to settle disputes (most of which now involve out-of-wedlock pregnancies) and perform all *adat* ceremonies in the village. However, the criteria for election to the council may have little to do with an individual's command of *adat* ceremony, a fact that often becomes apparent to those attending. The village mayor (*lurah*), for example, may be an appointed civil servant from a different ethnic group. Rather, individuals are elected to the *adat* council because of their extensive kinship and *posintuwu* networks, and hence their control over social reproduction. That is, these individuals are not elected because of their knowledge of *adat* liturgies but because of their positions within the feasting economy.

Ironically, their control over social reproduction can not be exerted until the decision has been made to hold an *adat* wedding. Since the *adat* wedding ceremony is no longer exclusive in its claims to adherence, many couples postpone it. The reasons given for holding the ceremony are complex and often do not originate with the couple themselves but with their families, village government, or the *adat* council. Their performance of the ceremony appears to stem from its wider implications in terms of local power relations as they are manifested in the ceremony itself, not from its stated function – namely, to marry the couple. It was said that those who had not performed the *adat* wedding did not feel the implications until they had marital problems. Marital problems inevitably concern the *adat* council in its role as village peace-maker. Members of the council act as mediators in disputes between quarrelling spouses or neighbours; their role as familial mediators is specifically contrasted with that of the police and the criminal justice system. The *adat* council will not interfere in a marriage where the *adat* ceremony has not yet been completed. The wedding ceremony is perceived as a commitment to the entire *adat* process, and hence the *adat* council may call on a couple to fulfil this requirement as part of its efforts to save a marriage.

This was clearly evident in the wedding of Aono (a man) and Uayu (a woman). Aono was a Manadonese civil servant who had married Uayu over her family's objections – hence the failure to perform the *adat* ceremony. After a number of children and numerous arguments over his gambling habit, Uayu fled to the *adat* council for assistance; they demanded the two undergo an *adat* wedding. The wedding was not, however, a formality performed before their peace-making efforts but itself their major disciplinary effort. An entire village was mobilized to construct the temporary shelters, provide the required bridewealth, and cook and serve at the feast. Placed at the centre of an *adat* spectacle, the couple were subjected to public rebukes by the chair of the *adat* council, by a prominent kinsman, and by the minister. In a rare display of public anger, the chair of the *adat* council lectured the couple and the unmarried people at the wedding on the need for respecting the *adat*. The failure to have such respect had led to the crisis the couple had found themselves facing. The groom was reduced to tears, and the young unmarried men in the audience recognized this wedding as the object lesson it was meant to be.

This example underscores that the social implications of undergoing the wedding ceremony extend beyond the status considerations of *adat* spectacle. The performance of the spectacle provided a stage upon which specific relations of super- and sub-ordination were renewed. The ritual did not 'express' or 'reflect' some more real political structure or order but constituted it through the ceremony itself; *posintuwu* exchanges, and the hosting, staffing, and participation in the wedding feast, created a host of dyadic relationships. That is, the feast does not, as Leach asserts of ritual, simply 'make explicit what is otherwise a fiction,' reminding its audience 'at least in symbol, of the underlying order that is supposed to guide their social activities' (1964, 16). Rather, feasting itself temporarily 'creates an order and freezes it for a moment' (Atkinson 1989, 8). The multiple ties of super- and sub-ordination created through feasting form the basis of social order. In the case of Aono, the performance of the *adat* wedding ceremony served to situate him, an outsider, in a dependent position within the village kinship network created by the ceremony itself. Feeling a moral debt to those who generously staged the wedding, Aono finally submitted to their requests that he stop gambling and attend church.

The Women's Christian Organization

The church wedding, or *pernikahan*, stands as an unabashedly Western imposition amid the complex negotiations of status and power that surround the *adat* ceremonies. Its liturgies and customs are direct imports from the Netherlands Reformed Church, and make no reference to local cultural realities or to the patterns of shared poverty or *posintuwu* exchange. Yet, the apparent isolation of the church from these local traditions hides its extensive influence over how those traditions are organized and performed (and vice versa). The liturgical isolation of the *pernikahan* hides the role of the religious bureaucracy in organizing the *adat* wedding and in subordinating *adat* prescriptions to those of the church. In a process that is described in more detail in the next two chapters, these complex negotiations of status have been encapsulated within the church.

This process of encapsulation cannot, however, be simply viewed as the cynical policy initiative of a culturally isolated church attempting to cloak itself in the legitimacy of 'tradition'; rather, it is equally the result of excluded groups seeking to utilize processes lying outside of church control to reassert their relevance and authority. As I noted in chapter 2, women were purposively excluded from positions within the church. However, the power and authority of women in village society continued to be exercised through their role in the social reproduction of their kin groups. As these practices of social reproduction increasingly became embedded in the church, women were able to parlay their 'secular' roles as the *seksi konsumpsi* (the 'feeding department') into religious authority. This church-sponsored group has played a central role in the development of the modern forms of feasting, the reception, and *posintuwu umum*. Here then, I briefly review the role of the Women's Christian Organization (Komisi Wanita) in the transformations of the wedding so far described and their utilization of this role to gain admission to positions of authority within the church.

The Women's Christian Organization was established shortly after Independence (both national, and of the Christian Church of Central Sulawesi from the mission). The original group, the Christian Ladies' Association (Persatuan Ibu Kristen [PIK]) was an independent organization formed in various congregations around Tentena by a local minister and a number of prominent women *kabosenya*. Membership was voluntary, and the aims of the group were to raise women's religious knowledge and consciousness. The women thus met once weekly for a religious service. Meeting simply for a service was judged insufficient to draw new members; hence, over time the organization has broadened its mandate to increase its relevance to its members. The local board of the Tentena branch took on the responsibility of organizing the weddings and funerals (the largest feasts) of its members. Until that time, weddings had been organized by the families concerned, and there were frequent difficulties, especially in the organization of voluntary labour. The PIK provided an ideal solution, an established group that could be utilized on a consistent basis. Its members were assigned to various standing committees (*seksi*) that oversaw specific tasks, such as cooking and setting tables. The evolution of the PIK, from religious service to service organization, thus illustrates how the social logic of leadership in Tentena is tied to feast giving.

The exceptional organizational ability of the association's local chapter president (and later village mayor) ensured that fewer difficulties occurred. More and more people turned to the PIK for assistance, and the president has become a standing member of the committee formed to oversee each wedding. This committee, as both it and the reception have evolved, is headed by three chairs. The first chair is selected by the bride's family and is usually a prominent individual noted for his or her organizational ability who is in charge on the day of the wedding. The second chair is a prominent family member (but not the parents) of the bride and acts as a liaison between the family and the committee. The third chair is always the head of the PIK and is in charge of staffing the various subcommittees. The average wedding requires about 130 workers, divided into subcommittees responsible for tasks such as borrowing plates, boiling water, cooking rice, and washing dishes. The successful coordination of these workers is itself dependent upon ties of super- and sub-ordination created through numerous previous weddings.

Voluntary labour for weddings is considered a form of *posintuwu*; hence, the logic of *posintuwu* has become an important factor in PIK membership and patterns of leadership. Since a return of some kind is required if a *posintuwu* relationship is to be continued, the women within the PIK were involved in the mutual exchange of voluntary labour for each other's weddings, but not involved, as a group, in the weddings of non-members. The need for labour at weddings was explicitly stated by some to be one reason for joining the PIK. By entering its organized *posintuwu* exchanges, they ensured that their own children's weddings would not be an unnecessary burden to their families at a time when the size of weddings ceremonies was rapidly expanding. Those who were most generous with their time and organizational ability at weddings became the 'natural leaders' of the PIK, as they are of the *adat* council. They are often the same individuals.

The involvement of the Christian Ladies' Association (PIK) in weddings created its own difficulties for the church. The PIK's assistance was lent only to registered members who had paid dues. This excluded those who were unable to pay. Further, as an independent organization, the PIK was answerable to its own divisional leaders and not to the local congregation. When some of the PIK activities clashed with congregational activities, the local church council appealed to the synod to reorganize the PIK and bring it to heel. The resultant reorganization of the PIK as a *komisi* (commission) did not fundamentally alter its aims or programs, but directly subordinated them to the local congregations. The PIK was 'democratized'; membership was now automatically granted to all women members of the congregation, and the committee of management (the *komisi*) now reports to a church elder (always a woman) who acts as liaison with the congregational council. Although answerable to local church councils, *komisi* programs are increasingly being rationalized as universal denominational programs through a hierarchy controlled by the synod, which appoints a (woman) minister to lead the organization. Congregations that had never had a Women's Group are now being encouraged to form one, and to form it on the model of those originally formed in Tentena, the synod headquarters. Most *komisi* have followed Tentena's lead, building their own meeting halls and establishing kindergartens as one of their programs. The PIK has thus been directly incorporated within the institutional framework of the church, while the role and power of women within the church has been commensurately increased.

The regularization of the staffing of feasts and of the giving of *posintuwu umum* have both occurred as the church has extended the membership and geographical scope of the Women's Christian Organization. This rationalization of feasting by women has served to give women a new source of power within the church hierarchy. Given their central role in the giving and collecting of *posintuwu umum*, and staffing all feasts, women have been able to assert their control over government and church policies established primarily by men. The role they have assumed mirrors that of the wife as *to popagampi*, or household manager, within the household. This managerial role, which includes control over the cash resources of the household, makes the implementation of policy dependent upon their acquiescence. What began then, as an attempt to tame the Women's Christian Organization has served, rather, as the back door through which they now control how ritual events, such as weddings and thanksgiving feasts, are conducted.

Class and Marriage

In this and the previous chapter I discussed how the introduction of *sawah* has fundamentally transformed the local economy and introduced a class dynamic to the kinship system. Both the creation of shared poverty and the extension of *posintuwu* exchange can be tied to this new class dynamic. My discussion of shared poverty in particular emphasized that, by restricting 'sharing' to social reproduction rather than to the means of production, class formation continued unhindered. Social reproduction has been commodified, which leaves the wealthy in control of the process yet subordinated to a kinship ideology that emphasizes generosity while legitimating inequality. There are two implications I will focus upon here.

First, social reproduction has been commodified; hence, feasting is the economic cost of the local political system as has emerged from the interaction among mission, state, and *kabosenya*. Economic resources my informants claimed they could ill afford were, in their own words, 'wasted.' Many looked upon the lighter ritual burdens of other ethnic groups with envy while acknowledging that their own social identities were defined in terms of the *adat* and their ritual responsibilities to others. To end one's *posintuwu* exchanges would be to break one's kin ties as they are locally constituted, and hence unthinkable.

Before the colonial period, *kabosenya* arranged marriages to solidify the alliances among the various extended kin groups to which they belonged. Strategic marriages of this sort have no further function since neither the church nor the state recognizes kinship-based politics. Both the church and the state have specifically attacked arranged marriages and perpetuated a model of marriage based upon romantic bonds (*cinta*). 'Dating' (*momungge*) is a relatively new and popular innovation, despite running counter to traditional norms on cross-gender socializing. Within these changing social mores, some marriages continue to be arranged, utilizing the ideological resources of this earlier era but now serving class interests. A 'generation gap' has thus emerged, focusing specifically on the issue of spouse selection.

The ideal of romantic love has been fanned by the growing Indonesian mass-cultural industries, and especially by pop music, although it found fertile ground in indigenous culture. My older informants attributed the changes in 'dating' to the Japanese occupation during the Second World War (*waktu Jepang*), which they presented as a period of rapid change and severe deprivation. Cloth and rice became scarce, so villagers were forced to revert to bark-cloth clothing, and many fled to the forest to open swiddens. To keep their unmarried daughters from being appropriated for Japanese 'service,' many set up arranged marriages. This return to tradition, however, was accompanied by rapid cultural changes introduced by the Japanese. The pace of imposed changes led one man to conclude that the period of the Japanese occupation was the first time the villagers 'felt colonized.' Of particular importance was the rapid breakdown of some aspects of the gender segregation typical of the traditional period. At that time, no opposite-sex pair was allowed to be alone, an injunction that extended to those already married, but not to each other. Public activities were (and generally remain) firmly segregated by gender; in church, for example, the women sat together separate from men. Most of my elderly informants insisted they had never spoken with their spouses before their marriage, whether the marriage had been arranged or not. Courting in the pre-war period was accomplished by subterfuge and subject to *adat* fine. These curbs were strong because indigenous notions of 'love at first sight' were also powerful. The Japanese introduced cultural innovations that weakened this rigid segregation and created a new public space for courting.

The initial focal point of courting came to be the *dero*, a ring dance performed after most public ceremonies such as weddings or on New Year's Eve. The *dero* is also a kind of competition. Traditionally, dancers formed a ring, divided in two equal parts by gender, swung their arms in unison. The leader of the one half would sing a verse, to which the other half of the circle must sing an appropriate response. This continues back and forth until one or the other side is defeated and can no longer respond. During the Japanese occupation, the dance was changed so that participants held hands rather than swinging their arms in unison and the strict segregation of the sexes in opposing arcs of the circle was broken up, creating numerous opportunities for young men to hold hands with young women. Many older people, scandalized by the changes, refused to take part, leaving the dancing to the unmarried young, although these elders continued to supervise the dance closely. A whole courting etiquette has thus arisen within the niches of the *dero*. Young men and women can select the spot in the ring at which they enter – never next to the person they're interested in, but close by, waiting for the people in between to tire and drop out. A set of hand signals, made possible by the new hand-holding style and made necessary by the watchful gaze of elders, transmits messages: when to drop out, where to meet. Many of the verses now sung carry veiled (and not so veiled) courting messages.

The public courting space opened by the *dero* has been expanded, most notably by the church, and to a lesser extent by the schools. Schools are not segregated by gender, and hence provide an ideal opportunity for courtship; but since the majority of To Pamona do not go on to high school, this opportunity is limited to a select few. Although the church has always firmly argued that marriage is a voluntary bond between the couple involved, the mission did not feel they could attack indigenous morals on sexual conduct (Kruyt 1970, 302–3). During the colonial period, the mission simply refused to enforce gender segregation or to punish anyone for its transgression unless it was explicitly and publicly brought to their attention. Since Independence, these sexual mores have weakened somewhat, allowing for greater interaction among young people. In the minds of parents, the results are equivocal at best, as they have watched the premarital pregnancy rate soar. Young people, I noted above, have often utilized pregnancy as a means of forcing parents to allow them to marry the person of their choice (although not all pregnancies are so intended). Parents have responded by restricting dating, except within the framework of the church youth group and the 'church friend' (*teman gereja*).

This new courtship dynamic has been captured by a new word: *momungge*. A young man, smitten by the looks of a young woman, may approach her only within the narrow limits set by school or the church youth group. If they wish to pursue the relationship, that is, take the first step towards marriage, the young man must call on the young girl at home, where their interaction will be carefully scrutinized by her parents. This provides the parents with the first opportunity to discourage an inappropriate suitor. The young couple will be allowed out of the house only if they are accompanied by a 'church friend,' another trusted member of the church youth group, who acts as chaperone. Preferred chaperones include the older, male cousins of the young woman, since they will be concerned to protect the kin group's honour. Wherever they go, the couple's behavior is carefully monitored and reported back to the girl's parents. Any breach of strict decorum may end the relationship. All of these rumours will be resurrected in the deliberative meetings for preparing and accepting the marriage proposal, since the entire kin group's honour is at stake. On one occasion, an uncle was so enraged that his nieces had arranged a special *dero* for visiting students from

Java (and so gave the impression of chasing men) that he ended the *dero*, chased the girls into the house, and irreparably damaged the door they locked behind them. The only appropriate public display of To Pamona dance as 'culture' is the *raego*, which is not associated with courting.

Courtship has developed as the extended kin group has decreased in importance as a basic political unit of To Pamona society. There are few incentives other than broad, preferential marriage rules for marrying within the extended kin group. The emphasis now falls on whom a child may *not* marry, and the courtship and proposal processes are used to exclude those who parents deem unacceptable. Arranged marriages of the traditional sort are now gone, and parents will, at most, provide their children with a restricted number of candidates whom they consider acceptable. Even those parents who claimed, in principle, that they would allow their children to marry whomever they fell in love with thought painfully long before granting their approval. This reticence stems from the fact that the marriage now voluntarily contracted by the couple continues to represent an alliance of kin groups, an alliance that must be cemented by ongoing *posintuwu* exchanges. The demands of the family's existing *posintuwu* network, as well as the family's available resources, play a role in this decision; a child who marries too high or too low may create problems with a family's feasting strategy. Since these exchange patterns reflect class differences, the selection of an appropriate spouse reflects a pattern of class consolidation. Parents also want their children to marry someone capable of supporting them in their old age, since marriage is frequently the point at which they divide their estate. The tendency for like to marry like ensures that the children of the wealthy consolidate their parents' position.

The selection of a spouse has thus become a major source of tension between parents and their children, with each using the economic and ideological resources available to them. I have already noted the means by which parents are able to discourage unacceptable suitors long before the topic of marriage comes up. Oftentimes, it is as simple as pointing out an unacceptable genealogical tie. One man retold of the horror he experienced when his mother disapprovingly pointed out that he should refer to his new girlfriend as 'grandmother.' He immediately broke off the relationship, despite the fact this same man's uncle (of nearly the same age) married a classificatory grandmother with his parents' full blessing. In the rest of this section, however, I recount the means by which young couples combat parental strategies, frequently leading to public disputes. Despite general acknowledgment that the young couple is in the wrong, they can still draw on the considerable ideological resources of church and state.

I have already repeatedly noted that one strategy adopted by thwarted couples desiring marriage is to get pregnant. This is by no means a foolproof strategy. In one case, a man's family simply paid the *adat* fine, thus indicating their contempt of the pregnant woman's family, who approved of the marriage. The young man was an engineer from a prominent family, and she a farmer's daughter. The woman's family pressed the matter, taking the case to court and insisting on marriage. The young man lost the case, but his family considered the six-month jail sentence preferable to the marriage. During his incarceration they arranged a marriage with a more suitable partner.

The young couple can escalate the dispute, if their parents continue to disapprove, by living together. This requires the tacit approval of at least one set of parents, usually the young woman's, since few couples can afford to establish their own household without the aid of their families. The preference for living with the young woman's family probably arises from the fact that, without the payment of bridewealth, the man's family has no rights in the children of the union. Living together is only a temporary situation at best, since neither church nor state tolerates 'common law' unions and both exert enormous pressure on families to allow the wedding. A prominent patron of the young man may sponsor an *adat* forgiveness ceremony (*mesumbo'o*), which requires the payment of a water buffalo to the parents by the errant child. Before independence, giving the water buffalo meant automatic forgiveness, but now there has to be some sign of willingness to receive. A sponsor is needed both to act as intermediary and to provide the water buffalo since few newly established couples can afford the gift. In short, no matter what the route taken, new linkages of dependency on familial patrons are created. This is true even if the wedding proceeds without a reconciliation due to government pressure, as the following example demonstrates.

Alima and Tatogo, an unmarried couple, had been living together for a year. This couple initially had not married because of the objections of Alima's mother. Alima had already had one child out of wedlock when he asked his mother's permission to marry a second woman. The arrangements were made, but before the wedding could be completed Alima backed out and began living with Tatogo, a Sundanese woman, in the back of a small market stall they rented. His mother, publicly embarrassed, washed her hands of her son's affairs. Alima and Tatogo had no plans to marry, stating they could not afford the ceremony. The village mayor, however, stated that the government could not tolerate a couple living together without at least having completed the civil marriage ceremony. She told me she was especially concerned about the future of Tatogo should Alima's eye start roving again. Unless married Tatogo had no rights. After the couple agreed to the civil ceremony, Alima's aunt requested he undergo the *adat* ceremony at the same time so that their children would be subject to the *ada mPamona*. The rapidly expanding ceremony carried with it an expanding cost. The young couple had no established *posintuwu* network and therefore could not count on much in the way of public contributions. They called on a family patron, a third cousin, who mobilized her *posintuwu* network on their behalf. She provided both material support as well as the required labour for a small but acceptable wedding. The government demand that the couple marry thus ended with the completion of the *adat* ceremony and the broadening of the patron's *posintuwu* network to include the young couple now in her debt. Tatogo began to turn increasingly to her patron, as she would to her mother, who attempted to instruct her in To Pamona *adat*.

The selection of a spouse is thus the major means of class consolidation in To Pamona society. The disputes between parents and children arising out of the new class dynamics of spouse selection have thus been successfully circumscribed within the patronage system described in the previous sections. While children may contest their parents' decisions and be aided and abetted by the state and church in so doing, the completion of the wedding is still dependent upon a patron with a well-developed *posintuwu* network. The voluntary nature of current spouse selection creates problems only for parents who must discourage ties with families that present too great a challenge as *posintuwu* partners. Patrons are unaffected by these considerations, since they are investing only in the young couple themselves.

The Role of Church and State in Marriage

Weddings, I noted earlier, are an arena within which the interests of the state, the church, and indigenous patrons are articulated. Throughout this chapter, I have tried to outline two complex, historical processes. The first of these processes is the reification of *adat*, which has been transformed from practice to law, to ceremony. This reification of *adat* has been accompanied by the creation of *adat* spectacles and bridewealth inflation. The impetus behind this transformation has been the efforts of the colonial and New Order states to subsume local political relations and marginalize their importance. As the wedding has been transformed into an ever larger spectacle, a second subordinate process becomes discernible; the solidification of a system of social reproduction through *posintuwu* exchange, shared poverty, and feasting. This process emerges in the margins of officially sanctioned *adat* procedures. Its impetus arises from the mission's attempts to 'inculturate' Christianity within the feasting complex, a topic discussed more fully in the chapters that follow.

The example of *posintuwu umum* was indicative of how the state, through the 'motivated misrecognition of local cultural realities,' subsumed *posintuwu* exchange within a national tradition, *gotong-royong*. This formal subsumption of *posintuwu* exchange is part of a wider state policy directed at establishing the universal principles underlying *adat* law traditions of Indonesia (Wignjodipoero 1983, 40–61). The rationalization of *adat* law prioritizes these universal values over local interpretations, and marks a shift from colonial rule through *adat* mechanisms to Indonesian rule and the establishment of a unitary state. *Adat* as 'law' has ceased to have any meaning, as was frequently pointed out to me by those disappointed by the *adat* dispute-settlement process. The *adat* council's rulings are restricted to 'family law.' Since the members of the *adat* council themselves achieve their position on the council through their kinship networks, this formal restriction of the *adat* appears natural and coincides with the emerging ideological contrast between *posintuwu* exchanges among kin and market exchange in civil society. These formal limits constrain *adat* discourse to a restricted and newly developed kinship sphere and isolate this sphere from the wider political and legal realms with which it was once associated.

While *adat law* has been marginalized, the state has encouraged the development of *adat* as 'culture' (*kebudayaan*), a new dynamic alternatively driven by the politics of ethnic management and the needs of a burgeoning tourist industry. The government has thus fuelled the creation of *adat* spectacles and, with it, the definition of *adat* as a 'traditional' *liturgy*. The creation of *adat* spectacle, of culture as ceremony, song and dance, thus serves to perpetuate indigenous power relationships in a sphere denied a meaningful political role within the state apparatus itself. By freezing 'culture' in family-focused *adat* liturgies and performative skills, indigenous political relations and discourse are locked into their 'traditional' concerns and made irrelevant to the normal operations of the state.

A similar argument can be made for church policy. The mission sought to 'inculturate' Christianity by incorporating indigenous modes of worship within the liturgical forms of the church. However, while providing the framework for feasting, the Christian liturgy remains insulated from it. The liturgy makes no reference to either the event of feasting or its organization. Like the *adat* spectacle, the Christian liturgy provides the framework within which feasting takes place yet isolates it as specifically 'non-liturgical'; the feast is a means to a liturgical end. In the case of both church and state, feasting, a particularly local preoccupation, is limited to a 'sideshow' of a liturgical event sanctioned by a larger bureaucratic polity.

Weddings are thus an arena within which the interests of the state, the church, and indigenous patrons are articulated. In some cases their interests have coincided with processes such as the transformation of wedding feasts described in this chapter as a result. However, there are also real tensions between the New Order's definition of *adat* in terms of pre-Christian traditions and the church's definition of a Christian *adat*. Government policy is thought to encourage *sukuisme* (communalism) within the church, threatening Christian unity and abetting the creation of ethnic churches. The state, in turn, is caught between religiously based challenges to its legitimacy and a fear of the kinds of ethnic separatism that fanned the regional rebellions of the 1950s and early 1960s. These conflicting goals thus set the limits on the strategies the To Pamona can use to maintain their kinship networks. It must be emphasized, however, that the villagers' strategies, no less than that of the church and the state, are not uniform. The generation gap in spouse selection and the class dynamics of *posintuwu* exchange amply demonstrate the different interests of the various segments of To Pamona society.

PART THREE

HIGHLAND CHRISTIANITY

5

Ritualization

But I have prayed for thee, that thy faith fail not: and when thou art converted, strengthen thy brethren.

Luke 22: 32

When the missionaries perceived the implications of community life and the solidarity that binds the group together, they realized that the christianizing of the people would never be attained by merely personal decision ... We soon discovered that in our preaching to individuals we had to take into account the collective aspect of the community. For he only is a Christian personality who stands out sharply against the world and all that is of the world, because he knows with absolute certainty he is a child of God, perfectly hidden in Jesus' mercy and a member of the community of which Jesus Christ is the head and leader. The Christian who has converted from animism little realizes the first part of this qualification. This realization must grow in him, and this is only possible if he has become a member of a new community which exercises the same strengthening and leading influence as the old one did, but now in another direction, in another spirit – the spirit of Christ.

Kruyt 1936b, 246

The Netherlands Missionary Society (NZG) was founded as an independent corporation in 1797, shortly after its inspiration, the London Missionary Society. Its independent status was aimed at keeping it free of narrow sectarian ties to particular denominations (Randwijck 1981, 156). This laudable attempt to remain free of church politics soon foundered, however, as more orthodox Calvinists grew increasingly restive with the 'modernist' theological leanings of many of the members of the board of directors; these aristocratic followers of the Reveil seceded, to form the Netherlands Mission Association (Nederlandsche

Zendingsvereeniging) in 1858, and the Utrecht Mission Association (Utrechtsche Zendingsvereeniging) in 1859 (which eventually came under the direction of Nicolaüs Adriani's father, Ds. M.A. Adriani; Randwijck 1981, 77–80). These various theological streams and the mission organizations that adhered to them did not initially give rise to an equal diversity of missiological methods.

Before Kruyt's innovations, missions in Indonesia were closely associated with the establishment of churches for civil servants: the state-supported Indische Kerk. Chistianity was clearly the religion of the *overheerser* (rulers). By 1900, there were also about 230,000 indigenous members, primarily in Minahasa, Ambon, and Timor (Randwijck 1981, 190). The missionaries sent by the independent missionary corporations were not, however, entitled to establish autonomous churches for their indigenous congregants; whereas the Ethical Policy specificly sought to hinder the formation of pan-Islamic identity in the archipelago, a pan-Christian identity was positively being encouraged by the Indische Kerk. To further this goal, preaching was conducted in Malay, the *lingua franca*, its ministers were regularly rotated throughout the Netherlands East Indies (NEI), and little effort was made to understand, or incorporate, local cultural practices (Randwijck 1981, 196). Conversion to Christianity, closely associated with colonial rule and Western education, was the first step in 'becoming Dutch' (for a discussion of a NZG mission that initially continued in the same vein, see Kipp 1990, 1993).

Kruyt's greatest innovation as a missionary was to reorient these broad policies, and change the subject of conversion from the individual to the ethnic community. His mission methodology was predicated upon Ethical Theology, which emphasized the role of an encompassing *volkskerk* in shaping and moulding individual piety. Kruyt legitimated this shift on cultural grounds; that a true pietistic Christianity could not be created out of an imposed, alien culture. Christianity had to develop out of indigenous systems of meaning and action, the *adat*, and hence had a social as well as an individual component. His mission methodology thus encouraged the preservation of as much of the *adat* as was compatible with Christian principles to ensure 'true' faith, as well as the preservation of the wider community as a *volkskerk* to support that faith.

It is in this light that we must examine Kruyt's descriptions of the communal unity of the To Pamona (1924a, 1929, 1936a, J. Kruyt 1939), and his attempts to preserve this unity within the church. Kruyt rooted To Pamona communalism in the *adat*. 'Each community lives in a village or in a district and the members regard themselves as part of a corporate whole. They form one family – grandparents, children, grandchildren. In such a circle the thoughts and wishes of the individuals are formed according to a common standard; all action is dominated by the slogan "What the ancestors did, so do we"' (1936a, 242). Yet, Kruyt provided more than enough evidence that this communal unity was not the spontaneous product of adherence to the *adat*. He frequently noted cases of extreme egoism and described how consensus arose out of factional bickering (1936a, 244). By prioritizing the unity of the community and emphasizing the lack of individualization, he masked this political process behind a façade of established consensus, the *adat* as law. The mission's attempts to preserve communal unity were thus tantamount to preserving the authority of the *kabosenya* within the church while masking its true source.

This chapter turns, then, to the political process by which an inculturated Christianity creates a faith community. I argue, however, that this faith community is not characterized by its shared beliefs, a form of communal unity predicated upon a Christian *adat*. Rather, this faith community emerges out of an indigenous political process incorporated within the bureaucracy of the church. The role of *kabosenya* has been unwittingly altered but not eliminated. These two political systems have articulated at the point of contact, a ritualized practice known as *monuntu* (to advise). *Monuntu* was the principal means of dispute settlement in the pre-colonial period, which the mission incorporated as 'preaching the word.' Interpreted in this way, the practice restricts who may appropriately speak and express communal 'consensus,' which is somewhat different from assuming that members 'share beliefs.' As many late-night conversations made clear, the ease with which those of low status are silenced does not translate into automatic acquiescence; they are as likely to go their own 'egoistic' way and continue 'sinning.'

Ritual Theory, Ritual Practice

The argument presented in this chapter attempts to supplement those approaches that treat religion as a 'cultural system.' My analysis of mission methodology and my own fieldwork led me to realize that the explanatory power of 'what ritual does' and 'how it does it' was somewhat more limited than that proposed by those interpretive approaches which treat culture as an autonomous realm outside of, yet shared by, social actors (e.g., Geertz 1973d). On the one hand, these models treat ritual as the basic mechanism by which shared values are internalized by ritual participants, and serve to inculcate dispositions to act in prescribed ways; ritual is the essential means by which 'culture' is transmitted and given its emotive force. On the other hand, the anthropologist finds that ritual also serves an analytic function, reintegrating belief and behaviour, cultural and social analysis. Ritual is presented as an enactment of public thought; hence, it is similar to culturally produced 'texts,' which can be 'read' to endow meaning upon social experience; ritual's meanings are public, and thus we need not concern ourselves with what's going on in our informants' heads. It is for this reason that ritual has proven a popular device for the organization of ethnographies.

Interpretive models of ritual treat it as a form of behaviour distinguishable from technical action in that it is symbolic, and thus equivalent to 'culture,' in opposition to instrumental behaviour. This transformation of ritual from action into symbol is predicated upon the analyst's ability to identify the instrumentality of action and distinguish it from that which is truly symbolic and hence readable as text. Ritual is transformed from an action that *does* something into *saying* something. Talal Asad argues that this transformation is an inheritance of anthropology's Reformation theological roots in the nineteenth century. Interpreting ritual (a linguistic act) is predicated upon the theological distinction between the 'outward sign' and the 'inward meaning,' a distinction meant to prioritize the outward sign as the authorized expression of established doctrine. Even where no such doctrine exists, theologians and anthropologists have asserted that these outward signs may embody meanings not evident to the ritual participant. 'The claim that the unsophisticated who employ "outward signs" in formal behaviour and speech do not understand the entire meaning being signified or expressed has served as an important principle of anthropological interpretation' (Asad 1988, 77).

Interpretive models of religion focus upon ritual because it plays a key role in bridging the gap between culture and participant, and between analyst and culture. First, ritual serves to reintegrate a publicly articulated symbol system with individual dispositions to act in culturally prescribed ways. 'By enacting the symbolic system, ritual is said to integrate two irreducible aspects of symbols, the conceptual (worldview) and the dispositional (ethos)' (Bell 1992, 31). Through the medium of ritual, symbolic concepts are inculcated and create individual predispositions to act in culturally prescribed ways outside of the ritual setting. The reintegration of symbol and action in ritual is a form of social control or socialization, perpetuating shared public values and behaviours by an unexplained psychological mechanism of internalization. In the older theological terminology, participation in ritual in some way acts to model individual action, to internalize 'outward signs' as 'inward meanings' that guide behaviour.

Second, the ability of ritual to bridge the gap between the thought and the action of participants is said to also provide the theorist with privileged access to the 'culture' of the Other; since rituals consist of publicly inscribed symbol systems, they are readily accessible to the anthropologist, who need not be concerned with the hidden, psychic aspects of the inculcation of dispositions. However, this 'culture' is nothing but that autonomous realm created by the theorist's initial assumption that ritual action simply dramatizes or enacts a system of symbols (Bell 1992, 32). This assumes that activity is the physical expression of thought, as *parole* is to *langue*. The search for meaning at the core of the interpretative program at once constitutes its methodology and its object of analysis by the systematic distinction between thought and action, subsuming the latter to the former. Ritual is specifically defined as symbolic action as opposed to instrumental behaviour and, as such, is interpretable as meaningful text by both social actor and anthropologist.

This hermeneutic circle can be criticized on a number of grounds. First, a growing number of practice theorists question the methodological soundness of reducing 'doing' to 'saying' (Asad 1993; Atkinson 1989; Bell 1992; Bourdieu 1977). They question a definition of ritual as symbolic action that precludes an analysis of its instrumentality. Second, Asad in particular questions the underlying theological suppositions of the search for meaning.

> The idea that symbols needed to be decoded ... plays a new role in the restructured concept of ritual that anthropology has appropriated from theology and developed. For by this idea anthropologists have incorporated a theological preoccupation into an avowedly secular intellectual task – that is, the preoccupation of establishing authoritatively the meanings of *representations* where the explanations offered by indigenous discourses are considered ethnographically inadequate or incomplete. In the case of Christianity, it is the Church that embodies the authority to interpret the meanings of scriptural representations ... In societies which lack the notion of authoritative exegesis, the problem of interpreting 'symbolic actions' is quite different. The most important difference relates not to the greater uncertainty in the interpretation of symbols in such societies, but to the fact that things have first to be construed as 'symbolic' before they become candidates for interpretation, and in the fieldwork situation it is the ethnographer who identifies and classifies 'symbols,' even where he or she then draws on the help of indigenous exegetes to interpret them. (Asad 1988, 77–8)

I have discussed the assumptions underlying anthropological theories of ritual in these general terms because of the particular role that theories of religion and ritual played in the Dutch mission to the To Pamona. I pointed out earlier that the Kruyt's sociological mission methodology was predicated upon early evolutionist anthropological theories (see chapter 1). Kruyt's model of 'animism' objectified a set of beliefs and practices as a 'religion' where the To Pamona themselves had no such conception. Kruyt asserted that 'animism' was a pre-logical mode of thought that made the To Pamona incapable of formulating the abstract tenets of a religion themselves. They directly embodied their thoughts in rites. Since these thoughts were directly manifest in rituals, they could be interpreted and systematized by the logical Western observer as a 'cultural system.'

This act of interpretation was not neutral, but one of active imposition of Western categories upon the To Pamona, the creation of a 'religion' where none existed. Kruyt's method thus transgressed the first rule of interpretation, which is, after all, based upon 'taking the native's point of view.' Kruyt did so because the definition of animism was central to his methods of effecting a conversion. Ethical theological injunctions prevented Kruyt from imposing a logically coherent theology and its associated rites upon the 'animist-thinking' To Pamona since the imposition of such an alien cultural tradition would lead to a superficial Christianity that would not reach or transform their animist inner beings. Kruyt thus welcomed animist interpretations of Christian rites and dogma as a sign that Christianity had become a meaningful part of their lives. Since animist interpretations of the 'outward signs' of Christianity were tolerated, these signs were made locally meaningful while simultaneously being captured within an objective category, 'religion,' under mission purview. The mission also attempted to incorporate the 'outward signs' of 'animist religion' within its own liturgies, and hence transformed elements of To Pamona ritual into officially sanctioned Christian rites. This emphasis on questions of meaning, however, ignores the instrumental aspects of ritual action. Hence, Kruyt provides a catalog of liturgies (symbolically conceived outward signs having no instrumental action) but fails to note, or discuss, the role of *posintuwu* exchange. By treating animism as a symbol system or mode of thought, another side of To Pamona ritual was rendered invisible.

To uncover those aspects of To Pamona ritual incorporated, yet analytically ignored, by the mission, I turn to practice theory. Practice theorists such as Bourdieu (1977) have focused upon the body as both subject and object of ritualized action, as the performer that both creates the formalized structure which is ritual and is the object of the structure so created. This conceptualization of ritual is not unlike the notion of discipline, well known through the work of Foucault (1979; cf. Asad 1993). The object of ritual discipline is the inculcation of embodied knowledge, the creation of a 'sense of ritual' on a par with the sense of hearing, the sense of direction, the sense of balance, and the sense of duty (Bourdieu 1977, 124; cf. Comaroff 1985, 6). The socially informed body bears the habitual dispositions required to improvise a ritual; it follows the unthought cues of when to bow and where to stand, what to bring and how to offer it. This embodied knowledge is not, however, limited to the ritual itself but constitutes an enduring predisposition to act in those ways in normal social intercourse. Thus, both interpretative and practice theorists root the power of ritual in its ability to perpetuate dispositions to act, but practice theorists tend to place more emphasis on the limits that can be expected of the 'practice of virtue' both in and out of ritual events. As Asad concludes, 'for symbols, as I said, call for interpretation, and even as interpretative criteria are extended, so interpretations can be multiplied. Disciplinary practices, on the other hand, cannot be varied quite so easily, because learning to develop moral capabilities is not the same thing as learning to invent representations' (1988, 87). The inherent limits to changing this internalized sense of ritual has important implications in the study of missions, conversion, and the process of 'inculturation' (a term now applied to missiological methods like those of Kruyt). Intellectualist models of conversion define the process in terms of the substitution of systems of meanings or cosmologies. These approaches prioritize European concerns with belief and orthodoxy, leading, for example, to the analysis of cosmologies and the 'indigenous theologies' enacted in Christian services (for example, see Aragon 1992). While not ignoring these aspects, at this point I would like to emphasize the embodied knowledge, the sense of ritual, carried from the practice of one 'belief system' to the other. Rather than begin with an analysis of the adoption (or usurpation) of 'meaningful' aspects of indigenous rituals such as *padungku* (thanksgiving) usually cited as the hallmark of inculturation (see Anggui and Lambe' 1985, for example) I start with the continuity of practice, specifically because Kruyt did never did so.

This approach to ritual postpones analysis of systems of meaning. Kruyt's toleration of animist interpretations of Christian symbols allowed for heterodoxy and the multiplication of interpretations. Yet, his usurpation of indigenous ritual practice served to highlight or prioritize his interpretation by granting himself a voice while denying others theirs. This seems to me the key to Leach's assertion that ritual 'makes explicit what is otherwise a fiction,' reminding its audience 'at least in symbol, of the underlying order that is supposed to guide their social activities' (1964, 16). I argue that this 'symbolic order' is a theoretical fiction perpetuated by both ritual leader *and* the anthropologist, like Kruyt, who reads ritual as an expression of shared belief. Social activities do not match the symbolic order expressed in ritual because that order is ideological, an attempt to create an orthodoxy which is best analysed in terms of hegemony and resistance (Comaroff 1985, 79). The diversity of interpretations of supposedly shared beliefs and values opens up new areas of concern.

To differentiate this approach from interpretive ones, analysis focuses on ritualization, not ritual (Bell 1992, 197–223). Ritual, a category, is defined in terms of formal symbols. By shifting the focus from ritual to ritualization, analysis is shifted from 'meaningful' public discourse to the means by which it is said. That is, the authorized speech of the leader is reduced to but one type of action among the many by which participants become both subject and object of the ritual, at once creating a formal event through their own actions as well as becoming the object of the structure they have themselves created. Emphasis is thus shifted from the conscious actions and intentions of ritual leaders to the *shared, unthought, everyday discipline by which the leaders' speech acts and actions are prioritized*. The emphasis is shifted from Western preoccupations with belief or a shared interpretation of common symbols that must be consciously affirmed, to the practical strategies utilized to meet certain ends, such as communing with God.

Conversion and the inculturation of Christianity thus represents the meeting of two forms of ritualization, that of the To Pamona and that of the mission. Each had their own unique, embodied sense of ritual. In this meeting, one form of ritualization was dominant, the other subordinate and contingent. Within the discourse on ritual that arose from this meeting, the mission's form of ritualization achieved dominance since it was in a position to define ritual as a category of experience within the larger, colonial political framework. And as I noted above, the mission's definitions of ritual were convergent with those of the nascent discipline of anthropology that emphasized beliefs. As a result, To Pamona forms of ritualization were rendered invisible to the mission during the process of conversion except in so far as the mission officially sanctified and incorporated elements of them. In speaking of the To Pamona mode of ritualization, I am not speaking of these co-opted, and hence highlighted, ritual elements. Rather, I am speaking of their sense of ritual that survived in the niches of the Christian worship service, unremarked and unremarkable because of its continuity with non-ritual activity.

One implication of the subordinated status of To Pamona forms of ritualization is that it rendered the means by which the *kabosenya* maintained their positions of power increasingly invisible, and hence hegemonic. I noted earlier that Kruyt's emphasis on communal unity led him to mistake an active political process, the establishment of consensus by the *kabosenya*, as a dead expression of a shared *adat*. An underlying assumption of Kruyt's analysis of the basis of *kabosenya* authority is that of shared 'belief' (in the Western sense) in the *adat*. Belief, in the Western sense, implies an affirmation of systematically formulated and articulated tenets. In contrast, I will attempt to show that this authority was the product of the practical logic of feasts of social reproduction. In co-opting the person of the *kabosenya* in Protestant forms of ritualization, the mission simultaneously, but unknowingly, co-opted the indigenous form of ritualization, feasting. Working together to create new ritual forms, both the mission and the *kabosenya* utilized their respective 'sense of ritual' in a unified ritual act to prioritize their own hegemonic discourses. The *kabosenya* were able to prioritize their interpretations of the Christian *adat* through feasting in a way that prevented a traditionalist resistance from their subordinates. The mission, assuming communal unity, mistook the lack of resistance for 'shared belief' in their doctrinal pronouncements in the new Christian *adat*. Political subordination based on feasting now masks an authority legitimated ideologically by Christian discourse.

The *kabosenya* thus emerge as pivotal figures in the meeting of these two forms of ritualization. It is the *kabosenya* who, in debate with the mission, determined what elements of To Pamona *adat* were to be incorporated within the Protestant liturgy. In so far as their authority was contested in the transition to a Christian *adat*, the *kabosenya* sought to incorporate those elements of the indigenous form of ritualization upon which their authority rested. It is this process that has led to the dominance of one particular form of Protestant worship, the thanksgiving service (*pengucapan syukur*), in the Christian Church of Central Sulawesi. The thanksgiving service is a key means by which feasting was legitimated, and hence central to the *kabosenya* patronage networks discussed in the previous chapter.

The Indigenous Form of Ritualization

Every culture has its own ways of ritualizing events, of distinguishing them from everyday activity and privileging their importance. In the To Pamona case I have attempted to link one form of ritualization, feasting, with the process of inculturation. Feasting is a means of privileging certain kinds of activity and not a 'rite' in itself; it refers, rather, to an aspect of the way many rituals that involved communal eating were conducted. A shamanic tradition that utilized a special priestly 'language of the heavenly powers,' and headhunting are illustrative of alternative ritual traditions (Adriani 1925). Feasting, however, was the only aspect of To Pamona ritualization compatible with Christian worship: the aspect most easily rendered invisible because it 'says' little.

Feasts are easily improvised because they are an extension of everyday practices that simultaneously constitute hierarchy and dependency through sharing, production, and reproduction. Feasting is common to the most basic of productive activities as well as the largest feasts of social reproduction because it is an implicit, practical 'strategy,' a set of situationally effective schemes and tactics for accomplishing specific practical objectives as varied as planting, marrying, or honouring the dead (Bourdieu 1977, 79). These strategies are not the product of logical thought, of problem solving, but the utilization of known and familiar techniques applied anew in each situation. As Bourdieu notes, 'the principles em-bodied in this way are placed beyond the grasp of consciousness [... and hence] are capable of instilling a whole cosmology, an ethic, a metaphysic,

a political philosophy, through injunctions as insignificant as "stand up straight"'
(1977, 94). The hierarchy created through the feast thus has its roots in the daily
inculcation of politeness behaviours and the coercive power of parents.

In the traditional longhouses (*banua*), and continuing well into the 1940s, all
households ate together, making communal eating the basic social act. The now
retired village mayor described such a meal just before the Second World War in
his grandfather's house, where eight families co-resided. Each family had its
own hearth and cooked its own meals (i.e., they were not living *sanco-ncombori*
[in a simple family household]). Eating, however, was done together, sitting in a
circle on one side of the room, with his grandfather, the *kabosenya*, sitting alone
on a raised platform on the other side. Women generally sat behind their
husbands. The spatial structuring of the participants followed a set of ordered
oppositions that mutually reinforced each other. Thus, higher was to lower, man
was to woman, older was to younger, as served was to server. The *kabosenya*, the
most senior family member, sat highest, and it was impolite for any junior to
raise his or her head above his. Any junior who had to move was forced to adopt
a crouched position and beg forgiveness (*tabe*) in a low voice. Juniors served
seniors; the youngest thus brought food to the *kabosenya* on their knees. Each of
these oppositions was internalized (by countless parental commands, 'Crouch!')
and hence could be improvised without thought in new circumstances as individuals assumed the positions to which they know their status entitles them. No
one was allowed to leave until the most senior member was finished, and had
taken the opportunity to *monuntu* (advise) his juniors on matters of common
concern. Kruyt emphasizes that *monuntu* was the primary 'legal' process (i.e.,
means of dispute settlement) of traditional villages (1950, 1: 196–8). As will be
made clear in a subsequent section, by inculturating preaching as *monuntu* Kruyt
incorporated this political process within the religious service.

Although every family cooked its own foods, eating together specifically
encouraged sharing. This is even more true today, when the occasions for
communal eating are rarer; brought together for special events such as a farewell
dinner, the collected extended family will eat 'pot-luck.' I have already underlined the role of various kinds of generalized exchange crucial to *mosintuwu*
among members of a *santina*; the act of eating together and sharing food
symbolizes these wider exchange networks. These forms of exchange are predicated upon this one basic act, which provides the practical template for the
feasting complex as a whole. Successively larger feasts pull together successively larger segments of the kin group. All participants bring their own rice (just
as every household within a longhouse cooked its own food), and those who have
more (such as a meat animal) contribute this as *posintuwu*. The exchanges that
take place at a feast, and indeed, make the feast possible, are simply magnifica-

tions of the sharing that takes place at a meal within a longhouse. The larger feasts take advantage of the practical strategies inculcated in everyday activity.

In holding a feast these two aspects of communal eating, hierarchy and sharing, are combined. This common logic links all the types of generalized exchange, whether 'shared poverty,' labour exchanges, or *posintuwu*. Feasting, by constituting kinship groups as groups and by providing the structure and reason for these generalized exchanges, creates relations of super- and subordination between specific individuals. All participants order themselves according to the known elements of their social environment, reimposing hierarchy within their small kinship segment. Their segment, in turn, is oriented by the position of their *kabosenya*, who is himself entrapped in relations of seniority and subordination with other *kabosenya*. The feast thus displayed the social hierarchy within a longhouse, village, or village confederacy at a particular moment and froze it under the collective gaze of the participants who unwittingly created it while performing the practical tasks of preparing and eating a meal. One's relationship of dependency to one's *kabosenya* was ordered within a larger social universe such that one's deference to one's *kabosenya* was now extended during the feast to deferring to those to whom that *kabosenya* defers.

These basic strategies order all forms of group activity. The same practical logic of feasting was thus imposed on both production and social reproduction. Traditional forms of agricultural production were dependent upon labour exchanges, and access to land was limited to those who could engage in these exchanges (i.e., married couples who could reciprocate the gendered labour needed to work a field). Each labour exchange had its host, who called on kin for assistance. To avoid scheduling conflicts, the rotation of labour exchanges was organized by the kin group's *kabosenya*, who also played a role in the allocation of land and supervising the assembled workers. Each of these leadership functions involves *monuntu*, advising. The power relationship is limited and the decisions are consensually arrived at, with the *kabosenya* serving as broker. It is the limited nature of the *kabosenya*'s power that necessitates feasting. Ritualization is a means of setting off particular activities as different, and privileging them. The feast held during the labour exchange spatially displayed the social order and thus served to highlight the discourse of the *kabosenya* who took that opportunity to *monuntu*. Deference and hierarchy, central to the serving of the communal meal, socially and spatially set the *kabosenya* apart. The *kabosenya* were served first, in the largest amounts, and sat at a higher elevation. From this position as first among equals, their words were privileged, their opinions prioritized, their authority to regulate productive activities displayed.

Feasting also served to socially situate this form of ritualized leadership within a network of reciprocal exchanges. The hierarchy that the feast imposes is predicated upon sharing among those present. As at any meal, each family cooks its own rice. The labour exchange, however, has a host for whom the work is being done. This host demonstrates his appreciation for this assistance by slaughtering an animal and providing the meat for the communal meal. The meat is by no means payment for the labour rendered, since this must be reciprocated at a latter date. The provisioning of meat follows the same logic as sharing at a meal; those who have extra share among those present. Slaughtering any animal occurs rarely and provides more meat than one family could eat. Doing so at a labour exchange raises people's spirits and energy levels, and so the work is accomplished more quickly. A host's status is thus tied to his generosity, since it is he who makes the feast possible.

This pattern was still strongly evident during the time of my fieldwork, in greatly altered circumstances. My research assistant had cleared a one-hectare swidden, which he was unable to plant with labour exchanges because of his commitments to me. His own wages allowed him to hire a work group, supplemented by his own extended family, including his father, Ngkai Bose, who directed the day's activities. Because a combination of unpaid and paid family was used, it was thought unseemly to underscore the difference, and all were treated as if they were participants in a labour exchange. All workers had brought their own cooked rice, which was supplemented by two extraordinary five-kilogram carp (*ikan mas*). The meal was prepared in a field hut on a small hill overlooking the field. The thirty or so people collected inside, and immediately outside the doors and windows, easing the passage of food, and allowing them to hear. The appearance was of concentric circles around Ngkai Bose, who began the meal with a prayer, and concluded it with *monuntu*, offering direction as to what was to be planted where, how labour was to be divided, and what tasks needed to be prioritized. The day's work seemed remarkably 'unsupervised,' since no one behaved like a *bos* (boss) in the field; work relations remained egalitarian, with no field marshal issuing orders. Work discipline was accomplished through example, with Ngkai Bose setting a pace that others would have been ashamed not to meet. Given this egalitarian approach to labour organization, the role of feasting, and the hierarchy it lays out, are crucial to the success of *monuntu*.

In the past, as now, this same combination of hierarchy and sharing was also found in feasts of social reproduction, weddings, thanksgiving (*padungku*), and funerals. Recall that a core element of the wedding feast (*resepsi*) is the regaling of the bridge and groom with advice by *kabosenya* from both sides of the family. I have emphasized that these feasts involved successively larger groups of kin and ordered them within a larger social universe. The larger feasts differ, however, in that there is no clear host. The various *kabosenya* each sought to centre their *santina* around themselves and did so through their control of the elite goods, cattle and cloth, needed for feasting. *Posintuwu* exchanges determined the social order imposed during the feast, and hence which *kabosenya* would *monuntu*. Feasts of social reproduction thus served to privilege and accentuate the discourse of these *kabosenya*, broadening their audience beyond the small group with whom they came in daily contact.

Inculturation and *Monuntu*

The mission decision to adopt the idiom of *monuntu* and incorporate it within the 'religious' sphere was based upon ethnocentric criteria. Kruyt and Adriani acknowledged that the To Pamona had no indigenous category of experience called religion. For reasons elaborated upon in chapter 1, the mission was forced to distinguish religion from *adat* as a means of delimiting institutional spheres of competence. Kruyt reified two forms of traditional religion, that is, 'religions without tenets': animism and spiritism. These tenets were assumed to be expressed directly through rites that the 'rational Westerner' could read like text and (having superior rationality) systematize as a religion. In reading Toraja (To Pamona) ritual, Kruyt constructed cosmological systems that he could fit within an evolutionary trajectory which placed Christianity as the most developed form. His definitions also privileged spiritism over animism, men's religion over women's. In effecting a conversion, he sought to incorporate only the cultural system he called spiritism or ancestor worship.

This selective definition of religion was in large part predicated upon one factor: gender. To Pamona society maintained rather rigid gender distinctions that allowed for little mixing between genders in most activities. That which Kruyt defined as animism was closely tied to a female-dominated shamanic tradition, which he interpreted as a survival of the older matriarchal social order. Since Dutch Protestantism was patriarchal, female forms of power were symbolically and institutionally subordinated by the mission (Willemsen 1990). Kruyt defined ancestor worship, and hence feasting, as the evolutionary superior of his two abstract 'cultural systems' and sought to incorporate its rituals within the Christian tradition he was constructing.

In inculturating Christianity, Kruyt transformed *monuntu* to fit Protestant notions of 'preaching of the word.' Feasting served to differentiate and privilege the significance of the *kabosenya*'s discourse. Kruyt simply substituted Christian sermons for the traditional ancestor-focused discourse within the feasting complex. He named the gospels, for example, the *nuntu ngkatuwu*, or 'advice for living' (note that Kruyt's son translates this with the common Dutch Christian phrase 'word of life,' which Kruyt was trying to render into Pamonan [1970,

269]). By de-emphasizing a theology that utilized a logic the To Pamona did not understand, and focusing upon biblical narrative, Kruyt attempted to provide concrete examples of Christian principles and how they should be applied in To Pamona society. However, even the simplest of examples was subjected to multiple interpretations; 'as interpretative criteria are extended, so interpretations can be multiplied.' For example, 'animist' assumptions led some To Pamona to a 'superstitious' interpretation of baptism as a form of 'medicine' to strengthen infants (Kruyt 1936b, 93). On the other hand, even though the 'rational' message preached was often not understood by these 'animist' thinkers, they were forced to treat his discourse seriously because their own embodied strategies of ritualization re-created hierarchical relations that privileged what he said. Feasting, and the discipline it imposed, was not dependent upon shared meanings. Rather, feasting imposed a discipline that could not 'be varied quite so easily, because learning to develop moral capabilities is not the same thing as learning to invent representations' (Asad 1988, 87).

As he used an existing tradition to deliver his sermons, Kruyt's authority became dependent upon its preservation, since undermining feasting would be tantamount to undermining the only mechanism that could make his 'rational' message meaningful to 'animist thinkers.' The mission took as long as it did to impose a liturgy upon services for just this reason. It was not until 1925 that a simple liturgy was adopted by the Conference of Missionaries. During this time, the organization of the weekly religious services, no less than labour exchanges, weddings, and funerals, was dependent upon the utilization of the *kabosenya*'s strategies of ritualization. When Kruyt transformed the *wa'a ngkabosenya* (council of village elders) into a consistory, or board of church elders, these elders became responsible for weekly evangelization groups, to whom they would *monuntu*. It was the *kabosenya* who negotiated with the mission to define Christianity in To Pamona terms, and their negotiations were conditioned by the fear of loosing what little power and authority they had. The end result was the preservation of feasting as the means of privileging the 'religious' discourse of *kabosenya*, the patrons of extended kin groups.

Since the imposition of a liturgy in 1925, feasting has become a subordinated form of ritualization within the dominant form, the Protestant *kebaktian* (religious service) marked by hymn singing, a sermon, and a collection for the church. Like the spectacle of an *adat* wedding, the liturgy of the church is played out before a feasting audience. Feasting itself is not a fixed element of the liturgy but the way the liturgy happens when a service is held anywhere other than the church building. Thus, the standard liturgical performances common to the evangelization, men's, women's and youth groups all utilize their members' embodied knowledge of feasting.

The seating arrangements of an evangelization group amply demonstrate the continuity of practice discussed above. The evangelization groups meet on a rotating basis in the homes of members. Since few houses are large enough to seat all participants inside, a temporary shelter or roof extension is usually built the day before. The pulpit will be centrally located so all can hear, but the finest chairs are located inside the house, in the front room. Benches, often borrowed from the school, will be placed outside. Even before the members arrive, they will group themselves, with, for example, women frequently arriving together, separate from their husbands. They will be greeted by the hosts, who will urge them inside. All women will enter, but move through, the house, to the back. The more prominent women will seat themselves at the back of the front room; others closer to the kitchen, perhaps out of view of the speaker. Similarly, *all* men, as they arrive, will be urged to sit inside. Even though I was repeatedly told 'all seats are equal,' I noted that lower-status men would *mundur* (retreat) to the benches outside, with the explanation that such a fine seat might be needed for an unexpected high-status guest. No high-status individual should be seated behind someone of lower status. The end result is the seating of the *ngkai* (grandfathers) inside, and low-status men outside. The stratification of space is thus self-imposed by each participant's appraisal of his or her own status. Such appraisals may be wrong in the eyes of others, but no one is corrected for overestimating his or her own status. The end product only serves to reinforce the self-stratification of space as a public phenomenon, such that I could note the pattern despite the insistence that all seats were equal. Misreading my own status, I attempted to retreat, to join the other young men outside. It was only the continued invitations of the host to move inside that confirmed my high status as honoured guest. The other low-status men received no such continued invitations. On another occasion, I sat outside, behind the low-status, poor, elderly host of a service; he invited me to sit inside, and, on my polite refusal, perplexed as to what to do, himself moved back two rows. The seating spontaneously created stratifies the group by gender and status.

After the elder has preached (*monuntu*), the meeting concludes with refreshments. At its simplest, these consist of coffee and at least two different kinds of home-baked cakes or cookies. Guests are provided with small plastic bags and encouraged to take extra for their children at home. Even at its simplest, such hospitality attempts to emphasize the generosity of the host; the costs of hosting a service are substantial, and include purchased coffee, sugar, flour, and plastic bags for about forty to seventy guests. The event is so expensive, in fact, that many groups have formed rotating credit associations (*arisan*), each family putting aside a little each week so that they have a large lump sum on hand for their turn to host the group. A substantial number of host families will use their turn in the rotation to hold a much larger thanksgiving service with the money they accumulate in this way. The rationale for feasting on such occasions is that the family has been blessed in some way; by feasting they alternately praise God for the blessing and share its benefits with their extended family. Although the thanksgiving service is a distinct liturgical category, it is important to note that its liturgy is exactly the same as in a regular service. The differences all lie in the size of the accompanying feast.

The size of the feast varies in terms of both the number who attend and the variety of foods served. A number of evangelization groups may thus be combined for the event, and the foods vary from the simplest – noodles and chicken – to the most expensive – *beko*, a meat dish. As the size of the feast grows, a minister instead of an elder may be asked to preach. I would thus argue that, if feasting is intended to privilege the discourse of the preacher, increasing feast size serves to further accentuate his message. Since each sermon is contextual, related to the circumstances of the event, the size of the host's blessings are explicitly extolled by the minister, a validation of the host's status. This became most clear to me when I held my own celebratory feast on the publication of my first book, which occurred while I was in the field. I asked for the assistance of my landlord, a high-ranking civil servant, who acted as co-host. He, in consultation with his wife, utilized their sense of ritual to improvise what was appropriate for me in these circumstances. It was determined that the two evangelization groups with which I most closely worked, plus a number of high-status acquaintances, including the chair of the synod, and the Dutch missionaries, should be invited. The status of the guests in turn determined the quality of food, as my landlady would have been embarrassed if there weren't at least two kinds of meat served. As my feast was transformed into a major event (as I worriedly checked my pocketbook), it required an equally prominent minister, no less than a member of the synod commission. That such a noted minister would agree to preach and, in preaching, extol my accomplishment validated the size of the feast.

The hierarchy created by the feast was predicated upon my 'sharing' my good fortune. This 'sharing' also has a second aspect as well. The feast, because of its size, meant drawing on my landlord's extensive *posintuwu* network; numerous volunteers worked for days to prepare the temporary shelter, butcher the animals, cook the meal, and serve it. Their willingness to help reflects his past assistance to them. The limits to the size of a feast are thus closely related not only to the financial ability of the hosts, but to the size of their exchange network, their past history of helping. The success of my landlord's feasts thus contrasts with the experience of another, rich, retired civil servant who had just returned to the village after years away, but who had not devoted himself to building a *posintuwu* network, expecting his status as a civil servant to carry the day. Indeed, his direct requests for help were honoured (how could they be refused?), but only a polite minimum was forthcoming and no one volunteered. A same-sized feast may articulate different degrees of dependency within an exchange group. Status is acquired not only by hosting a large feast, but through one's utilization of the *posintuwu* networks that make any feast possible.

The continuity of indigenous feasting practice, and hence the perpetuation of the exchange networks by which a *kabosenya*'s authority is established, is, as I pointed out above, subordinated to the primary liturgical event, the sermon. As a subordinated form of ritualization, feasting continues to exist in the margins of the Protestant service, only occasionally emerging to overwhelm that service. Feasting is not directly incorporated in the liturgy, and hence is not defined as a specifically religious activity. The Protestant liturgy, however, is rarely enacted outside the church building without invoking this subordinated form of ritualization, and vice versa.[1] This linkage of the two forms of ritualization has tied the church to kinship and its attendant encapsulation of hierarchy and dependency. The church has grown and prospered because its incorporation of To Pamona 'religion' simultaneously captured a kin-ordered political process.

Dominance and the Protestant Worship Service

The interpretive act by which *monuntu* was construed 'religious' was not neutral but an active imposition of a Western category upon the To Pamona. As noted above, this incorporation was selective, assimilating the act of speaking as 'religious,' as preaching, while ignoring the cultural means by which those speech acts were highlighted. I argued earlier that this emphasis upon the spoken word, and upon meaning, is a distinctive feature of the Western, specifically Dutch Protestant, form of ritualization. Kruyt, like most theologians of his day, conceptualized ritual as the 'expression' of belief, or dogma. Ritual was a *leervorm*, a lesson of instruction in God's will as expressed in his word, the Bible, to those assembled. Dutch Protestant worship is thus centred around this fundamental act, the 'preaching of the Word.'

Preaching the Word is a transformative event. In Protestant theology, the preaching of God's word is accompanied by the action of the Holy Ghost upon the listener so that they are made receptive to the Truth. The outward sign's transformative power, its ability to create significant inward meanings, is predicated upon the actions of the spirit of God. This theological inner orientation, the emphasis on belief, ignores the structured social circumstances by which shared belief is created. It is significant, then, that Kruyt himself came to reject a model of conversion based upon the transformative power of the Word and instead recognized it as a political process (Kruyt 1910). In so doing, he de-emphasized the importance of shared belief in defining Christian identity. Of greater importance was submission to the 'word of God.'

Kruyt's theological and theoretical reasoning for this radical change in mission methodology is discussed more fully in the next chapter. Here, analysis is directed at his methodology, the political means he utilized to prioritize the speech acts of the minister. The first method, the selective incorporation of *monuntu*, has already been discussed. However, in 1925, Kruyt slowly began adding distinctive Protestant liturigal features of worship, marking this particular form of *monuntu* as specifically 'religious,' as a ritual. The Conference of Missionaries imposed a basic Protestant liturgy upon the services they had been holding in the *monuntu* style and, as the Protestant liturgy was foregrounded, those aspects of feasting that did not fit the Western model were increasingly ignored and marginalized. Thus, speaking was included within the liturgy, whereas eating was not.

The first change to be introduced was hymn singing. In 1912, Kruyt introduced a hymnbook containing thirty-six hymns in Bahasa Pamona (Sura mPongayu). These distinctive Western hymns were taught in village schools, although only later, when they were introduced as a part of the funeral service, did they become widely used (Kruyt 1970, 273). So distinctive were these hymns within the local tradition that the entire funeral service, including Bible reading, sermon, prayer, and hymns, were referred to as *mongayu* (singing). Hymn singing was so distinctively Christian that when Talasa, the animist king of Poso, died in 1948, Jan Kruyt refused to allow hymn singing at his funeral, despite his children's desire for a 'Christian burial.' Kruyt's funeral sermon, in itself, was considered insufficient to constitute a Christian service. Hymn singing was incorporated in the order of worship developed in 1925 and so lent a distinctive feature to all Christian worship services.

With the introduction of the order of worship, other changes also took place. Sunday worship services, which had been taking place in homes, were moved to the schools, and, eventually, to church buildings. Jan Kruyt emphasized that this change was significant in that it shifted the balance away from the indigenous sphere towards Western models. When services had been held in homes, the missionaries were considered guests and had to adhere to indigenous norms. When services were moved to the schools, the missionaries became hosts and thus determined the nature of the gathering. 'People sat on benches, could no longer spit between the floor joists but had to go to the window, and you came into a strongly regulated space where you had to speak in turn and therefore said nothing' (J. Kruyt 1970, 271). The religious services ordered space in a manner that further prioritized the speech of the minister. Rather than congregants sitting in a circle, benches were arranged church fashion, facing a pulpit, and invoked a discipline inculcated in school. Whereas the traditional seating formation emphasized inner versus outer circle, with those of the inner circle speaking, the new seating arrangement divided congregation from minister, singers from speaker. The consultative process of *monuntu* was thus transformed into a one-sided conversation.

The historical evolution of the religious service presented so far emphasizes the contingent nature of the Protestant form of ritualization. It was dependent upon the slow transformation of elements of the indigenous form of ritualization with the gradual overlay of hymn singing, and the backgrounding of the shared meal as 'non-liturgical.' Unlike the indigenous form of ritualization, the Protestant form of ritualization was not an extension of everyday 'virtues'; it was, rather, a colonial imposition predicated upon Western Christian norms. How then, can we describe the Protestant form of ritualization as dominant within the To Pamona social formation?

The question of dominance relates to who controls access to that particular form of ritualization. Over the last century that control has shifted from the colonial mission to an indigenous elite. As discussed in the previous chapters, as the To Pamona made the transition from swidden to *sawah* agriculture, a class dimension was introduced, and control of social reproduction became dependent upon the ownership of property. Class differentiation was blunted by two factors. First, the fragmentation of landholdings has meant that To Pamona society is not divided into landowners and workers, but into 'just-enoughs' and 'not-quite-enoughs.' Second, class differentiation has been blunted by 'shared poverty.' Hierarchy and dependency within a kin group are created through control of social reproduction and not the means of production, through control of *posintuwu* exchange networks (a function of wealth), rather than land per se. The economic and political constituency created through 'shared poverty' is preserved through feasting and now articulated with the church.

This new rural elite are like the old *kabosenya* in that their political constituency is created through their control of social reproduction. They dominate within the church because the feasts through which they exercise control of the social reproduction of their extended kin groups are themselves encapsulated within the church. That the evangelization groups continue to encapsulate kinship was driven home to me by local reaction to a synod directive to redistribute membership of the groups by streets, 'by straight lines,' so as to ensure a consistent size. The redistribution rapidly faltered, however, as cut-off kinsmen flouted the directive and continued to attend the services of their physically distant, 'close' kin. 'When we see them everyday, how can we turn our backs on them when it is their turn to host the evangelization group?' Members spoke of 'feeling at home,' and of long-standing obligations to help, as of greater practical importance than the need to even out the numbers in each group.

Unlike the old *kabosenya*, the new elite's control of social reproduction is based on their property – although not on relations of production per se. Since they are the wealthiest members of the community, they have greater access to the educational system, which guarantees salaried jobs in both the church and state. Ministers and civil servants are overwhelmingly drawn from this class. It is this small group that has negotiated the reformation of the feasting complex and its consolidation within the church as the church became a more powerful institution within the To Pamona community. As this new elite has achieved an entrenched position within the church hierarchy, its members have more clearly subordinated feasting to the liturgical forms of Christianity. Their reasons for doing so can be tied to the transformations of *monuntu* by the mission, which further accented the elders' speech, and hence their ability to define the Christian *adat*. As elder or minister, they were no longer just one speaker among several in the inner circle, but *the* speaker from a pulpit. The religious service offered no opportunity for opposition; nor for alternative conceptions or interpretations to be discussed. The *kabosenya*'s word, like the mission's word, became God's word, a sermon.

The minister's increasing ability to define ritual situations comes as the greatest shock, perhaps, to those who do not normally submit to its discipline. Papa Dori, for example, was a peripheral member of the church community, noted more for his band than for his piety. On his daughter's first birthday, however, even he felt the need to 'praise God for his blessing.' He requested that the evangelization group meet in his house that week, and set about building a large shelter for the many guests. A pig was to be slaughtered. And the size of the event was such that it required a minister as preacher, not the elder. But here, Papa Dori outreached himself. He called on the classis minister, a distant uncle with whom he had lived as a child (and whom he therefore called 'Papa'), to preach. This minister, his 'father,' did the unthinkable. He began his sermon with praise for Papa Dori for finally taking part in the evangelization group and for feeling the need to praise God. But he quickly moved on, in pointed fashion, to the self-agrandizing aspect of Papa Dori's feast and his poor track record in church attendance. When I later spoke with the minister about the harshness of his words, he argued that he could not have spoken that way with any other member of the congregation; it was specifically because this was his 'son' that he could take him to task, thereby underscoring how kin relations are embedded within the church. But, the only place he could discipline his son was in the evangelization group, where Papa Dori's very investment prevented him from leaving or reacting in anger. The ritual allowed for a one-sided interpretation of

Papa Dori's piety, which could not be argued with. The patron–client aspect of their families' relationship, first made manifest through the minister's fostering this poorer kin member, was further clarified here; try as this poor man might to engage in the status-bearing activities of the church, he must remember his place and not overstep his bounds.

The process of inculturation thus involves more than the imposition of an ideology, a system of meanings and values expressing particular class interests. Inculturation is, rather, an extension of hegemony or of the distribution of power and influence (Williams 1977, 108). I have noted that the mission tolerated multiple interpretations of the outward signs of Christianity. Its ideological control was weak, but this mattered little, since 'what is decisive is not only the conscious system of ideas and beliefs, but the whole lived process as practically organized by specific dominant meanings and values' (Williams 1977, 109). These relations of power are what Kruyt sought to capture after his realization that individual conversion was an impossibility. In placing the emphasis in his mission methodology upon the spiritual community, which exercised a 'strengthening and leading influence' (1936, 246), Kruyt denied the individual the ability to say 'no' to conversion.

As an extension of hegemony, the utilization of *monuntu* as preaching is predicated upon the unthought, the unremarked, the everyday – that is, culture. 'It is a lived system of meanings and values – constitutive and constituting – which as they are experienced in practices appear as reciprocally confirming. It thus constitutes a sense of reality for most people in society, a sense of absolute because experienced reality beyond which it is very difficult for most members of the society to move, in most areas of their lives. It is, that is to say, in the strongest sense a 'culture,' but a culture which has also to be seen as the lived dominance and subordination of particular classes' (Williams 1977, 110). Culture in this sense creates relations of power that grant unequal access to the expressive aspects of ritual. It does not guarantee acceptance of that which is expressed, only of the right of the powerful to speak. It is in this sense that I interpret the actions of young friends, the subjects of *monuntu*, who silently accepted the advice proffered, then did otherwise with a muttered, 'It is better to just remain silent' (*Lebih baik diam saja*).

Within the network of relations of power created through the meeting of these two forms of ritualization, the ideological definition of which parts of the *adat* were 'religious' was thus determined by those with a voice, the mission and the new elite. Both interest groups attempted to incorporate those elements of their form of ritualization upon which their authority rested. This new category of experience granted ideological priority to Dutch definitions based upon preaching the Word. The indigenous elite, on the other hand, incorporated feasting within the liturgy as a thanksgiving service. The Dutch emphasis on belief, meaning, and expression (that is, on ideology) specifically ignored those social practices (that is, feasting) upon which the ideology's authority rested. The act of *monuntu* was thus incorporated as a ritual act, but feasting and *posintuwu* exchanges were not.

Transformations

Ritualization refocuses attention on the way embodied knowledge is freshly applied to each situation rather than examining ritual as the enactment of a fixed and unchanging structure. Each ritual event is thus a subtle interplay of competing strategies, some expected, some not, which challenge and mould existing relations of power. Hegemony 'does not just passively exist as a form of dominance. It has continually to be renewed, recreated, defended, and modified. It is also continually resisted, limited, altered, challenged by pressures not at all its own' (Williams 1977, 112). The shift in focus from ritual to ritualization thus highlights the transformative power of ritual, its ability to usurp, transform, and adjust to change as its claims to authority are challenged and appropriated (Comaroff 1985, 4–6). The new situations created by the colonial presence, the transformation of the economy, household and political relations, all have their impact upon the ritual event. As with the wedding feast, it is thus possible to examine trends in the transformation of current ritual practice.

These general trends involve the individualization, modernization, and extension of feasting, processes that can be related to the subordination of feasting to the Protestant liturgy, as well as to general changes in household and kinship structure. As fewer and fewer households co-reside in a single house, communal eating (*molimbu*) has been increasingly restricted to feasts. Wage labour and the commodification of the local economy have limited ties of generalized reciprocity between households primarily to those exchanges conducted during feasts. And the traditional political functions of kin groups have disappeared as these groups became hierarchically organized within the church bureaucracy. This reordering of the kinship sphere and its incorporation within the evangelization group transformed the available means of accomplishing ritual and tipped the balance of power towards those who controlled the new sources of wealth. The new elite hold the largest feasts and introduce new elements emulated by others. For example, the introduction of a floor value for *posintuwu keluarga dekat* (*posintuwu* from 'close' family) was introduced by a respected feast-giver renowned for his generosity. So, too, it is the wealthier families who are responsible for the wide-scale adoption of the thanksgiving service (*pengucapan syukur*). The trends towards the individualization, modernization, and extension of feasting are thus the crucial means by which the hegemony of this elite is asserted, and its disciplinary hold over its genealogical juniors deepened.

The growth in the number of thanksgiving services held and the use of the service by new groups and in new situations is thus the most significant change in ritual performance, with the greatest implications for the extension of church power. Whereas the evangelization-group format was applied to just-married couples, similar weekly groups have now been formed catering to women, to men, and to young people. The size of the feast is a test of the abilities of the host family. Even at its simplest, hosting the evangelization group is a major expense. But increasingly, families have been caught in a kind of 'feasting inflation' in which the reasons for a thanksgiving service have multiplied. When the men's group in one village elevated their weekly meetings to a full thanksgiving service with slaughtered pig, it proved such a burden on their members that membership declined precipitously.

Children's birthday parties held in the form of a thanksgiving service attended solely by the child's friends were the latest innovation. Parents expressed their despair at having to disappoint their children, eager to match the size and sumptuousness of a friend's feast. When I first heard of a planned party for a neighbour's five-year-old child, I had expected that the format would have been adapted, with the emphasis on games; yet this was not the case. Although there were balloons, the thirty or so children were seated in rows around the pulpit, from which a fifteen-year-old preached in a service nearly identical to that of their parents.

Closely associated with the extension of feasting is its individualization. The church's attempts to preserve 'community' through the incorporation and Christianizing of annual communal feasts such as the harvest festival (padungku), or the creation of new communal feasts on the occasion of mass rites such as baptism and the confession of faith, have ironically been a general failure. What had once been community feasts with hosts competing for status have now become multiple feasts, each with its individual host. A parallel with the general move to the mebolai marriage ceremony can be drawn. For example, the harvest festival was celebrated in successively larger groups, first in the fields among a swidden group, then by the village as a whole. Over the years, the communal village feast has been replaced with a pattern of rotating home visitations. Elders told me that the communal feast was too unwieldy to organize for the now larger village, although they did so several years ago on government orders. I attended one such 'traditional' padungku in a neighbouring village. Since the village has a population of more than 150 families, only one representative from each family could attend. Seated in the village soccer field, these representatives were fed out of small woven baskets with bamboo glasses by servers in adat costume. The district government was hoping to foster a rebirth of local traditions, which would serve as a draw for tourists, much like the secondary funerals of Tana Toraja. The government quietly dropped its plans the following year; given the expense, the difficulty in finding appropriate meat animals, the time required to prepare disposable utensils such as the bamboo glasses (when the women's group had several hundred glasses in its communal stock), and the fact that only a small part of the village could attend, resulted in a rapid reversion to the pattern of individually sponsored feasts.

As *padungku* is currently practised, a special church service is held at which farmers bring their 'expression of thanks' (a portion of their harvest, piled next to the pulpit), followed by individual families providing meals for all visitors. The first sitting is formal, and followed by a more casual succession of visits to family and patrons, lasting all day and night. One may eat six or seven times in an afternoon at the harvest festival, on New Year's Day (when baptisms are held), or when confessions of faith are heard. The harvest festival is held at different times in different villages on a rotating basis, thus allowing for extended kin groups to meet regularly. Who one visits reflects ties of super- and subordination, as those with higher status tend to play host, leaving only to visit those of higher status yet. Low-status, unmarried men, in contrast, form roving bands, moving from house to house, unworried about the need to reciprocate. These visits are accompanied by gifts of special feast foods, like *inuyu*, sticky rice cooked in a bamboo steamer, which are given to visitors by the bundle for those back home, unable to come. The individualization of the harvest festival, as of other communal feasts, has transformed it from a village-wide into a kindred-centred feast in which patron–client relations are solidified.

As the example of *padungku* demonstrates, it is becoming increasingly difficult to feast in the original style; feasting has thus been 'modernized.' The use of plates, cutlery, and buffet-style serving has come to replace the older pattern of *molimbu*. Just as the church service strictly orders space in rows, not circles, so this social order has been applied to feasts. The 'modernization' of feasting styles can be tied to a number of factors. The practice is, first, closely associated with the adoption of *posintuwu umum* and the overall expansion in size and number of guests invited. This bundle of innovations have a 'middle-class' air about them; *posintuwu* in an envelope, a Sunday dress in a chair, a plate and spoon, are all valued as higher-status variants of the bowl of threshed rice, sitting on the floor, and eating with your fingers out of a leaf. And as the women's group has invested in large sets of cups and plates, it has become more practical to reuse these readily available communal supplies rather than having to search for sufficient bamboo and banana leaves. The style of feasting that originated with the wedding reception has thus gradually become the dominant form.

The increasing numbers of thanksgiving services has also been matched by the extension of *posintuwu* exchanges. The original narrow definition of *posintuwu* as a gift given only at weddings or funeral feasts is slowly being transformed by *posintuwu umum*. *Posintuwu umum* was first collected to assist the bridal family in hosting the wedding feast. As *posintuwu umum* has become increasingly important in weddings, the exchange networks thus created have been extended to feasts held on other occasions. Many of the wealthier families will bring *posintuwu umum* to any feast to which they are invited, especially to those of poorer families who have extensively helped them in the past. The spread of *posintuwu umum* is closely tied to the increasing individualization of feasting as even the poor are forced to host feasts to maintain their status as full exchange partners; and to feasting's extension to new occasions as the reasons for thanksgiving services multiply.

These transformations in feasting all serve to adapt the practice to the changes in local political relations. Individualized feasts serve to define a salient kindred around a centre, a prominent patron who, through his largess, controls the rituals of social reproduction of that kindred. Establishing leadership within this kinship group has thus served as the primary motor for the individualization of feasting, as well as the extension and expansion in size of feasts. Since leadership is established only through relative differences in feast size, asserting one's independence (and the subordination of others) through an enlarged feast fuels 'feasting inflation.' 'Genealogical amnesia' limits the knowledge of descendants of the exact ties binding them within an extended kin group. These ties are remembered only if they are constantly renewed through *posintuwu* exchanges; hence, those with greater wealth are able to maintain a wider network of exchanges.

The preservation of kinship ties is thus predicated upon feasting, and simultaneously establishes relations of super- and sub-ordination. The political ordering of the kinship group, the establishment of leadership, elevates prominent feast-givers to the point where they are granted a voice in the ritual event as an elder. However, since the expansion of feasting has taken place within the church-sanctioned evangelization groups, these ideological expressions are moulded by the larger demands of the church. *Kabosenya* are no longer *kabosenya*, but church elders. I was informed in a number of villages that 'there were no more *kabosenya* in our village,' although an accusing finger was pointed at neighbouring villages said to be more 'traditional.' These mutual accusations simply highlight the changed nature of the *kabosenya*, who no longer wish to be identified with a 'feudal' system.

It should be evident, then, that the Protestant service is much like the *adat* spectacle performed during the wedding, since it, too, is carried out during a similarly backgrounded feast. The abstraction and reification of the *adat* as a liturgical performance is a part of the wider process of inculturation. In both cases, Western modes of domination have been predicated upon the incorporation of 'tradition' and its subordination to a larger bureaucratic organization, whether state or church. The gradual imposition of a Protestant liturgy upon *monuntu* preserved indigenous relations of dominance and subordination within a kinship framework while simultaneously prioritizing mission ideology, 'the Word of God.' Similarly, the transformation of *adat* into a liturgical spectacle also serves to preserve indigenous relations of dominance and subordination but limits *adat* law to a 'cultural' sphere, where it poses no threat to the civil state. As I argued earlier, Kruyt's sociological mission method utilized the techniques of domination developed by the secular liberal state to religious ends; but this commonality of methods does not imply common goals. Kruyt's very success in inculturating Christianity among the To Pamona thus established a familiar dynamic, a tension between church and state, that laid the groundwork for 'pillarization.'

6

The Rationalization of Belief

How then shall they call on him in whom they have not believed? and how shall they believe in him of whom they have not heard? and how shall they hear without a preacher?

Romans 10: 14

Religion was a key component in early variants of modernization theory. As societies develop, it was argued, they not only become more complex and institutionally specialized, but evolve more universalistic notions of deity, morality, and community. These deparochialized commitments cut across the segmentary attachments of family, ethnicity, and traditional religion, muting their divisiveness, and providing a unified 'civic' consensus for the modern nation-state. In terms of religious content, in other words, modernization involved two things: a Weberian disenchantment of local worlds, and the emergence of a universalistic and explicit religiosity, roughly Durkheimian in form. Development in this view was thus a long march toward a rationally-constructed and, in essence, educated religiosity.

Hefner 1989, 2

Kruyt's model of conversion had explicit evolutionary undertones. The conversion of the To Pamona would lead to the gradual abandonment of animistic ways of thinking, with a concomitant increase in 'rationalism.' Kruyt shared Weber's expectation of a unilinear evolution of 'traditional religions' into rational, bureaucratic 'world religions.' The end product of this evolutionary progression or rationalization of religion is an interiorized, essentialized religion defined in terms of a rationally applied, abstractly formulated system of beliefs. In this chapter, I argue, in contrast, that the emphasis on the rationalization of systems of belief is misleading and that the priorization of meaning in the study of ritual reduces a complex phenomenon to a unilinear process, a move from less to more rationality (which thus begs the question whether such a universal standard actually exists; Habermas 1984, 8–42). I argue that greater attention should be paid to the institutional changes that motivate and sustain the development of religious discourses (cf. Asad 1983, 252). Among the To Pamona, there was no rationalization of a belief system, despite conversion to a world religion and problems of meaning continued to be addressed piecemeal. This was the result of the de-emphasis on systematic dogmatics by the mission. Religious discourse, however, took place within an increasingly rationalized bureaucratic system that extended and universalized the relations of power embodied in the practical logic of ritual activity, as described in the last chapter.

Conversion and Shared Belief

Most Christian models of conversion focus on changes in beliefs, and thus prioritize both the propositional character of specific doctrines and a mental state or conviction that such propositions are true (Tooker 1992, 802). Indeed, one's salvation is said to be dependent upon holding true beliefs that negate errors in the practical application of those beliefs (i.e., sin). Animist traditions, as Kruyt noted, are not propositional; they are tied to a practical or embodied logic whose sense is tied to culturally specific practical activities. This is not to argue that 'animists' are incapable of propositional logic, just that the Western concept of 'religion' is intimately tied to propositional belief. This is the underlying assumption of Weber's distinction between traditional (non-propositional) and world ('rational') religions (Tooker 1992, 809). In discussing the conversion of animists to Christianity, we need a vocabulary that distinguishes between these abstractly formulated propositions (beliefs) and the more general cultural category of belief (or faith) which denotes a mental attitude of exclusive affirmation of the truth of these propositions. In the case of the To Pamona, I will argue that rational beliefs (i.e., a systematic theology) were relatively underemphasized in the conversion process and that the inculcation of the wider category of 'belief' or 'piety' was prioritized.

Kruyt was an early advocate of a process now variously referred to, in English, as the indigenization, contextualization, or inculturation of the Christian message.[1] As Kruyt formulated this process, there was little point in utilizing a propositional-oriented Christian theology that was not accessible to animistic thinkers; Kruyt explicitly rejected intellectualist accounts of religious conversion. The intellectualist model views conversion as a change in religious beliefs 'where beliefs are viewed as instruments of explanation and control of actual time–space events' (Hefner 1993, 102). In the intellectualist tradition, conversion occurs when the convert compares the relative coherence and explanatory force of two competing belief systems and selects one on the basis of its superior ability to address absolute problems of meaning. Christianity, in this model, as a rationalized world religion with universalized doctrines and a superior rationality should be the obvious choice over an animist tradition that met the problems of 'evil, suffering, frustration, bafflement, and so on – piecemeal' (Geertz 1973c, 172). Kruyt's rejection of the intellectualist tradition of missiology was slow in coming, the product of fifteen years of mission failure. The key to this rejection was his experiences with Papa i Wunte, his first convert.

Papa i Wunte was the *kabosenya* of Kasiguncu, a coastal village near Kruyt's mission post. Kruyt developed a warm friendship with the man; his adopted son, Pancali, eventually married Papa i Wunte's daughter. The man also became one of his primary informants on *adat* and culture: '"Tua Boba (N. Adriani) is the oldest of you all," Papa i Wunte once said to me, "but you are my oldest son. You were the first to call me father and after you, all the ministers and their wives, all the civil servants and officers have done so"' (Kruyt 1910, 16). Papa i Wunte was the first *kabosenya* to allow a Christian school to be built and, according to Kruyt, was already convinced of the veracity of the Christian message as early as 1904 (ibid., 25); yet he refused to convert. His reticence stemmed from the question 'When I become a Christian, what must I leave behind?' (ibid., 21). Abandoning the cult of the ancestors would have undercut his authority within his village and village confederacy. Kruyt thus came to recognize that conversion was not a matter of simple intellectual acknowledgment of Christianity's veracity, of propositional assent, but a political process integrally tied with the extension of Dutch colonial rule. This was a factor long recognized by the To Pamona themselves: '[Kruyt] did not lose heart, but as he had asked the help of Papa i Wunte when he attempted to start the school at Buyu-mBayau, so now he tried to profit from Ta Lasa, a headman of the To Lage. He called a meeting with this sharp orator at which all of the headmen of Kuku appeared. Without reserve, they all gave as their opinion that the missionary was like a tame buffalo cow with which the Netherlands government would entice and capture them, the wild buffaloes' (Adriani 1919, 178). Though long convinced of Christianity's veracity, Papa i Wunte postponed his conversion until after the Netherlands East Indies (NEI) government's invasion in 1905. It was not until several months after the Dutch colonial government had guaranteed his continued political influence by appointing him district head of the coastal region that Papa i Wunte was baptized, on Christmas Day, 1909 (*Regeerings-Almanak* 1909; Kruyt 1970, 109). It is important to point out that the entire village was baptised together. This does not mean that all were as intellectually receptive to Christianity as was Papa i Wunte. As Kruyt himself emphasized, the majority of the new converts had no intellectual appreciation of the totality of the Christian message. They were making a leap of faith. By having the village convert as a unit, the mission took advantage of existing relations of power to maintain a guiding spiritual community that would provide the functional replacement for an interiorized theology. The religious community so created would inculcate Christian values without the mission having to impose a set of rational beliefs that most villagers did not (or, according to Kruyt, could not) understand. Indigenous relations of power would provide external guides in a situation where an interiorized set of theological propositions to guide behaviour were lacking.

Kruyt's most original contribution to missiology was thus to sever the conversion process from the issue of propositional beliefs. This was a daring move in a religious climate dominated by acrimonious divisions within the Dutch churches on issues of doctrinal orthodoxy. His methodology was explicitly evolutionary, taking advantage of what he saw as the natural progression of social change from its lowest matriarchal and animistic forms to the superior, patriarchal Christian form. Conversion could not imply an understanding of the Christian message in its totality (cf. Hefner 1993, 122). Animistic thinkers, he stated, had a great deal of difficulty in expressing the tenets of their religion, and so placed their unsystematic conceptions directly in rites. As their thinking matured, a disjuncture developed between their rites and belief. For example, the logic of an animistic rite was clear to animistic thinkers who saw the link between the ritual action and the intended result. As that group developed an ancestor cult (*spiritisme*), its thinking evolves in 'dynamistic' directions. Because the original rite was never explicitly related to a codified system of beliefs, as the mode of thinking of individual members of the group changes, so, too, does their interpretation of the meaning and intent of the rite. This new mode of thinking, no less than animism, was unable to formulate a rational set of tenets. There is thus a disjuncture between the animistic rite and its new dynamistic interpretation, or, more generally, between rite and dogma. Kruyt thus found pre-animistic and animistic residues in the rites of the dynamistic To Pamona and proposed a theory of survivals not unlike Tylor. The conversion to Christianity, he argued, should take advantage of this and allow animistic and dynamistic interpretations of Christian rites so that these new rites became meaningful to their participants in their own terms. As their thinking evolved, they would eventually acquire a 'rational' appreciation of Christian dogma through the Christian rites they had long participated in.

Kruyt rationalized these methodological innovations in terms of Ethical Theology. The imposition of a theologically focused Christianity would simply breed a syncretism; Christianity would have no impact on animistic ways of thinking and would remain an unintegrated part of the To Pamona cultural psyche. Since Kruyt's ministry was firmly based in the pietistic traditions of the Netherlands Missionary Society, such empty formalism was untenable. The only alternative was to initially accept animistic interpretations of Christian rites. Kruyt used the honouring of the sabbath as an example (1925, 160). Christian doctrine holds that the Lord declared the sabbath a day of rest and that the avoidance of work is intended to honour his creation. The To Pamona accepted the prohibition of work on Sunday but interpreted this prohibition in magical terms: work done on Sundays would cause crop failures. Kruyt argued that such 'superstition' *must* be tolerated, since it is a sign that the rite has acquired meaning for them (1925, 164). All converts had to work through a 'magical phase' of Christianity, and hence the mission should welcome the superstition surrounding Christian rites as an indication of the new role Christianity was gaining in their lives. He compared this paternalistic approach to an experience he had with a European child before entering the mission field:

> When, as a young missionary, I sojourned for a few months in Gorontalo [North Sulawesi] there also lived a European teacher's family with two wonderful sons. I was quickly on good terms with them. But then I noted that the youngest had become frightened of me and hid when I came. I asked his mother what the reason could be and she finally got a confession from her son: 'Mr. Kruyt is a minister, and he can send Frits to heaven or hell, whatever he wishes.' This had been told him by the native nanny. I could only calm my little friend with the assurance: 'Now, Frits, if I had that power then I would certainly bring you to God in heaven.' I have never forgotten this, and have taken the same course with my Torajas. (Kruyt 1925, 166–7)

It is important to underscore the root assumptions that guided Kruyt's new methodology. By reducing a cosmology (animism) to a 'mode of thinking,' Kruyt's model of religious evolution could be easily articulated with the dominant colonial ideology of the 'primitive.' This evolutionary perspective (which has been rephrased but unchallenged in the traditional-versus-rationalized religion literature) only recognizes difference against the measure of Western religion and its favoured mode of theological argumentation. In rejecting the intellectualist model of conversion, Kruyt de-emphasized theology in favour of piety, thus allowing for conversion without altering the subordinate position of the 'child-like' To Pamona.

An important corollary of this point is that the congregation cannot be considered a group with shared beliefs. Recognizing his inability to alter a 'mode of thinking,' Kruyt sought to establish an orthopraxy rather than an orthodoxy. Regular attendance at services was of greater importance than correct belief since it was only in the religious service that individuals could be induced to reform themselves. This led some government officials to the dismissive claim that 'the influence, either good or bad on character, disposition, morality and custom of the people is unnoticeable' (Son MVO 1935, 7). This inability to enforce a standard system of beliefs betrays the essential lack of power of the mission. Kruyt emphasized that he could never contradict the beliefs of his congregation, a sentiment reflected by every minister and elder I interviewed. A direct attack on someone's heartfelt belief would only elicit anger and a refusal to listen. Toleration of divergent opinion on central matters of faith was a necessity as long as a significant proportion of respected elders refused to embrace Christian cosmological concepts (the last conversions in Tentena occurred in the late 1940s). This toleration has itself been institutionalized with theological concerns neglected in favour of homiletics. Indeed, a large proportion of those who preach (elders and those elders elevated to pastor) have little or no theological training. The standardization and systematization of beliefs is considered a long-term project, always seemingly postponed because of the congregation's lack of education.

Within this relaxed theological atmosphere a number of distinctive indigenous cosmological concepts have entered local Christian discourse in an uneven manner. Aragon (1996) and Adams (1993) have argued that in nearby areas in Central and South Sulawesi, similar concepts fill in unresolved aspects of the Christian canon in relation to local concerns. They argue that the existence of these beliefs does not reflect superficial or incomplete conversion or arbitrary survivals. Rather, as Hefner argued in relation to Muslim conversion in Java,

> in studying the transition from locally-based faiths to 'world' religion we need to examine the cultural content of both religious discourses in relation to the social scale, political organization, and cultural diversity of the communities to which each would appeal ... From this perspective, the distinction between traditional and world religions is best understood not in terms of a Weberian contrast between 'traditionalism' and 'rationalization,' but in terms of the primary cultural diversity of each religious community, and the shared tacit knowledge its idioms can assume. (1987, 55)

The persistence of specific indigenous cosmological concepts should not be interpreted as the eruption of animism through the façade of incomplete Christian conversion. Rather, the utilization of these concepts in Christian discourse is based upon their continued saliency in other contexts. This shared tacit knowledge is formulated and inculcated in non-ritual contexts but may systematically invade Christian discourse where no alternative is readily available to address local concerns.

A case in point is the indigenous notion of *puloru* (to suffer from divine justice). The concept of *puloru* is central to local power relations between elders and juniors. One becomes *puloru* through disrespect or disobedience to elders; divine retribution is considered automatic, a result of the threat, although it is now said to be the working of God rather than of the ancestors. Punishment comes in the form of accident or illness. For example, Ito, a newly waged twenty-year-old truck driver who spent his money on drink rather than supporting his mother, was warned by her that he was *puloru*. He ignored her threat until months later, when he was involved in an accident that earned him six months in jail. On his return to the village after serving his sentence, the entire village buzzed over the contrite transformation in his behaviour; a more attentive son could not have been found. The object lesson quickly made the rounds, an evident token of the power of God, and of his proxies – parents.

The ministers and elders of Tentena generally denied having used the concept in sermons, as it has no theological basis.[2] Despite the absence of theological support for the notion, it remains unquestioned and frequently invoked in every-day church life; it is, for example, *puloru* for anyone other than the designated minister or elder to preach from the pulpit (*naik mimbar*). An anecdote related by a Classis Minister is typical of its usage. Siding with another minister in a dispute with his church council, this minister threatened the council with *puloru* if they did not accept his ministerial right to arbitrary authority in the matter; they quickly backed down. *Puloru*, like most other indigenous cosmological concepts (particularly ghosts, such as the *ringgiana* and *angga*), are thus more accurately extra-theological. These concepts address local problems of meaning ignored by the 'universalizing message' of Christianity as the missionaries interpreted it. The lack of theological rigour applied to sermons ensures that no overt contradictions are found between theological and extra-theological cosmological principles, but also serves to preserve Christian theology from syncretic accretions. When theology is de-emphasized, a wide range of individual extra-theological beliefs can be easily articulated with official doctrine and does not have to be incorporated in the Christian canon. Since these beliefs lie outside the official canon, their use becomes a matter of individual interpretation; some may dismiss a particular application of an extra-theological concept as superstition, while others believe wholeheartedly. As Lambek notes of a similar situation in Mayotte, 'it is a mistake to conceive of responses to misfortune as having a unified comprehensive logic. Instead of fully elaborated systems of thought, there are fragments drawn from various traditions and reproduced in various disciplines, fragments which are brought together rhetorically in moments of narration or conversation' (1993, 391).

Perhaps the clearest example I encountered of this polyglot approach to issues of belief was an elder who sought to bring some theological rigour to his sermons. A well-read university graduate, he explained that an educated audience could tolerate sermons on more abstract theological issues. His sermons to an educated audience were thus finely crafted expositions of the finer points of Reformed Christian doctrine. Yet, this same man also related to me his experience with a *tau mepongko* (werewolf, changeling) some decades before. *Tau mepongko*, through the long use of black magic (*doti*), change shape while sleeping. An immaterial aspect of their being will leave their body (or the body itself, according to others) and appear as an animal or a flying head with dangling entrails before their victim, whose liver[3] they covertly eat. The victim will die a few days later. This elder related how a *tau mepongko* appeared in his dreams (not in body, nor as a waking apparition) for three nights in a row and how he chased him off in the name of Jesus. The *tau mepongko* (a neighbour) died two weeks later. He also showed me a stick of fragrant wood he kept because its smell was said to be intolerable to *tau mepongko*. This blending of traditional and Christian beliefs subordinates pre-Christian cosmological concepts to Christian conceptions without their either entering the Christian canon or being dismissed as inconsistent with Christian discourse. Individuals are free to integrate them with their own Christian beliefs in their own way. Others carried a picture of Jesus in their wallets as a talisman, much like the foul-smelling splinter of wood, and still others proclaimed that their faith in itself accomplished the same ends. Other than the fact that most villagers believe in *tau mepongko* and agree on their ability to change shape, I could obtain no consensus on their ontological basis, that is, what exactly the 'immaterial aspect' of the *tau mepongko* was and how it related to Christian notions of body and soul.

Every individual situationally attempts to create a consistent cosmology centred on a personal understanding of the Christian faith within which he or she struggles to resolve 'problems of meaning.' Despite its universalistic claims, the mission thus left a host of specifically local 'problems of meaning' unaddressed. These problems are primarily health-related concerns. The church eliminated the indigenous shamanic tradition and substituted expensive, secular Western-style medicine, which does not always work as predicted. The interpretation of disease may thus invoke concepts such as *puloru*, *kasalora* (affliction resulting from leaving while another person is eating), *doti* (magical poisons and spells), and a host of ghosts (*angga*, *ringgiana*, *tau mepongko*, *setan*). An ill person and his or her family will struggle to understand the 'signs' available to them, as 'fragments which are brought together rhetorically in moments of narration or conversation' consistent with their remembered behaviour (Lambek 1993, 391).

When the cousin of a friend fell ill with what seemed a clear case of chronic (chloroquine-resistant) malaria, I insisted he be brought to the local hospital for treatment. To my surprise, ten days of medical care brought no improvement. His family concluded that it was clear from the medication's failure that malaria was not the cause. They suspected that he had encountered a ghost (*angga*) when wandering alone in the forest just before he fell ill. Few will walk alone in the forest precisely out of this fear; my penchant for napping in field huts far from the noisy village was considered irresponsible (and stupid), necessitating that a companion be present to prevent harm coming to me. The serendipity of the walk in the forest, the illness, and the failure of hospital treatment was thus sufficient to lead them to seek the help of a *topagere* (masseur).

The *topagere*, unlike a shaman, generally does not use prayer, and hence has not been banned by the church. Some of these *topagere* now ascribe their effectiveness to Christian prayer (a form of laying on of hands), whereas others state they are massaging out *kantu* (objects embedded in the victim's flesh by means of evil spells). Yet others claim they are massaging out the ill person's appendix, which the mission had so often blamed for many of the deaths otherwise attributed to *tau mepongko*. The *ad hoc* nature of these local solutions to problems of meaning is not a reflection of some 'animistic survival.' Rather, it is within these situations that the shared tacit knowledge of extra-theological concepts are developed, propagated, and articulated with Christian beliefs. Theological and extra-theological conceptions are part of a single discourse and subjected to rules of logical consistency. Importantly, this quest for consistency allows for multiple interpretations. The masseur thus treated my friend's cousin, rubbing his limbs in search of the responsible *kantu*, which he finally 'worked out.' His family took the man's subsequent recovery as proof of the truth of their original suspicions. Such empirically derived proofs are not easily shaken.

Another example of this last point was the reporting of visions throughout Central Sulawesi about a decade ago. The visions, usually of the face of Christ, but also of crucifixes and other religious symbols, were first seen in the Kulawi district to the west, where the Salvation Army church predominates. The visions rapidly spread along the major roads, first appearing in Poso to the north, then in Tentena about a month later. As people first heard the miraculous tales, a few began vigils in the local churches. After one sighting was made, the whole village would congregate, hoping to see their own vision. Problems arose when some prominent church figures did not see the vision and that was interpreted by others as a failure of faith. The elder discussed above did not contest the reality of visions per se, but only whether this particular manifestation was real. He did not see the image and was racked by guilt and self-doubt, and finally saw his authority as an elder challenged for his lack of faith. Yet, in the arguments that followed, he came to the conclusion the visions were fake because those who had seen them did not treat the images with enough awe: 'Another elder challenged me, "Don't you see the image of Christ here on the wall? Look, here's his eye, and here his ears!" and he poked the wall. And that's when I knew the vision wasn't real. Would you poke Christ in the eye if he appeared before you?' His own wife, however, saw the vision and continued to believe in their verity; she listened to his logical deposition with a simple nod to me, adding 'I saw.'

The visions thus became a major political problem for the church and demanded a definitive resolution. The Synod Commission's response was to separate the question of the reality of the vision from the issue of faith, and hence from the internal political challenges being mounted on some of its prominent ministers and elders. The church had little to say about the veracity of the phenomena but emphasized that blessings are not distributed according to merit, but by the grace of God. Seeing the vision was thus not a proof of faith, and the failure to see not a failure of faith. Shortly after this pronouncement was read in every church, the visions ceased. To this day villagers are divided as to whether the visions were real or not.

Simply put, the difficulty I have outlined is that ritual does not necessarily ensure shared belief or a shared interpretation. It can, as the visions cited above make clear, lead to public discord. Problems of meaning are experienced by individuals, and it is individuals who attempts to explain these problems, with their own disparate theological and extra-theological resources, only some of which enter the public discourse of the church. Even the supposedly absolute doctrinal stance of the church is subjected to individual interpretation; those who accept the doctrines of the church may nonetheless contest a particular application of them in certain circumstances. Rather than requiring adherence to a consistent set of doctrines, the church has demanded faith in the process by which religious knowledge is constructed. Although individuals may differ in their interpretations, they will differ within the institutional confines of the church and its ultimate test of biblical authority. This faith is fostered by how ritual is done, rather than what it says.

The Construction of Ritual as Text

The austere forms of Calvinist ritual are ideally suited to being 'read' like text. The emphasis on preaching 'the Word,' the practice of biblical exegesis, and the lack of what might be termed 'performative flourishes' all serve to make the written sermon the focal point of the ritual event. This point was driven home when the Chair of the Synod described to me the opposition she faced after sanctioning a seemingly innocuous Christmas pageant. This performative event, she was told by a fellow Synod member, lacked a 'teaching' element. The two-hour-long performance was allowed to proceed only after an hour-long sermon was added to 'explain' its significance. Yet, as the discussion in the previous section showed, the purpose of preaching is not to perpetuate a systematic set of propositional beliefs. If this is so, how is the ritual as text constructed and what is its point?

Kruyt's utilization of the idiom *monuntu*, to advise, was not accidental but followed from Dutch Protestant conceptions of the sermon as a *leervorm*, a teaching format, and the minister as a teaching presbyter (a teaching elder). Ethical Theologians emphasized that the arid, rationalist practice of teaching propositional knowledge did not reform the spirit or the emotions, and that it was these emotions which provided the dispositions to act. Ethical teaching was thus intended to evoke self-reflection, personal critique, and a desire for personal change centred on biblical truth. This form of biblical exegesis requires little in the way of theological knowledge, and hence is ideally suited to the conditions of the Gereja Kristen Sulawesi Tengah (Christian Church of Central Sulawesi), where untrained elders assume much of the burden of preaching. This model for the construction of the sermon as text is known locally as 'contextualization' (Papasi 1992, 161).

An elder, preaching at a thanksgiving service celebrating the conclusion of my research, chose as his text 'The fear of the Lord is the beginning of knowledge: but fools despise wisdom and instruction' (Proverbs 1: 7). He emphasized how the acquisition of technical knowledge, whether theological, scientific, or artistic, is not the basis of wisdom. Wisdom arises out of fear of the Lord, a fear like that a 'child feels for a parent who loves them, who always gives them advice. A fear accompanied by longing to be near them, a loyalty consisting of faith, hopes, honour, awe and pride.' Wisdom does not rise out of specialist's knowledge rooted in theory but in deference to a parental God and deference in turn to parents; this elder, my landlord, I called 'Papa.' This sermon, though generally phrased, was explicitly intended to encourage me to defer to 'local knowledge,' to local models for the construction of texts, and the acquisition of religious knowledge.[4]

The emphasis on the contextual nature of sermon writing led me to explore the process of the production of specific texts and the situations that evoked them. I interviewed the ten elders and ministers who preached in the various services in which I took part, an average of two to four services a week over a two-year period. These preachers had a wide variety of educational backgrounds. The group included several elders with no theological training other than some 'helpful hints' they received from ministers; theological students who regularly preached in youth groups; graduates of the local theological seminary who now led congregations; and graduates of higher schools of theology who served as congregational ministers, the Classis minister, and members of the Synod Commission. There were four women and six men. Despite the differences in background, gender, and role, there was a great degree of consistency to the process of producing a sermon. Significantly, preaching was an Indonesian language skill; only two elders and one minister occasionally preached in Bahasa mPamona, the local language.

Surprising to me at the time was the shared aversion to theological abstractions despite a general, strong positive valuation of higher theological education. This positive valuation of theological education stemmed from its recognized importance in gaining a true understanding of the meaning of biblical texts, as well as for gaining a paid position within the church, the second-largest employer in the area after the government. Theological education also legitimated the clear hierarchy of church offices; hence, ministers with masters degrees became 'natural' candidates for Synod jobs. While theological knowledge was deemed helpful in the preacher's creation of the text, the text itself was to studiously avoid abstractions. Although these preachers emphasized that the reason for avoiding theological abstractions was the congregation's inability to understand, as the sermon cited above emphasized, the avoidance of such abstractions is also a positive injunction. 'You should not use complicated terms (*istilah tinggi*) so that the congregation goes home without hope'; wisdom is not gained through learning propositional knowledge but through the application of biblical knowledge in practical situations. Even where the congregation has greater-than-average educational qualifications, the sermon must address their specific needs in simple, straightforward terms.

The second general principle by which a sermon is produced is that it be contextual. The specific needs of the hosts of the service must be established and the sermon should offer hope or provide a solution to those needs. Mama Anangodi, for example, was an elder called to preach the weekly evangelization service for a newly married couple who had just joined the group. Although newly married, the couple had two children. After the woman had become pregnant, his father refused to allow them to marry – until the couple had the second child. The woman had been raised by an uncle with whom she did not get along. The basis of the new family thus seemed shaky, and 'the peace' just established between family members needed to be strengthened. She thus chose Galatians 5:13 as the text from which she would preach: 'For brethren, ye have been called unto liberty; only *use* not liberty for an occasion of the flesh, but by love serve one another.' This text, she argued, emphasized that a true love allows liberty; however, this liberty had limits. It was not a licence to sin. We are, rather, to use this liberty to serve one another through love (not lust) in the name of

Christ. The verse was utilized to legitimate the young couple's desire for self-determination, to establish their own household over the objections of their parents, while also placing limits on that liberty which comes with responsibilities and duties towards kinsmen.

The hope proffered usually focuses upon the grace of God and salvation through Jesus. One creative example I witnessed was the use of the Christmas liturgy for a 'Comforting Service' (*penghiburan*). This service is usually held on the third evening after a death, marking the end of mourning. In this case the minister utilized the Christmas liturgy with the lighting of candles on a Christmas tree as a consolation for the family of the deceased that the deceased had found his salvation in the birth of the Emmanuel, 'God with us.' The Christmas carols that followed directly pointed to the celebration which must accompany the saviour's birth, the source of salvation, just as the candles furnished a physical symbol of the light he provides in the darkness. Since the evangelization services rotate among forty households, it is inevitable that the hosts will have experienced a birth, death, or 'blessing' of some kind in the interval since they last hosted the event. This tends to stereotype the 'needs' that are addressed in sermons. In the case of the *pengucapan syukur* (the thanksgiving service), it is the family itself which determines the topic of the sermon by indicating the 'blessing' for which they are thankful; the most common reasons given included birthdays, recovery from illness, graduations, and anniversaries of deaths.

Although the sermon is narrowly focused on the needs of the host, it must be phrased generally so as to benefit all members of the congregation. Mama Anangodi's sermon on liberty, for example, was also tailored for the upcoming Independence Day celebrations. The assumption of the congregation that the sermon's message is intended for the host can create problems for the sermon writer who wishes to address wider social problems. One elder stated she had to avoid sermons of the 'Thou shalt not ...' type, because the hosts assumed they were being accused of the sin being discussed. Such direct attacks 'hardened the heart,' she argued, and they refused to listen. This served to further narrow the kinds of needs addressed. This elder felt it limited her to preaching only on the subject 'love.' Another stated that there are a host of sins that could not be directly addressed in a sermon, but that require a different approach to combat; sins such as harshness and violence required social measures as provided by the various church-affiliated institutions. A congregational minister insisted that the only way he could address 'animist survivals' in agricultural practice was to join farmers in their work and provide a Christian alternative through prayer; sermons that directly branded such acts as superstition were an affront to people's beliefs and resulted in no changes. These self-imposed limits on what can and can't be said in sermons leave a number of locally constituted 'problems of meaning' unanswerable, leading to the infusion of indigenous cosmological concepts, such as *puloru* (incurring divine retribution), to fill the gap.

Having identified the subject of the sermon, the preacher then searches for an appropriate citation from the Bible. Biblical authority is tantamount in the production of the sermon, and all that is said must be legitimated by the verses cited. All of the preachers I interviewed made ready use of published collections of verses bearing titles such as *The Right Verse* and *Such Is the Word of God*, which are divided into sections by subject, such as 'Praising God' and 'Mourning.' Since elders and ministers may be writing two sermons a week on top of other duties, these collections saved them time. They also made use of published biblical commentaries (*tafsiran*) that explained the meaning and intent of the selected verses. Indeed, it is these published works that make up for most elders' lack of theological training.

In writing the sermon, preachers attempt to relate the verse selected and their understanding of it to the needs they have identified as the subject. The format of a sermon is simple, starting with the reading of the Bible, moving to exegesis on the biblical context of the verse, and then broadly comparing that context with the local context. The verse cited is thus intended to serve as a model for emulation. Knowledge of the Bible is highly valued, since it provides one with the direct templates for right action in a way that theology does not. This template approach is thus geared towards producing 'practical advice.' These preachers all emphasized that they had to keep the sermon simple, short, direct, and practical.

The use of biblical narratives as a template for action may invoke both positive and negative injunctions, although negative injunctions, of the 'Thou shalt not ...' type are generally avoided, lest the host be offended. Positive injunctions may be either dispositional, of the 'Love thy neighbour' type, or specifically chart a course of action, such as the call to 'witness' (*bersaksi*), that is, to spread the Word to non-Christians. Given that thanksgiving services are among the most common form of worship, the call to 'praise God' supplies both legitimation and message for this particular action.

The character of religious knowledge in Tentena is thus particular, not systematic. It is built out of numerous case studies drawn thematically from the Bible to fit a stereotypical set of local needs. To paraphrase Geertz on animism, it meets problems of meaning 'piecemeal,' its logic being dictated by practical activities such as birth, marriage, and death, rather than the logic of some theological text. That is, the verse chosen as the basis for the sermon follows from the local context, not the reverse. The verse should offer a concrete solution to the situation rather than conveying propositional knowledge about Christianity as a system of thought. This contextual style of sermon can be contrasted, for example, with the sermons produced in conservative Dutch Calvinist churches in North America. Here, the subject of the weekly sermon is determined by the church calendar and the Heidelberg Catechism. The doctrines of the catechism are divided into fifty-two 'Lord's Days' or sections, to be preached on fifty-two successive Sundays. Each section of the catechism addresses a specific theological issue, such as 'original sin' or 'trinitarianism.'

"Belief" as it is locally constituted de-emphasizes dogmatics and emphasizes biblical knowledge and its ad hoc application. 'To believe' means to accept the Bible as 'the word of God,' having ultimate authority. The implications of direct interpretation of the Bible, rather than theology, as the ultimate guide for religious understanding was underscored for me by a conversation with a young man on the subject of eating pork. A butcher, he stated he did not understand why his Islamic neighbours were revolted by the thought of eating pork. Drawing on Leviticus, I pointed out that God had defined the pig as 'unclean' and that the Jews were also forbidden to eat pork. Unbelieving, he asked me to show him in the Bible. On reading the verse, he was thrown in a quandary and proclaimed that he, too, would give up pork. It took another half-hour and multiple references to the Letters of Paul to demonstrate to him that Jewish dietary law did not apply to Christians.

As this experiment in biblical exegesis makes clear, multiple interpretations of particular biblical passages are easily arrived at. This range of interpretations is narrowed, however, in that only one interpretation is preached in a religious service and it is tied to a specific situation. During the ritual, the embodied knowledge of the congregation creates those relations of deference that prioritize this one interpretation if not eliminating others. Its truth is not established with reference to a systematic body of propositional knowledge but through its applicability to their practical needs. Its veracity as the Truth is assured by the Church, whose institutional procedures offer the guarantee that only those to whom the congregation should rightfully defer are allowed to preach from the pulpit; for anyone else to even approach the pulpit is *puloru*.

Rationalization

The production of religious texts in Tentena follows a pietist methodology introduced by Kruyt and intended to meet specific mission ends. Kruyt was attempting to teach not only a set of religious beliefs (i.e., intellectual propositions), but the category of *faith* itself (i.e., the self-disciplining of behaviour in accordance with the Word of God). To say one has faith in Christ carries specific behavioural and dispositional implications. According to Kruyt, the behavioural implications of being Christian would make sense to the To Pamona only in relation to their own set of spontaneous dispositions to act, the *adat*. The Christian *adat* as it was developed by the To Pamona was to remain a cultural whole, but a whole subjected to and judged against the Bible. By rationalizing their spontaneous dispositions to act as a 'Christian *adat*' rather than imposing systematic dogmatics upon them, a specifically To Pamona form of Christianity, their own *volkskerk* would result.

Conversion to Christianity in this case can be likened to the rationalization of animist traditions in Indonesia as it has occurred among the neighbouring To Wana of the northeast arm of Sulawesi (Atkinson 1983). The rationalizing animist traditions of Indonesia are not simply abstracting the tenets of their faith like the anthropologist who reads ritual as text. Their selective abstractions of specific 'religious propositions' are moulded by church and state definitions of what constitutes a 'religion' (*agama*). The dominant religious traditions of Indonesia, Islam and Christianity, are 'religions of the book,' defined in terms of an abstract system of theological beliefs that stands in a 'distant and problematic' relationship with civil society (i.e., are 'disenchanted'). The spontaneous abstraction of 'religion' by animists such as the To Wana, that is, their formulation of a set of 'religious propositions,' is based upon their understandings of these dominant definitions, and hence has less to do the systematic interpretation of their own previously unrationalized belief system than with propagating indigenous versions of the dominant forms (Atkinson 1983). Among these 'rationalizing' animist traditions, the abstract propositions that define their new 'religious belief systems' are preordained by the world religions. Given the predetermined nature of the abstract principles by which religion is defined in Indonesia (in terms of monotheism, a book, a prophet), both 'rationalizing' animists and Christian converts are faced with the same tricky task of 'rationalizing' their now' disenchanted' *adat* in relation to the new religious sphere. Christians such as the To Pamona must also situate their 'spontaneous dispositions to act' within the category of 'religion' as they have received it.

I have set 'rationalization' within quotation marks because of the dual sense of the word, playing off both 'rationality,' a way of thinking, and 'to rationalize,' to make more efficient through the systematic elimination of waste. Kruyt defined the process of conversion and the abstraction of belief as solely dependent upon the development of a new mode of thinking. Weber, in contrast, emphasized both sides of this essential duality. As Peletz interprets Weber, the rationalization of religion refers to 'both institutional changes involving the differentiation, specialization and development of hierarchical forms of social organization; and to intellectual or attitudinal trends entailing, in negative terms, "the disenchantment of the world" (the displacement of "magical elements of thought"), and, in positive terms, processes by which "ideas gain in systematic coherence and naturalistic consistency"' (Peletz 1993, 66–7). Studies of the rationalization of religion in Indonesia have, following Geertz, tended to emphasize the rationalization of systems of cultural meaning. In defining religion, they, like Kruyt, have prioritized thought over action, rationality over political rationalization. Kruyt's own emphasis on animism as a mode of thought prevented him from noting how indigenous relations of power were inculcated through ritual practice. Kruyt's formulation of the rationalization of a Christian *adat* similarly hides the systematization of these relations of power within a larger bureaucratic entity, the church.

Weberian definitions of rationalization root the systematization of beliefs in the 'institutional or social organizational changes that help motivate, buttress, or sustain this rethinking and reconfiguring' (Peletz 1993, 66). However, Weber's model is unilinear, with increased 'rationality' emerging in lock-step with these institutional processes of rationalization. I have emphasized that the religious service invoked a 'logic' tied to practical activity that cannot be characterized as more (or less) 'rational.' I found it necessary to examine this body of knowledge in terms of 'power–knowledge' relations (Foucault 1980), that is, in terms of social relations, rather than as the 'mode of thinking' of the individual who produced it. Changes in the forms of religious knowledge we find among the To Pamona can only be understood as the application of knowledge in a relationship where the perpetuation of that knowledge establishes a relationship of power (Foucault 1979, 27). That is, we can understand the creation of a 'religious *adat*' only in terms of the relationship established by *monuntu*, which simultaneously creates both knowledge and deference. This knowledge is not developed through the application of propositional logic, but through the ad hoc application of case studies. It at once declares itself dominant and subordinates all 'civil *adat*,' yet admits its powerlessness in addressing specific issues.

It is within the inherent limits of this power relationship that 'problems of meaning' develop as the particular interpretations of a preacher are challenged and some problems ignored altogether. Geertz rooted the rationalization of belief systems in such problems, which thus demanded a 'sweeping, universal, and conclusive' symbolic resolution (1973c, 173). Here, however, I will show that such problems of meaning have not been met by grand theory, by the rationalization of propositional knowledge, but with a more refined application of the particularist approach of the mission. The constant challenges to the hegemony of the church that constitute 'problems of meaning' call for a refinement of the mechanisms of deference by which the particularist solutions to those problems are definitively reached and the social body disciplined. Rather than reacting with a change in basic strategy, the church has extended and rationalized its power through the claim that its particularist biblical knowledge is applicable to all aspects of life. The basic model for the application of this knowledge, the religious service, remains unchanged, but is applied in new situations to newly formed interest groups. The *kebaktian* (religious service) was first extended to the evangelization groups, then to the women's groups, and finally to youth's and men's groups. What I called 'feasting inflation' is related to this process of extending the basic model of power/knowledge to new situations, of refining and universalizing its application. The expansion of feasting is closely tied to a rationalizing church bureaucracy that seeks to systematically extend its authority through the inculcation of biblical knowledge.

Church Discipline

Religious rationalization involves the refinement of the church's methods for reforming the self, of fostering a faith in which the individual abdicates power to authorized interpreters of the Bible. Kruyt's methodology sought to shape the spontaneous dispositions to act, the *adat*, of To Pamona through the process of *monuntu*. Christian *monuntu* called for self-reflection and examination, and voluntary self-reformation. *Monuntu* did not forbid, and hence Weberian defini-tions of power that stress the repressive aspects of the relationship, 'the probabil-ity that one actor within a social relationship will be in a position to carry out his own will despite resistance,' obscure the conditions within which voluntary compliance can be fostered. This compliance is fostered by the structured nature of the ritual occasion, which demands deference to the speaker. This voluntary deference, the practice of a virtue, a valued spontaneous disposition to act, prioritizes the words and commands of the preacher. Further, these words are contextualized and legitimated in terms of the Bible, the recognized source of the Truth, the Word. Thus, the relationship established through the practice of *monuntu* is not characterized by one member exerting his or her will despite resistance. Rather, the relationship is characterized by the voluntary abandon-ment of resistance. The relationship is not predicated upon coercion, but upon hegemony.

This limited power is most effective when it is systematically utilized, when it is part of a sustained disciplinary program that regularly inculcates voluntary deference and thus naturalizes it. It is in this light that we must examine the general transformations in the practice of *monuntu* discussed in the last chapter. These transformations were characterized by the individualization and moderni-zation of feasting and the extension of *posintuwu* exchanges and the occasions for holding a feast. Feasting is the means by which deference to genealogical seniors is fostered. The extension and modernization of feasting can thus be related to challenges to their authority. Resistance to elders is *puloru* and calls for a renewal of attempts to ensure compliance through further *monuntu*. Resistance calls forth a more systematic application of the power relationship in an attempt to quell this resistance, to foster voluntary compliance in the faithful follower of Truth.

It is the equivocal nature of this power relationship that requires the institutional rationalization of its application. This is clearly seen through the example of gender relations within the church. Kruyt's incorporation of feasting, and exclusion of shamanism, was explicitly intended to exclude women from positions of authority within the church. Shamans (almost all women) were the initial focal point of traditionalist resistance to the mission. Such was the case in Tentena, where the village shaman refused to convert and continued to hold curing ceremonies invoking the *lamoa* (spirits) until her death in the 1940s. The village minister's response was to encourage her son to enter the ministry over her objections. The son later returned to become the minister in Tentena. This selective recruitment of men to positions of power was at once the source of the problem of women's continuing traditionalism and the initial attempt to resolve it. By recruiting the son to Christianity, the mother's authority was undermined. Yet this strategy was not totally effective (the shaman never converted) and women remained the 'problematic' repository of *adat* ceremonies requiring reformation.

As discussed in chapter 4, it was the perception of women as a problem in the church that led to the formation of the first women's group in Tentena in 1953 by the local minister. The intent of the group was to foster a greater degree of Christian consciousness (*kasadaran*) among the women of the village through educational, health, and service programs (Lumentut 1991, 28–9). The group's first programs involved weekly religious 'services.' The English word 'service' aptly summarizes both aspects of these programs, which included worship as well as 'serving' the minister's guests (PIK 1985, 2). Shortly after the group had established an independent governing body in 1954, its priority program became setting up the Sekolah Kepandaian Putri (Girls' Skills School) in Tentena, which taught secretarial skills and enabled its graduates to obtain positions in the civil service. The group also expanded its role and membership in village society through the regularization of labour and *posintuwu* exchanges for members' weddings (see chapter 4). This program has fuelled the overall modernization and extension of feasting, although it also reinforced the image of the women's group as the cooking department (*seksi konsumpsi*).

The growth of feasting within the women's group is closely related to the form of its leadership. Historically, women were not excluded from the role of *kabosenya*; they took part in *posintuwu* exchanges and had their own sources of elite goods (i.e., payment for shamanic service). Leadership within the women's group, like that of elders within the church, has been based upon their reputation for *mosintuwu*. It is for this reason that the local leadership of the Women's Group (Komisi Wanita) became involved in the management of weddings, a role traditionally performed by *kabosenya*. As one leader, a graduate of the Girls' Skills School and civil servant, put it, 'they were coming to me anyway [to arrange weddings] so I made weddings a Women's Group program.' The weekly religious services provided these women leaders with their first opportunities to *monuntu* on a regular basis. The Women's Group thus became the crucible within which women's authority was melded with a presbyterial bureaucracy, much like the men in the consistory.

This form of leadership and the *posintuwu* exchanges are two complementary aspects of social reproduction in Tentena. Leadership emerges out of *posintuwu* exchanges, and *posintuwu* exchanges are made necessary by life-cycle ceremonies such as baptisms, marriages, and funerals. The normal cycle of social reproduction, subordinated to *monuntu*, thus necessitates a 'voluntary' deference to the leaders who organize these feasts of social reproduction as religious services. Leadership is not a class phenomenon specifically because it is manifested through its control of social reproduction, not through the means of production. A leader's power is attenuated, not absolute, and therefore requires a constant renewal; without feasting there is no enactment of deference, no power.

In turn, the women submitting to the discipline of the women's group find that they are subordinating the social reproduction of their families to the demands of the church. The principal demand is that the women submit themselves to the reforming power of the Word. Each ritual of social reproduction is accompanied by a sermon written to fit their circumstances, to address their sins. The sermon cannot coerce compliance to the ideal 'good Christian life.' The leader of the Women's Group emphasized that they organize the rituals of social reproduction of *all* families, irrespective of the women's participation, since the group had a 'responsibility' to ensure the event is correctly performed. This 'responsibility' ensures that all women are subjected to the same discipline whether they accept it or not. The performance of such a ritual thus combines ideological pressure, the call to attend to the Word, with moral persuasion, the creation of debts of gratitude through *posintuwu* exchanges. In chapter 4, I discussed a number of 'disciplinary' problems whose resolution was found in the performance of the wedding feast and the creation of debts of honour and gratitude which predisposed them to 'listen' thereafter.

The overwhelming success of the Women's Group has effectively reversed the church's perception of women as a problem. They are now a well-disciplined cadre of faithful followers of the Word. Women outnumber men in participation in all church services. Women candidates consistently garner the largest number of votes in elections for elders. Women applicants for the theological seminary now outnumber men. And even the chair of the Synod Commission is now a woman. The tables have been effectively reversed, and it is the men who are now perceived to be a problem. Widespread social problems, such as gambling, drunkenness, and its attendant violence, are specifically male-centred problems. I met few women who drank and never saw a woman drunk; some men, on the other hand, drank frequently and to excess, and a number of domestic disputes were tied to this problem. This was also cited as the reason why the *dero* (ring dance) had to be carefully supervised after weddings.

It is significant that this 'social problem' was approached within a religious framework, as an issue of sin that needed to be met through attendance of religious services; since these sins of proscription could not be directly attacked in sermons without offence being given, its attempted resolution was thus by the inculcation of faith. The Women's Group thus introduced a new program, Pekan Keluarga (Family Week), which was later expanded as a Synod-sponsored event. As the name suggests, the program was designed to strengthen family values, narrowly defined in terms of the household. These family values are closely associated with motherhood and nurturing, *kasih ibu* (mother love). Family Week involves nightly religious services in the church or in each household, following a preset liturgy combined with a number of competitions for children such as tests of biblical knowledge and sporting events. During the household services the streets of Tentena are deserted, and all the *warung* (market stalls) where alcohol is sold are closed. For a solid week all households are brought together as a group in a ritual context to celebrate the family as a unit. The liturgy specifies the ideal roles and associated behaviour expected of each family member and, through participation, calls on them to recognize this ideal as a model for their behaviour. The sermons provided a call for the maintenance of a pious life and tie this to nurturing and responsibility for children's upbringing. They in no way directly attack drinking.

It is important to note the innovation introduced by Family Week. The difficulty with previous attempts to address the problems of drink and domestic violence was that those with the problems rarely attended church services. Family Week circumvented this difficulty by extending the discipline of the church into the household itself, where it could not be so easily avoided. By individualizing the service to each household and repeating the message daily for a solid week, each husband was forced to discipline himself. The hope of the Women's Group was that such imposed self-discipline, bolstered by a renewed sense of responsibility for their families, would foster a self-reformation and a new piety in men. The renewed piety of husbands would lead to their greater attendance at other services, to their voluntary submission to the authority of elders and ministers, and to a more regular application of *monuntu* and its calls for self-reformation. To some extent, the effort has been successful, and the men's group has flourished as it rarely had before.

The extension and rationalization of the power relationship embodied in *monuntu* in no way changes its essential nature. Ministers and elders recognize the limits of their power and avoid difficulty by not addressing specific issues, specific sins, in tailoring their sermons to their audience. Their power is not predicated upon an ability to coerce, but on a deference inculcated through congregational self-reformation in response to their message. The deference offered may be self-interested, concerned only to meet the imminent needs of certain rituals of social reproduction. Yet, self-interested or not, such voluntary submission subjects the individual to *monuntu*, to a call for self-reformation that attempts to inculcate a 'true faith,' that is, a faith that no longer requires motives of immediate self-interest. A preacher's message is not systematized and abstracted as a 'rational' theology, but individualized and concretized to meet the specific needs of a parishioner. The use of such practical 'biblical templates' necessitates a rationalization of their application, not of their message. Ministers' power is thus dependent upon the constant extension and broadening of the application of their discipline to create a true piety grounded in biblical authority.

Institutional Rationalization

Geertz's phrase 'internal' conversion, used in reference to the rationalization of traditional religion, contrasts with models of conversion to the world religions and prioritizes the abstraction of a shared, consistent, belief system and its ability to address universal 'problems of meaning.' Here, I have argued that the process of conversion, whether 'internal' or to a world religion, must address the issue of how the reproduction of religious knowledge creates a power relationship; the creation of a body of knowledge can take place only within institutional or social-organizational constraints. The 'rationalization' of this knowledge need not imply the systemization of its propositional content. Rather, as the case of the conversion of the To Pamona to Protestantism has shown, systematic dogmatics may be set aside in favour of the rationalization of the application of this knowledge. This emphasizes the institutional side of Weber's concept of religious rationalization rather than intellectual coherence.

Geertz, following Weber, links the process of religious rationalization to the eruption of 'problems of meaning' resulting from widespread social and cultural change. In Tentena, these problems of meaning were not addressed by sermons, *nor could they be* without accusing and alienating parishioners. These epistemological breaks were resolved through individual 'rationalizations,' that is, through the ad hoc application of diverse cosmological concepts to explain particular events. On the one hand, this has perpetuated the use of certain indigenous concepts such as *puloru* and *tau mepongko*, which are subordinated to, but articulate with, Christian beliefs. On the other hand, these explanations are ad hoc and individual, and engendered intense debate, much like in the case of the Balinese villagers Geertz describes as engaging in 'a full-scale philosophical discussion' (1973c, 183). As the example of the visions of Christ demonstrate, such philosophical discussion may lead to challenges to established authority within an existing institution. I have argued that these political challenges were resolved by the acceptance of the actual diversity of beliefs combined with an extension and intensification of church discipline. The extension of religious services, feasting, and *posintuwu* exchanges over the last three decades has served to regularize deference, to encourage acquiescence, to discipline the social body. The church is less interested in perpetuating a definitive theological formulation than it is in reinforcing submission to the process by which religious knowledge is created. As the head of the church's institutional development office told me, the ultimate goal is for every household to meet daily for worship in a nested set of services ultimately rooted in the congregation, the spiritual community as a whole.

This is not to argue that institutional rationalization has been a conscious policy; it has, as I emphasized above, emerged out of specific problems of meaning and particularist attempts to resolve them. Challenges to ministerial authority denote an absence of faith, and hence engender renewed efforts to preach the Word. When the traditionalist beliefs of women were perceived as a problem, the women's group was formed to 'strengthen them in their Christian Faith.' When men's drinking and gambling began to be perceived as a problem, they became the focus of individualized attention through household religious services. In neither case were the villagers' beliefs or actions directly attacked; rather, local ministers and elders sought to build their *faith*, and so gain voluntary submission and reformation. As a particularist response to a social problem, the institutional form that they assumed was originally ad hoc. However, as these social movements gained in numbers and importance, their independence resulted in further challenges to the church. Insofar as possible, the church has thus attempted to usurp these independent movements and incorporate them within its own Presbyterial structure and, in so doing, standardize and universalize their programs. Unplanned and ad hoc, the end result has been institutional rationalization. Again, the institutional history of the Women's Group is instructive.

The Women's Group took institutional form in 1955 after three years of informal activities in and around Tentena. At that point, the governance of the existing groups assumed presbyterial form, with its boundaries following the church's congregational and Classis boundaries. This presbyterial body held its own weekly religious services and implemented its own programs, independent of local congregations. It represented, in effect, the creation of an independent church within the church. As the Women's Group rapidly grew in numbers during the early 1960s, it instituted a number of highly successful programs such as the construction of their own village meeting halls and the establishment of a kindergarten school system in 1968. The Women's Group also administered or lent support to a number of government programs such as the PKK (Pendidikan Kesejahteraan Keluarga [Family Welfare Education]) and POSYANDU (an infant health and nutrition program). Their success in these endeavours left the committee of management in Tentena critical of both government and consistory inefficiencies: 'Komisi Wanita lebih teliti kebutuhan masyarakat daripada pemerintah yang ada di sini' (the Women's Group pays greater attention to the needs of society than the local government here). The male-dominated village government was said to be disorganized and incapable, and the male-dominated Consistory considered them to be nothing but the church's 'cooking department.'

The independent and critical attitude of the Women's Group led to several disputes with the local Consistory in Tentena and elsewhere over the scheduling of events and finances. The Women's Group argued that they were responsible only to their own Classis, not to the local church. These local consistories thus appealed to the Church Synod to curb the independence of the Women's Group and to directly subordinate it to the local congregation. This was finally done by the Synod Meeting of 1989. The Chair of the Synod Meeting (a woman) emphasized that the integration of the Women's Group did not change its purpose or programs, but gave it a greater role in pushing the growth of the church as a whole. The group's integration within the church made every woman within the congregation an automatic member and subordinated the local boards of management to a church elder, who was to act as an intermediary between the Consistory and Women's Group. All finances were to be handled by the Consistory. In practice, the Women's Group has retained a great deal of autonomy as well as control over its own finances after finding the congregational budgeting process too cumbersome.

The integration of the Women's Group within the Synod structure of the church had two implications. First, as a Synod program, the disciplinary power of the Women's Group was extended to all the women within the congregation as well as to all the congregations of the church. Previously, not all women within a congregation joined, if for no other reason than that they could not afford the dues. Further, not all congregations had an established Women's Group. The incorporation's effect was, as the Synod Chair argued, to vastly broaden the role

of the Women's Group within the church. The second implication of the incorporation was the centralization of power within the Synod. The men's and youth's
groups were also integrated at the same time. These were the last three independent Christian organizations in the area. The other independent organizations, the
yayasans controlling education, health, and development, had been directly
subordinated to Synod control in 1981 when members of the Synod Commission
took over the daily operations of the foundations. The Synod Commission, once
responsible for the administration of only its ministerial staff, has now integrated
a host of previously semi-independent religiously oriented groups providing
educational, economic, and health-related services within a single bureaucratic
order.[5] The institutional rationalization of the church may thus be likened to the
process of state formation.

The ideological foundation of this 'state formation' is the 'comprehensive
approach' adopted by the Gereja Kristen Sulawesi Tengah at the instigation of
the Dutch Reformed Church in the early 1960s. Simply put, the comprehensive
approach is based on the premise that the 'good news' is spread by deed, not just
by word. As the chair of the Synod Commission told me, 'The good news must
be experienced in all aspects of life, from schools on, to build a good world to live
in.' The missionary from the Dutch Reformed Church at the time, the Reverend
Visser, was more blunt: 'We get nothing from religion if the people are unhealthy
and we get nothing from healthy people if they don't know how to earn money;
and you get nothing from people who only know how to earn money, but have a
rotten attitude' (Berge and Segers n.d., 1). The comprehensive approach was a
practical application of 'Social Gospel' theology, as developed by the influential
Dutch missionary H. Kraemer. Its intent, unlike 'inculturation,' was to effect
socio-economic change (Koetsier 1975, 72–3), not preserve tradition. The comprehensive approach has thus provided both the legitimation and the funding for
the expansion of the church bureaucracy into areas of civil society generally
controlled by the state elsewhere (but not in the Netherlands). It was this
increased revenue that gave the Synod the financial security to establish Synod
offices to supervise the women's and other groups.

The expansion of the 'social' mission is, however, less a change in policy than
a change in ideological emphasis *for the mission*. Kruyt's mission included the
establishment of an extensive network of more than 300 schools as well as a
hospital in Tentena. The schools taught, among other things, appropriate farming
techniques for the newly established *sawah* fields. The missions' emphasis on
the comprehensive approach stems rather from the loss of their old role,
'missionization' or 'conversion' (*penginjil*) to the independent daughter church
in 1947. With the day-to-day operations of the church now controlled by indig-

enous ministers, the mission turned its emphasis to the larger problem of 'development.' Development projects sponsored by a variety of mission organizations are funnelled through the church-directed *yayasans* (foundations) such as the Foundation for Social Development (Yayasan Pembangunan Masyarakat), the Foundation for Social Health Services (Yayasan Pelayanan Kesehatan Masyarakat), and the Foundation for Christian Education and Teaching (Yayasan Pendidikan dan Perguruan Kristen).

The drive towards the institutional centralization of the church can also be tied to the professionalization of its clergy. As elsewhere in Indonesia, development since Independence has been accompanied by structural specialization; local congregational ministers (*guru injil*, gospel teachers) who served as schoolteachers as well were forced to assume one or the other role when most of the Christian school system was transferred to the state. Most *guru injil* became teachers, leaving the church with few professional ministers. In 1981, the GKST had only 138 ministers for 135,000 members in 308 congregations. Most congregations were led by a *pendeta angkat*, an elder who assumed ministerial duties. With Dutch support, the theological academy in Tentena was expanded, first in 1968, and then again in 1986 and 1992, to meet the need for ministers (Papasi 1992, 158). The first expansion increased the number of new ministers without changing their qualifications. It accepted graduates from junior high schools, who completed a further six-year program before being ordained. In 1986 the academy was upgraded, accepting only high-school graduates and offering a college diploma (*sarjana mudah*). In 1992, the academy began offering a bachelor's degree (*program strata satu*). A small but increasingly larger number of ministers have acquired their degrees from the Sekolah Tinggi Theologia INTIM (Theological University for East Indonesia) in Ujung Pandang which, until 1992, was the only higher theological school in Sulawesi.

The restricted number of ministers meant that they were generally reserved for wealthier urban congregations and for supervisory positions, such as Classis ministers, or for Synod offices. The church hierarchy is thus a meritocracy, with educational qualifications serving as the primary status marker. It is important to note that these ministers were the best-educated persons in a district where the majority of individuals still have only a primary-school education. Although having a specifically theological education, ministers were deemed best able to organize and run the health, education, and development foundations. This pattern had been established by the colonial government that had regularly elevated *guru injil* (such as Pancali Sigilipu) to upper civil-service positions for the same reason. Lastly, this pattern also fits with the 'comprehensive approach' that sees these activities as alternative forms of 'spreading the Word' through deed. It was thus a very short step from appointing the better-educated ministers to run these foundations to assigning the ministers who sat on the Synod Commission to run them.

The increasingly tight Synod control over the church foundations since 1981, when members of the Synod Commission took over their daily operations, has immeasurably broadened the patronage powers of commission members. The extension of the church into social development has thus been responsible for institutional rationalization, or the centralization of church management. This institutional rationalization in turn has allowed for a refinement of 'church discipline,' for the universalization and systematization of church intervention in everyday life. The growth of the church bureaucracy and the extension of its 'mission' thus derive, on the one hand, from internal challenges to its proclaimed authority as an adjudicator of all aspects of life, and, on the other hand, from primarily Dutch sponsorship of its 'social' programs. In other words, the rationalization of the church emerges out of challenges to 'traditional' authority at the local level, supported by the 'modernist' social service–oriented Synod.

From a comparative historical perspective, the rationalization of the church bureaucracy bears a striking if not surprising resemblance to the 'pillarized' Dutch church that created it. The structural features of the GKST, its presbyterial form, and its associated educational, health, and development agencies emulate those of the mother church. More telling, perhaps, is the manner in which Ethical Theology (and now the comprehensive approach) has served to entrench old political elites in new roles within a *volkskerk* and thereby preserve local ethnic identities. The articulation of religious services with feasting has made the church an essential part of the social reproduction of households and kinship networks as well as establishing hierarchy within those networks. These political elites are subordinated in turn to the church bureaucracy. This bureaucracy is staffed by the children of these elites since only they can afford the fees for advanced education. The church bureaucracy has been increasingly centralized, while extending and universalizing the application of its discipline through the multiplication of religious services.

The pillarization of the GKST differs, however, in one marked respect from the Dutch case: under the New Order, the church has been forced to abandon its political wing. This enforced abandonment of politics does not mean that the church has lost sight of its political priorities, nor that its members support the current status quo of 'religious state' and 'secular' political parties. Rather, the field of contestation has shifted; politics, as under the colonial regime, are conducted through sorties in the realm of 'culture.' The church has thus ironically prospered, given its position of strength as an 'inculurated' *volkskerk*. The rationalization and extension of feasting over the last twenty-five years, combined with the bureaucratic centralization of the church, has pillarized its congregants at a time when, temporarily at least, they have been without a political voice. It remains to be seen whether the collapse of the New Order will result in a new 'emancipatory movement' by Christian parties, and a rebirth of religious *aliran* in Indonesia.

7

Rationalizing Religion in Indonesia

Then saith he unto them, Render therefore unto Caesar the things which are Caesar's; and unto God the things that are God's.

Matthew 22: 21

Instead of approaching religion with questions about the social meaning of doctrines and practices, or even about the psychological effects of symbols and rituals, let us begin by asking what are the historical conditions (movements, classes, institutions, ideologies) necessary for the existence of particular religious practices and discourses. In other words, let us ask: how does power create religion? To ask this question is to seek an answer in terms of the social disciplines and social forces which come together at particular historical moments, to make particular religious discourses, practices and spaces possible.

Asad 1983, 252

The highlands of Central Sulawesi have the reputation of being isolated, inaccessible, and irrelevant to the larger social movements that have troubled Indonesia. To those in urban centres such as Jakarta and Ujung Pandang, Central Sulawesi is a dangerous backwater, a source of such archaic threats as sorcery and headhunting, an area that has made little contribution to the state's obsessive goal, development (*pembangunan*). Within the national imagination, Central Sulawesi plays the role of an exotic Other, ideal for anthropological study. And yet, this reputation is ill deserved, a fact drawn home by a short conversation in a small village on Lake Poso.

I was speaking with a farmer in his kitchen about the idyllic conditions of his surroundings, the kind of flattering small talk by which one shows one's appreciation for the cup of coffee just presented. He nodded his head, noting that this village was the 'rice basket' of the region, its prosperity assured by an *adat* proscription on the shedding of blood within the village bounds.

And without missing a beat, he smiled, and concluded, 'And that's why, when the Darul Islam rebels invaded in the late '50s, we waited until they left the village.'

This conversation was not without its context. The allusion was not just to an invasion from the Islamic south some forty years earlier, but to the anticipated foray of political partisans expected to attend the twenty-fourth anniversary convention of the Indonesian Democratic Party (PDI) in the nearby Lake Poso Festival Grounds. The PDI is one product of the New Order's coercive restructuring of the political landscape after the divisive decade of 'Guided Democracy' under past president Sukarno. The PDI was an amalgamation of Sukarno's Nationalist Party and the various Christian parties, including Parkindo, the Indonesian Protestant Party. The PDI had been successfully galvanized in the 1991 elections by Sukarno's charismatic daughter Megawati, whose message of democratic renewal found a burgeoning audience in the new urban middle classes. So popular was this message that the state engineered her replacement with a more pliable politician, Suryadi. Outraged partisans subsequently occupied the party headquarters in Jakarta, and riots resulted. The subsequent party conventions in Java and Sumatra also resulted in riots. Looking for a safe site for the twenty-fourth anniversary party convention had led organizers to consider, and reject, successively smaller urban centres in Sulawesi such as Manado, Ujung Pandang, Palu, and Poso, and eventually settle on the rural Lake Poso Festival Grounds in Tentena. Tensions mounted as the event (and the expected chaos) drew near.

Portentous signs abounded. Local pranksters had already discovered the value of the newly installed telephone system; the minister received an anonymous call in the dead of night conveying a threat to fire-bomb the largest church in Tentena. As reports had just begun to circulate of a series of church burnings in Java and Kalimantan, the prank was treated with great seriousness. A watch was instituted at the church, with a minimum of twenty men a night standing guard. The district head imposed a similar nightwatch throughout the area in anticipation of PDI partisans; night-time patrols of villagers armed with machetes would maintain the tense peace until the convention was over. The festival grounds themselves were surrounded by army troops. This apparently fortuitous overlap of religious and political tensions was very much heightened by perceived threats and escalating ripostes.

In the boredom of the empty nights, many hasty words were spoken (and now, no doubt, regretted). A good friend, otherwise non-confrontational, was very specific about the danger from within and the measures that would be taken. 'Of course the threat came from some hot-headed Muslim youth! But let them actually try something. We will be ready. We control both ends of the valley. We will sweep them before us!'

These images stick in my mind, a constant reminder of the implications of the incorporation of the highlands in larger social movements; almost every adult in Tentena had experienced personal loss through the ongoing eruptions of larger social movements into the highlands. Ngkai Osi, the oldest villager, had been six when the Dutch came; he lost an uncle at the battle of Tamungkudena. Every adult over age sixty remembers the atrocities of the Japanese occupation; of daughters taken into 'service,' of the shortage of food, and of forced labour. Every adult over age fifty remembers the incursions of Darul Islam and Permesta rebels and the mortar bombs that rained down on the village from the surrounding hills. Every adult over age forty remembers the slaughter of the leaders of the Youth Movement of Central Sulawesi and the birth pangs of the New Order; the children of those stigmatized as 'communists' continue to pay the price for their parents' political activities decades ago. These intermittent outbursts are interspersed with longer periods of more destructive cultural violence, such as the banning of animist funerary rituals, the enforced cultivation of wet-rice fields, and the break-up of longhouses; Kruyt attributed the 30 per cent drop in population in the early colonial period to a cultural ennui bred by rapid social change (Kruyt 1950, 1: 78). These changes were not haphazard but introduced new forms of exploitation to the highlands, which increasingly defined them as the periphery of now distant centres.

Local fears of outside forces have been only marginally relieved by recent history. More than thirty years of New Order rule have thoroughly integrated the region under a national government, national media, and national economy. The road running through the village is now part of the Trans-Sulawesi Highway. Television, newspapers, and magazines keep residents abreast of national movements, and telephones and letters rapidly convey all the news that's 'not fit to print' (such as church burnings). The arrival of the ministers of the Interior, and of Defence, by helicopter during the PDI convention simply highlighted how hollow the claims of isolation are at the '22nd nationally designated tourist destination.' The world is beating a path to their door.

The rapid extension of the New Order state into its rural periphery has not, however, brought an end to the tensions of the past. These tensions are in many ways the very product of that extension, and the threat it poses to local elites, to local livelihoods, and to their 'faith.' Yet, as I have been at pains to demonstrate, this tension cannot be interpreted within the meta-narratives of secular modernization theory; this is no conflict between a secular modern state and a successionist ethnic periphery whose identity is rooted in 'primordial' sentiments. The Indonesian state and its local representatives explicitly reject the secular label and consider themselves the rightful protector of 'religion.' The 'ethnic periphery' is a diffuse group with no clear boundaries, no primordial *ur*-identity. Rather, local identities are anchored in 'religion,' itself a recent, trans-ethnic phenomena. This local identity is rooted in a *volkskerk*, a modernist institution that has fostered a particular brand of religious nationalism. The tensions I have described result from the competing nationalist discourses of church and state, discourses that have blurred the ideological boundary between the rightful realm of each. In such conditions, it is no simple matter to 'render therefore unto Caesar the things which are Caesar's; and unto God the things that are God's.'

In the remainder of this chapter, I underscore the exemplary aspects of the processes transfiguring the Christian Church of Central Sulawesi. This small church in a largely Islamic country is by no means unique, an insignificant colonial legacy growing in an unwatched niche of the state apparatus. It is rather, typical of the historical conditions that have created the discourse on religiosity in Indonesia. By choosing a Christian example, I hope to have underscored the colonial origins of that discourse; rather than essentializing the inherently political nature of an Islamic Other, I aim to point out its parallels with the Dutch churches and their colonial progeny. The processes by which secular modernization has been emasculated and religious pillars created in both the Netherlands and the Netherlands East Indies have been shaped by colonial institutions, including a colonial anthropology whose ideal models were translated into prescriptive policy. The grand sweep of Weber's 'rationalization of religion' thesis thus requires tempering, a more historically rooted analysis of the relationship between power and religion.

In relating this particular example to the larger issues of the 'politics of *agama* (religion)' in Indonesia, I argue that those political strategies that attempt to authoritatively define the scope of religiosity are rooted in institutional concerns. It is in the political struggle to answer particular questions of bureaucratic competence that the church's rationalization is either aided and abetted or peters out into irrelevance: Is religious education better delivered by special classes in state schools or through independent religious schools? Should political principle be subject to religious authority? Does the health of the 'spirit' need to be nursed in hospitals, and if so, how? The Christian Church of Central Sulawesi, following the lead of the Netherlands Missionary Society, has a vested interest in extending its Bible-based particularist discipline into all aspects of social life. Yet, each claim is contested, subject to the demands of state institutions and policies that shape and mould the public role which religious organizations may legitimately assume. The transformation and multiplication of wedding ceremonies is one example of how this struggle has been played out on cultural terrain;

both church and state have sought to reform the household through successive incursions on the processes by which it is ritually constituted.

Increasingly, the church has found its social programs under pressure; its schools, hospitals, and development initiatives have all faced the dual threat of regulatory hurdles and better-financed state competition. Yet, the clipping of the church's modernist wings has by no means slowed its rationalization. The multiplication of worship groups and the extension of feasting and *posintuwu* exchange to new constituencies have served to entrench the church ever further in the 'traditional' sphere. The state's attempts to delimit religion to a specifically spiritual realm has meant the steady expansion of worship services. Since these hierarchically organized services are embedded in local processes of social reproduction, in the maintenance of kinship and of access to land and labour, the church's power is increasingly centralized; this offers it a new base for resisting the state.

The Christian Church of Central Sulawesi thus swings between a 'modernist' pole and a 'traditionalist' post; it is a Janus-faced fellowship whose 'inculturation' is its strength. A similar dynamic arguably underlies both 'new school' (*kaum muda*) and 'old school' (*kaum tua*) Islam in Indonesia as well. (I avoid using the usual oppositional glosses applied to these theological orientations, 'modernist' and 'traditionalist,' since these terms hide common processes of rationalization and modernization affecting both.) Tradition is not a perpetuation of the past in the present but a constantly reinvented discursive resource available for local manipulation. It is this latter process that I believe Geertz sought to capture with the phrase 'internal conversion,' thus pointing to the reinterpretation and reorganization of 'tradition' in new, more 'rational' forms. As both the new and the old school have established broad-based religious bureaucracies rooted in local communities, their utilization of 'tradition' serves as one point of intersection with the state; as religious communities and the state engage in contentious debates on the boundaries of religiosity, 'tradition' serves as a potent resource within which religious bodies may retreat when their 'modernist' incursions in civil society are threatened. It is to this dynamic that the growth of 'cultural Islam' during the New Order may be ascribed (see Hefner 1997b).

The multiplicity of strategies adopted by religious institutions in the 'politics of *agama*' challenges both the assumed inevitability of secular modernization and the liberal stereotypes of an essentialized, monolithic, and antimodern 'Islamic politics.' Rather than essentializing either religion or Islam, we need to recognize that the 'region's diverse history demonstrates that the nation-state and nationalism have been as decisive an influence on Muslim politics as have any timeless principles of Muslim governance' (Hefner 1997a, 26). The same is equally true of Christian politics. It is, then, to these historically particular transformations that the remainder of this chapter is devoted. By first addressing the colonial discourses on religion by which the religious pillarization in Indonesia was fostered, I set the stage for a discussion of their transformation under the New Order; rather than argue for some evolutionary trajectory from animist religion (or the 'traditionalist' variants of the 'world' religions) to the rationalized, disenchanted religion of secular modernity, I emphasize their common transformations and the alternative modernities they offer.

Colonial Discourses on Religion in Indonesia

The late nineteenth-century contests between secular Dutch liberals and the confessional proponents of the 'Great Protestant Nation' challenge the ideological presuppositions of the Weberian concept of the 'rationalization' of religion (1963). Weber describes rationalization as the objectification of religion as a system of beliefs and the disarticulation of that system of beliefs from everyday activities (i.e., the 'disenchantment of the world,' or secularization). Religion is, in other words, defined in terms of a restricted discursive field that has an ambiguous relationship with practice (in particular, politics and economy); it does not directly inform practice (a characteristic of the 'enchanted world') but, through ritual, creates general and flexible mental 'dispositions' – ethical imperatives – to act in culturally specific ways. 'Rationalization' stands in evolutionary contrast to tradition. 'Rationalization' is not, however, a simple representation of a process, but also a prescriptive liberal, ideological position; the process can be tied to enlightenment definitions that impute a distinct essence to religion that is opposed to, and exclusive of, politics and economics. As Asad notes, 'the insistence that religion has an autonomous essence – not to be confused with the essence of science, or of politics, or of common sense – invites us to define religion (like any essence) as a transhistorical and transcultural phenomenon. It may be a happy accident that this effort of defining religion converges with the liberal demand in our time that it be kept quite separate from politics, law, and science – spaces in which varieties of power and reason articulate our distinctively modern life' (1993, 28). This prescriptive liberal constitutional position is the norm by which Orientalism surveys its ethnographic Other, Islam, and finds it wanting; no longer for theological reasons, but for its transgression of those 'natural' boundaries necessary for the good governance of the modern democratic state (cf. Said 1979, 120). Islam is assumed to couple the otherwise autonomous essences of religion and politics, a move that encourages Orientalists to view their 'religious discourse in the political arena ... as a disguise for political power' (Asad 1993, 29). Such tired ideas have acquired new life in the post–cold war era, where ideology and economic interests are said to have been supplanted by the 'clash of civilizations,' between the secular West and an equally monolithic Islam (cf. Huntington 1993).

The religious pillarization of the Netherlands stands as a marked exception to the secular modernization thesis and denaturalizes the assumptions of liberal political theory. In making the 'Kingdom of God' more than a metaphor, the Dutch Confessional political parties provide a compelling example that undermines essentialist definitions of religion. I would, however, go further with regard to Islam. This Christian oddity is of importance not because 'the exception proves the rule' but because it leads us to question the presuppositions of secular modernization; an anti-essentialist interpretation of Islam cannot assume that it, any more than Christianity, is inherently 'political' (Hefner 1997b, 79–80). We must seek the particular institutions, ideologies, and social movements that, as in the Netherlands, allow religious organizations to successfully challenge the hegemony of the secular state in the political sphere. We need to examine how debates between the confessional parties and the liberal state in the Netherlands East Indies inadvertently fostered the religious rationalization of Islam, Christianity, and Balinese Hinduism, and hence ultimately shaped the particularly modern forms of political organization in Indonesia.

The introduction of the Ethical Policy in 1901 marks a key transitional period in which the confessional politics of the Netherlands first began to transform the colony. 'Ethical imperialism' brought the entire archipelago under the uniform rule of the Dutch, the 'Pax Neerlandica.' Simultaneously, Van Vollenhoven's pluralistic legal reformation of the state apparatus through *adat* law studies severed 'tradition' from 'religion,' allowing the Dutch to rule through the first while granting Indonesians 'freedom' in the latter. The colonial state sought to undermine the potential political claims that Islam could legitimately make by defining religion as a 'transnational essence' distinct from the local cultures (*adat*) through which they chose to indirectly rule (i.e., by institutionalizing *adat* rather than *shari'ah* law).

However, it was precisely this transcultural status that freed Islam (and to a lesser extent, Christianity) from the taint of colonial collusion and made it an ideal forum within which to grapple with emerging questions of modernity and tradition. Since religion was defined by the colonial state as a 'non-political' sphere, as a delimited social domain rooted in individual rights, it offered greater room for local agency than the political realm itself. The churches of the Netherlands progressively expanded the boundaries of these religious rights at the turn of the century and increasingly limited the purview of the secular state; religious rights, hard-won in the Netherlands, were actively pursued by Christians in the Netherlands East Indies (Randwijck 1981, 264–88). Christianity became a means through which 'loyal opposition' to the colonial state could be voiced (Haire 1981, 60–2). This religious expansion into civil society was particularly modernist in focus precisely because it was viewed as transcultural and not rooted in local tradition. The successful strategies adopted by Christians were quickly emulated by Muslims seeking parity. Rationalized religious bureaucracies offered them the only legitimate means of wresting control over large areas of everyday life out of Dutch colonial hands.

The usage of common methods and of extended debate between the Dutch confessionals and the liberals itself implies an agreed-upon set of terms and assumptions; the Ethical Policy was less a radical innovation than the form that the liberal state took under confessional tutelage. We cannot ignore the effect of Ethical Theology and the concept of the *volkskerk* on the development of the Ethical Policy. The Ethical Policy was an attempt to sever distinct religious and political spheres that, initially at least, conformed to the demands of liberal political theory. However, this religious sphere was not defined in narrow 'spiritual' terms predicated upon individual 'belief.' Snouck Hurgronje, the Dutch adviser who formulated the new policy towards Islam, differentiated three arenas of potential religious influence: the spiritual arena, within which absolute freedom should be granted; the social sphere, within which the colonial state should systematically favour *adat* over religion but within which Islamic organizations would be given freedom to operate as in the Netherlands; and the political sphere, from which religion was to be banned (Suminto 1985, 12). This tripartite division opened up an area of contestation between 'religion' and the secular 'culture' (*adat*) favoured by the Dutch, which allowed organized religion to invade key areas of civil society such as education, the press, social welfare, and economic associations, as it had in the Netherlands. To ensure compliance, the boundaries between these spheres of activity were carefully policed by a number of governmental ministries (Noer 1978), and a new advisory body under Hurgronje's direction, the Office of Native Affairs (Kantoor voor Inlandsche Zaken), was created to coordinate general policy (Suminto 1985).

Local Islamic leaders, like the Christian missions, were thus able to form associations with social-welfare or cultural ends while being actively discouraged from any overt form of political action (Suminto 1985, 122). These associations were formed on Dutch models and became the major means by which Islam was rationalized in Indonesia; it was not a homogeneous and 'inherently' political Islam that later entered the political fray in the republican era but these particular Islamic cultural organizations. As the form of colonial rule changed in the Ethical period, these organizations faced new questions about the relationship between religion, now defined as a transcultural essence, and local culture, now reconceptualized as *adat* law; the two major responses have been glossed here as 'new school' and 'old school.' It was this same dynamic that had also impelled missionaries such as Kruyt to so carefully use ethnographic methods to document local culture so that they could better protect the religious sphere under their control from governmental constraints.

The most prominent Islamic organizations to invade this arena of contestation were Sarekat Islam (Islamic Union) and Muhammadiyah ('Way of Muhammad'), followed later by the 'old school' Nahdatul Ulama (Association of Muslim Clerics). These innovative Islamic associations rejected earlier organizational models and adopted Dutch (usually glossed as 'modern') forms of bureaucratic organization. As specifically mass organizations, they spread across the archipelago, gaining a visibility that both underscored the potential threat they posed and eased the burden of colonial supervision. While each is usually carefully cited in the lineages of later political parties, they were born within that arena of cultural contestation opened up by the Ethical Policy; these religious organizations were not founded to meet specific 'political' goals (a proscribed and policed domain), but as a means by which a 'modern' transcultural Islam could come to grips with the newly defined secular world. This secular world was defined through state-regulated *adat* law studies that carefully delimited local traditions which cross-cut religious identities. *Adat* law studies and the administrative divisions they sanctioned encouraged the solidification of long-standing ethnic identities, thereby confronting this 'modern' Islam with its cultural Other in a new way. This state-imposed Weberian dynamic disenchanted the colonial world; religious concepts, once intertwined with the concrete details of ordinary life, now stood 'apart,' 'above,' or 'outside' of them in a distant and problematic way. That which was 'religious' now required its explicit scriptural reasons (Bowen 1993, 25–9). This transformation of Islam thus amounts to its 'internal conversion' in the Geertzian sense, a move to systematically define universal, sweeping, and conclusive scriptural principles[1] that address generally posed problems of meaning, socially conceived; a specifically theological project undertaken by a rational–legal bureaucracy for whom collective, rather than individual, answers were sought.

Muhammadiyah was founded in 1912 in East Java, but rapidly spread throughout Indonesia, chiefly through the efforts of West Sumatran traders and teachers; it represented the 'new school' wing (*kaum muda*) of Indonesian Islam (Ricklefs 1981, 162–3). The 'new school' emphasized the self-sufficiency of Scripture, a distinctive position only because it denied authority to other written religious texts such as theological commentaries (Bowen 1993, 22). The group advocated the adoption of Western educational and administrative methods to further the chances of Indonesian Muslims in the Dutch East Indies. Its initial priority was the establishment of religious schools on the Christian model, teaching 'modern' subjects such as mathematics and geography, as well as those religious subjects usually taught in the traditional Islamic schools, the *pesantren*. These schools also adopted Western educational methods such as classroom seating and black-boards. Muhammadiyah also established separate social organizations for women (Aisyiah) and age groups (Nasyiatul Aisyiah for girls, and Hizbul Wathan for boys). Lastly, the organization also sponsored numerous social-welfare activities such as orphanages and the distribution of alms. Muhammadiyah was introduced to South Sulawesi in 1926 (Rössler 1997, 276), and from there spread to the highlands of Central Sulawesi with Bugis migrants; Muhammadiyah now oper-ates both a primary school, and a junior high school in Tentena (competing with both Christian and state schools), as well as an orphanage.

Muhammadiyah fits the ideal typical model prescribed by the Ethical Policy. Engaged in activities designed to further the social welfare of the *umat* (commu-nity of believers), Muhammadiyah adopted a modernist stance to religion that allowed for a clear separation between that which was Islamic, sanctioned by Scripture (narrowly defined) and hence 'religious,' and that which was not, and hence optional, within limits. This attitude was not dissimilar from Adriani's insistence that for Christian converts the civil *adat* should be distinguished from the sphere of religion, but that the two together had to be viewed as a 'Christian *adat*' since they could not be allowed to conflict with each other (1932, 1: 369). Yet, despite the more limited role left to 'religion,' it was still able to serve as a potent critique of the colonial state; Bowen notes in his study of Gayo Muslim religiosity in Sumatra that the rationalization of a public sphere of religion which Muhammadiyah fostered was

> religious, social, and political in varying mixes and degrees. Although the history of this process requires further study, it appears to have been largely through events designated 'religious' that Gayo began to engage in critical public discussions about society ... Because open political activity was prohibited during most of the colonial period, the most effective way to gather together townspeople was under the banner of religion ... Speakers ... urged Gayo men and women to rationally rethink how they ordered their lives, from matters of dress and hygiene to what sort of music and literature they read. (1993, 326)

While the colonial state had interpreted the demand 'to render unto Caesar the things which are Caesar's; and unto God the things that are God's' to mean an absolute separation of spheres of influence, Muhammadiyah, like the Dutch Protestant churches, recognized the distinction between church and state but believed that the state should be subject to religious principle where such principles had relevance. And the spheres of relevance were not to be determined by the secular state, but by the absolutes of Scripture – and its ambiguous interpretation. Hence, Muhammadiyah has historically fought for the establishment of an Islamic state (the implementation of *shari'ah law*), actively supported the Darul Islam rebellions that sought to establish this state, and have provided leadership for the banned modernist Islamic party Masyumi (Liddle 1996, 73–6). However, Muhammadiyah itself has never directly entered the electoral fray. Like the Christian churches, it remained within the modernist liberal parameters established by the Ethical Policy.

Importantly, these same modern bureaucratic organizational methods were later adopted by the 'old school,' who otherwise appeared to reject western influence; they were not unlike the Dutch Confessionals who rejected the Enlightenment values of the French Revolution yet adopted its administrative methods to beat the liberals at their own game. Nahdatul Ulama, now the largest social-welfare organization in Indonesia, was founded in East Java in 1926 as an association of religious teachers who operated *pesantren*, the only generally available common schools in Java (Feillard 1997). The clerics who operated these schools were figures of great authority within rural *santri* communities. These clerics argued that ambiguities in the Scripture made dependence upon the interpretations of established scholarly traditions necessary; the 'new school's' call for individual understanding and interpretation of Scripture was thus rebutted. Most follow the Shafi'i tradition, which offers a coherent legal framework (*shari'ah law*) that they believe should be the ultimate basis of government. The organization formed after the spread of 'new school' Muslim and secular colonial schools began to undermine their position within their communities. They avoided open political confrontation with the colonial government (indeed, in 1938 they proclaimed the Netherlands East Indies an 'Islamic realm' on the grounds that *shari'ah* law was being administered by government-sanctioned Islamic officials [Feillard 1997, 131]); they directed their energies towards establishing a broad network of upgraded religious schools with an expanded curriculum.

The question of religious education was thus a key area of cultural contestation in both the Netherlands and Netherlands East Indies; such contests similarly sparked the growth of Dutch religious associations during the 1860s and 1870s to counter secular, liberal plans for a national school system. A similar state-funded Christian school system was created in Central Sulawesi and elsewhere before Indonesian Independence by the Netherlands Missionary Society. The emphasis on education is indicative of the 'religious' priorities of these organizations distinct from the political problem of voter mobilization. As Hefner notes, '*Nahdatul Ulama* was "nonpolitical" only in the conventional understanding of politics. From its own perspective, the party's actions showed clear political priorities and an astute awareness of how best to achieve them. While eschewing confrontation with the government, it quietly promoted Islamic regeneration. In its eyes, after all, Java's ills were a product not simply of infidel colonialism but of irreligious Javanism as well' (1994, 83). These Islamic and Christian educational organizations took shape when electoral franchises were very restrictive and devoted their efforts towards those *not enfranchised*. They were, in other words, not concerned to extend their hegemony through overt political means, but through the better and more regular application of disciplinary methods to their religious subjects through a broad array of social-welfare experiments. In each case, liberal attempts to separate church and state, and hence deny religious organizations power, foundered on the issue of the relationship between a now-distinct religious sphere and culture. Islamic clerics found their authority challenged by an irreligious Javanism actively supported by the state as *adat*. Their innovation was to combat such 'traditions' with 'modern' organizational methods borrowed from their colonial competitors. Similarly, in the case of the To Pamona, 'irreligion' was defined through challenges to the traditional elites entrenched in the church. They thus rationalized church programs such as the evangelization groups to extend their disciplinary hold. Politics, when resorted to at all, was a subsequent means to that end and not a priority until the political franchise was extended.

The success of Muhammadiyah and Nahdatul Ulama in navigating the contested terrain of secular tradition without appearing overtly political contrasts with other suppressed organizations, such as the Masyumi, which failed in that respect. Their success depended upon constructing viable bureaucracies within the clearly policed boundaries of civil society, their incursions outside the spiritual realm requiring constant scriptural legitimation in the view not only of colonial authorities, but increasingly of their own members. Such new rationalizing demands placed the emphasis on religion as ideology, as a system of 'tenets' that specified a cognitive attitude that stands 'apart,' 'above,' or 'outside' of 'culture' for its 'believers.' The processes by which 'religion' was embedded in practice (a 'religious culture,' or the 'inculturation of religion') were ignored. The disenchantment of the 'tradition,' on the one hand, and the rationalization of religion, on the other, must thus be seen as an interpretive artefact, the product of prescriptive colonial demands.

This studied ignorance of embedded practice was crucial, I argued, to the means by which Kruyt masked his incorporation of indigenous power relations within the mission bureaucracy. Similarly, 'modern' Muslim bureaucracies such as Muhammadiyah and Nahdatul Ulama proclaimed a set of 'shared beliefs' but made no reference to the indigenous political processes that lent their bureaucracies power; the social meaning of their doctrines and practices needs to be understood within the wider 'political economy of meaning' (Bowen 1993, 30), the 'movements, classes, institutions, ideologies' that made such discourses possible (cf. Asad 1983, 252; Hefner 1985, 9–17).

Post-Colonial Discourses on Religion in Indonesia

The 'Ethical Period' of colonialism is thus marked by the successful institutional separation of church and state but the unsuccessful separation of religion and power. In the immediate post-Independence period, it was these modern religious bureaucracies and not an amorphous 'political Islam' that were turned to explicitly political (electoral) purposes due to the rapid extension of the franchise. Islam in Indonesia (but oddly enough, not Christianity or Hinduism) was described in terms of its confessional political streams (*aliran*). Geertz described these *aliran* during the short-lived democratic and 'guided democracy' period as

> not merely loose conglomerates of people with similar voting habits. Rather they are social, fraternal, recreational, and religious organizations within which kinship, economic, and ideological ties coalesce to press a community of people into the support of a single set of social values which are not just concerned with the proper exercise of political power but condition behaviour in many different areas of life. To join a Moslem political party is to commit oneself to one or another of the variant interpretations of Islamic social doctrine. (1960, 163)

It was only at this point that explicit comparisons were made between *aliran* formation in Indonesia and *verzuiling* in the Netherlands (generally, only in the Dutch literature, see Gunawan and Muizenberg 1967; McVey 1971; Gunawan 1971; Wertheim 1973). Here, however, I have argued that limiting discussions of pillarization to this period of democratic-party politics is imbued with liberal political presuppositions and ignores this wider tie between religion and power. What Geertz describes as the extension of religiously based political parties into the body politic is a theoretical and historical inversion; it was, rather, the rapid colonization of the electoral field by pre-existing religious organizations. I have also underscored that this is a 'religious' and not an Islamic phenomenon; the Christians in Sulawesi, and the Hindus in Bali, were also pillarized/rationalized, like their Muslim neighbours.

While the religious pillars were not the immediate target of Suharto's military-backed New Order, they have been subject to radical restructuring following the elimination of the Indonesian Communist Party. The army was dominated by secular Javanese generals who had gained their credentials in putting down the Darul Islam rebellions in Java, Sumatra, and Sulawesi in the 1950s. Despite the aid of Muslims in eliminating the Communist Party in the pogroms of 1965, the

New Order has consistently sought to limit the political power of the Islamic parties. A number of analysts have pointed out the similarities between the New Order and the colonial state, particularly in its religious policies (Anderson 1983b; Lev 1985). Like the colonial state, the New Order has sought to limit the political activities of independent Muslim organizations while simultaneously encouraging a 'cultural Islam.' This continuity may, however, be overdrawn; the New Order does not conceive of itself as a secular liberal state. In recent years it has actively supported Muslim *dakwah* (missions), the building of mosques, the practice of Islamic law, and established a government-sponsored association of Islamic intellectuals that counts many cabinet members among its supporters (Hefner 1997b). Rather than viewing the New Order as a simple continuation of the colonial state, I would argue that it has usurped the successful policies of 'pillarized' Islam and seeks to establish itself as the sole legitimate religious pillar.

The New Order interpretation of 'Pancasila democracy' (SNRI 1983) has been established as the permanent form of the constitutional state. The Pancasila (the five pillars) are the five principles upon which the constitution is based, the first of which is 'belief in *Tuhan*' (a Supreme Being, God). The five pillars of the Pancasila are a careful allusion to (and ideological replacement of) the five pillars of Islam; similarly the use of the non-denominational term *Tuhan* rather than the Islamic (and Christian) *Allah* bases the state on monotheistic religion rather than Islam, and thus guarantees freedom of religion to those adhering to other 'world religions' (*agama*, non–ethnically based scriptural religions) (Kipp and Rodgers 1987, 17). However, the first pillar does more than guarantee religious freedom; in the New Order's interpretation, it is not simply a determination of limited individual rights, but it also specifies the state's corporate responsibility. The first pillar prescribes the state's role in protecting and promoting 'world religions' (*agama*) and in discouraging traditional tribal or ethnic 'belief systems' (*kepercayaan*).

In one sense, the Pancasila thus blurs the boundary between religion and the state. Instruction in a world religion is mandatory at all levels of the educational system (state as well as confessional). The State Islamic Institute Colleges (IAIN) have standardized the qualifications and curriculum of increasingly large numbers of those trained in Islamic law, theology, the arts, and pedagogy at higher levels (Hefner 1997b, 88). The Department of Religion, a full cabinet portfolio with separate sections for each recognized religion, is charged with managing the Haj, registering Islamic marriages, and encouraging the building of mosques, churches, and temples. Many teachers in the religious school system and health professionals in the religiously based health-service organizations are civil servants paid by the state. Its most recent move has been to support a new, influential association of Islamic professionals, ICMI (Ikatan Cendekiawan Muslim se-Indonesia; Indonesian Muslim Intellectuals' Union), in an attempt to co-opt a pious but restive middle class. These policies and others have greatly strengthened the reach of Christian, Islamic, and Hindu/Buddhist organizations in the New Order. It is these state-directed policies that have sparked the wave of religious rationalization among the 'traditional religions' in the periphery (Atkinson 1983; Kipp 1993; Schiller 1997; Steedly 1993), as well as making large inroads in the heterodox *abangans* of the Javanese heartland, the traditional supporters of the Communist Party.

Viewed in this light, the New Order's avid support of religion can be seen as the last step in removing the threat of communism. In a simple-minded equivalence, the state has clearly linked atheism with communism, leading to widespread 'statistical' conversions to Islam and Christianity among the former supporters of that group. Religion provided one of the few safe havens in the dangerous first decade of the New Order. Yet as Kipp (1995) has shown, once subject to the discipline of the now-strengthened religious bureaucracies, these opportunistic converts soon become indistinguishable from those who convert for other more 'spiritual' reasons.

This transformation in the state was the succeeding step in the New Order's 'floating mass' policy towards political parties. It was initially viewed as a continuation of colonial policy, as the primary means of depoliticizing Indonesian society and, perforce, the religious political parties (Amal 1994, 218). As Anderson says, 'the semi-official doctrine of the "floating mass" (originally coined in 1971) in effect says that Indonesia's unsophisticated rural masses are not to be distracted from the tasks of development by political parties, except in brief state-defined preelection campaign periods. Under a law established in 1975, political parties are formally banned from establishing branches below the regency level' (1983a, 490). The 'floating mass' policy has been used to prevent religious parties from developing grass-roots organizations. The negative connotations of *politik* have been emphasized by the state, and linked to the chaos of the Guided Democracy period and the attempted 'communist coup' of 1965. Political parties make their appearance once every five years in strictly limited ritualistic election campaigns (*pesta demokrasi*, festivals of democracy: Pemberton 1994, 5) only to disappear from sight shortly thereafter. The religious parties have also been subject to political engineering, and were amalgamated into two polyglot organizations fraught with internal tensions and disputes, and shorn of their religious symbols and names. Their leadership is subject to government review. The New Order state, in contrast, enters the electoral fray through Golkar (*Golongan Karya*, Functional Groups), an explicitly 'non-political' political party representing the military and the civil bureaucracy. Golkar is not hindered by the 'floating mass' policy since its structure, from its provincial to its village branches, is virtually identical to the institutions of local government. All civil servants and their spouses, including those working for religious organizations, must join KORPRI (the Indonesian Civil Service Corps) or the Dharma Wanita (Association of Retired Civil Servants and Wives of Civil Servants), and are expected to vote for Golkar. As a 'non-political' political party, its sole function is to deny a parliamentary majority to the other parties (Liddle 1996, 19). As further protection against this eventuality, a large number of parliamentary seats are reserved for military and presidential appointees.

It is by these means that the New Order has attempted to eliminate its competition on both the left and the right: by physically eliminating the Communist Party and establishing itself as the sole legitimate sponsor of 'religion' as it had come to be defined in Indonesia. The New Order is driven, in other words by impulses towards statism, centralization, and uniformity (Liddle 1996, 81). The ideal to which their political policies are working would appear to be a variation of one-party rule in which the 'diversity' of Indonesian 'functional groups' (political interests) would be moulded into 'unity' through particularly Javanese cultural ('non-political') values of consensus building (*musyawarah*) and 'benevolence-obedience' as embodied in the Pancasila. In this ideal formation, effective executive power would lie with a strong president, the dispenser of benevolence, the king-like centre from whom direction would flow.

The establishment of 'consensus' in the New Order has a coercive edge that reveals the military roots of the regime. As Liddle argues, this ideal model of political leadership encouraged statism: 'most government departments have agencies charged with *pembinaan* (development, building, in the sense of guidance) as in ... the Department of Information's directorate for the guidance of the press. Newspapers and magazines, mostly privately-owned, are told to behave in a "free and responsible" way, and are first warned, then shut down if they don't' (1996, 80). Such 'guidance' is offered to all the 'functional groups' (including religious groups) that make up the state and its electoral representative, Golkar, as well as to the other political parties. Their leadership is subject to regular review, and all decisions are made from the centre, not Parliament.

The New Order state has thus attempted to establish itself as the sole legitimate *aliran* in Indonesia; its aggressive support of religion in the abstract has been equalled by its aggressive debilitation of independent religious organizations and their incorporation within Golkar. Its positive incentives are combined with policies meant to undermine the provisioning of services by independent religious organizations. By teaching religion in state schools, it makes the more expensive religious school system redundant. In Tentena, the church's hospital was almost closed when the government pulled the staff (all of whom were civil servants paid by the state) for use in its own, newly established Puskesmas (People's Health Clinic). Similarly, all funds for the improvement of local schools were issued through special 'presidential orders' rather than the Ministry of Education, and thereby directed solely at state schools. The promise of new buildings was combined with the teaching of religion in state schools as an incentive to persuade the GKST to turn over the bulk of its primary-school system to the government. These initial attempts to undermine the institutional basis of the religious pillars was carried a step further in 1984, when all organizations, including the state-amalgamated Muslim and Christian political parties, were forced to abandon their sacred texts as their 'philosophical' basis (*asas tunggal*), and to acknowledge the ideological principles of New Order rule (the Pancasila) as the sole foundation of their organizations. This subsumption of the Quran, the word of God, to the word of man, evoked widespread resistance from many Muslim organizations (Ramage 1995, 35–9). Faced with the overwhelming military supremacy of the Suharto regime, some groups have prioritized pragmatism over abstract theological principle (Hefner 1997b). It is such pragmatism that led Nahdatul Ulama to 'leave politics' and, ironically, throw its support behind the 'non-political' Golkar in 1984.

The New Order's policies are not, however, without contradiction. Its support of 'religion' has led to a widespread resacralization of civil society and the deepening of popular piety. This piety can be made to serve the state only as long as the New Order can successfully present itself as the sole legitimate *aliran* in Indonesian society, as the protector of those religious bodies it seeks to co-opt; this bolstered piety otherwise supports the very organizations the state seeks to undermine. It is to this contradiction that we now turn; the surprising growth of 'rationalizing' religions under New Order rule. The process of rationalization in these conditions is, I have argued, an attempt by locals to capture control of the realm of 'discursive tradition' on their own, not state, terms. The importance of these discursive traditions for the continued social reproduction of a peasantry composed of 'just-enoughs' and 'not-quite-enoughs' has been pointed out, and forms the root of local resistance. As the contest of representations surrounding the Lake Poso Festival Grounds cited at the beginning of this book makes clear, the arena of struggle has shifted from the modernist bureaucracies of educational, health, and welfare organizations to 'culture.'

Culture as Contested Territory

In the first section of this book, I dwelt on the irony of a colonial power whose civilizational mission was based on its responsibility to shepherd its wards along a unilineal path to modernity, yet did so in a 'culturally sensitive' manner within the confines of traditional *adats*. In this chapter, and elsewhere, the NEI state's ironic use of 'culture' as a discursive resource to limit and cross-cut the power of religion has been repeatedly emphasized. However, the segregation of religion entailed the disenchantment of 'culture' and opened up a complex area of contestation; religious organizations now had to justify their actions in the cultural sphere in scriptural terms. This demand encouraged their rationalization as 'religions,' on the one hand, and their conflicting 'inculturation' in the new cultural sphere, on the other. The success of religious bodies in colonizing 'culture' – and the relative failure of the state in accomplishing the same – underlies the process of pillarization in both the Netherlands and Indonesia.

'Culture' in this sense is a discursive phenomenon, the product of ethnographic representation, and not a simple perpetuation of the past in the present. 'Tradition' in this sense is the product of modernization, and not its predecessor. As a discursive resource, its uses are not bound by the intents of its authors. I have, for example, highlighted how the various classes of To Pamona village society have utilized an innovative tradition of 'shared poverty' (*mosintuwu*) to provide 'free' labour for their peasant enterprises in a commodified market economy. Yet the price of their utilization of 'tradition' is that they can no longer contest state discourses on 'tradition' that blame it for the failure of state-directed development. Multiply authored, 'culture' has an apparent objectivity that encourages us to view it as the product of 'shared meanings' rather than in terms of its strategic manipulation for alternative ends. Hence, the ideological separation of religion need not preclude the strategic use of 'culture' to shore up and buttress 'modern' religious bureaucracies, as the example of the Christian Church of Central Sulawesi made clear; feasting, *posintuwu* exchange, and kinship remained extra-liturgical elements of worship yet underwrote the way in which worship was performed.

In this book, I have been particularly concerned with how religion relates to those elements of 'culture' that are economic: agricultural production, and 'gift' and market exchange. At issue was the apparently contradictory economic 'development' of the To Pamona, their increasing embeddedness in commoditized relations of production and exchange, with their increasing dependence upon a 'moral economy' tied to kinship, feasting, and hence the church. In this contest, 'tradition' is generally portrayed as 'the past in the present,' which is increasingly attenuated by the state's forced march to modernity and economic 'take-off.' This duality is usually conceived in evolutionary terms, as contraries, as local non-market relations are 'supplanted' in the 'transition to capitalism.' Yet, as Bloch and Parry (1989) have argued, there is no necessary opposition between market and non-market economic exchange mechanisms. The moral economy of the To Pamona is a 'transactional sphere' that has arisen within a market context;

it is not an attenuated tradition facing extinction under the threat of market forces, but a mutualistic, strategically invoked discursive tool necessary for the market to work at all.

This approach thus draws on recent critiques of both 'dual economy' models of peasant society and those 'spheres of exchange' theories rooted in Polanyi's substantivist analysis of markets (Kahn 1993; Ferguson 1994). The dual-economy model was popular in those Dutch colonial circles that were heavily influenced by the work of Chayanov (Kahn 1993, 75–109). Their work was given new life by Geertz's 'involution' thesis (1963) and Scott's 'moral economy' model (1976), described in chapter 3. The dual-economy model views peasant economic behaviour as couched within a protective cultural cocoon that isolates 'traditional' values and patterns of behaviour from capitalist inroads. Whether conceived in Geertz's culturalist terms, or as 'articulated modes of production,' the dual-economy model presumes the 'traditional' peasant sphere will slowly die out as an increasing number of peasants 'jump ship' from 'traditional' to 'modern' economies. A similar sense of transition underlies the 'spheres of exchange' approach derived from Polanyi's institutional analysis of markets. Distinct spheres of exchange, such as 'traditional' *posintuwu* exchange and the commodity market, are said to temporarily coexist; at least until money, the ultimate acid of traditional social relations, allows for interchangeability between the spheres, leading to the breakdown of 'tradition.'

Posintuwu exchange provides an important corrective to this perception of the ultimate triumph of the market, and the gradual elimination of 'tradition.' This exchange sphere has blossomed to the same extent as the market has encroached on To Pamona society. It is certainly not unique in its ability to decommodify the 'social acid' of tradition, money, and transform it into a 'gift' (cf. Carsten 1989). But *posintuwu* exchange also highlights that interchangeability between these economies is critical to their functioning, and not a sign of 'traditions' ultimate demise; the same objects may regularly attain or shed their commodity status in different contexts (cf. Appadurai 1986). What requires emphasis is not just that the objects of local exchange, including labour, may enter either sphere of exchange; but that, once within a sphere, they must follow the rules that structure it (cf. Ferguson 1994, 137). Within the one sphere, the calculation of costs and benefits is forbidden; in the other, it is crucial. Regardless of the degree of 'economic rationality' of individuals, however, it is to their advantage to emphasize their adherence to the ideological rules structuring an exchange sphere; for generous gift-givers eager to maintain their reputation, the ideal of the free gift underscores their magnanimity. For 'calculating' gift-givers attempting to benefit from the generosity of others, the ideal of the free gift limits their obligation to repay.

This discursive tradition, this product of modernity in To Pamona guise, is thus not the survival of a natural economy; nor is it an entirely invented tradition. It is, rather, the product of the differentiation in land holdings, the commodification of labour, and asymmetrical market relations that leave even the wealthier villagers at the economic margins. Thus situated, the presuppositions of liberal economists hold; rational economic choices are imperative due to limited means. And so, too, the presuppositions of the moral economists on the need for subsistence insurance; the 'rural population' is like 'a man standing permanently up to the neck in water, so that even a ripple is sufficient to drown him' (Scott 1976, 1). It these dual constraints that condition a particularly 'peasant' form of rural capitalism; a form of capitalism without capitalists, where economic choices are thoroughly commoditized, but where poverty necessitates the exploitation of every uncosted 'traditional' input possible. Kahn (1993, 65) thus describes the continuum of peasant economic behaviours as lying between the 'traditional' peasant whose activities are made possible only through commoditized inputs and wage work and the 'capitalist' peasant whose success lies in maximizing the exploitation of uncosted 'traditional' resources such as land and kin labour. The viability of To Pamona households depended largely on the amount of uncosted resources they had at their command; but their dependence on these resources inevitably tied them to their unviable brethren, from whom they derived uncosted labour in exchange for subsistence insurance. These ties, which constitute the 'moral economy' of the To Pamona, also established hierarchical kinship relations, and transformed economic inequality into genealogical seniority.

The utilization of this discursive tradition thus transforms local class relations from a clear-cut differentiation of haves and have-nots into the more delicately shaded 'just-enoughs' and 'not-quite-enoughs' described by Geertz in Java. Class divisions are blunted, and an ideology of economic and political egalitarianism asserted, while class is translated into kinship terms. This translation process is accomplished, I argued, through the process by which economic goods are decommodified and transformed into gifts: through *posintuwu* exchanges that define the boundaries of a kin group while simultaneously establishing its centre around a wealthier patron. These exchanges, and the establishment of patronage ties, take place in the series of church-sponsored worship services that encapsulate this 'traditional' kinship hierarchy within the 'modern' bureaucracy of the church. The church, for its part, sought to extend these ties because of their disciplinary potential; through these power/knowledge relations, they were able to foster 'faith,' adherence to the church's procedure for establishing 'Truth,' if not 'belief.'

In the case of the To Pamona, the 'problematic' relationship between an abstractly formulated, rational religion and a disenchanted secular tradition has thus been bridged by patron–client relations unrecognized by the church's liturgical order (cf. Hefner 1985, 182–8). This relationship allows the church to proclaim itself an inclusive fellowship, yet establish hierarchy; to 'inculturate' itself within a traditional *volk* largely of its own making, while maintaining its modernist credentials as an organization. While it cannot be assumed that the Protestant To Pamona are typical of the rest of a religiously diverse country, this case study should at least point to a new direction in the interpretation of the melding of economic dualism, legal pluralism, and religious nationalism that marked the Ethical Policy.

What Next?

I began this book by questioning the essentialist roots of expressions of To Pamona ethnicity that claim to represent the group's authentic 'origins.' By focusing upon how these 'representations,' in the sense both of 'image of' and as 'speaking for,' have been constituted, the political, economic, and cultural discourses that made the ethnic category 'To Pamona' salient have been underscored. To Pamona ethnicity cannot be rooted in some 'primordial sentiment' and opposed to nationalism; rather, there are two divergent conceptions of ethnicity that are themselves part of nationalist discourses rooted in competing institutional orders. The one nationalist discourse is tied to a theological conceptualization of the *volkskerk*; the other, to the Indonesian nationalist project, 'Various But One.' Both discourses can be traced back to their colonial roots: Ethical Theology and the Ethical Policy. Both projects posit unique and sometimes contradictory solutions to the problem of the relationship among nation, state, and church.

Such encompassing yet contradictory discourses cannot help but open up marginal spaces, the silences that greet a sermon, the cynicism of flag-waving on Independence Day. Throughout this book, I have drawn on such episodes to indicate how local realities exceed the totalizing discourses of church and state. It is, however, difficult work to fill in the silences, and harder yet to re-present them without stirring a new totalizing discourse into the pot. Though 'participant observation' over the course of two years offered numerous opportunities to fill these gaps, to record the 'voices' of those who struggled against the disciplines that constrained them, I could never shake the realization that they themselves never spoke up; and that repeating these conversations in public had implications which neither they nor I would be willing to live with. 'Don't write this down yet.'

These previously silenced voices may now finally be heard. On 21 May 1998, Suharto suddenly resigned as president of Indonesia after weeks of widespread rioting throughout the country. An economic crisis born of corruption, cronyism, nepotism, and the domino-like collapse of the so-called Asian Tiger economies of Indonesia's neighbours led to the massive devaluation of its currency, the failure of its ruined financial institutions, vast unemployment, and huge hikes in the cost of basic necessities. The military, until then an unswerving pillar of support for the regime, delivered the ultimatum that Suharto would be impeached if he did not resign immediately. His immediate successor, Vice-President B.J. Habibie, has liberalized the electoral system in preparation for the first free national election since 1955, to be held in June 1999. Forty-eight political parties have been registered; twelve have explicitly declared Islam as their foundation. Still others are Islamic in orientation but accept the bounds of Pancasila democracy. Both Protestant and Catholic parties have entered the fray as well. *Aliran* may yet be reborn.

It is, however, too early to tell what choices the voiceless may make in the privacy of the polling booth. We must be careful not to confuse pillarization with 'resistance' to the state or infer that the collapse of the New Order is an automatic vote of confidence in the religious parties. The rationalization of religious bureaucracies is itself a state-building project that encapsulates local hierarchies; and this hierarchy may also have crumbled in the economic collapse that took down Suharto. All bets, as it were, are off. What will happen then, when the silenced may finally represent themselves?

Notes

Introduction: On Origin Stories in a Postmodern World

1 See, for example, Pakan 1977, on the Toraja, among whom he includes the To Pamona. The work is entitled 'The Toraja People: Identification, Classification and Location.'

1: Missions in Colonial Context

1 All translations from the Dutch are mine.

2: The Reformation

1 Although Kruyt and Adriani adopted local custom in naming a language group after its word for 'no' (Bare'e), the indigenous population found the name 'No Speaking Toraja' nonsensical. Although it had some currency beforehand, the name Pamona was first officially used in reference to the group about 1973 (Pakan 1986, 19), when it was applied to the two administrative districts around Lake Poso.

2 Among the slave-holding lemba such as the To Onda'e and the To Lage, each *sombori* built their own house, although daughters would build their houses next to their parents'. Since the Dutch proscribed the building of longhouses, this has become the predominant pattern in the region.

3 Other missionaries also adopted former slave children and gave them superior educations in distant schools. See Schuijt-Mansvelt 1919.

4 The Darul Islam movement in Sulawesi had ties to a similarly named movement which began in West Java in 1948, and in Aceh in Sumatra in 1953.

5 After the government made it clear that they would not tolerate Megawati within

the leadership of the PDI, a rump PDI congress in Medan, Sumatra, elected Suryadi as party president, resulting in the splitting of the party into pro- and anti-Megawati camps. Megawati's supporters controlled the PDI headquarters in Jakarta and refused to leave, holding rallies throughout July 1996. On 27 July so-called Suryadi supporters (widely believed to include soldiers) invaded the PDI headquarters to rout out Megawati. The move sparked massive rioting in the streets of Jakarta, including an attempt to burn down the headquarters of a state bank in central Jakarta.

6 The use of the Indonesian word *Tuhan*, rather than the Islamic (or for that matter Christian) *Allah* was intended to allow for a limited religious diversity. It thus allowed the framers of the constitution to avoid accusations of secularism, while also avoiding rooting the state in Islamic law (the rejected Jakarta Charter to the Constitution of 1945) (Atkinson 1987, 177; Ramage 1995, 14–19).

3: The Household, Kinship, and Shared Poverty

1 The selection of the study group was specifically designed to examine the various factors influencing the transfer of kin within *santina*. Rather than retain the focus on Tentena, I explored the kin ties linking the villages of Tentena, Petirodongi, Taripa, and Kamba.

2 This arbitrary division summarizes a number of variables. Those classified as well-to-do had incomes above Rp. 250,000 per month, usually owned their own concrete-walled homes. Most obtained their incomes from civil-service jobs, which many reinvested in petty trade. On average they had the largest landholdings. Middle peasant households had incomes between Rp. 125,000 and 249,000, and lived in their own, usually wooden-walled houses. The poorest households had cash incomes below Rp. 125,000. They usually lived in inherited houses, shared a house, or had a bamboo slat–walled house, and the smallest landholdings.

3 Although see Schrauwers 1998 for a discussion of the neighbouring village of Buyumpondoli, which differed in some respects.

4 Pamonan customary law specifies that all children have an equal right to a parental inheritance. However, parental property is usually divided while the parents are still alive, as their children marry, and hence is subject to uneven distribution in an attempt to ensure the viability of the new households. The inequalities that result have led to some bitter rejections of *adat* law, and To Pamona ethnicity by the dispossessed.

5 See the discussion on this system as it operates in Buyumpondoli (Schrauwers 1998), where it is most developed.

6 This liberal policy has been consistently applied during the eighty-five years I have

examined in this chapter, first by the Dutch colonial government, and successively by the Japanese and Indonesian governments. Present Indonesian government programs all assume a nuclear-family household with a male household head as their basis. Space limitations have precluded any analysis of how this policy was applied in each regime.

7 The term 'denuded' refers to a household in which one or more of the minors of the core nuclear family is not co-resident with their biological parents.

8 Kruyt (1899; 1950) commented on adoption (*adoptie*), but made no mention of fosterage (*opkweking*).

9 The reference was inappropriate in that the 'real' Cinderella was a full daughter disenfranchised from her inheritance by her stepmother, whereas, as will be made clear, foster children are distinctive precisely in that they are not eligible.

10 Wawo Ndoda differed from most To Onda'e villages. It had no slaves, and its *kabosenya* was a woman. In the war between the To Napu and the To Onda'e at the turn of the century, the people of Wawo Ndoda refused to take sides; thus, even though they were themselves To Onda'e, they faced punitive raids from their own people. This is the reason that this village moved to the territory of the To Wingke mPoso rather than settle with the other To Onda'e at Taripa in 1908.

11 The 'official' *adat* guide (Santo 1990) prepared by a conference of *adat* experts organized by the assistant to the Bupati's office for the Pamonan-speaking areas of Kabupaten Poso follows the Indonesian Supreme Court's ruling that equal inheritance among siblings is common to all *adat* systems. This guide has attempted to resolve differences in *adat* between the various village confederacies, resulting in a great deal of controversy. It has not yet been officially accepted by the Bupati. An alternate source (Sigilipu 1993) and other informants told me that, in practice, sons tend to receive less land than daughters since they can obtain other jobs to support themselves. This is only a rough guide, however, since unequal division depends on the compliance of all siblings. Unequal division is thus usually done by the parents themselves before their deaths, precisely to prevent any disputes between their children.

12 Given my statement that there is no common household development cycle, it may seem ironic that, for much of the period of my fieldwork, Ngkai and Tu'a Bose lived *sanco-ncombori* with my landlord. This was a temporary measure that resulted when Ngkai Bose co-signed a loan for his divorced son's business endeavours. When the son went bankrupt, Ngkai Bose became liable for the loan and had to give up a large part of his pension for its repayment. When I returned to the field two years later, Ngkai Bose had re-established his independence after repaying the defaulted loan, only to once again end up living *sanco-ncombori*; this time, not as a dependent, but with the now-remarried divorcée who was unable to support his

new family. The ease with which households slide from the viable to unviable category is an indication of how economically marginal peasant livelihoods in the area are.

4: Marriage, Kinship, and *Posintuwu* Networks

1 Kruyt's diaries demonstrate he gave *posintuwu*, but his failure to analyse it as a practice can be tied to his definitions of culture as '*adat* liturgies.' My thanks to Gert Noort for pointing this out.

2 Kruyt (1912, 2: 23) notes that in some areas the bridewealth was called *saki mporongo*, which he translates as the 'wedding fine.' This 'fine' is paid to the bride's father, who divides it among those who contributed to his own bridewealth. The bride's mother's family would itself impose 'fines' (ask for presents). I noted such practices only in the village of Kamba in the Laa river valley.

3 Patronyms were introduced to the area by the Dutch missionaries. Each baptised convert was given his or her father's name as a family name; hence, the supposed common ancestor of these two families was the grandfather of my informants. Although the two families in this example shared the same family name, my informant's grandfather was a To Tino'e, the other from Mori (several hundred kilometres apart).

5: The Ritualization

1 I had supposed that communion (the "Lord's Supper") held within the church might also be interpreted in the same terms, but received mixed responses from parishoners.

6: The Rationalization of Belief

1 Kruyt's term was *toeeigenning*, appropriation.

2 I did hear at least one ad-lib usage of the term in a minister's spontaneous translation, in Bahasa Pamona, of his written text in Bahasa Indonesia.

3 As in much of Indonesia, the liver is considered the seat of the soul in the same manner as we refer to our 'heart.'

4 In nodding (in an unsatisfactory way) to this call, my text has utilized specific biblical verses as a foil to my more theoretical musings.

5 Significantly, the only independent Christian organization that has not been incorporated within the Synod is Parkindo (Partai Kristen Indonesia, the Indonesian Protestant Party). The New Order amalgamated this party with the nationalist and Catholic parties to form the PDI (Partai Demokrasi Indonesia). Like all politi-

cal parties, the PDI is not allowed to build a grass-roots organization, and its leadership is under tight governmental control.

7: Rationalizing Religion in Indonesia

1 This is, of course, a relative phenomenon; I am not implying that Islam was theologically unsystematized in the earlier period. Rather, that the Ethical Policy sparked a bureaucratic revolution within Indonesian Islam by which an organizationally determined set of theological principles was developed to specify a relationship towards 'secular' culture, which entailed a shift from embedded practice to publicly proclaimed ethical principles (see Bowen 1993, 321–4).

Bibliography

Manuscripts (MVO, Memorie van Overgave)

Engelenberg, W.G. 1906. 'Bijdrage voor de memorie van overgave van den Resident S.J.M. van Geuns, voorzoover betreft de afdeeling Midden-Celebes, bevattende een overzicht van de gebeurenissen van 13 Mei 1903–1 Juni 1906.' MMK 302, Algemeen Rijksarchief, The Hague.

Hengel, J. van. 1910. 'Afschrift van de Memorie van Overgave van de Resident van Manado, J. van Hengel.' MMK 303, Algemeen Rijksarchief, The Hague.

Son, E.L. van. 1935. 'Aanvullende Memorie van Overgave der Onderafdeling Poso.' KIT 1212, Algemeen Rijksarchief, The Hague.

Tideman, J. 1926. 'Memorie van Overgave van het Bestuur van het Aftredenen Resident van Menado, J. Tideman.' MMK 305, Algemeen Rijksarchief, The Hague.

Winkelman, A.W. de Haze. 1935. 'Algemeene Gegevens over de Afdeeling Poso door A.W. de Haze Winkelman.' KIT 1213, Algemeen Rijksarchief, The Hague.

Published Works

Abbreviated titles for frequently cited journals:

BTLV	Bijdragen tot de Taal-, Land- en Volkenkunde van Nederlandsch-Indië
IRM	International Review of Missions
KS	Koloniale Studien
KT	Koloniaal Tijdschrift
MNZG	Mededeelingen van Wege het Nederlands Zendelingen Genootschap
TNAG	Tijdschrift van het Koninklijk Nederlandsch Aardrijkskundig Genootschap
TTLV	Tijdschrift voor Indische Taal-, Land- en Volkenkunde

Aass, Svein. 1980. 'The Relevance of Chayanov's Macro Theory to the Case of Java.'

In *Peasants in History: Essays in Honour of Daniel Thorner*, ed. E.J. Hobsbawn, Witold Kula, Ashok Mitra, K.N. Raj, and Ignacy Sachs, 221–48. Calcutta: Oxford University Press.

Acciaioli, Gregory. 1985. 'Culture as Art: From Practice to Spectacle in Indonesia.' *Canberra Anthropology* 8/1&2: 148–71.

Adams, Kathleen M. 1993. 'The Discourse of Souls in Tana Toraja (Indonesia): Indigenous Notions and Christian Conceptions.' *Ethnology* 32/2: 55–68.

– 1998. 'Domestic Tourism and Nation-Building in South Sulawesi.' *Indonesia and the Malay World* 26/75: 77–96.

Adatrechtbundels. 1910–38. Series O, 'Het Toradja-Gebeid,' in each volume, issued yearly. *Adatrechtbundels bezorgd door de commissie voor het Adatrecht en Uitgegeven Door het Koninklijk Instituut voor de Taal-, Land- en Volkenkunde van Nederlandsch-Indië*. The Hague: Martinus Nijhoff.

Adriani, Dr Nicolaüs. 1919. *Posso (Midden-Celebes)*. The Hague: Boekhandel van den Zendingsstudie-Raad.

– 1920. 'The Effect of Western Rule on Animistic Heathenism.' *IRM* 9/1: 81–5.

– 1925. 'The Peculiar Language of the Heavenly Powers.' *IRM* 14/1: 59–72.

– 1928. *Bare'e-Nederlandsch Woordenboek met Nederlandsch-Bare'e Register*. Leiden: Koninklijk Bataviaasch Genootschap van Kunsten en Wetenschappen.

– 1931. *Spraakkunst der Bare'e-Taal*. Bandung: A.C. Nix & Co.

– 1932. *Verzamelde Geschriften van Dr N. Adriani*, 3 vols. Haarlem: De Erven F. Bohn N.V.

Adriani, Nicolaüs and Kruyt, Albert C. 1912–14. *De Bare'e-Sprekende Toradja's van Midden-Celebes*. 3 vols. Batavia: Landsdrukkerij.

– 1913. 'De Economische Toestanden, de Handel en Nijverheid der Toradja's, op Celebes.' *Tijdschrift voor Economische Geographie* 4: 403–9.

Alexander, Jennifer, and Alexander, Paul. 1978. 'Sugar, Rice and Irrigation in Colonial Java.' *Ethnohistory* 25 (3): 207–23.

– 1982. 'Shared Poverty as Ideology: Agrarian Relationships in Colonial Java.' *Man* n.s. 17 (4): 597–619.

Amal, Ichlasul. 1986. 'Central Government–Regional Relation: The Cases of West Sumatra and South Sulawesi.' *Prisma* 42: 88–103.

Anderson, Benedict R. O'G. 1972. 'The Idea of Power in Javanese Culture.' In *Culture and Politics in Indonesia*, ed. Clair Holt, 1–69. Ithaca, NY: Cornell University Press.

– 1977. 'Religion and Politics in Indonesia since Independence.' In *Religion and Social Ethos in Indonesia*, ed. Benedict R. O'G. Anderson, 21–61. Clayton, Victoria: Monash University Press.

– 1983a. *Imagined Communities: Reflections on the Origin and Spread of Nationalism*. London: Verso.

- 1983b. 'Old State, New Society: Indonesia's New Order in Comparative Historical Perspective.' *Journal of Asian Studies* 42/3: 477–96.

Anggui, A.J., and I.P. Lambe'. 1985. 'Experiments of Inculturation in the Toraja Church.' *Reformed World* 38/7: 366–73.

Appadurai, A. 1986. 'Introduction: Commodities and the Politics of Value.' In *The Social Life of Things: Commodities in Cultural Perspective*, ed. A. Appadurai, 3–63. Cambridge: Cambridge University Press.

Aragon, Lorraine V. 1992. 'Divine Justice: Cosmology, Ritual, and Protestant Missionization in Central Sulawesi, Indonesia.' Unpublished PhD thesis, Department of Anthropology, University of Illinois at Urbana-Champaign.

- 1996. 'Reorganizing the Cosmology: The Reinterpretation of Deities and Religious Practice by Protestants in Central Sulawesi, Indonesia.' *Journal of Southeast Asian Studies* 27/2: 350–73.

Arts, J.A. 1985. 'Zending en bestuur op Midden-Celebes tussen 1890 en 1920. Van samenwerking naar confrontatie en eigen verantwoordelijkheid.' In *Imperialisme in de Marge: De Afronding van Nederlands-Indië*, ed. J. van Goor, 85–122. Utrecht: HES Uitgevers.

Asad, Talal. 1979. 'Anthropology and the Analysis of Ideology.' *Man* n.s. 14/4: 607–27.

- 1983. 'Anthropological Conceptions of Religion: Reflections on Geertz.' *Man* n.s. 18/2: 237–59.

- 1988. 'Towards a Genealogy of the Concept of Ritual.' In *Vernacular Christianity: Essays in the Social Anthropology of Religion*, ed. Wendy James and Douglas Johnson, 73–87. Oxford: JASO Occasional Papers No. 7.

- 1993. *Genealogies of Religion: Discipline and Reasons of Power in Christianity and Islam*. Baltimore, MD: Johns Hopkins University Press.

Atkinson, Jane M. 1983. 'Religions in Dialogue: The Construction of an Indonesian Miniority Religion.' *American Ethnologist* 10/4: 684–96.

- 1989. *The Art and Politics of Wana Shamanship*. Berkeley: University of California Press.

Bakry, K.H. Hasbullah. 1978. *Kumpulan Lengkap Undang-Undang dan Peraturan Perkawinan di Indonesia*. Jakarta: Penerbit Djambatan.

Bank, J. 1981. '"Verzuiling": A Confessional Road to Secularization, Emancipation and the Decline of Political Catholicism, 1920–1970.' In *Church and State since the Reformation*, vol. 7, Britain and the Netherlands series, ed. A.C. Duke and C.A. Tamse, 207–30. The Hague: Martinus Nijhoff.

Barr, Donald F., Sharon G. Salombe, and C. Salombe. n.d. *Languages of Central Sulawesi: Checklist, Preliminary Classification, Language Maps, Wordlists*. Ujung Pandang: Hasanuddin University.

Barth, Fredrik. 1981. 'Ethnic Groups and Boundaries.' In *Process and Form in Social*

Life: Selected Essays of Frederick Barth, vol. 1, ed. Fredrik Barth, 198–226. London: Routledge & Kegan Paul.

Bell, Catherine. 1992. *Ritual Theory, Ritual Practice*. Oxford: Oxford University Press.

Berge, Tom van den, and William Segers. n.d. 'Dominee Visser moest van de Indonesische millitairen na acht jaar Sulawesi (Celebes) verlaten: "Het was een vergissing Dominee Visser."' Unpublished interview.

Beurden, A.I.P.J. van. 1985. 'De Indische "Goldrush," goudmijnbouw en beleid.' In *Imperialisme in de Marge: De Afronding van Nederlands-Indië*, ed. J. van Goor, 179–226. Utrecht: HES Uitgevers.

Bigalke, Terance. 1984. 'Government and Mission in the Torajan World of Makale-Rantepao.' *Indonesia* 38: 85–112.

Blink, H. 1905–7. *Nederlandsch Oost- en West-Indië: Geographisch, Ethnographisch en Economisch Beschreven*, 2 vols. Leiden: E.J. Brill.

Bloch, Maurice. 1975. 'Property and the End of Affinity.' In *Marxist Analyses and Social Anthropology*, ed. Maurice Bloch 203–22. London: Tavistock.

Boeke, J.H. 1953. *Economics and Economic Policy of Dual Societies*. Haarlem: H.D. Tjeenk Willink.

Bourdieu, Pierre. 1977. *Outline of a Theory of Practice*. Trans. by Richard Nice. Cambridge: Cambridge University Press.

Bowen, John R. 1986. 'On the Political Construction of Tradition: Gotong Royong in Indonesia.' *Journal of Asian Studies* 45/3: 545–61.

– 1988. 'The Transformation of an Indonesian Property System: Adat, Islam, and Social Change in the Gayo Highlands.' *American Ethnologist* 15/2: 274–93.

– 1993. *Muslims through Discourse: Religion and Ritual in Gayo Society*. Princeton, NJ: Princeton University Press.

Breman, Jan. 1982. *Control of Land and Labour in Colonial Java: A Case Study of Agrarian Crisis and Reform in the Region of Cirebon during the First Decades of the 20th Century*. Dordrecht: KITLV Press.

Brouwer, K.J. 1951. *Dr A.C. Kruyt: Dienaar der Toradja's*. The Hague: J.N. Voorhoeve.

Brouwer, R.A.M. 1912. 'The Preparation of Missionaries in Holland.' *IRM* 1: 226–39.

Burchell, Graham, Colin Gordon, and Peter Miller, eds. 1991. *The Foucault Effect: Studies in Governmentality*. London: Harvester Wheatsheaf.

Burns, Peter. 1985. *The Decline of Freedom for Religion in Indonesia*. Townsville, Queensland: James Cook University of North Queensland.

Carsten, Janet. 1989. 'Cooking Money: Gender and the Symbolic Transformation of Means of Exchange in a Malay Fishing Community.' In *Money and the Morality of Exchange*, ed. J.P. Parry and M. Bloch, 117–41. Cambridge: Cambridge University Press.

Collier, William L. 1981. 'Agricultural Evolution in Java: The Decline of Shared

Poverty and Involution.' In *Agriculture and Rural Development in Indonesia*, ed. Gary E. Hansen, 147–73. Boulder, CO: Westview.

Comaroff, Jean. 1985. *Body of Power, Spirit of Resistance: The Culture and History of a South African People*. Chicago: University of Chicago Press.

Comaroff, Jean, and John Comaroff. 1991. *Of Revelation and Revolution: Christianity, Colonialism and Consciousness in South Africa*, vol. 1. Chicago: University of Chicago Press.

Coté, Joost. 1996. 'Colonising Central Sulawesi: The "Ethical Policy" and Imperialist Expansion, 1890–1910.' *Itinerario* 20/3: 87–108.

Crystal, Eric. 1974. 'Cooking Pot Politics: A Toraja Village Study.' *Indonesia* 18: 118–52.

de Kat Angelino, A.D.A. 1931. *Staatkundig Beleid en Bestuurszorg in Nederlandsch-Indië*, 3 vols. The Hague: Martinus Nijhoff.

Department of Education and Culture (Departemen Pendidikan dan Kebudayaan). 1977/8. *Adat Istiadat Daerah Sulawesi Tengah*. Jakarta: Departemen Pendidkan dan kebudayaan, Proyek Penelitian dan Pencatatan Kebudayaan Daerah.

– 1979. *Sejarah Daerah Sulawesi Tengah*. Jakarta: Departemen Pendidikan dan Kebudayaan.

– 1980. *Pengaruh Migrasi Penduduk Terhadap Perkembangan Kebudayaan Daerah Sulawesi Tengah*. Jakarta: Departemen Pendidikan dan Kebudayaan, Proyek Penelitian dan Pencatatan Kebudayaan Daerah.

– 1982. *Sejarah Revolusi Kemerdekaan Daerah Sulawesi Tengah*. Jakarta: Departemen Pendidikan dan Kebudayaan.

– 1982/3. *Sejarah Perlawanan Terhadap Kolonialisme dan Imperialisme di Daerah Sulawesi Tengah*. Jakarta: Departemen Pendidikan dan Kebudayaan.

– 1983. *Sistem Gotong Royong Dalam Masyarakat Pedesaan Daerah Sulawesi Tengah*. Jakarta: Departemen Pendidikan dan Kebudayaan.

– 1983/4. *Ungkapan Tradisional Daerah Sulawesi Tengah*. Jakarta: Departemen Pendidikan dan Kebudayaan.

– 1984. *Upacara Tradisional (Upacara Kematian) Daerah Sulawesi Tengah*. Jakarta: Departemen Pendidkan dan Kebudayaan, Proyek Inventarisasi dan Dokumentasi Kebudayaan Daerah.

– 1984/5. *Sejarah Pengaruh Pelita Terhadap Kehidupan Masyarakat Pedesaan di Daerah Sulawesi Tengah*. Jakarta: Departemen Pendidikan dan Kebudayaan, Proyek Inventarisasi dan Dokumentasi Kebudayaan Daerah Direktorat Sejarah dan Nilai Tradisional.

– 1985. *Sistem Ekonomi Tradisional Daerah Sulawesi Tengah*. Jakarta: Departemen Pendidikan dan Dokumentasi, Proyek Inventarisasi dan Dokumentasi Kebudayaan Daerah.

– 1986. *Dampak Modernisasi Terhadap Hubungan Kekerabatan Daerah Sulawesi*

Tengah. Jakarta: Departemen Pendidkan dan Kebudayaan, Proyek Inventarisasi dan Dokumentasi Kebudayaan Daerah.

Departemen van Economische Zaken. 1936. *Native Population in Borneo, Celebes, the Lesser Sunda Islands and the Moluccas*. Batavia: Landsdrukkerij.

Downs, Richard E. 1956. 'The Religion of the Bare'e-Speaking Toradja of Central Celebes.' PhD thesis, Rijksuniversiteit Leiden.

Drewes, G.W.J. 1957. 'Oriental Studies in the Netherlands: An Historical Survey.' *Higher Education and Research in the Netherlands* 1/4: 3–13.

Dreyfus, Hubert, and Paul Rabinow. 1983. *Michel Foucault: Beyond Structuralism and Hermeneutics*, 2d ed. Chicago: University of Chicago Press.

Ellen, Roy F. 1976. 'The Development of Anthropology and Colonial Policy in the Netherlands: 1800–1960.' *Journal of the History of the Behavioral Sciences* 12: 303–24.

End, Th. van den. 1992. 'Rencana Gereja Kesatuan Sulawesi Tengah pada Masa Zending.' In *Wajah GKST*, ed. Pdt. Dj. Tanggerahi et al., 17–29. Tentena: Gereja Kristen Sulawesi Tengah.

Errington, Shelly. 1989. *Meaning and Power in a Southeast Asian Realm*. Princeton, NJ: Princeton University Press.

Fabian, Johannes. 1986. *Language and Colonial Power: The Appropriation of Swahili in the Former Belgian Congo, 1880–1938*. Berkeley: University of California Press.

Fasseur, C. 1979. 'Een Koloniale Paradox: De Nederlandse Expansie in de Indonesiche Archipel in der Midden van de Negentiende Eeuw.' *Tijdschrift Voor Geschiedenis* 92/2: 162–86.

Feillard, Andrée. 1997. 'Traditionalist Islam and the State in Indonesia: The Road to Legitimacy and Renewal.' In *Islam in an Era of Nation-States: Politics and Religious Renewal in Muslim Southeast Asia*, ed. Robert W. Hefner and Patricia Horvatich. Honolulu: University of Hawaii Press.

Ferguson, James. 1994. *The Anti-Politics Machine: 'Development,' Depoliticization, and Bureaucratic Power in Lesotho*. Minneapolis: University of Minnesota Press.

Fortes, Meyer. 1969. *Kinship and the Social Order: The Legacy of Lewis Henry Morgan*. Chicago: Aldine.

Foucault, Michel. 1979. *Discipline and Punish: The Birth of the Prison*. Trans. by Alan Sheridan. New York: Vintage.

– 1980. *Power/Knowledge: Selected Interviews and Other Writings*. New York: Pantheon.

– 1991. 'Governmentality.' In *The Foucault Effect: Studies in Governmentality*, ed. Graham Burchell, Colin Gordon, and Peter Miller. Chicago: University of Chicago Press.

Fraassen, Ch. F. van. 1991. 'De Positie van Luwu in Zuid- en Centraal-Sulawesi.' In *Excursies in Celebes*, ed. Harry A. Poeze and Pim Schoorl, 1–20. Leiden: KITLV Uitgeverij.

Friedmann, Harriet. 1980. 'Household Production and the National Economy: Concepts for the Analysis of Agrarian Formations.' *Journal of Peasant Studies* 7/2: 158–83.

Gallas, P.A. 1900. 'Bijdrage tot de Kennis van het Landschap Posso.' *TNAG* 17: 801–14.

Geertz, Clifford. 1960. *The Religion of Java*. Chicago: University of Chicago Press.

– 1963a. *Agricultural Involution: The Process of Ecological Change in Indonesia*. Berkeley: University of California Press.

– 1963b. *Peddlers and Princes: Social Development and Economic Change in Two Indonesian Towns*. Chicago: University of Chicago Press.

– 1965. *The Social History of an Indonesian Town*. Cambridge, MA: MIT Press.

– 1972. 'Religious Change and Social Order in Soeharto's Indonesia.' *Asia* 27 (Autumn): 62–84.

– 1973a. 'Ethos, World View, and the Analysis of Sacred Symbols.' In *The Interpretation of Culture*, ed. Clifford Geertz, 126–41. New York: Basic.

– 1973b. 'The Integrative Revolution: Primordial Sentiments and Civil Politics in the New States.' In *The Interpretation of Culture*, ed. Clifford Geertz, 255–310. New York: Basic.

– 1973c. '"Internal Conversion" in Contemporary Bali.' In *The Interpretation of Culture*, ed. Clifford Geertz, 170–92. New York: Basic.

– 1973d. 'Religion as a Cultural System.' In *The Interpretation of Culture*, ed. Clifford Geertz, 87–125. New York, Basic.

– 1983. 'Local Knowledge: Fact and Law in Comparative Perspective.' In *Local Knowledge: Further Essays in Interpretive Anthropology*, ed. Clifford Geertz, 167–234. New York: Basic.

– 1984. 'Culture and Social Change: The Indonesian Case.' *Man* n.s. 19: 511–32.

– 1984 [1956]. 'Capital-Intensive Agriculture in Peasant Society: A Case Study.' *Social Research* 51/2: 419–36.

George, Kenneth M. 1996. *Showing Signs of Violence: The Cultural Politics of a Twentieth-Century Headhunting Ritual*. Berkeley: University of California Press.

Gerdin, Ingela. 1982. *The Unknown Balinese: Land, Labour and Inequality in Lombok*. Gotherburg, Sweden: Gothenberg Studies in Social Anthropology 4, Acta Universitatis Gothoburgensis.

Gereja Kristen Sulawesi Tengah (Christian Church of Central Sulawesi). 1973. 'Benih Yang Tumbuh: GKST.' Unpublished.

– 1988. *Kumpulan Tata Ibadah Gereja Kristen Sulawesi Tengah*. Tentena: Badan Pekerja Sinode Gereja Kristen Sulawesi Tengah.

– 1989. 'Refleksi: Laporan Penelitian Karakteristik GKST.' Unpublished.

Geschiere, P.L. 1973. 'The Education Issue in the Dutch East Indies in the Twentieth Century: Opinions on the Question of "Western Education" versus "National Education."' *Acta Historiae Neerlandicae* 6: 146–74.

Gintu, Afrida M. 1991. 'Padungku Merupakan Ungkapan Syukur Dari Masyarakat

Suku Pamona: Suatu study tentang kebudayaan masyarakat suku Pamona yang diambil alih oleh Gereja ditinjau dari perspektif Pembinaan Warga Gereja.' Unpublished thesis, STT INTIM Ujung Pandang.

Goedhart, O.H. 1908. 'Drie Landschappen in Celebes.' *TTLV* 50: 442–548.

Goody, Esther N. 1971. 'Forms of Pro-Parenthood: The Sharing and Substitution of Parental Roles.' In *Kinship*, ed. Jack Goody 331–45. Hammondsworth, Middlesex: Penguin.

Goor, J. van. 1986. 'Imperialisme in de Marge?' In *Imperialisme in de Marge: De Afronding van Nederlands-Indië*, ed. J. van Goor, 9–18. Utrecht: H & S Uitgevers.

Gordon, Alec. 1992. 'The Poverty of Involution: A Critique of Geertz' Pseudo-History.' *Journal of Contemporary Asia* 22/4: 490–512.

Gordon, Colin. 1991. 'Governmental Rationality: An Introduction.' In *The Foucault Effect: Studies in Governmentality*, ed. Graham Burchell, Colin Gordon, and Peter Miller, 1–51. Chicago: University of Chicago Press.

Gunawan, Basuki. 1968. *Kudetá staatsgreep in djakarta: de achtergronden van de 30 september-beweging in indonesië*. Meppel: J.A. Boom en zoon.

– 1971. 'Aliran en Sociale Structuur.' In *Buiten de Grenzen*, ed. W.F. Wertheim, 69–85. Meppel: Boom.

Gunawan, Basuki, and Muizenberg, O.D. van den. 1967. 'Verzuilingstendenties en Sociale Stratificatie in Indonesie.' *Sociologische Gids* 14: 146–58.

Habermas, Jürgen. 1984. *The Theory of Communicative Action*, vol. 1: *Reason and the Rationalization of Society*. Trans. by Thomas McCarthy. Boston: Beacon.

Haive, James. 1981. *The Character and Theological Struggle of the Church in Halmahera, Indonesia, 1941–1979*. Frankfurt am Main: Lang.

– 1985. 'Indigenous and Reformed – The Meeting between Christianity and Pre-Literary Religions and Islam on an Eastern Indonesian Island.' *Reformed World* 38/7: 374–84.

Hammar, Lawrence. 1988. 'The Philosophy of Shared Poverty: Rethinking Agricultural Involution and the Culture of Geertz.' *Journal of Historical Sociology* 1/3: 253–77.

Harris, Olivia. 1982. 'Households and Their Boundaries.' *History Workshop* 13: 143–52.

Hart, Gillian. 1992. 'Imagined Unities: Constructions of "The Household" in Economic Theory.' In *Understanding Economic Process*, ed. Sutti Ortiz and Susan Lees, 111–29. Lanham: Society for Economic Anthropology/Monograph in Economic Anthropology No. 10.

Harvey, Barbara S. 1977. *Permesta: Half a Rebellion*. Ithaca, NY: Cornell Modern Indonesia Project Monograph Series No. 57.

Hefner, Robert W. 1985. *Hindu Javanese: Tengger Tradition and Islam*. Princeton, NJ: Princeton University Press.

– 1987. 'The Political Economy of Islamic Conversion in Modern East Java.' In *Islam* and the Political Economy of Meaning: Comparative Studies of Muslim Discourse, ed. William Roff, 53–78. Berkeley: University of California Press.

– 1989. 'Redefining Divinity: State-Sponsored Religious Education in Indonesia.' American Anthropological Association Annual Meeting, Washington, DC.

– 1993. 'Of Faith and Commitment: Christian Conversion in Muslim Java.' In Conversion to Christianity: Historical and Anthropological Perspectives on a Great Transformation, ed. Robert W. Hefner, 99–128. Berkeley: University of California Press.

– 1994. 'Reimagined Community: A Social History of Muslim Education in Pasuruan, East Java.' In Asian Visions of Authority: Religion and the Modern States of East and Southeast Asia, ed. Charles F. Keyes, Laurel Kendall, and Helen Hardacre, 75–95. Honolulu: University of Hawaii Press.

– 1997a. 'Islam in an Era of Nation-States: Politics and Religious Renewal in Muslim Southeast Asia.' In Islam in an Era of Nation-States: Politics and Religious Renewal in Muslim Southeast Asia, ed. Robert Hefner, 3–40. Honolulu: University of Hawaii Press.

– 1997b. 'Islamization and Democratization in Indonesia.' In Islam in an Era of Nation-States: Politics and Religious Renewal in Muslim Southeast Asia, ed. Robert Hefner, 75–127. Honolulu: University of Hawaii Press.

Henley, David. 1996. Nationalism and Regionalism in a Colonial Context: Minahasa in the Dutch East Indies. Leiden: KITLV Press.

Hirosue, M. 1981. 'The Transformation of the Eastern Toraja Society in Central Sulawesi and Its Religion.' Southeast Asia: History and Culture 10: 142–73.

Hitchcock, Michael. 1998. 'Tourism, Taman Mini, and National Identity.' Indonesia and the Malay World 26/75: 124–35.

Hoekstra, D.J.F. 1896. 'Het Possomeer.' TNAG, 2d ser. 13: 439–45.

Hoëvell, G.W.W.C. Baron van. 1893a. 'Bijschrift bij de Kaart der Tomini-Bocht.' TNAG 2d ser. (10): 64–72.

– 1893b. 'Todjo, Posso en Saoesoe.' TTLV 35: 1–47.

Hollan, Douglas. 1988. 'Pockets Full of Mistakes: The Personal Consequences of Religious Change in a Toraja Village.' Oceania 58/4: 275–89.

Horsting, L.H.C. n.d. Uit Het Land Van Kruyt: Wat Midden-Celebes Ons Hollanders Leeren Kan. Bandung: A.C. Nix & Co.

Hoskins, Janet. 1987. 'Entering the Bitter House: Spirit Worship and Conversion in West Sumba.' In Indonesian Religions in Transition, ed. Rita Kipp and Susan Rodgers, 136–59. Tucson: University of Arizona Press.

Hunt, D. 1979. 'Chayanov's Model of Peasant Household Resource Allocation.' Journal of Peasant Studies 6/3: 247–85.

Huntington, Samuel. 1993. 'The Clash of Civilizations?' Foreign Affairs 72 (Summer): 22–49.

Hutajulu, Rithaony. 1995. 'Tourism's Impact on Toba Batak Ceremony.' *Bijdragen* [KITLV] 151/4: 639–55.

Inta, Ch. 1992. 'Yayasan Pendidikan dan Perguruan Kristen GKST.' In *Wajah GKST: Buku Kenangan 100 Tahun Injil Masuk Tana Poso*, ed. Dj. Tanggerahi et al., 137–53. Tentena: Gereja Kristen Sulawesi Tengah.

Jacobsson, Bengt. 1991. 'Heads, Buffaloes and Marriage among the To Pamona of Central Sulawesi (Indonesia).' In *A Conciliation of Powers: The Force of Religion in Society*, ed. Goran Aijmer, 34–50. Göteborg: Institute for Advanced Studies in Social Anthropology at the University of Göteborg.

Jansen, Rien. 1989. 'De Economische Ontwikkeling van Celebes, 1900–1938.' *Jambatan* 7/2: 65–79.

Jongeling, Maria C. 1966. *Het Zendingsconsulaat in Nederlands-Indië, 1906–1942*. Arnhem: Van Loghum Slaterus.

Ka'bah, Rifyal. 1985. *Christian Presence in Indonesia: A View of Christian-Muslim Relations*. London: The Islamic Foundation.

Kahn, Joel S. 1978. 'Ideology and Social Structure in Indonesia.' *Comparative Studies in Society and History* 20/1: 103–22.

– 1985. 'Indonesia after the Demise of Involution: Critique of a Debate.' *Critique of Anthropology* 5/1: 69–96.

– 1993. *Constituting the Minangkabau: Peasants, Culture and Modernity in Colonial Indonesia*. Providence, RI: Berg.

Kano, Hiroyoshi. 1980. 'The Economic History of Javanese Rural Society: A Reinterpretation.' *The Developing Economies* 18/1: 3–22.

Kato, Tsuyoshi. 1989. 'Different Fields, Similar Locusts: Adat Communities and the Village Law of 1979 in Indonesia.' *Indonesia* 47: 89–114.

Kaudern, Walter. 1925a. *Migrations of the Toradja in Central Celebes*. Götenborg: Elanders Boktryckeri Aktiebolag.

– 1925b. *Structures and Settlements in Central Celebes*. Göteborg: Elanders Boktryckeri Aktiebolag.

Kearney, Michael. 1996. *Reconceptualizing the Peasantry: Anthropology in Global Perspective*. Boulder, CO: Westview.

Keeler, Ward. 1987. *Javanese Shadow Plays, Javanese Selves*. Princeton, NJ: Princeton University Press.

Kennedy, Raymond. 1944. 'Applied Anthropology in the Dutch East Indies.' *Transactions of the New York Academy of Sciences*, ser. 2 (6): 157–62.

Kieve, Ronald A. 1981. 'Pillars of Sand: A Marxist Critique of Consociational Democracy in the Netherlands.' *Comparative Politics* 13/3: 313–37.

Kipp, Rita S. 1990. *The Early Years of a Dutch Colonial Mission: The Karo Field*. Ann Arbor: University of Michigan Press.

– 1993. *Dissociated Identities: Ethnicity, Religion, and Class in an Indonesia Society*. Ann Arbor: University of Michigan Press.

Kipp, Rita S., and Susan Rodgers. 1987. 'Introduction: Indonesian Religions in Society.' In *Indonesian Religions in Transition*, ed. Rita Kipp and Susan Rodgers, 1–31. Tucson: University of Arizona Press.

Kloos, P. 1989. 'The Sociology of Non-Western Societies: The Origins of a Discipline.' *Netherlands Journal of Social Sciences* 25/1: 40–50.

Knight, G.R. 1982. 'Capitalism and Commodity Production in Java.' In *Capitalism and Colonial Production*, 1–30. London: Croom Helm.

Koentjaraningrat. 1975. *Anthropology in Indonesia: A Bibliographical Review*. The Hague: Koninklijk Instituut voor Taal-, Land-, en Volkenkunde.

Koetsier, C.H. 1975. *Zending Als Dienst Aan De Samenleving: De houding van zending en kerk ten opzichte van sociaal-economische vraagstukken in Indonesie, in het bijzonder op Midden-Java*. Delft: W.D. Meinema B.V.

Kraemer, Hendrik, ed. 1935. *Dr N. Adriani*. Amsterdam: H.J. Paris.

Krammerer, C.A. 1990. 'Customs and Christian Conversion among Akha Highlanders of Burma and Thailand.' *American Ethnologist* 17/2: 277–91.

Kruyt [Kruijt], Albert C. 1893a. 'Eenige feesten bij de Poso-Alfoeren.' *MNZG* 37: 115–29.

– 1893b. 'Grammaticale Schets van de Bare'e-Taal.' *BTLV* 42: 203–33.

– 1894. *Woordenlijst van de Bare'e-Taal*. The Hague: Martinus Nijhoff.

– 1895-7. 'Een en Ander aangaande het Geestelijk en Maatschappelijk Leven van den Poso-Alfoer.' *MNZG* 39: 3–36, 106–53; 40: 7–31, 121–60, 245–82; 41: 1–52.

– 1899a. 'De Adoptie in Verband met het Matriarchaat bij de Toradja's van Midden Celebes.' *TTLV* 41: 80–92.

– 1899b. 'De Weerwolf bij de Toradja's van Midden-Celebes.' *TTLV* 41: 548–67.

– 1906. *Het Animisme in den Indischen Archipel*. The Hague: Martinus Nijhoff.

– 1910. *Papa i Woente*. Rotterdam: M. Wyt & Zonen.

– 1911. 'De Slavernij in Posso (Midden-Celebes).' *Onze Eeuw* 11: 61–97.

– 1913. *Ta Lasa: Een Tegenhanger van Papa i Woente*. The Hague: Boekhandel van den Zendings-Studie Raad.

– 1915. 'The Presentation of Christianity to Primitive Peoples: The Toradja Tribes of Central Celebes.' *IRM* 4: 81–95.

– 1918. 'Measa, Eene Bijdrage Tot het Dynamisme der Bare'e-Sprekende Toradja's en Enkele Omwonende Volken.' *BTLV* 74: 233–60.

– 1919. 'Measa, Eene Bijdrage Tot het Dynamisme der Bare'e-Sprekende Toradja's en Enkele Omwonende Volken-Vervolg.' *BTLV* 75: 36–133.

– 1920. 'Measa, Eene Bijdrage Tot het Dynamisme der Bare'e-Sprekende Toradja's en Enkele Omwonende Volken-Vervolg.' *BTLV* 76: 1–116.

– 1923a. 'Het Volksonderwijs in Beheer bij de Zending.' *KT* 12: 426–33.

– 1923b. 'Koopen in Midden Celebes.' *Mededeelingen der Koninklijke Akademie van Wetenschappen*, Afdeeling Letterkunde 56, Serie B: 149–78.

– 1924a. 'The Appropriation of Christianity by Primitive Heathens in Central Celebes.' *IRM* 13: 267–75.
– 1924b. 'De Beteekenis van den natten Rijstbouw voor de Possoers.' *KS* 8/2: 33–53.
– 1924c. 'De Hoofden in Midden Celebes onder het Nederlandsch-Indisch Gouvernment.' *Koloniaal Tijdschrift* 13: 23–44.
– 1924d. 'Het Huwelijksrecht in Posso en Zijne Ontwikkeling.' *KT* 13: 466–82.
– 1924e. 'De Rechtspraak der Possoers onder het Indisch Gouvernment.' *Koloniale Studien* 8/1: 401–20.
– 1925. *Van Heiden tot Christen*. Oestgeest: Zendingsbureau Oegstgeest.
– 1929. 'The Influence of Western Civilization on the Inhabitants of Poso (Central Celebes).' In *The Effect of Western Influence on Native Civilisations in the Malay Archipeligo*, ed. B. Shrieke, 1–9. Batavia: G. Kolff & Co.
– 1933. 'Lapjesgeld op Celebes.' *TTLV* 73: 172–83.
– 1936a. 'Communal Unity in Central Celebes.' *World Dominion* 14/3: 242–52.
– 1936b. *Zending en Volkskracht*. The Hague: Boekhandel en Uitgeverij voor Inwendige en Uitwendige Zending.
– 1937a. 'Het Leggen van een Knoop in Indonesie.' *Mededeelingen der Koninklijke Akademie van Wetenschappen*, Afdeeling Letterkunde Deel 84, Serie B(4): 147–66.
– 1937b. *Het Leven van de Vrouw in Midden-Celebes*. Oegstgeest: Het Zending-bureau.
– 1938. *De West Toradjas op Midden Celebes*. 4 vols. Amsterdam: Verhandelingen der Koninklijke Nederlandse Akademie van Wetenschappen, Afdeling Letterkunde, new series, vol. 40, Noord Hollandsche Uitgevers Maatschappij.
– 1950[1912]. *De Bare'e Sprekende Toradjas van Midden Celebes (de Oost Toradjas)*, 3 vols., 2d ed. Amsterdam: Verhandelingen der Koninklijke Nederlandse Akademie van Wetenschappen, Afdeling Letterkunde, new series, vol. 54, Noord Hollandsche Uitgevers Maatschappij.
Kruijt, J.P., and Walter Goddijn. 1968. 'Verzuiling en Ontzuiling als Sociologisch Proces.' In *Drift en Koers: Een halve eeuw sociale verandering in Nederland*, ed. Dr A.J.N. Hollander et al., 227–63. Assen: Van Gorcum & Comp.
Kruyt, Jan. 1924. 1939. 'Community and Individual in Central Celebes.' *IRM* 28: 231–9.
– 1970. *Het Zendingsveld Poso: Geschiedenis van Een Konfrontatie*. Kampen: Uitgeversmij J.H. Kok N.V.
Kuitènbrouwer, Martin. 1991. *The Netherlands and the Rise of Modern Imperialism: Colonies and Foreign Policy, 1870–1902*. New York: Berg.
Kuper, Adam. 1988. *The Invention of Primitive Society: Transformations of an Illusion*. London: Routledge & Kegan Paul.
Lambek, Michael. 1993. *Knowledge and Practice in Mayotte: Local Discourses of Islam, Sorcery, and Spirit Possession*. Toronto: University of Toronto Press.

Langenberg, M. van. 1986. 'Analysing Indonesia's New Order State: A keywords Approach.' *Review of Indonesian and Malaysian Affairs* 20/2: 1–47.

Langkamuda, Hr. 1992. 'Pengembangan Masyarakat dalam Pelayanan GKST.' In *Wajah GKST: Buku Kenangan 100 Tahun Injil Masuk Tana Poso*, ed. Dj. Tanggerahi et al., 179–89. Tentena: Gereja Kristen Sulawesi Tengah.

Langley, McKendree R. 1984. *The Practice of Political Spirituality: Episodes from the Public Career of Abraham Kuyper, 1879–1918.* Jordan Station, ON: Paideia.

Leach, Edmund R. 1964. *Political Systems of Highland Burma: A Study of Kachin Social Structure.* London: Athlone Press (London School of Economics Monographs on Social Anthropology No. 44).

Lev, Daniel S. 1985. 'Colonial Law and the Genesis of the Indonesian State.' *Indonesia* 40: 57–74.

Li, Tania Murray. 1996. 'Household formation, Private Property and the State.' *Sojourn* 11/2: 259–88.

Liddle, R. William. 1996. *Leadership and Culture in Indonesian Politics.* St Leonard, NSW: Allen and Unwin, in association with the Asian Studies Association of Australia.

Lijphart, Arend. 1968. *Verzuiling, Pacificatie en Kentering in de Nederlandse Politiek.* Amsterdam.

Lindblad, J. Thomas. 1989. 'Economic Aspects of the Dutch Expansion in Indonesia, 1870–1914.' *Modern Asian Studies* 23/1: 1–23.

Locher-Scholten, Elsbeth. 1981. *Ethiek in Fragmenten.* Utrecht: HES Publishers.

– 1991. '"Een gebiedende noodzakelijkheid": Besluitsvorming rond de Boni-expeditie 1903–1905.' in *Excursies in Celebes*, ed. Harry Poeze and Pim Schoorl, 143–64. Leiden: KITLV Uitgeverij.

Lumentut, Connie. 1991. 'Kedudukan Wanita Dalam GKST.' Unpublished BA thesis, Akademi Theologia GKST, Tentena.

Magido, A. 1987. *Tata Cara Perkawinan Adat Suku Pamona di Kabupaten Poso.* Poso: Privately published.

Marcus, George, and Michael Fischer. 1986. *Anthropology as Cultural Critique: An Experimental Moment in the Human Sciences.* Chicago: University of Chicago Press.

Martin, Luther, Huck Gutman, and Patrick Hutton. 1988. *Technologies of the Self: A Seminar with Michel Foucault.* London: Tavistock.

Mauss, Marcel. 1970[1925]. *The Gift: Forms and Functions of Exchange in Archaic Societies.* Trans. by Ian Cunnison. London: Cohen & West.

Mazee, G.W. 1911. 'Over Heksen-Moord en de Berechting Daarvan.' *Tijdschrift van het Binnenlansch Bestuur* 41/6: 396–402.

McVey, Ruth T. 1971. 'Nationalism, Islam, and Marxism: The Management of Ideological Conflict in Indonesia.' In *Nationalism, Islam, and Marxism*, ed. Ruth McVey, 1–33. Ithaca, NY: Modern Indonesia Project, Cornell University.

Meulin, P.J. van den. 1923a. 'Antwoord op het Artikel van Dr Alb. C. Kruyt.' *KT* 12: 434–40.

– 1923b. 'Het Volksonderwijs in Beheer bij de Zending, en de te Dien Aanzien Bestaande Regeerings-Voorschriften.' *KT* 12: 243–67.

Millar, Susan B. 1989. *Bugis Weddings: Rituals of Social Location in Modern Indonesia*. Berkeley: Center for South and Southeast Asia Studies, University of California.

Moore, Henrietta. 1994. *A Passion for Difference*. Bloomington: Indiana University Press.

Muratorio, Blanca. 1980. 'Protestantism and Capitalism Revisited in the Rural Highlands of Ecuador.' *Journal of Peasant Studies* 8/1: 37–60.

Noer, Deliar. 1978. *Administration of Islam in Indonesia*. Ithaca, NY: Cornell Modern Indonesia Project Monograph Series No. 58.

Noorduyn, Jacobus. 1991. *A Critical Survey of Studies on the Languages of Sulawesi*. Leiden: KITLV Press.

Pakan, Priyanti. 1977. 'Orang Toraja: Identifikasi, Klasifikasi dan Lokasi.' *Berita Antropologi* 9/32–3: 21–49.

– 1986. 'Bibliografi Bernotasi Folklor Toraja.' *Berita Antropologi* 12/42: 1–195.

Pangku, Diana A. 1987. 'Gereja dan Posintuwu dalam Masyarakat Pamona.' Unpublished BA thesis, Akademi Theologia GKST.

Papasi, P.M. 1992. 'Pendidikan Theologia GKST.' In *Wajah GKST: Buku kenangan 100 Tahun Injil Masuk Tana Poso*, ed. Dj. Tanggerahi et al., 154–63. Tentena: Gereja Kristen Sulawesi Tengah.

Parmentier, Richard. 1987. *The Sacred Remains: Myth, History, and Polity in Belau*. Chicago: University of Chicago Press.

Parry, Jonathan, and Maurice Bloch. 1989. 'Introduction: Money and the Morality of Exchange.' In *Money and the Morality of Exchange*, ed. J. Parry and M. Bloch, 1–32. Cambridge: Cambridge University Press.

Peletz, Michael G. 1983. 'Moral and Political Economies in Rural Southeast Asia: A Review Article.' *Comparative Studies in Society and History* 25/4: 731–9

– 1993. 'Sacred Texts and Dangerous Words: The Politics of Law and Cultural Rationalization in Malaysia.' *Comparative Studies in Society and History* 35/3: 66–109.

Pemberton, John. 1994. *On the Subject of 'Java.'* Ithaca, NY: Cornell University Press.

PIK (Persatuan Ibu Kristen Tentena). 1985. *Sejarah Berdirinya PIK GKST Cabang Tentena*. Tentena: Privately published.

Rahman, Wan A. 1985. 'Aliran: Its Relevance in Analysing Javanese Society.' *Jurnal Antropologi dan Sociologi* 13: 47–52.

Ramage, Douglas E. 1995. *Politics in Indonesia: Democracy, Islam and the Ideology of Tolerance*. London: Routledge.

Randwijck, S.C. Graaf van. 1981. *Handelen en Denken in Dienst der Zending: Oegstgeest, 1897–1942*, 2 vols. The Hague: Uitgeverij Boekencentrum bv.

Rasker, A.J. 1974. *De Nederlandse Hervormde Kerk Vanaf 1795: Haar Geschiedenis en Theologie in de Negentiende en Twintigste Eeuw*. Kampen: Kok Uitgeverij.

Rauws, D.J. 1916. *Midden-Celebes*. Rotterdam: Uitgave van het Zendingsbureau.

Redfield, Robert. 1960. *The Little Community/ Peasant Society and Culture*. Chicago: University of Chicago Press.

Reenders, Hommo. 1991. *Alternatieve Zending: Ottho Gerhard Heldring (1804–1876) en de verbreiding van het Christendom in Nederlands-Indië*. Kampen: J.H. Kok.

Regeerings-Almanak. 1909. *Regeerings-Almanak voor Nederlandsch-Indië Deel II: Kalender en Personalia*. Batavia: Landsdrukerij.

– 1918. *Regeerings-Almanak voor Nederlandsch-Indië Deel II: Kalender en Personalia*. Batavia: Landsdrukerij.

Ricklefs, M.C. 1979. 'Six Centuries of Islamization in Java.' In *Conversion to Islam*, ed. Nehemia Levtzion, 100–27. New York: Holmes & Meier.

Riedel, J.G.F. 1886. 'De Topantunuasu of Oorspronkelijke Volksstammen van Centraal Selebes.' *BTLV* 35: 77–95.

Robinson, Kathryn M. 1986. *Stepchildren of Progress: The Political Economy of Development in an Indonesian Mining Town*. Albany: State University of New York Press.

Roseberry, William. 1989. *Anthropologies and Histories: Essays in Culture, History and Political Economy*. New Brunswick, NJ: Rutgers University Press.

Rössler, Martin. 1997. 'Islamization and the Reshaping of Identities in Rural South Sulawesi.' In *Islam in an Era of Nation-States: Politics and Religious Renewal in Muslim Southeast Asia*, ed. Robert W. Hefner and Patricia Horvatich. Honolulu: University of Hawaii Press.

Rouffaer, G.P. 1907. 'Alb. C. Kruijt. Het Animisme in den Indischen Archipel.' *TNAG* Tweede Series (24): 266–71.

Rozali, L.H., Ahmad Asri-Saro, and Amir Lumentut. 1984. *Struktur Bahasa Pamona*. Jakarta: Pusat Pembinaan dan Pengembangan Bahasa Departemen Pendidikan dan Kebudayaan.

Said, Edward W. 1979. *Orientalism*. New York: Vintage.

Sanjek, Roger. 1982. 'The Organization of Households in Adabraka: Towards a Wider Comparative Perspective.' *Comparative Studies in Society and History* 24/1: 57–103.

Santo, D.J., et al. 1990. *Kasingkandomu Ada mPamona: Pompatoka Gombo Ada mPamona*. Tentena: Kantor Bantu Bupati Kabupaten Poso, stensil.

Sarasin, Paul, and Frits Sarasin. 1905. *Reisen in Celebes ausgefuhrt in den Jahren, 1893–1896 und 1902–1903*, 2 vols. Wiesbaden: Kreidel.

Schiller, Anne. 1997. *Small Sacrifices: Religious Change and Cultural Identity among the Ngaju of Indonesia*. New York: Oxford University Press.

Schoor-Lambregts, A.J. van den. 1992. '"Het Heerlijke en Schoone Werk der Zending": Alb. C. Kruyt over Celebes.' *Indische Letteren* 7/3: 98–108.

Schrauwers, Albert. 1995. 'The Household and Shared Poverty in the Highlands of Central Sulawesi.' *Journal of the Royal Anthropological Institute, incorporating Man* n.s. 1 2: 337–57.

– 1997. 'Houses, Hierarchy, Headhunting and Exchange: Rethinking Political Relations in the Southeast Asian Realm of Luwu." *Bijdragen KITLV* 153/3: 356–80.

– 1998. '"Let's Party": State Intervention, Discursive Traditionalism and the Labour Process of Highland Rice Cultivators in Central Sulawesi, Indonesia.' *Journal of Peasant Studies* 25/3: 112–30.

Schryer, Frans J. 1998. *The Netherlandic Presence in Ontario: Pillars, Class and Dutch Ethnicity*. Waterloo, ON: Wilfrid Laurier University Press.

Schuyt-Mansvelt, A.M. 1919. *Padjangko: Een Toradja-'Boefje.'* The Hague: Boekhandel van den Zendingsstudie Raad.

Schwarz, Adam. 1994. *A Nation in Waiting: Indonesia in the 1990s*. Boulder, CO: Westview.

Scott, David. 1994. *Formations of Ritual: Colonial and Anthropological Discourses on the Sinhala Yaktovil*. Minneapolis: University of Minnesota Press.

Scott, James C. 1976. *The Moral Economy of the Peasant: Rebellion and Subsistence in Southeast Asia*. New Haven, CT: Yale University Press.

Siagian, T.P. 1985. 'Some Notes on Christian Education in Indonesia.' *Prisma* 38: 33–43.

Sider, Gerald, and Gavin Smith. 1997. 'Introduction.' In *Between History and Histories: The Making of Silences and Commemorations*, ed. Gerald Sider and Gavin Smith, 3–28. Toronto: University of Toronto Press.

Sigilipu, P. 1993. *Mabaresi Polimbayo Lemba mPamona i Piamo*. Tonusu: Privately published.

Simatupang, T.B. 1984. *Iman Kristen dan Pancasila*. Jakarta: BPK Gunung Mulia.

Smith, Gavin. 1985. 'Reflections on the Social Relations of Simple Commodity Production.' *Journal of Peasant Studies* 13/1: 101–8.

– 1989. *Livelihood and Resistance: Peasants and the Politics of Land in Peru*. Berkeley: University of California Press.

SNRI (Sekretariat Negara Republik Indonesia). 1983. *Undang-Undang Dasar, Pedoman Penghayatan Dan Pengamalan Pancasila (Ketetapan MPR No. II/MPR/1978), Garis-Garis Besar Haluan Negara (Ketetapan MPR No. II/MPR/1983)*. Jakarta: Sekretariat Negara Republik Indonesia.

Soebadio, H. 1985. *Cultural Policy in Indonesia*. Paris: Unesco.

Stange, Paul. 1986. '"Legitimate" Mysticism in Indonesia.' *Review of Indonesian and Malaysian Affairs* 20/2: 76–117.

Steedly, Mary M. 1993. *Hanging without a Rope: Narrative Experience in Colonial and Postcolonial Karoland*. Princeton, NJ: Princeton University Press.

– 1996. 'The Importance of Proper Names: Language and "National Identity" in Colonial Karoland.' *American Ethnologist* 23/3: 447–75.

Steinberg, David J., ed. 1987. *In Search of Southeast Asia: A Modern History.* Rev. ed. Honolulu: University of Hawaii Press.

Steininger, R. 1977. 'Pillarization (verzuiling) and Political Parties.' *Sociologische Gids* 77/4: 244–57.

Strathern, Marilyn. 1985. 'Kinship and Economy: Constitutive Orders of a Provisional Kind.' *American Ethnologist* 12/2: 191–209.

Stuurman, Siep. 1983. *Verzuiling, Kapitalisme en Patriarchaat: Aspecten van de Ontwikkeling van de Moderne Staat in Nederland.* Nijmegen: Socialistiese Uitgeverij Nijmegen.

Suminto, H. Aqib. 1985. *Politik Islam Hindia Belanda.* Jakarta: Lembaga Penelitian Pendidikan dan Penerangan Ekonomi dan Sosial.

Suryadarma, P.P. 1986. 'Bibliografi Bernotasi Folklor Toraja.' *Berita Antropologi* 12/42: 1–195.

Swellengrebel, J.L. 1978. *In Leijdeckers Voetspoor: Anderhalve Eeuw Bijbelvertaling en Taalkunde in de Indonesische Talen, 1900–1970.* The Hague: Martinus Nijhoff.

Tanggerahi, Dj. 1983. 'Pengharapan Atas Kematian: Suatu Studi Perbandingan Antara Kepercayaan Suku Pamona Dengan Iman Kristen.' Unpublished dissertation, Sekolah Tinggi Theologia untuk Indonesia Bahagian Timur, Ujung Pandang.

Tobondo, A.R. 1992. 'Pelayanan Kesehatan Masyarakat di Wilayah GKST.' In *Wajah GKST: Buku Kenangan 100 Tahun Injil Masuk Tana Poso*, ed. Dj. Tanggerahi et al., 164–78. Tentena: Gereja Kristen Sulawesi Tengah.

Tooker, Deborah E. 1992. 'Identity Systems of Highland Burma: "Belief," Akha Zan, and a Critique of Interiorized Notions of Ethno-Religious Identity.' *Man* n.s. 27/4: 799–820.

Tsing, Anna L. 1987. 'A Rhetoric of Centres in a Religion of the Periphery.' In *Indonesian Religions in Transition*, ed. Rita S. Kipp and Susan Rodgers, 187–210. Tucson: University of Arizona Press.

– 1993. *In the Realm of the Diamond Queen: Marginality in an Out-of-the-Way Place.* Princeton, NJ: Princeton University Press.

Verkuyl, J. 1990. *Ketegangan Antara Imperialisme dan Kolonialisme Barat Dan Zending Pada Masa Politik Kolonial Etis.* Jakarta: PT BPK Gunung Mulia.

Volkman, Toby A. 1984. 'Great Performances: Toraja Cultural Identity in the 1970s.' *American Ethnologist* 11/1: 152–69.

Wal, S.L. van den. 1971. 'De Nederlandse expansie in Indonesie in de tijd van het modern imperialisme: de houding van de nederlandse regering en de politieke partijen.' *Bijdragen en Mededeelingen Betreffende de Geschiedenis der Nederlanden* 86/1: 47–61.

Warren, Carol. 1986. 'Indonesian Development Policy and Community Organization in Bali.' *Contemporary Southeast Asia* 8/3: 213–30.

Waterson, Roxanna. 1984. *Ritual and Belief among the Sa'dan Toraja.* Canterbury: University of Kent, Centre for Southeast Asian Studies, Occasional Paper No. 2.

Weber, Max. 1963. *The Sociology of Religion.* Ed. by Ephraim Fischoff. Introduction by Talcott Parsons. Boston: Beacon.

Weiner, Annette B. 1980. 'Reproduction: a Replacement for Reciprocity.' *American Ethnologist* 7/1: 71–85.

Weinstock, Joseph A. 1981. 'Kaharingan: Borneo's "Oldest Religion" Becomes Indonesia's Newest Religion.' *Borneo Research Bulletin* 13/1: 47–8.

– 1987. 'Kaharingan: Life and Death in Southern Borneo.' In *Indonesian Religions in Transition,* ed. Rita S. Kipp and Susan Rodgers, 71–97. Tucson: University of Arizona Press.

Wertheim, W.F. 1972. 'Counter-Insurgency Research at the Turn of the Century – Snouck Hurgronje and the Acheh War.' *Sociologische Gids* 19/4: 320–8.

– 1973. 'From Aliran towards Class Struggle in the Countryside of Java.' In *Dawning of an Asian Dream: Selected Articles on Modernization and Emancipation,* ed. W.F. Wertheim, 94–115. Amsterdam: Afdeling Zuid- en Zuidoost Azie, Antropologisch-Sociologisch Centrum, Universiteit van Amsterdam.

Wesseling, H.L. 1987. 'Knowledge Is Power: Some Remarks on Colonial Studies in the Netherlands.' In *Dari Babad dan Hikayat sampai Sejarah Kritis,* ed. Ibrahim Alfian et al., 351–68. Yogyakarta: Gadjah Mada University Press.

White, Ben. 1983. '"Agricultural Involution" and Its Critics: Twenty Years Later.' *Bulletin of Concerned Asian Scholars* 15/2: 18–31.

Wignjodipoero, R. Soerojo. 1983. *Kedudukan serta Perkembangan Hukum Adat setelah Kemerdekaan.* Jakarta: PT Gunung Agung.

Wilken, G.A. 1912a. 'Het Animisme bij de Volken van den Indischen Archipel.' In *De Verspreide Geschriften van prof. Dr G.A. Wilken,* vol. 3, 1–287. The Hague: G.C.T. van Dorp & Co.

– 1912b. 'Over de verwantschap en huwelijks- en erfrecht bij de volken van den Indischen Archipel, beschouwd uit het oogpunt van de nieuwere leerstellingen op het gebied der maatschappelijke ontwikkelingsgeschiedenis.' In *De Verspreide Geschriften van Prof. Dr G.A. Wilken,* vol. 3, 411–44. The Hague: G.C.T. van Dorp & Co.

Willemsen, Marie-Antoinette. 1988. 'Het Pad van de Vrouw: Veranderingen in de positie van Pamona-vrouwen vanaf de eeuwwisseling tot 1987.' Unpublished MA thesis, University of Breda.

– 1990. 'Cirkels worden Kleiner. Veranderingen in de Positie van Pamona-Vrouwen vanaf de Eeuwwisseling tot 1987.' *Jambatan* 8/2: 88–100.

Williams, Raymond. 1976. *Keywords: A Vocabulary of Culture and Society*. London: Fontana.

– 1977. *Marxism and Literature*. Oxford: Oxford University Press.

Wintle, Michael. 1987. *Pillars of Piety: Religion in the Netherlands in the Nineteenth Century*. Hull: Hull University Press, Occasional Papers in Modern Dutch Studies No. 2.

Wolf, Eric. 1982. *Europe and the People Without History*. Berkeley: University of California Press.

Woodward, Mark R. 1989. *Islam in Java*. Tucson: University of Arizona Press.

Wong, Diana. 1987. *Peasants in the Making: Malaysia's Green Revolution*. Singapore: Institute of Southeast Asian Studies.

– 1991. 'Kinship and the Domestic Development Cycle in a Kedah Village, Malaysia.' In *Cognation and Social Organization in Southeast Asia*, ed. Jeremy Kemp, 193–201. Leiden: KITLV Press.

Woud, Auke van der. 1987. *Het Lege Land: De Ruimtelijke Orde van Nederland 1798–1848*. Amsterdam: Meulenhoff Informatief.

Yanagisako, Sylvia J. 1979. 'Family and Household: The Analysis of Domestic Groups.' *Annual Review of Anthropology* 8: 161–205.

Zahn, Ernest. 1989. *Regenten, rebellen en reformatoren: Een visie op Nederland en de Nederlanders*. Amsterdam: Uitgeverij Contact.

Index

abstention, policy of, 45–6
Aceh, 19, 41, 45, 47
adat (*see also* customary law), 7, 8, 19, 20, 62, 65, 173; Christian, 57–8, 64, 78, 80, 132, 172, 178–9, 212, 234; costume, 134, 139, 142; council, 63, 89, 134, 137, 140, 156; as culture, 88–90, 166, 241–5; and ethnic identity, 62, 70–1, 90, 130, 160, 233; and mission, 34, 42–4, 50, 53, 58, 77, 178; Pamonan (*ada mPamona*), 71, 76, 164, 249; rationalization of, 71, 76, 140, 144, 165–6, 196; seculariza-tion of, 78, 232, 242; spectacle, 90, 142–3, 148, 153, 165, 195–6
Adriani, Nicolaüs, 9, 10, 47, 51, 61, 70 104; on religion, 32, 78, 234; schol-arly influence, 11, 54; youth and education, 52, 172
agama, 7, 18, 57, 228, 238
agriculture, and patronage, 26, 129; *sawah*, 71, 100, 110–16, 127; swidden, 67, 71, 110, 127; and tradition, 21–2, 71, 98–9, 242; work groups (see *pesale*)
aliran (see *also* pillarization), 14, 42, 82, 88, 91, 223–4, 228, 237–42

angga (spirits), 56, 203–5
animism, 12, 17, 18, 22, 32, 54–8, 68, 90, 175, 200; and beliefs, 198, 212; and church 77–8, 131, 176, 183–4
anitu (ancestors) 56–7, 68
anthropology: discourse on religion, 11–12, 43, 54–8, 228; and ethnicity, 59, 63; and missions, 9, 42–4; and representation, 3–4, 8, 10–16, 31, 50, 54, 61; interpretive, 173–5
Anti-Revolutionary Party, 14, 17, 39, 41
arisan (credit association), 149, 185
army, 83–4
arts (*kebudayaan*), 6, 7, 88, 161
Asad, Talal, 174–7, 225, 230
Atkinson, Jane, 32

Bachofen, J.J., 55
Bali, religion in, 17–18
banua. See longhouse
belief, shared, 16, 173–9, 187–8, 198–206, 211
biblical authority. *See* scriptural auth-ority
Boeke, J.H., 21, 100
Bourdieu, P., 176
bridewealth, 58, 67, 130, 137–8, 143–4,

148, 249; and social reproduction, 105–7, 111, 118; and kinship ideology, 131; inflation, 138, 144, 165

Bungkundapu, Asa, 83

bureaucracy, colonial, 40–4, 77–81; church, 84–6, 91, 221, 232; Indonesian, 23–4, 88–9; Islam, 232–6, 250

bureaucratization, 17–20, 42–3, 48, 232–4

capitalism, 21, 60, 63; and agriculture, 91, 98–9, 103, 107–8, 127, 244; and secularism, 27

Catholics, political role, 39–40

Chayanov, A., 101, 103, 113, 128, 243

Chinese merchants, 111–13

Christian Church of Central Sulawesi (Gereja Kristen Sulawesi Tengah), 24, 63–4, 84–7, 158, 207, 221, 228, 241

Christian Reformed Church, 13, 15

Christianity, conversion to, 9–10, 12, 172, 183–4, 200; and culture, 53–4, 63, 157–8, 232; indigenous, 44, 50; political aspects, 3, 14–15, 17, 18, 19, 33–40, 41–2, 172, 229–32

Church (see also Christian Church of Central Sulawesi, Indische Kerk): bureaucracy, 192, 221–3; and ethnicity, 7–8, 10, 16, 21, 25, 61, 172; and feasting, 22, 73–5, 86, 129, 183–7; and gift economy, 22, 129–30, 132; institutional logic, 20–1, 23; leadership, 22, 73–5, 99, 159–60, 173, 178, 189–90, 208; and modernism, 86, 229; and state, 4–8, 13, 14, 20, 34, 39, 54, 78, 84, 92, 160, 222, 228–30; wedding, 141, 157, 165–7

Cinderella analogy, 119, 126, 154–5, 249

class, 21–2, 28, 86–7, 132, 216, 244; consolidation, 160, 163, 189; differ-

entiation, 99–103, 107, 111, 115, 117

classis, 84–5

colonialism, 8–10, 11, 19, 27

Comaroff, Jean and John, 11, 12, 58

commodification, 21; of local economy, 100, 102–3, 110–16, 131; and weddings, 129

communalism, 55–6, 99, 105, 113, 129, 172–3

comprehensive approach, 87, 221–3

confessional politics. See Christianity, political aspects

consistory, 73, 84, 184, 220

conversion, 9–10, 12, 18, 19, 34, 42, 50, 56, 200; intellectualist models of, 198–9; internal, 213, 233; methods (see also sociological mission method), 172, 176–7, 187–8, 191, 197; and politics, 47, 239; in Tentena, 77

corvée labour, 72, 78–9, 110

council of elders (wa'a ngkabosenya), 68, 72–3, 89, 184

culture, brokers, 77–82; objectification of, 6, 8, 10–11, 19, 58, 64, 89–90, 242; and politics, 15–16, 223–4; and religion, 8–10, 19–20, 42–3, 53–4, 173–4, 191, 232–3, 236

Darul Islam, 82, 87–8, 226–7, 235, 247

dancing (dero), 161–3, 217

dating, 134, 160–5

development, 21–2, 34, 48, 87–8, 225, 239; and agriculture, 71, 242; and church, 86, 222, 242; and rationality, 27; and tradition, 97–8, 242

disciplinary practices, 19–20, 36–7, 156, 176–8, 189, 214–19, 236, 244

dispute settlement, 173

district head (mokole, camat), 71, 89, 133, 140

divine justice (*puloru*), 203, 210–11, 214, 219, 249
doctrine, 18, 38; and ritual, 174, 198–206

economy, dual, 21, 27–8, 98, 100–2, 243–4; moral (*see also* gifts, shared poverty), 28, 98–104, 242, 244; natural, 99, 244. *See also* market
education, 39, 53, 57, 70; and religion, 77, 92, 228, 235–6; and state, 79, 238–41
elders, church, 73, 81, 84, 86, 184, 195, 207; and women, 216–17
elections, church, 84, 86–7; national, 87–8, 236–7, 246
elites (*see also* patronage), 4, 23–6, 117, 191, 222, 227; Dutch, 35–6, 38, 191; and tradition, 20–1, 25, 28, 65–9, 86–7, 149, 173, 236, 244
Ethical Policy, 10, 21, 33, 41, 45, 48, 59, 71, 76, 90, 97; and religion, 231, 234
Ethical Theology, 34, 39–40, 43–4, 52–3, 90, 172, 222, 232; and pietism, 200, 207
ethnic groups, definition of, 59, 61–2; identity and church, 5–8, 10, 32, 63, 130, 222; and state, 5–8, 44, 63, 70, 90
ethnography. *See* anthropology
Engelenberg, W.G., 47–8, 70–1, 78
Envangelization group. *See* worship groups
evolutionism, 55–7, 60
exchange. *See* economy; gifts; *pesale*; *posintuwu*

Fabian, J., 60
faith, 77, 198–202, 211–12, 214, 219, 244

family week (*pekan keluarga*), 217–18
feasting, 22, 28, 68–70, 129; and church, 74, 86, 144, 149, 157–60, 165–7, 178–83, 214–15, 242; and Javanese, 74–5; modernization, 142–4, 148, 192–6, 229, 242; and status, 75–6, 131, 151–2; wedding, 130, 141–4
floating mass policy, 15, 239–40
fosterage, 105, 113–14, 117–19, 127, 249
foundations (*yayasan*), 86, 222
Foucault, Michel, 19, 36, 176, 213
functional groups. *See* Golkar
fundamentalism, 3, 16
funerals, 188; secondary, 68–9, 74, 79, 130, 153, 227

Geertz, Clifford, 17, 21, 100–3, 114, 118, 128, 213, 218–19, 243–4
gender, 183, 185, 215–18
gifts (see also *posintuwu* exchange), 22, 99, 242
Golkar, 16, 239–40
gotong royong, 75, 145, 147–8, 165
Groen van Prinsterer, Guillaume, 38–9
Gunning, J.W., 52

Habermas, Jürgen, 19
headhunting, 68–70, 74, 79, 179
headman, village (see also *kabosenya*), 72–3, 140, 147, 155–6, 164; *lurah*, 89, 156
health care: indigenous, 204–5; religious, 221, 228
hegemony, 177, 191–2, 213–14
Heldring, Otto G., 38–9
Hervormde Kerk. *See* Reformed Church
hierarchy, 68, 146, 222; and feasting, 75–6, 144–5, 157–8, 179–81, 194; and kinship, 117, 127, 129, 152–7

history, 62
Hoëvell, G.W.W.C., Baron van, 46, 51,
    53
households, 26, 67, 98–9; development
    cycle, 117, 120–7, 249; and feasting,
    74–5, 130, 142, 160, 217; functions,
    103, 105, 116, 118, 142; and kin-
    ship, 116–20; To Pamona (*sombori*),
    104–10, 247;
Hurgronje, Snouck, 232
hymns, 184, 188

Idenburg, A.W.F., 42
ideological articulation, 60, 63, 109
Ikatan Cendekiawan Muslim se-Indo-
    nesia (ICMI), 239
illness, 204–5
imperialism, 34, 45–50
inculturation, 8, 132, 145, 177, 198, 242,
    250; and feasting, 165–6, 179–83,
    229; and *monuntu*, 183–7
Independence, 82, 91, 158
indirect rule, 19, 41–2, 48, 50
Indische Kerk, 172
Indonesian Academy of Sciences (LIPI),
    23
Indonesian Council of Churches (PGI),
    24
Indonesian Democratic Party (PDI; *see
    also* Parkindo), 91, 226, 248, 249
Indonesian Nationalist Party (PNI), 88,
    226
inheritance, 111, 118–19, 125
involution, 21, 100–1, 103, 243
Islam: conversion, 202; and ethnicity,
    32; law, 42, 231, 235, 248; new
    school, 229, 232–4; old school, 229,
    232, 235–6; pillarization of, 14,
    16–19, 229–30, 232–3, 237; political
    aspects (*see also* Darul Islam), 3, 19,

31, 87–8, 92–3, 237–41; threat from,
    46, 226–7

Javanese, 74, 83, 89, 100, 102

kabosenya, and church, 73–4, 89, 160,
    173, 178–9, 195; and kinship, 99, 130;
    and nationalism, 76; and state, 79–81,
    160; traditional, 67–70, 153; women,
    158, 215–16
Kahn, Joel, 244
Kaudern, Walter, 61, 64
kepercayaan (belief systems), 7, 18, 92,
    238
kinship: and gift economy, 22, 26, 69;
    and household, 102–3, 116–20; ideol-
    ogy, 104–5, 112–13, 116, 129–30; and
    leadership, 65, 67, 69, 99
Komisi Wanita (Women's Christian
    Organization), 85, 157–60, 193–4,
    219–21; and mission, 57, 215–18
Kraemer, H., 221
Kruyt, Albert C., 4, 5, 10, 98, 129;
    education, 51–2, 55; and imperialism,
    47, 51, 70; model missionary, 9, 46,
    172, 200–1, 211–12; on religion,
    175–6, 183, 187–8, 198–202, 233;
    scholarly influence, 11, 13, 19, 31–59,
    63
Kruyt, Jan, 10
Kuyper, Abraham, 33, 41

Lake Poso festival, 4–6, 23–4, 89–91,
    93, 226–7
Lambek, Michael, 203
land claims, 72, 83
law, civil, 88; customary (see also *adat*),
    8, 19, 42–4, 50, 248; customary law
    area (*adatrechtkring*), 43–4; custom-
    ary law studies, 50, 51–4, 59, 231,

233; and ethnic identity, 76, 88;
  Islamic, 42, 231, 235, 248
Liberals, 36, 39–40, 230–1
liturgies, 133; *adat*, 143, 148, 154,
  166, 249; church, 144, 176, 184, 186,
  188
longhouse, 67–9, 99, 180, 247
Lumentut, Pdt., A. 24
Luwu, 46–8, 61, 64, 82

magic, 204–5
market, 22, 98–100, 131, 242
marriage, alliance, 69, 121, 163;
  arranged, 137, 155, 160, 163; feast,
  68, 130; and status, 130–1
Masyumi, 235–6
Michielsen, W.J.M., 45
ministers, 84–5, 87, 186, 190, 207, 221
missions, home, 38–40
modernity, 21, 27, 71, 76, 86–7
modernization, 22–3, 27, 63, 100; and
  conflict, 91, 233, 236; and culture,
  142, 236, 241–5; and feasting, 148,
  150, 158, 194–5; and secularism, 3,
  16, 27, 33, 35, 39, 79, 227–9, 231–3
Molindo L., 73, 80–1
monuntu. See preaching
mosintuwu, 67, 73–5, 130, 145, 151–2,
  180
Muhammadiyah, 233–5

Nahdatul Ulama, 233
nationalism, Christian, 7, 10, 14–16, 28,
  44, 59, 76, 81, 228; ethnic, 76–7, 228,
  245; Indonesian, 6–7; and state, 70, 88
Netherlands, 11, 14–18, 20, 32–40, 58,
  231
Netherlands Bible Society, 51, 52
Netherlands East Indies 11, 15–16, 33–4,
  45

Netherlands Mission Association (Nederlandsche Zendingvereeniging), 171–2
Netherlands Missionary Society (Nederlandsch Zendeling Genootschap), 24,
  46, 51, 52, 171, 201, 228, 235
Netherlands Reformed Church, 19, 36–7,
  86, 141, 157, 221
New Order government, 15, 16; and
  development, 88–90, 227; and
  politics, 226–7, 237–41; and religion,
  223–4, 230
Ngkai Bose, 107–9, 113, 117, 121–6,
  154, 181, 249

padungku. See thanksgiving
Pamona, kingdom of, 61, 62; village,
  125
Pamona Utara, 21, 64, 81
Pancasila, 88, 92, 238, 241
Papa Ian, 154–5
Papa i Wunte, 79, 199
Parkindo (Indonesian Protestant Party),
  15, 84, 91, 226
paternalism, 44, 50
patronage, 22, 99, 120, 127–32, 153–4,
  164, 184, 191, 194–5, 244–5
Pax Neerlandica, 42, 231
peasantization, 100, 127–8
Peletz, Michael, 212–13
Pemberton, John, 6, 11, 23
Permesta, 13, 82–3, 88, 124, 227
pesale (labour exchange), 73, 101, 106,
  113–15, 148, 180–1
Petirodongi, 83, 111, 124
pietism, 38, 53, 172, 201, 241
Pierson, N.G., 52
pillarization, 14–16, 33, 35–40; in Indonesia (see *aliran*)
Polanyi, Karl, 243
posintuwu: exchange, 22, 26, 67, 104–5,

145–52, 243–4; and feasting, 73–5, 129–31, 159, 180, 186–7; ideology of, 75, 132, 149, 242; *keluarga dekat*, 149–50; *umum*, 147–50, 165, 194–5
Poso, mission post 46; kingdom of, 49, 50, 62, 70–1, 76; town, 71, 122
power (see also *tanoana*), 68, 191–2
practice theory, 175–7
preaching, and inculturation, 183–7; as political process, 173, 180–2, 213
pregnancy, 137, 155, 162–4
proposal process, 133–7, 153, 155

rationality, 20, 27, 53–4, 56; market, 98–100, 101, 107, 129, 243; and religion, 197–8, 200, 212
rationalization: of *adat*, 71, 76, 140, 144, 196; institutional, 218–24, 229; of Islam, 232–4, 237–8; of religion, 17–20, 27–8, 50, 64, 78, 92–3, 159, 197–8, 212–24, 225–46; of state bureaucracy, 41, 43, 81, 88–90
reciprocity, 106, 117, 131, 146–7, 180, 181–2, 192
relativism, 44
religion, discourses on, 11–12, 19–20, 32, 43, 53, 78, 81–2, 173–6, 183, 187, 228, 237–41; and politics, 15, 16–20, 92; and culture, 8–10, 19–20, 44, 53, 57, 173; and economy, 27
representation, 245; and anthropology, 3–4, 12, 28, 175, 228, 242; and church, 8, 12, 87, 178; and politics, 16, 90; and state, 8, 12
revival (Reveil), 17, 38, 171
Riedel, J.G.F., 31, 60, 62, 63
ritual, 157, 173–6
ritualization, 177–8, 192
Roskes, J.W., 55

Sangele, 72
santina, 75, 180, 248; economic functions, 104–10, 116–19, 120–1, 125, 145; and weddings, 139, 143
Sarekat Islam, 233
Saussaye, Prof. P.D. Chantepie de la, 51–2
schools, 72, 79–80, 86, 110, 199, 221, 233–5
scriptural authority, 210–11, 214, 233
sermons, 184, 187–92, 206–11
service (religious) (*see also* thanksgiving service): comforting, 209; and discipline, 214–18; and feasting, 74–5, 132, 184–7
shamanism, 57, 179, 204, 215
shared poverty, 21–2, 98; and hierarchy, 127–8, 132, 181, 189; and kinship, 100–4, 112, 132; and *posintuwu*, 104–5, 145, 152
siblings (*to saana*), 107, 130, 132
Sigilipu, Pancali, 77–81, 121, 199, 222
slavery, 65, 67–8, 247
sociological mission method, 4, 9, 19, 27, 34, 51, 53–4, 57, 196; and ethnicity, 63, 87
social reproduction, 105–7, 111, 118, 241; and feasting, 152–8, 160, 165, 183, 195, 216, 229
sombori. See household
space, ritual, 180, 185, 188–9, 194
spiritism, 55–8, 183
state: and agriculture, 98–9, 242; colonial, 19; and economy, 22, 28; ethnic management by, 6–7, 21, 61–3, 76, 88; and feasting, 130, 132, 147, 160, 165–7; formation (*see also* rationalization), 41–2, 45; institutional logic, 20–1, 23, 43; and local leaders

(see also *kabosenya*), 72–3, 76,
78–81, 113; post-colonial, 82–3, 88,
248; and religion, 7–8, 13–16, 20,
33, 54, 78, 88, 90–3, 160, 227–30,
237–41; and women, 220
structure and agency, 12, 14, 20–3, 219
Suryadi, 91, 226, 248
Sukarnoputri, Magawati, 91, 226, 247–8
symbol, 174
syncretism, 34, 74, 200
Synod, 84–5, 159, 206; sessions, 24–5,
220

tadulako (see also *kabosenya*), 139–42
tanoana, 56, 57, 68, 131
tax, 46
teachers, 72, 73, 77
Tentena, 63, 65, 89, 92, 205, 215, 220,
240; settlement of, 71–2, 98–9;
school, 79, 215, 234
thanksgiving (*padungku*), 68; service,
74–5, 148, 179, 186, 192–4, 209
Tomini, Bay of, 45, 46, 65
To Pamona: ethnic identity, 4–9, 12, 59,
61–2, 63, 245; incorporation of, 19,
27, 62, 64–5
Toraja, and *adat* law studies, 50, 54, 59;
Bare'e-speaking (*see also* To Pamona),
32, 51, 61, 69, 247; defined, 31, 247;
and religion, 32, 42–4, 54–8; Sa'dan,
18, 61; West, 61
tourism, 5, 6–7
tradition (see also *adat*, customary law):
discursive, 71, 99–100, 107, 127–9,
241; and development, 98, 101, 194;
perpetuation of, 21–2, 26–8, 63, 91,
98, 109, 127
Tu'a Bose, 107–9, 113, 117, 121–6
Tumonggi, Az. (*see also* Papa Ian), 24,
25

Tylor, E.B., 55

United Development Party (PPP), 92
Utrecht Mission Association (Utrechtsche Zendingvereeniging), 51, 172

verzuiling. *See* pillarization
village confederacies, 65–77, 140
Village Government Law, 89
visions, 205–6, 219
volkskerk, 4, 8, 10, 12, 16, 43–4, 61, 77,
81, 86, 90–3, 212, 232, 245

wage labour, 111–14
Wawo Ndoda, 65, 72, 79, 121, 249
Weber, Max, 17–19, 27, 197–8, 218–19,
230
wedding, 23, 25–6, 28, 228–9; ceremony, 133–44; church, 141, 157;
civil registration, 139–40, 155; and
posintuwu exchange, 130; reception,
141–3
werewolf, 79, 204–5, 219
Wijck, J.C.W.D.A, van der, 45
Wilken, G.A., 55, 97
women's worship group. *See* Komisi
Wanita
Woodward, Mark, 74
worship groups, 25, 85, 229; Evangelization group, 73–5, 84, 184–7; household, 217–18; and kinship, 22,
189–90; men's, 85, 193, 218, 221;
women's (*see* Komisi Wanita);
youth's, 85, 162, 193, 221

Youth Movement of Central Sulawesi
(GPST), 83, 227